Education

and

Social

Problems

Education
and
Social
Problems

Carl Weinberg

FP The Free Press, New York
Collier-Macmillan Limited, London

THE FREE PRESS
A DIVISION OF THE MACMILLAN COMPANY
866 Third Avenue, New York, New York 10022

Collier-Macmillan Canada Limited, Toronto, Ontario

Library of Congress Catalog Card Number: 72-129289

printing number
1 2 3 4 5 6 7 8 9 10

For Marca and Hayley
So that these problems shall not be theirs

CONTENTS

3 *Problems of Drug Taking* 66

PREFACE

FOR SEVERAL YEARS now publishers' representatives have been stopping by my office to explore the possibility of my contributing a small work on some specific social problem. The topic was to be decided by the winds of public sentiment. Most persons who specialize in the social aspects of education have probably received the same requests. Many have apparently yielded to the temptation. My shelves are currently overflowing with books on the slum child, mid-city education, and cultural deprivation.

The areas of interest have shifted as one problem diminishes in urgency and another emerges. For several years education was absorbed with a concern about juvenile deliquency, then the dropout was fashionable, after which the slum and its schools gained ascendancy in the competition for the attention of the educational community. The culturally disadvantaged, deprived, or differentiated have currently outstripped all other issues as the subject most worthy of consideration.

My resistance to plunging into an analysis of any of these issues was a function of a basic suspicion I have held about the permanence of a work that was dictated by the urgencies of a moment in time. Education as an institution has always been susceptible to *ad hoc* deployments of resources on a crisis basis. The best current example is the vast expenditure of money, time, and effort to embark hastily upon remedial programs for lower class children. The intellectual rationale for Headstart, Upward Bound, the Job Corps, and other programs tied to federal support could not have been wisely and carefully conceived, given the rush to action. At best these programs will have effects which we cannot intelligently evaluate. At worst the funds provided by the federal and local governments will go mostly to support the research interests of academicians who wish to be professionally mobile. Lacking a basic interest in the problem itself, researchers have and will continue to regard financial support and the culturally deprived as the means and the sample by which they can conveniently test their notions about individual and social behavior.

The concern about the educational advantages of the poor, as well as the other issues mentioned, are important of course and well deserve the attention of scholars and researchers. From the standpoint of integrating academic and educational interests, however, this one-topic-at-a-time approach may be shading our perception of the necessity of looking at a wide range of social strains within some common framework.

This has been the appeal of this project for me. Rather than begin with the notion that a given area of social conflict has consequences for educational behavior and the reorganization of educational structures, I have been able to ask a more general and, to me, more interesting question. This is: What are the current strains in American social life which affect the schools, and is there some organizational famework which can be applied to the analysis of these strains which can order our thinking about the relationship of these and education?

This work represents a modern conception of social problems

insofar as the form rather than the history structures the analysis. Social deviation takes different forms at different stages of social evolution. The focus of this analysis is on that form and on the idea of change itself. The reader will observe frequent references to forms of conflict which do not yet represent the particular manifestations of the problem area under consideration. I believe that certain projections based on some assessment of where the society is moving are necessary if educators are to have some conceptual preparation to anticipate the strains on their resources.

Carl Weinberg

INTRODUCTION

U N L E S S   O U R   S O C I E T Y sees fit to create a new institution devoted exclusively to the exploration and amelioration of social conflict, the school will not be free to pursue academic ends without first unraveling the strands of disorganization which inhibit its task. Education in America has never doubted or challenged its commitment to expend much of its resources on producing the good citizen. The dimensions of this functional problem have been so great and so complex that barriers to the goal are resolved in highly institutionalized ways, through a manifest set of formal regulations and patterned sanctions. But these are no longer adequate for many reasons.

First, the form of strain or conflict often has no covering regulation to which we can legitimately appeal, so that the problem is automatically regulated. What, for example, covers dissension borne of racial strain? What policies show us the way to arbitrate student protests? By what authority can we restrain students from dressing or wearing their hair as they like? School administrators tackle each conflict on an *ad hoc* basis by appealing to the intentions of a diffuse and often inappropriate set of rules.

Second, the members of the society are not always in accord about the legitimacy of the school's response to issues of conflict. Issues dealing with prayer, busing, and student dress have split the sentiments of the community in such a way that the school can no longer base its procedures on reliable predictions of public support.

Third, the culture is changing faster than the school in its tolerance of violations of the Protestant ethic. Historically this has always signaled a shift in the major institutions in the direction of the new values. But institutions move more slowly than the culture, and for periods of time the two are incompatible. It is during this lag in incompatibility that the role of the school in combating those aspects of social strain which impinge upon the educational task is most seriously handicapped.

Fourth, ecological transformations in community life are occurring at a rapid rate, with a concommitant shift in abilities, aspirations, socialized styles and manners, attitudes toward restraint, and prejudices about the major institutions. The school, which is rigidly organized to accommodate one kind of population, discovers that its methods and expectations are incompatible with the qualities of the new community. Traditional negative sanctions such as detentions, additional homework, or even physical punishment for deviant behavior may no longer be effective mechanisms for student control. If a student has no interest in doing homework, either for its own sake or for the sake of gaining the approval of the teacher, then giving him three times as much the following day is futile. This may have worked with students who are highly motivated to conform but not with those who view deviance as the best defense against controls which they view as illegitimate.

The educational structure which has emerged to solve the functional problems of socialization, to develop respectful attitudes toward traditional goals, and to internalize allegiance to the value of conformity is, for the reasons mentioned, obsolete. A superstructure which appeals only to the dictates of control is blind to the subtle ways that social problems infiltrate and sabotage the best laid plans. Reliance upon this superstructure has always been an appealing way to avoid the rigorous inspection of the social conflicts which daily frustrate the efforts of educational functionaries. Only now, when the superstructure is experiencing an accelerating erosion, can the role of the school in relation to social conflict be constructed on the basis of appropriate and intelligent response patterns. These response patterns will evolve out of an independence of activities functionally related to specific forms of conflict. This book represents an attempt to provide educators with organized knowledge about separate forms of social disorganization in the hope that such knowledge can become a part of their working apparatus to remove barriers to educational attainment.

Students of society and students of education are becoming increasingly aware of the role of the school as an agency of ameliorative action in the solution of social problems. Problems arising out of marginal urban living and out of the social and psychological consequences of minority group membership and economic deprivation were brought to public attention as part of the sweeping concerns of the "Great Society." Substantial funds have been made available to explore the ways in which the culturally deprived can be provided greater access to the mechanisms by which social mobility is achieved. All eyes turn automatically to education as the great equalizer. When new functions are conceived out of a shift in the value structure of a culture, some institution is either newly conceived to accommodate such functions or old institutions are defined as reasonable recipients of the new responsibility. Education has cooperated with social demands to incorporate into its already overloaded structure activities devoted to the problem of equal opportunities.

The pattern will probably remain the same for some time. A given social problem will emerge in the public consciousness and the school will be assigned the responsibility for reorganizing its facilities to deal with it. Presumably patterns of organization within the school devoted to the amelioration of some specific area of social conflict are effected on a topical basis. Today's concern is unequal opportunities; tomorrow's may be mental health, drugs, or an alienated adolescent society. The organization of an education facing a commitment to solve problems of social conflict is best achieved through a conception of social problems as general phenomena. Poverty may be a substantively different condition from mental illness, as heart disease is different from leukemia, but institutional structures within hospitals are organized to combat both conditions. In the same way if the amelioration of social problems is to become a manifest role of the schools, then the school needs to conceive of the kind of organization which can accommodate a range of demands in this area.

STRUCTURE FOR ANALYSIS

Our main concern here is with the organization of a framework within which we can explore the relationship between social problems and educational structures. Our secondary concern, but one crucial to the purpose of the book, is the organization of a framework within which the various problems can be prescriptive of educational innovation.

Two approaches to the study of social problems have ceen conceived in the evolution of sociological inquiry. One approach attempts to view social problems as special cases of social disorganization, to be studied from the perspective of social facts or conditions which could account for or be related to the specific manifestation. This involves studying disorganization to arrive at an understanding of what the norms and values in a society actually are. This approach looks at one manifestation of disorganization through the kind of conceptual framework that would provide insights into other types. In the tradition of Durkheim[1] suicide was of interest only insofar as this phenomenon could extend our knowledge of the consequences of certain forms of social organization. The importance of Durkheim's *Suicide* was that it demonstrated a procedure of analysis, that it revealed certain ideas about group membership, such as degree of cohesiveness, which could be used to explain rates of suicide. The fact of suicide itself as a specific form of social strain or disruption was secondary.

The first approach seeks to augment knowledge about social organization through the study of conflict; the second approach regards the exploration of social problems as legitimate in itself and necessary to the understanding of specific segments of social life. Whereas the first approach wishes to generalize findings to a range of social disorganization, the second approach has no such intention. The first approach attempts to develop conceptual tools to be utilized in the analysis of a class of phenomena; the second approach regards the exploration of social problems as an implemen-

[1] Émile Durkheim, *Suicide: A Study in Sociology* (New York: The Free Press, 1951).

tation of knowledge about a specific time and place. Becker[2] views the distinction as being between understanding the nature of man and society in the abstract and an understanding of what is actually happening in social life.

For example if the problem area under investigation happened to be drug addiction, the first approach would attempt to isolate certain conditions in the organization of society, such as economic organization, stratified positions, or cultural values, out of which an abstract explanation of the phenomenon would emerge. The second approach would seek to present a descriptive survey of the incidence of the problem, the characteristics of users, the ecological conditions associated with drug use, the behavior of addicts, and the organization of legal and medical facilities to deal with the problem.

According to Merton and Nisbet,[3] the first approach, which is generally more respectable within sociology insofar as explanation is more respectable than description, focuses upon important social processes which are utilized as explanatory conceptual factors. They cite four such processes: (1) *conflict* of institutions, where institutional loyalties come into conflict as a result of change, confusion, or incompatible goals; (2) *social mobility,* where persons strive for the rewards of the system and experience differential success; (3) *individuation,* a process of shifting from a communal, familial form of social organization to a stage of bureaucratic impersonalization; and (4) *anomie,* a process during which norms and values become ambiguous, conflict with each other, or lose their immediate relevance to persons.

These processes are classifications of social phenomena which help to order our understanding about the vast and complex network of social interactions. As classifications they provide useful conceptual tools for investigating specific problems of sociological interest. The specific research that follows the organization of ideas frequently provides data that reaffirm the utility of these ideas as well as indicating the necessity for continual reformulation.

Descriptive data of the kind that would be revealed in exploring the actual circumstances of specific problems have a similar utility. They may suggest conditions which would ultimately yield to broader classifications, which in turn could form explanatory hypotheses.

2 H. Becker, ed., *Social Problems, A Modern Approach* (New York: John Wiley & Sons, Inc., 1966), p.1.
3 R. Merton and R. Nisbet, *Contemporary Social Problems* (New York: Harcourt, Brace & World, Inc., 1961).

The fruits of both approaches are incorporated in the several treatments of this book. Both facts and interrelated ideas are useful in understanding the dimensions of a problem and, in this case, the way in which the school is involved. The fact that a certain percentage of high school students use drugs is as provocative to our concerns as the contention that drug taking is a function of differential peer associations, which can be productively explored.

Social problems are violations of the normative order associated with the regulations of institutions and the values of the culture. Human interaction occurs within a social context which orders that interaction. When that interaction produces disruptions in the normative order as a result of direct incompatibility or ambiguity of expectations, conflict results. This conflict occurs either in the form of deviance or aberrations resulting in personal disorganization, such as mental illness, broken homes, or alienation. Behaviors which are defined as problematic derive that definition from the evaluation of the society within which the behavior occurs. When a given social problem occurs in such a way as to threaten the stability of the majority of members of a society, certain ameliorative and regulatory actions follow. When this behavior either does not threaten the majority, or when it becomes so widespread that it begins to reflect a majority rather than a minority consensus, original definitions are modified and institutionalized regulative patterns dissolve. Drinking and divorce are two examples. When we speak of social problems, we want to consider that the substance of the "problem" lies not only in the outcome, such as poverty or mental illness, but also in the conditions which produce these outcomes.

HISTORICAL PERSPECTIVE

For our purposes any strain between persons and their institutions which affect the educational behavior of segments of the population is a sufficient condition for denoting such a conflict a "social problem." In this sense the diffuse and often incompatible expectations which affect the lives of adolescents are construed as a social problem. The increased number of controls over adolescent activities, such as curfews and regulations pertaining to dress, suggest that the adult society has been forced to make the same problematic definition of certain manifestations of adolescent life. Adolescence is only a recent addition to the ranks of social problems. This is due to the fact that teenagers required a long period of time to evolve into their own unique society, but the dimensions of conflict within and across age groups are beginning to emerge. History has caught up with a latent area of conflict and made it manifest. Other such areas will emerge as old tendencies erupt in new cultural soil.

The history of a culture in constant transition has shown that different problems dominate different stages of social history. At the turn of this century problems associated with immigration and industrialization were preeminent in making demands upon the resources of the school. The functional problems for that time were the integration of a diverse population into urban life, the molding of a common culture, child labor, clarification of women's role in society, and equipping persons to fit comfortably into a world being changed by machinery.

Following World War I the major institutions were called on to build stable goals into the consciousness of a society disillusioned and confused by war and rapid change. The roar of the Roaring Twenties was a decade-long aftermath of a war whose only meaning seemed to be a cause for temporary celebration. The breakdown of the moral and legal order left the society in circumstances of insecurity and aimlessness. The response to the resulting apprehension was indicated by widespread gangsterdom linked to the disorganizing effects of prohibition, the rise of the KKK, and the resurgence of witch hunts best represented by the Sacco-Vanzetti trial and the terror which followed it.

The market crash of 1929 ushered in a decade of demoralization. Faith in the stability of the economic cycle was shattered and persons found themselves pressed into circumstances which were beyond their control and which offered few alternatives for economic salvation. In 1935 4,200,000 youths were out of school and out of work. Delinquency was rampant. The dead end kids became a national stereotype. The functional problem for the school was to discover a basis for its own existence at a time when education did not appear to be linked to the job market. Training persons for work which did not exist, or for college which few could afford, or to espouse values which were not functional to the contemporary struggle for survival was a labor of tradition. How to live meaningfully with scant resources, to aspire for the sake of aspiration, and to discover the mechanisms by which the vicious cycle could be broken was a labor of love. A nation in a migratory mood, of men searching for work, and whole states uprooting and transplanting their populations, such as the victims of the dust bowl catastrophe, found little salvation in the school. Symptomatic of this mood was the plight of the American school teacher, paid little if at all, who himself was forced to seek an environment that could accommodate his lowly regarded skills.

The functional problem for the school for the first five years of the forties was linked to the disorganizing effects of World War II. War is a time of uncertainty, of fear, of sacrifice, of anger and hatred, and of death. It was to the amelioration of these social problems that the institutional resources of the school were directed. The aftermath of this war brought a new wave of disorganizing effects. Millions of men were liberated by their army and travel experiences from traditional loyalties, loyalties to institutions and loyalties to values of restraint. The world view replaced the community view; the pace in all social relations was quickened; mobility, both physical and social was rapid; stability and permanence were questionable virtues. The disorganized family, broken by death and divorce and strained by prolonged absence and new experiences, began to be viewed by the school as a major explanatory factor in accounting for educational difficulty of students. A long series of scholarly, and some not so scholarly, works on the family appeared for consideration by teachers and future teachers.

The past twenty years have witnessed the solidification of a society around values associated with affluence. At the same time a number of conflicts have emerged out of the fact that persons are differentially positioned with respect to access to this affluence. The children of the affluent generation, tied very loosely to institutional constraints, are free to seek their own purposes in a vastly complex and jet-paced society. Out of this condition there has proliferated a number of problems which confront the school as a watchdog of the public morality. The problems may differ, but many of them are products of the same social condition. It is with this view of social problems that this book has been written. The view is one of change, of new forms of old problems. It sees these forms as tied to the currents of changing social interaction.

Accompanying the emergence and disappearance of specific problems through time, certain areas of social strain remain constant, changing only in their form of disruption. Certain problems are inherent in a society which is populated by diverse ethnic groups, but segregation is not the same phenomenon as a race riot. New conditions give rise to new forms of conflict, which is to say that a book of this type can be rewritten every ten years and have available material for a totally new content. The phenomenon of drug addiction, for example, is not new, but today the infiltration of a drug-taking ethic has penetrated every social stratum and every age level beyond puberty. This is a vastly different circumstance from the isolated incidence of addiction, a condition affecting the lives of very few.

PROBLEM CHARACTERISTICS

The topics chosen for the content of the book are varied but they have several things in common. First, they are topical. That is, each area of conflict and strain is of significant concern to present-day reformers as well as the public at large. Each area has been discussed frequently in the popular press and the weekly periodical. Second, each area contains a manifestation which is relevant to our time. The form of disorganization can be specifically related to conditions which are uniquely configured in our stage of historical evolution. The major forms of crime, for example, have remained constant over the past several decades and while research into murder, theft, and embezzlement continues to occupy criminologists, the same kind of headlines dominate newspaper headlines today as they did twenty-five years ago. This is not the case with sexual "deviations." "Free sex" and "abolish abortion" movements are no longer underground. Homosexuality is the subject of television specials and birth control pills are disseminated in university student health centers. The times have changed and the strains have intensified. Third, each problem area has special relevance to and for education. The school in some way is both affected by and affects the incidence and form of the conflict. The fact that we can establish such relationships became an important criterion for the inclusion of each problem in the book.

The approach to the analysis of each problem area involves three major steps. The first step considers the fundamental parameters of the problem. It looks at the people affected, the form of conflict, and the circumstances surrounding the conflict. It examines some basic research and summarizes the state of present knowledge about the problem area. Finally it evaluates the conditions out of which the strain grows and is cultivated.

The second step involves an analysis of the way in which the problem has consequences for educational behavior, and the role which education has played in producing conditions conducive to the growth of the problem. Socio-educational research is examined and summarized, and further directions for empirical investigation are suggested.

The third step poses hypothetical directions for education, projecting consequent effects upon the state of the problem depending upon the alternatives chosen. It is here that the reader will need to make his own evaluation about alternatives and consequences. Suppose, for example, that we are considering the problem of suicide among college students. We have implied in our discussion that suicide appears to be functionally related to stress, ambiguity, and competition. We then assume that higher education will be moving in one of several directions: to a tutorial system; to a greater emphasis on depersonalization, such as is found in the monolithic multiversity; to a breeding ground for graduate education; to a scientific or a liberal arts emphasis; and so on. Our problem at this point is to assess, based on what we know so far about the problem, the direction which will be most conducive to a reduction of those elements out of which tendencies for suicide evolve.

In the last section the winds of political and cultural change will be estimated. Culture influences political directions, and these in turn influence directions for the school. It makes a difference, for example, whether the politics of a state or a nation are predominantly conservative or liberal for counterpart ideologies exist in the school. An emphasis on mental health versus an elitist humanities education can be described broadly as a liberal-conservative dichotomy. It is unlikely that a strong conservative strain in state politics will witness a liberal strain in education.

The place of the school in American life is paramount. Access to the rewards of a bureaucratic society is predominantly through the classroom. At the same time the school has assumed the function of unilateral socialization. The circumstance is one which has seen a heavy abrogation and delegation of functions once shared by the family. The family does not have the influence it once had. Too many problems of either survival or status striving have occupied the attention of the adults. Urban life is not conducive to the kind of family integration characteristic of rural life. The peer group competes successfully for the child's loyalties. Freedom for the children has become an ethic born of both a progressive ideology (and parents wish to appear progressive) and a rationalization for the inability to exercise strong controls. Only one other institution, the school, has the organization, the regulations, and the compulsory attendance to exercise the kind of social control which will inhibit childhood anarchy. It is for this reason that amelioration of large and small social conflicts is assigned to the school; and it is for the same reason that this work is directed to the attention of educators rather than parents or church leaders.

Social problems are not educational problems, but they are

problems for education. They are problems in two distinct ways. They may be problems insofar as they represent behaviors of student members of the school, such as participation in delinquent acts, or they are indirect problems insofar as they constitute social or psychological environments which affect educational performance. Examples are poverty, urban life, and family disorganization.

In some instances deviant behavior can be directly linked to environments, but it is important to keep in mind that conceptually the problems are not always the same as the environment. All children of the slums are not delinquents and all Negroes are not low achievers or rioters. To confuse this issue, as educators frequently do in assigning causes to disruptive behavior, is to lose one of the threads of order which this book hopes to achieve. The application of the fruits of sociological analysis is not necessarily found in data that we can use in planning programs. The main contribution rests in the ordering of social phenomena in such a way that the complex network of interaction of persons and attitudes in the school becomes conceptually clear and hence capable of being manipulated.

Education

and

Social

Problems

1

Problems and Solutions

INSTITUTIONS have problems. Some persons are victims of the failure of society to discover a way to make institutions safe for all people. We see the value of conforming to institutional patterns, and we are willing to surrender much personal freedom and choice because we do not see how to maintain social order and permit freedom at the same time.

Persons who experience unfavorable or difficult life situations as a result of their participation in institutional life are victims of

1

certain patterns of social organization. Reorganization is difficult because most persons believe that they are richly rewarded as a result of their affiliation with the American way of life as they know it. Children grow up believing in the core structure of American social life because their whole conception of human adaptation depends upon the existence of a stable set of values. Their rejection of these values is possible on a large scale only when the values are non-functional—that is, when regardless of one's belief, the society which protects those values does not return anything meaningful as a payment for loyalty, or when in return for this loyalty, persons experience pain, anxiety, frustration and deprivation, gradually withdraw their loyalty and look to new value systems to improve their condition. The new value systems may very well be those which support crime, delinquency, drugs, violence, and revolution.

The problems that we deal with in this book are problems of institutional life, and the solutions can be found only in the reordering of those institutions. This may be difficult, perhaps impossible. Institutions may be bigger than the human power which makes them work as they do. If this is true, then we have reached a point in social history when our most serious problem is that we have run out of time.

We will assume, however, that persons who understand the structure of social institutions are able to conceive of ways of reshaping those structures. Part of our problem in this book is to make sense out of the relationship between people and institutional structures. If we say, for example, that schools are racist and that the only way to solve the problem of racism is to change those educational structures which account for the racism, then what does that have to do with persons who exist in the school? We may find many schools where teachers and administrators pass attitude tests with flying colors, and yet, as we observe the mobility rates of students through these schools, we can see the white children moving on to higher education and the dark-skinned children moving to low skill occupations or to the streets. Since, however, persons move in and out of institutions but structures remain, the important focus must be upon those patterns which reflect the past and guide the present.

As we talk about solving problems in the school, we will talk only about changing the school, not changing people. Not that, in many cases, people do not need to be changed. Many do, but many others are sincerely trying to figure out what they can do to help solve the problems. Their intentions are solid; their knowledge is limited. An understanding of the way in which educational structures produce social problems is necessary. It is also important to understand the way in which educational structures emerge as a reflection of several significant value systems in society, and how problems emerge when these value systems are imposed on people's lives.

THE MANAGEMENT OF BELIEF SYSTEMS

Institutions, particularly those like the church and the school, which evolve a bureaucracy to service important social functions, reflect the prominent belief systems of a society. In the execution of certain beliefs the organization often experiences disruptions. This is not necessarily because the beliefs are problematic in themselves; it is ordinarily because organizations have not evolved structures mature enough to accommodate the belief system without at the same time producing social disorganization in the lives of many participants. We need to look at some of these belief systems and the way in which the school manages them.

Universalism

Americans believe in single standards. We believe that all persons, regardless of differences, should be required to compete against the same standard of excellence, be it in athletics, in seeking job promotions, or in the classroom on examinations. Educators recognize and accept the notion of individual differences, but they have not yet figured out a way to live comfortably with this understanding and the belief in the fairness of standards.

The Status Quo and the Inevitability of Social Justice

We believe, almost by definition, that a just society founded on democratic principles will ultimately produce social justice for all. We respect the social order in almost all its forms because it is inconceivable that a nation born out of democratic principles could evolve into something inconsistent with that notion. The school is the dominant social institution responsible for the perpetuation of the democratic ideal. Unfortunately educators have not discovered how to do it democratically. Again, differences are not accommodated, but under the guise of the democratic assumption everyone in the interest of social justice is treated alike. In order to treat persons differently the social order and its assumptions must be overhauled, but Americans believe in the status quo since everything will turn out to be just. If change is necessary to solve problems of social justice, then our basic assumptions about the American social order are thrown into doubt. Education has not yet learned to manage change within this framework.

Efficiency

We believe strongly in accomplishing tasks with the most efficient utilization of materials and personnel. To this end we have established bureaucracies to manage our functional tasks. As persons assume roles within the bureaucracies they are typed in line with those roles. Social interaction becomes defined by the functional and status components of these roles. This works fine up to the point where persons within the bureaucracies decide that they have to be more than the role prescribes. When many students in secondary schools and on college campuses walk out of class, they do so predominantly because they do not like the bureaucratic conception of the student role. Students may by definition be all the same, but human beings are different. It is inefficient to deal with different individuals. The school, like General Motors, operates on a mass production basis. This is another example of the school's inability to manage social or personal difference.

Moral Absolutes

Americans believe strongly in morals and confuse these with social conventions. Having a strong nationalistic pride and a typical ethnocentrism, Americans, like most other nationalities and cultures, believe that their beliefs are right and those which differ are wrong. American morality, couched in modern Calvinistic ethics, a minor variation of the Protestant ethic, forms the cornerstone of our educational institutions. If we believe generally in the value of industriousness, we reward this in students and punish laziness or what we define as laziness. If our moral absolutes are worthy outside the school, they are even more worthy within because the culture must survive, because children are young and cannot comprehend subtle variations, and because there are too many children to manage if there is a great deal of flexibility. Again, we see how differences are difficult to manage within a context of moral absolutes.

Common Sense

Americans believe in the common man and common sense. We elect politicians who run on a common sense platform. We feel that large states and even monolithic national governments can be run best by men with common sense. Common sense, within institutional contexts, is often referred to as conventional wisdom. The conventional wisdom of education is partly a belief that the way things were done in the past are best. Common sense is also intuition. In over a hundred years the teacher's role has actually changed very little. Teachers still tell students what to do and how to do it, reward them when they do, and punish them when they don't. The complexity of contemporary social life would appear to require that students be taught a more sophisticated basis on which to make decisions. As differences in personal and social experiences increase for children, the utilization of conventional wisdom or common sense would appear to be a highly inappropriate basis for decisions for many, if not most, students.

Order and Restraint

We believe that order in our lives and in the lives of others is intrinsically beneficial. Lack of restraint threatens our sense of order and stability. We mobilize our forces, which may mean more police or more rules for students, to guarantee us this stability. We put students on schedules and timetables. If some students wish to take more time to graduate than our sense of order allows, they are defined as strange and encouraged to return to sanity. Students differ in their capacity to fit ordered molds of academic as well as personal style. But our need for order requires all students to be the same. Conformity, while a haven for those students who have the capacity to conform, is the educational death knell for those who do not.

These are the beliefs which, when transferred into educational structures, often produce disruptions in the lives of students and close channels for many who might otherwise overcome their original disadvantages. The way in which persons are victimized by educational structures intended to help them "fit in" to the main stream of American society is one of the critical themes of this book. At the same time we wish to view the school as an environment in which the kinds of problems we talk about can be alleviated and possibly, in the cases of race relations, mental illness, sexual deviation, and alienation, be prevented. The remainder of this chapter will be devoted to a discussion of the kinds of structural reorganizations that are necessary in order for the school to make a difference in the whole spectrum of social disorganization.

The kinds of solutions we suggest here are general to all or several of the problem areas covered in the book. They are the framework within which the analysis of each problem area should be viewed. They reflect the problematic aspects of the management of belief systems which we discussed earlier. Many of the general suggestions are repeated in the context of the specific problem areas to follow. Such repetitions serve to link the specific with the general and help to provide the applied framework for the book. We are concerned here with a reconstruction of educational institutions. It is possible that no meaningful change of educational structures is possible without significant parallel changes within the larger society. But the general culture is changing, and rapidly. Its changes will be reflected in the schools, but as happened with earlier belief systems, the possibilty of similar mismanagement must be avoided. The assumption here is that the new values, the changes, are humanistic, that is, that persons are no longer able to accommodate themselves to the violence of everyday social living, in which one's human qualities are reduced to mechanistic conformity. The solutions or recommendations that are embodied in the following discussion are linked to that conception of change. If social change moves in a less humanistic direction, the suggestions made here will be totally incongruent with dominant cultural themes and may be viewed as an idealistic attempt to provide a direction.

The ideas which follow are conceived as the components of the preventive model by which education can be transformed into a therapeutic environment. It should be noted that a therapeutic environment need not conduct therapy in any sense. It is simply a context within which the daily experiences help students grow toward an understanding and acceptance of themselves in relation to others with whom they interact.

PERSONALIZED INTERACTION

We have evolved a long distance from the kind of interaction that characterized the rural town. Size, of course, was the key, and the patterns appeared to flow from that. The impersonalization of urban interaction was also a function of the density of population within an ecological context. In the midst of masses children as well as adults seek out a group of close friends to buffer the anxiety that emerges out of a depersonalized world. But because normal activities require persons who do not know each other or who do not know each other well (school, church, job, movies, parks, the beach) to congregate together, the friendship group dissipates as a potent cohesive force. If there is some value in reducing the social distance between persons in institutional life, particularly in educational and economic spheres where there is very little intimacy, the way to do it is to reduce the interaction structures to smaller components.

Students in early elementary classrooms look almost exclusively to the teacher for behavioral cues. Their relationship to the class is one of meaningless convenience. It is more practical to have one teacher and thirty-five students than one teacher and one student. The child accepts this, accepts that the other students in the class have as much right to their seat as he has to his. But the important person in the classroom is the teacher, and since there is no real understanding of the value for others besides himself being in the room, the child relates his behavior almost exclusively to the perceived expectations of the teacher. Young children will develop friends, but the friendship group itself is highly fluid in its boundaries and the mechanism of cohesion or support is still missing from the group structure.

The suggestion that emerges from this kind of analysis is, then, that students should understand something about why they are not alone in the class. They should be able to relate to others as partners in some activity and understand the value of the other's presence.

MULTIDIMENSIONAL STATUS SYSTEMS

Most emotional problems are linked to belief systems. These systems reflect the values of a particular culture. If economic success is personally important to an individual, it is likely that the culture within which he resides regards economic success highly. If popularity amongst peers or success in competition is important to an individual student, then we can usually affirm that the culture of the school esteems popularity and competition.

There are two routes we can take. One route is to work toward changing the values of the culture so that the goals are more available to more members. The other is to work within the framework of dominant value systems but open more channels to the attainment of traditional goals.

Schools, as we know, develop fixed status systems. Gordon's study of *The Social System of the High School* delineates the structure of these systems.[1] Status is achieved by performance in academic areas, through participation in highly valued extra-curricular

[1] C. Wayne Gordon, *The Social System of the High School* (New York: The Free Press, 1946).

activities (a popularity index), and through association with peer groups or cliques. The school can combat tendencies toward status consolidation of this sort by restructuring the three dimensions. First, the school can extend the criteria for academic performance; second, the school can employ strategies to uplift the evaluation of low status activities; and third, the school can institute activities designed to promote a greater variety of interpersonal interaction.

We have already considered the first problem and have suggested ways of extending the base of evaluation of academic performance. We know the second can be done because different activities have different status in different schools. In many predominantly Negro high schools the status of the choir is higher than in predominantly white schools. The history of music in the culture of the Negro and musical ways of achieving mobility in the larger system are circumstances which influence the evaluation of musical activities. In working class schools the value of athletics is high. In a middle class school the student council is esteemed above that of most athletic activities. In these schools debate carries prestige as an activity. This is not true in the working class school. The problem for the school is to conceive of ways to make activities which have low status more desirable to the students. The current practice is simply to organize activities around all possible interest categories. If we make a realistic assessment of the function of participation in these activities, we shall see that interest is only one focus for organization. Students can, for example, be asked to participate in several activities on a rotating basis and charged with the task of structuring the club or association in whatever way they think it can be made more attractive to the student body as a whole. This appears to be a more creative utilization of the system of activities in secondary schools.

Schools frequently make attempts to break up cliques that form around high school fraternities and sororities. In the absence of any organized system of interpersonal relations, however, the same cliques coalesce on an informal basis. The school needs to consider ways of producing effective interacting units among persons of different statuses. Work groups can be an effective strategy if the task involves different abilities. Ultimately some kind of basic encounter strategy will intrude upon the traditional structures of the school. Clique formation is often a matter of birds of a feather sticking together for mutual support, and the limitation of membership is often a function of the inability of persons to relate to those they do not know. One simple activity—having every student talk to (we can even provide students with an outline of things to say) another student that he does not know—will make the boundaries of friendship groups even more fluid than they presently are.

Status in the secondary schools, as well as in many colleges and universities varies according to the curriculum that one has chosen. Hollingshead's early study of a high school showed how many students chose the colloge preparatory curriculum even if they did not intend or expect to go to a college.[2] Status is king. This kind of separation of status curricula produces the frustration and inter-group aggression about which we spoke earlier. The school's task is to discover ways to remove the stigma associated with membership in such curricula as the industrial or commercial. One way of doing this can be to make the entrance requirements to special technical high schools as difficult as possible, using a wide range of criteria and advertising this fact. The status of an activity is always improved as access to it is made more difficult. More significantly, the schools need to organize a structure of interaction between persons in different programs. Teachers, who have long felt that their position in colleges of education were defined as inferior by other students, should be the first to realize the importance of interpersonal interchange where persons can honestly describe the kinds of challenges which are unique to their chosen fields. The importance of this kind of activity can partly be seen in the large number of people who are either unhappy in their work or in their academic pursuits. The source of this intrapersonal conflict often rests in the motivation for their choice of careers, which is often status.

RESTRUCTURING THE TIME FACTOR

Social mobility is ordinarily tied to a timetable. Students who are "left back" or "detained" at a particular grade level because they have not learned the material for that grade are quickly classified as failures. They know this themselves. It seeps into their self image. Poor people, for example, are often migratory people. They have a consistent history of high physical mobility. This pattern makes it difficult for their children to keep up in school. Many students are forced to repeat a grade. This is damaging because schools place such high emphasis on a patterned time progress. One should move through the first six grades in six years or less. Even when students do progress according to the normal time table in systems that subscribe to automatic passage regardless of content

---

[2] A. B. Hollingshead, *Elmtown's Youth* (New York: John Wiley and Sons, Inc., 1949).

mastery, many are damaged because they have not learned the content of one grade level and are thereby handicapped in the next.

The alternative to this pattern that is destructive to many children would be a new definition of progress and time. The non-graded school is one such plan. Deficiencies in goal attainment for this plan would occur if students are not convinced that time is unimportant. An educational system that withdraws from its traditional cycle of graduating groups of students at certain intervals, so that one, two, or three year delays are not viewed invidiously, might successfully combat this problem. At University Elementary School in Los Angeles, where John Goodlad, the proponent of non-graded schools is the director, students are grouped "sociologically." That is students are grouped according to both sociometric (friendship, play grouping) and achievement criteria. Teachers attempt to play down any individous distinctions based upon disparate age groupings.

It appears, however, that the success of this attempt is intricately related to gaining support from other institutions and groupings, such as the family and the friendship group. No resocialization can effectively occur when other institutions do not support the goals. Perhaps the school as a total environment for a period of time offers the only solution in a transition period between a time-scheduled status pursuit and an individually oriented, non-time-pressured, learning for knowledge environment.

ANOTHER CONCEPTION OF ORDER
AND RESTRAINT

Students are seldom asked about how they feel with respect to what they learn. They are asked only to describe what they know. The cognitive as well as the moral dimensions of the educational experience help to produce a non-affective climate. The obvious problem with this is that feelings need some kind of an outlet, and because there is no institutionalized vehicle for expressing feelings appropriately, they are either repressed or, when repression mechanisms are no longer functioning adequately to protect the child or the adult, they emerge in inappropriate and often self-destructive ways.

A reconstructive view of the educational experience is one that challenges the function of the old proprieties. It is a view that accepts the possibility that affective structures can be instrumental in producing healthy children as well as producing more meaningful learning experiences. If these kinds of affective structures can be organized so that children come to believe that it is not only appropriate but useful to allow feelings to be expressed in the course of the educational experience, then traditional role relationships will begin to erode. Critics of this view (usually those who are threatened by the potential disruption of the system and those who are unclear about how it will work) will, of course, object. They will appeal first to the potential disservice that we are doing to children, saying that when children take their place in the larger society they will be unprepared to conform to the normative system of adult life. It is at this point that educators will once again have to decide whether or not their role is to reflect the larger society with all its problems, or to play a leadership role in building the kind of personalities that will engage in an overhaul of the dysfunctional characteristics of that larger society. Since education has always played a passive and conservative role in social change, the prospects for affective education do not appear to be bright. At the same time educators should be aware that there are alternatives, and as persons concerned about the mental health of children they may be forced to play a more active role in the conception and implementation of new educational structures.

THE ORGANIZATION OF CONTROL

We spoke earlier about the punitive model on which educational control was based. A more general view is one that sees punitive techniques as instrumental only when tendencies toward deviance are potential or when deviant acts do erupt. The more general model is one that conceives of control as a function of seeking rewards from the system. Because competition is one structural component of the system, persons adhere to rules of decorum so as not to endanger their position in the race for status. Failure to succeed in the competition for status is perceived by children as both a social and a psychological failure. They fail in their maneuvering for a comfortable and highly esteemed position in the social system, and they experience rejection. Teachers introduce an affective dimension into their evaluation of students. The student not only loses ground in the status race; he is also told in effect that we do not like rule breakers. Like most control systems which are not totally autocratic, the school capitalizes on the children's need to be accepted and esteemed. In extreme cases, such as those reported by Henry, the teacher often plays one student against another in order to ritualize control.[3] Henry describes his research in elementary school classrooms as revealing a strong tendency on the part of teachers to encourage students to increase their own status by exposing the deviant behavior of others. In this way an informal police state emerges and forms what Henry calls the "witch hunt syndrome."

Competition, then, is utilized in education as both a motivational device and as a control mechanism. The alternative to competition as a strategy is, of course, cooperation. A cooperative model is one that conceives of motivation and control as functions of group solidarity. When deviant tendencies occur or when actual disruptions appear, the group must evaluate together the effect that such disruptions have upon the group goals. The value of this model over the competition model, in terms of reducing structurally the elements within the environment which are harmful to the emotional makeup of children, is that consensus and arbitration are activities and postures that are based upon communication between the people involved.

In general the notion of control is often conceived as being completely distinct from the cognitive educational routines. The cooperative model would not make this distinction since deviance and conformity are always evaluated by the group as part of the group's progress in approaching educational goals. Unfortunately the many attempts to employ a cooperative model in the classroom have been retarded in their effects because the school and/or the teacher permits only a limited amount of freedom to the group and holds the group accountable and responsible for performing its tasks in ways that are acceptable to the school and the teacher.

STRUCTURAL CHANGES IN HIGHER EDUCATION

Because of a number of factors already discussed, poverty children do not typically meet the entrance requirements of higher education. And since they do not attend college, their opportunities for mobility are limited. To some extent the junior college programs in many states have sought to provide a broader base of opportunity for such people. But for the most part this has provided little more than an extended public school education in which the normal rewards of college attendance are absent. In perhaps too drastic a view of the function of the junior college, Clark, for ex-

---

[3] J. Henry, *Culture Against Man* (New York: Random House, Inc., 1963), pp.293–296.

ample, has suggested that the predominant function of the junior college is to "cool out" a large group of marginal students who have aspirations but weak background.[4]

A serious review of the role of higher education in ameliorating social injustices is required. Proponents of a new role are talking about such possibilities as a reorganized set of entrance requirements, a pass-fail kind of evaluation, and a no-drop contract for the first year.

A more revolutionary restructuring which we might consider would be to provide higher education to all who want it and eliminate the invidious concept of the drop-out or flunk-out. This could be done by providing credit for all courses that are passed and no credit for all courses that are failed. Courses that are failed would simply mean that the student would have to take them again or pass them by examination whenever he is ready. For many students graduation would take more than four years, but the hope would be that such delays would not be considered negatively. We would hope that the university could resocialize students to new definitions of timetables as we suggested earlier. In a time of rapid social change and the confrontation of the structure of higher education by students across the country, such revolutionary possibilities are not out of sight.

THE MANAGEMENT OF DIFFERENCES

We spoke earlier in this introductory chapter of the school's inability to deal with social and personal differences. The problem of reducing the invidious consequences of these differences and suggestions for dealing with them were then discussed. But what about increasing the advantage of social and personal differences? The school must be a place where children build on their uniqueness rather than their similarities. A school is currently a place where children act like adults, adults (particularly in the lower grades) act like children, black kids act like white ones, poor kids act like rich ones, and everybody is always looking around to see what model he can imitate rather than be himself.

The kind of structure that encourages children to act in ways that are self-estranging and that emphasizes the negative view of social differences is one that emphasizes a single standard of approval. It is, moreover, a structure that orients its activities to the future

---

[4] B. Clark, "The 'Cooling Out' Function in Higher Education," *American Journal of Sociology* 65 (May 1960): 569–576.

rather than the present. Students are required to think about what they are going to be when they are older and the kinds of performance required to achieve future goals. Futurizing education deprives children of the opportunity of capitalizing upon and enjoying what they are in the present. If children could begin to believe that there is something special, something valuable about being children, perhaps they would not need to imitate adults in their frantic search for approval. If children can begin by believing there is something special about being a child, they might also extend this image to other aspects of being oneself.

In some way teachers need to express their individuality as adults and diminish the possibility of imitation. This can be done by emphasizing the differences between adults and children rather than the similarities. Children can be encouraged to discuss what it means to be a child. They can write about it, sing about it, draw children, act out being a child, and they can be shown beautiful works of and by children. If this is successful, then we can move on to male and female, black and white, poor and rich, Jew and Gentile. In the socialization of younger members of our society we do not have time to concentrate on differences. It is both inefficient or inappropriate because the school's job is to produce committed and moral adults. The consequence of producing individuals might be the reduction of the conflict and disorganization that are widespread in our society.

A HUMANISTIC APPROACH

Being non-human does not mean denying drives and inclinations in the interest of social stability. Man is a social being, and in order to live in society he must develop a sense of which behaviors will be harmful to society and which will not. The dehumanization of modern man has not occurred because there were controls over his behavior but because of the inability of institutional leadership to distinguish between appropriate and inappropriate restrictions on individual freedom. We have erred on the side of excess. This is apparent in the restrictions we have imposed upon sexual freedom in the interests of protecting the public morality. The consequence of this adaptation of major institutions has been the aberrations and problems that we observe in American life.

A humanistic approach to the education and socialization of the young is one that attempts to analyze the dysfunctions of institutional repression of human needs, desires, and curiosity. It is a view that does not distrust all because a few may take advantage of permissive attiudes in disapproved ways. All children, from the earliest school years, are required to bring to school a note from their parents certifying that the child was absent for some legitimate reason. Very few, if any, children challenge this expectation, because it is a rule and rules are to be followed. This practice, while helping to control the truant inclinations of some, force upon all the institutional mode of distrust. It is the beginning of a supersocialization process that makes it difficult for children to define their individuality. Within such an environment even the most sophisticated sex education program would meet with failure, because children and adolescents know that in school they are not free to be themselves.

The humanistic approach to education is one that conceives of extending human probabilities, rather than being directed by human possibilities. It says we will help children develop in a permissive atmosphere because most will benefit, even if a few might extend their "deviant" patterns. Further, this approach conceives of differentiating between involved and uninvolved learning. Involved, here, refers to the process of encouraging students to relate to learning experiences with feelings as well as cognition. It poses the most meaningful conception of being open to learning. And being open refers to a state of being uninhibited to pursue the kind of inter-personal interaction which is possible. The only way to produce such an attitude is, of course, to have persons interact on a close basis so that they can explore the feelings and attitudes of others, rather than producing interaction based on a complex of projections as to what others feel or think.

THE HUMANISTIC SCHOOL
—AN IDEAL AND A PREDICTION

It is to be expected that the issues of our times will polarize around the culture of economic efficiency and the culture of interpersonal relations. Industry is already beginning seriously to address the question of how to improve efficiency in bureaucratic functioning by improving the basis of interpersonal communication. This attempt will undergo brutal attacks as a cooling out and cooptation increase. It will be seen as a more efficient way of controlling dissent stemming from alienation. Technocrats will press for a conception of industry and education as technology, having nothing to do with individuals, and will scoff at humanistic activities. But both will change as a matter of survival. They will change because competition for personnel will become greater. Public schools will begin to lose teachers and students to progressive, Summerhill-type schools, and universities will feel the same strain. The agent for change will emerge from outside the mainstream of education. Some of those who are now boring from within will eventually give up their efforts to make schools an integrating experience and create competing educational structures. Others will continue the struggle, not wanting to throw the baby out with the dirty water.

The humanistic school will be concerned with knowledge, interpersonal relations, human potentialities, and social problems. Students will have an opportunity to be involved with all parts of their humanity in effecting change within the school and within the society. Education will be relevant because it will bring, in a meaningful way, the cognitive and affective processes together; and resistance to activities which prevent persons from being productive will become a commitment of students.

The humanistic school will be one where students and teachers together will deal with the question of relevance. It will be a situation in which group solidarity will offset the tendencies for intragroup hostility through competition. Students will learn with the help of others because the new conception of evaluation will relate to the extent to which one can give knowledge to others and help others become integrated into the learning experience and environment.

Students in the humanistic school will learn to question educational content from the perspective of developing capacities for aesthetic growth rather than from the perspective of preparation to compete for college entrance or rewards. College students will seek relevance by applying both knowledge and affective experiences to the problems of self-awareness and self-fulfillment, and to the solution of social problems.

The members of the humanistic school will cohere because it will orient its curriculum to purpose through human action. Activists have discovered that isolation dissolves when persons work together for something. And perhaps the latent function of radical action for the members is mainly that action requires cooperation; communication and liking usually flow from this. Young radicals are notoriously inefficient at their tasks and changes are seldom apparent, but the whole process of interacting with others to affect change is profoundly humanizing. The humanistic school is one in which the latent outcomes of activities which appear to show little in the way of product will be evaluated in terms of maturation in the area of inter-personal relations.

Scholars ordinarily mistrust the softness of affective education. Institutions have perpetuated this climate of distrust as a way of preserving existing patterns, but the results have been, for too many, disastrous. It is true that in many areas students as well as adults are rejecting rationality to pursue visceral dictates. It is a common example of how persons need to reject one structure completely in order to live comfortably with the other. Eventually experience leads persons to strike a happy medium between the rational and affective domains, and education should provide many of the experiences which can facilitate this process.

Persons need to be actively linked to their life space and their future, their future as persons, not as professionals or role types. They need freedom. . . . They need freedom to explore their potentialities. Mistakes are not as debilitating as alienation. In many ways mistakes in the organization of one's life can be productive in facilitating growth. Rational, impersonal, bureaucratic living denies one this opportunity.

Students in schools at all levels can be efficiently managed so that alienation does not disrupt the patterns of education on a broad or serious basis. Our conception of education is one which sees the stable school as one that manages conflict rather than one that has none. But management is becoming more difficult all the time. This is because the management structures of teachers, students, and administrators is impersonal. The school of the future will also need to manage conflict and alienation. The only hope for avoiding institutional anomie would appear to be the establishment of a new structure for solving institutional problems. This structure has to look like and be a participatory democracy. School must be a community of persons actively seeking common goals rather than a monolith of persons competing with each other for position and status.

If the educational scientist is to contribute to the process of educating the whole man, he must himself become a whole man, which he is not. The educator-scientist is a victim of the system which created him and which he is intent on preserving. If he must objectify the goals of classroom activity, let him begin by considering the human condition. Let him think about operationalizing the components of alienation in educational terms and establish programs devoted to reducing these. What a student is capable of, acting as a free and independent explorer of his own potentialities, cannot be known in advance. We do him a serious disservice if we allow him to live in terms of the limitations which our preconceived goals impose. It often apears that we act upon a basic distrust that, given such freedom, students will plant the seeds of their own and society's collapse. Therefore, we manage his life and in the process take most of the meaning out of it. Working on this assumption, we cannot possibly build the kind of community of mankind that our idealistic thinkers envision. Perhaps, left to their own devices, given power to create their own world, students will produce a fascist state. This is a theoretical possibility given our structure of cooperative self-determination. There is, however, no evidence that those who have taken this freedom are, as persons, interested in controlling the lives of others. The flower children of our times are being buried under a pile of bureaucratic manure, but there is no indication that they will not survive. More likely they will prevail, and spread their message until schools will find it no longer possible to dam up their human energies. Children will simply not permit it, even though their parents do.

2

Problems
of Poverty

POVERTY IS EVERYWHERE and poverty is nowhere.
At least, nowhere to be seen. These are important underlying no-
tions of two popular books on the subject of poverty in America,
Harrington's *The Other America*[1] and Bagdikian's *In the Midst of
Plenty*.[2] Harrington talks about the "invisible" poor and Bagdikian

---

[1] Michael Harrington, *The Other America* (New York: The Macmillan Company, 1962).
[2] B. H. Bagdikian, *In the Midst of Plenty: The Poor in America* (New York:
Signet Books, 1965), p.75.

emphasizes the "out of sight, out of mind," psychology of the American middle class.

The statistics which describe the poverty population are often mentioned within a context of awakening interest, as if the reader or listener is bound to be overwhelmed by how many poor people are walking around his country. Harrington talks about 40 to 50 million, and Bagdikian goes as high as 54 million, depending on the definition. Statistics may be dull, but the weight of numbers is politically potent, particularly when this weight lies heavily upon the conscience of the politician and his constituency.

The majority of poor people are white but the majority of non-whites are poor. Sixty per cent of persons living in rural areas are "poor," and twenty-five per cent of those who live in cities. Unemployment figures are higher for persons living in rural areas (Negroes, Mexicans, Puerto Ricans, and Indians) than for the white urban majority. Figures for Puerto Ricans and Indians show double the national unemployment average. It is through the lack of employment that persons become statistics of the poverty culture, but the significance of unemployment rests as much in the area of not having any work to do as it does in not having any money to spend.

THE EFFECTS OF POVERTY

The effects of poverty, as would be the case with almost any social condition, are differentially distributed throughout the poor population. We do not mean to make the argument that persons react differently to different experiences as a purely personal matter. The point is that the social psychology of different clearly defined social groups is bound to influence the adaptation members of these groups make to the condition of poverty. For example those persons who, reared within the main streams of the American culture, exposed and committed to the Protestant ethic, particularly such expectations of that ethic as industriousness and the intrinsic value of work, when suddenly cast into the doldrums of an economic depression, are bound to have different reactions from those with radically different experiences. For these persons (and the depression years of 1929–1939 saw legions of them scurrying for something to do) being out of work was as much a psychological hardship as it was an economic one.

There are some data on this issue. As early as 1937 James Plant, after observing the behavior of children from families with marginal or lower living standards, concluded that these children showed distinctly more insecurity symptoms than children from economically advantaged homes.[3] Later investigations led Plant to conclude that persons living on relief experienced lower morale, greater familial discord, and had more children who required psychological help than persons in the economic mainstream.[4]

Life magazine in March of 1961 decided to take a look at the unemployed, not so much from the statistical standpoint, as would be the approach of more scholarly periodicals, but from the point of view of the kind of human relations story that the average citizen relishes. The description rang with such purple statements as "the faces of the nation's jobless last week bespoke individual tragedies that were multiplied by the statistics of unemployment" and "Anxiety, hunger and hopelessness beset them and their families. They suffered the indignity of being useless and were ashamed at having lost their self-reliance."[5]

The onset of a period of leisure that accompanies decreased weekly hours is typically met by increasing amounts of moonlighting, currently a popular style in our society. It is not so much that people need more money than they make; this is a relative and highly individual motive. The problem is that people unaccustomed to extensive leisure and generally unequipped to deal with it fall back upon deeply internalized needs to work. This quality is the psychological downfall of men who are displaced by automation or unplaced because of the lack of skills. When workers exhaust their unemployment compensation, lose their skills or find their skills obsolete, and begin to approach late middle-age, the consequences can be expressed by a legion of social and psychological concepts which are very popular in the literature. Alienation, lack of self-esteem, self-estrangement, anomie, depression, withdrawal are some of the more popular.

Unemployment is, obviously, an important correlate of poverty and should be considered in order to aid us in our description of the effects of poverty. But at the same time poverty is not always a condition of unemployment. Many middle-class persons experience periods of unemployment and it is possible to show detrimental effects of this circumstance independent of conditions of poverty. Goodchilds and Smith, for example, demonstrated differential effects of unemployment, based upon social status. The higher the

3 James Plant, *Personality and the Cultural Patterns* (New York: The Commonwealth Fund, 1937), pp.204–205.
4 James Plant, *The Envelope* (New York: The Commonwealth Fund, 1950).
5 W. W. Heller, "Anguish of Men without Work," *Life* 50, No. 10 (1961): 18–25.

status of the unemployed, the greater was the tendency to be defensive and self-critical. The same study found that the unemployed of the lower social statuses were less self-criitcal and more hostile toward the society which produced their situation.[6]

The problem of unemployment for minority group members, such as Mexican-Americans and Negroes, is compounded beyond the considerations already discussed by the realities of discrimination. The effects for these persons of living under the hardships of poverty combines the frustration of unemployment, disillusionment with the American "land of plenty" ideal, the bitterness of racial antagonisms, and the hopelessness of acquiring any control over the conditions which bring it all about.

Poverty as a social problem has meaning only as one relates the facts of poverty, income, work, housing, and so on to the world in which they exist. In their interaction with the world around them, the poor develop certain biases and resentments, attitudes toward the major cultural institutions, and ways of approaching and avoiding the majority population. Whatever social regularities we have observed in the behavior of those in poverty, an understanding of these regularities may be aided by presenting a brief discussion of certain ambiguities which are bound to occur in the definitions and associations we have about the social facts we report. Three of these ambiguities occur in the context of relative deprivation, the poor family, and the culture of poverty.

Relative Deprivation

Poverty is often described as a "culture." In this context the poor are those who have been born into poverty and socialized by others who themselves have had to define their life styles and activities in terms of limited resources. The poor have been conditioned to a wide range of typical adaptations to each other and to the world outside their own culture. Attitudes toward marriage, sex, education, economic morality, work aspirations, drugs and alcohol, and entertainment are all shaped by the traditions of the poor. The patterns emerge in response to sociologically arranged interactions and concomitant conditions.

Poverty is also conceived as a set of circumstances and ecological arrangements within which the poor find themselves placed. One can look at income levels, types of jobs, condition of housing, educational and recreational facilities available, degree and type of illness, and statistics on divorce, desertion, and court records and

---

[6] J. D. Goodchilds and E. E. Smith, "The Effects of Unemployment as Mediated by Social Status," *Sociometry* 26 (1963): 287–293.

draw a clear distinction between the poor and others. The important point is, as far as confrontation of the poor with others is concerned, that the poor also have these clear distinctions before them.

The social psychology of poverty is concerned with the effects of position or circumstance on the collective psychology of persons living in similar economic and geographical locations. It is important, therefore, that as we begin to introduce and discuss the parameters of poverty we emphasize the contemporary approach by considering what has occurred in the last several years. One dimension of this attack is the phenomenon of violent rebellion. Insofar as this is a racial problem, we will reserve the peculiarly racial aspects for a later chapter. Insofar as this is a confrontation between the haves and have-nots it is necessary here, at the beginning, to clear the air of certain ambiguities. One such ambiguity arose around the extensive attempts to explain the Watts Riot in Los Angeles in the context of levels of deprivation. Anyone who has explored the ecological conditions of Harlem, of the black ghettos of Detroit, Philadelphia and Chicago and a dozen other northeastern and midwestern cities with large poverty pockets, if asked to predict where violent reactions to economic and social deprivations would occur, would probably have chosen Los Angeles last. Nonetheless the Watts riot occurred in the beginning (August 1965) and set the stage for comparable acts in the past several years. It becomes suddenly obvious to commentators on such events that the poor in one community do not compare themselves to the poor in other communities, that one's own discomfort is much less than the discomfort felt by others. Persons react to their own circumstances in relation to the circumstances of those around them. To those who have felt the differences of an August night in New York or Chicago and in Los Angeles the case is even clearer. The long, hot summer phenomenon is not the same. The conditions are different quantitatively in almost all respects. But the fact of rebellion of the haves against the have-nots, although certain general characteristics can be carried across the poverty board, is relative to the perception of the persons whose acts are being evaluated. The poor in Watts could point objectively to their disadvantages, but the salient internal frustrations must be evaluated with respect to perspective, what the poor see around them as well as the objective data of unemployment and income. The greater part of Los Angeles against which the residents of the southeastern part of the city (where the riot occurred) view their own circumstance is a landscape of affluence. The haves are seen as not only well off but pervasive. Millions are living in luxury, and the poor do not have a share. The sumptuous homes in Bel Aire, Beverly Hills, and Brentwood are owned, in the minds of the have-nots, by people who have supermarkets, department stores, and many other business enterprises in the neighborhoods of the poor. Relative deprivation as a consideration leads us neatly to the notion that poverty, regardless of precise quantification, is simply having less than everybody else. And when that "less" becomes a personally felt imposition, the stage for conflict is set.

The Poor Family

A second ambiguity about the culture of poverty resides in the definitions we make about problems associated with family structure and organization. Chilman describes the poverty home as containing high rigidity, poor impulse control, hostile aggression, loss of control of children at an early age, being crowded, and having low self-esteem.[7] Other qualities of the home she designates as apathy, low verbal communication, reliance on personal rather than skill attributes for vocational success, lack of goal commitment, fatalism, and magical thinking. In these homes behavior (particularly deviant behavior) is viewed in terms of pragmatic consequences, reasons or intent being not important.

One needs to be careful about sociological generalizations such as these in at least two respects. First, generalizations do not by definition apply to all cases. They are indications of tendencies and in no direct way suggest a cause–effect relationship. This is important to understand if one ultimately wishes to use sociological knowledge for applied purposes. If we can say that many poverty homes do not have the characteristics outlined above and argue also that such characteristics can be found in non-poverty homes, then we must search much deeper across socioeconomic lines for the real source of the problems.

Second, we must clearly understand that such conditions as poor impulse control, aggression, loss of control of children, and so on are not in themselves problems. They are merely signs of a different kind of socialization from that which occurs in most non-poverty families. If one wished to adapt other institutional contexts such as the school to different forms of socialization within families, our concerns about motivation, aspiration, and conflict would decrease. A good example of the way in which both of these generalization problems confound our attempts to aid children of

[7] Catherine Chilman, "Child Rearing and Family Relationships," *Welfare in Review* (January 1965) : 9–19.

the poor occurs in the case of the broken home. We do have statistics which demonstrate that divorce, desertion, and separation rates are much higher in poverty families than in the normal population. Many school teachers take this as a sign or an explanation of and for educational problems. Our interpretations of statistics, given that we are not cautious about these ambiguities, lead us to certain conclusions which are not only uncalled for by the data but are deterrants to seeking better solutions to problems than we now have. Given a superficial knowledge of the culture of poverty it is possible and even likely for teachers to define a child as (1) a product of a disorganized home, and (2) a victim of this disorganization. If we have evidence that a particular poor child does not in fact come from a broken home, it is possible that we will look for the kinds of disorganization which actually precede divorce or desertion. If we know that the home is broken, then we immediately assume that the problem emanates from this condition. This in practice frees us from responsibility, since we cannot put a father into the home or in any real way duplicate his function. Teachers do not typically focus on the fact that many broken homes are not accompanied by educational problems for the children, particularly in the middle stratum of the economic order. The meaning of a broken home is not always disorder and conflict. Often the sources of a more basic kind of conflict are reduced by the separation of the two parties to it, the father and the mother.

It was not the intention here to introduce the implications for education of the poverty data but rather to use the school and teachers as an example of the way ambiguities in our definitions of sociological knowledge lead to errors in our application of such knowledge.

The poor family is characterized by high rates of divorce and separation, short courtship periods (many marriages occurring due to pregnancy), many teenage marriages, and high mobility rates.

As social facts, divorce and desertion rates, courtship and marriage regularities, deviant patterns in sexual or economic matters, and mobility rates are purely descriptive. We have already discussed briefly the problems inherent in making the kind of sense out of broken home data that will aid our applied interests. In themselves facts have little meaning. When one attempts to look at the behavioral correlates of these facts we begin to suspect that something in the environment of the group we are discussing (in this case the poor) is not only associated with the facts but helps to explain the way the facts affect the persons who contribute their cases to the data. This is simply to say that divorce rates, for example, are not only descriptive of low income groups in general, they also help to explain the attitude that poverty people have toward the idea of stability in general. It is only when we draw our analysis out to encompass the significant components of the poverty group that we can begin to identify the problems upon which to focus. An insistence on the stability of marriage vows in this case only treats one of the symptoms of poverty, not the problem itself. If we are to be concerned with migration patterns of the poor, high mobility and transiency rates in particular, our problem is the same. High mobility rates are characteristic of business executives as well as migratory farm workers. In the former case physical mobility is associated with upward social mobility; in the latter, with unstable or downward social mobility. It is not so important that one move, but it is important why one moves. What a fact means in terms of the larger explanatory picture is the important dynamic of poverty. Ambiguities about these meanings can be clarified only if we consistently focus upon the actual context within which the descriptive factors occur.

The Culture–Sub-culture Notions

A final ambiguity which requires our attention is that which focuses on a socioeconomic condition as a cultural or sub-cultural experience. Oscar Lewis, for example, describes the sub-culture of poverty as a patriarchal system (except for Negroes, whom he describes as matriarchal), oriented toward distrust rather than trust, blaming the world rather than themselves, not interested in or a part of the institutions which regulate their lives, firm believers in experience rather than in books, and oriented to the slum rather than the national community.[8] It may be true that certain definitions of the world or the nation are distributed differently in the slums than in other communities, but these definitions must come from somewhere. A separate culture or a sub-culture appears to be, to the persons who like to play around with these concepts, a collection of persons who have some things in common with the large culture but a few things like age, economic status, delinquent patterns or race as differences. The attitudes and habits which describe these separate categories of persons emerge and are linked to the qualities which differ, rather than those they have in common with the general culture. To the extent that these terms convey a sense of difference which often establishes a

---

[8] Oscar Lewis, "The Culture of Poverty," *Scientific American* 215, No. 4 (1966): 19–26.

barrier for communication between the members of sub-cultures and members of the general culture (and this, too, may be a false division) the ambiguities inherent in our conception of these groups as sub-cultures need to be faced. The attitudes of poor people as well as many of their behaviors, such as those described by Lewis and others already discussed, are adaptations to conditions which are indigenous to our American culture. Differences in economic position are a function of the organization of our economy, and differences in race bring about conditions which are tied to our history of race relationships. The adaptations which persons make in response to their special circumstances with respect to economic organization or the history of race relationships are clearly representative of our institutionalized forms of conformity or deviation. To have been poor in India during the last century and the greater part of this one was, in terms of the cultural definition of one's stratum, met with a sense of fatalistic determinism. The adaptations of their differences, of the poor and of racial minority groups in this country, are chosen from the possibilities available to them as participants in our unique cultural history. Knowledge of the acceptable processes to success goals which all or most of the members of our society seek is related to the opportunity to utilize traditional channels. Those who do not find these channels available may turn to delinquent modes. In this sense the form of deviance is determined by the form of conformity. If hard work is the acceptable mode of achieving cultural goals, then not working for economic success becomes the deviant adaptation. If the problem is one of access to opportunities, then the definition of sub-groups, such as the poor or the Negro, as sub-cultures is misleading and perhaps dangerously so since our efforts to alleviate conflict seem to proceed on the basis of differences rather than similarities.

To talk about the poor or the Negro or the adolescent or the delinquent as a sub-culture is to emphasize the differences in such a way as to obscure their basic stake in the American way of life and their history in it. "Another culture" as a definition of persons carries the assumption that goals as well as means of achieving those goals are products of a separatism which does not and has not existed in America for the last fifty years, and perhaps, in the pure sense, has never existed. The interaction of persons with different social characteristics, while not a personal or integrative kind of interaction, has always occurred. It has occurred at the level of a communication of goals that are desirable and the means which are desirable and undesirable for attaining them. Race riots do not occur because the communication of the white world with the black world is not possible but because it is very possible and very complete. The poor, because they are very much a part of the culture of our country, are aware of our concepts of equal justice and our notion of the good life. Their adaptations in terms of personal and social disruption are deeply tied to their awareness of and consequent dissatisfaction with their place in relation to the standard cultural goals.

THE DEFINITION OF THE POOR

We know who the poor are and for the most part where they are. The more obvious descriptions of the poor in terms of their occupations as laborers and migrant workers, or non-occupations, do at times confine our conceptualization of the problems associated with poverty to rather gross categories which obscure the dynamics of poverty. The fact that clerics, dedicated to voluntary poverty, do not define their status as deprived but rather desirable, indicates that the association of poverty with a specific meaning and in a specific context is important in explaining the adaptations of persons to their situation. To be poor in a situation or a system which defines poverty either as desirable or religiously ordained, such as in India, is bound to have different consequences from a circumstance in which poverty is associated with the absence of valued qualities in persons.

Poverty is seldom described today as a virtue other than in religious circles. But the intellectual history of the West reminds us that there has been something of a tradition of valuing poverty, not for its own sake but for the sake of the society in which it exists. Many western traditions, particularly in Europe and in early American history, grew out of the need to rationalize poverty as a desirable quality, on the one hand to uphold the support of the church by the poor in terms of contributions and not losing faith with God, and on the other to maintain the economic order in equilibrium despite gross inequalities in rewards. This conversion of the definition of poverty was given powerful intellectual stimulus by the subsistence doctrine of real wages. According to this view, represented by Malthus, it was the want of necessities that induced the laboring poor to work at all.[9] If labor, as a class, rose above the poverty level, indolence would reign. Furthermore the provision for subsistence by public policy or even by private

9 T. R. Malthus, *An Essay on the Principle of Population* (New York: E. P. Dutton & Co., Inc., 1914).

charity would, by destroying the fear of want, destroy the incentive to work. So deeply rooted did these principles become in the culture of the North Atlantic world that they still represent the dominant orthodoxy of the twentieth century. Marx however looked on poverty as a vicious circle that degraded and debilitated the lower classes. He stated: "Accumulation of wealth at one pole is, therefore, at the same time accumulation of misery, agony of toil, slavery, ignorance, brutality, mental degradation at the opposite pole, *i.e.*, on the sides of the class that produces its own product in the form of capital."[10] The rich defend their position: "The poor deserve what they get." This embodiment of Social Darwinism enabled the rich to lead what they considered to be ethical lives. This individualistic presupposition of the doctrine did contain a germ of truth—just enough to establish it firmly in the dominant position.[11] As William Sumner stated: "We have our choice between survival of the strongest and survival of the weakest or we can go on as in the past vacillating between the two, but a third plan—the socialist desideratum—a plan for nourishing the unfittest and advancing in civilization, no man will ever find."[12] Perhaps the greatest deficiency on the part of the poor according to the traditional view was their presumed propensity to propagate. This population "principle" was the guarantee of poverty for the masses. In Malthus' first essay there was no hope for the poor, "irrational animals." As the threat dimmed, Malthus introduced the softer notion of the "preventive check" in later editions of the population essay.[13]

John Stuart Mill advocated higher levels of living for the lower classes for an entire generation, to be planned and engineered by the state.[14] This socialism sensed that rising living levels introduce their own incentive to generate a smaller family unit among the poorer classes. This is why the germ of truth in Malthusianism may apply today only in the vicious circle cultures of depressed and underdeveloped regions. Malthus' population argument was the cornerstone of the traditional view. Contemporary enlightened views of these matters have in common with the socialists the notion that poverty is primarily and institutionally a generated phe-

[10] Karl Marx, *Capital* (Moscow: Foreign Languages Publishing House, 1959, pp.640–650.
[11] R. E. Lane, *Political Ideology: Why the American Common Man Believes What He Does* (New York: The Free Press, 1962).
[12] A. G. Keller and M. R. Davie, eds., *Essays of William Sumner* (New Haven: Yale University Press, 1934), p.11.
[13] Malthus, *Principle of Population*.
[14] W. J. Ashley, *Principles of Political Economy* (London: Longmans, Green and Co. Ltd., 1909), pp.365–366.

nomenon, calling for a social approach to its extermination. The social reform approach differs from the socialist in its acceptance of existing institutional arrangements. In the United States today it is doubtful that a massive anti-poverty program could be a political threat to the established order. Poverty may have presented such a threat in the New Deal days of the thirties but that danger no longer exists. Today we are motivated to develop and expand our public anti-poverty programs more on the basis of humanistic grounds than from fear. However we recognize that the world is watching our performance and comparing it with the gains of the Soviet bloc.

THE PROTESTANT TRADITION IN THE UNITED STATES

The prominent strain of our current definition of poverty must be seen as originating in the social-religious conception provided by the Calvinist reformers in New England. Economic failure was certain to be associated with the fate of the non-chosen of God. As time passed, the purely secular society found that it was necessary to rationalize this view to accommodate the ego needs of the large masses who were economically unsuccessful. The distinction between being "poor but honest" and the "dregs of humanity" was forced into the breach between those who considered themselves legitimately part of the economic order and those who were to be used as models of an important difference. This distinction was embodied in the concern of the working man to be defined as an integrated member of society, integrated as a cog in the machinery of the community, and to be distinguished from those who had lost the right to this kind of dignity.

There is no dignity in poverty, and therefore there is nothing to lose. Without the struggle to maintain one's image in a society which approves of respectability, a major mechanism of social control disappears. Legal channels for maintaining social control are simply devices for discouraging deviance. The principal force that restrains persons from deviant acts on a grand scale is their commitment to the institutionalized means of achieving status and respectability in their social order. Lacking this commitment, or the opportunities by which it can be reinstated, the disenfranchised, those living in poverty circumstances, are forced to solidify the definition of others toward them in the direction of disapproval. But since disapproval is a functional sanction only in cases where persons rely on approval in their daily lives, it does not always work to discourage the aberrant behaviors which characterize the poor. The definition of the poor as deviant in their morals and remiss in their responsibilities to society does little, in the social-psychological sense, to improve the probabilities of integrating the poor into the mainstream of American life. At the same time the definitions we make of the poor do increase the potential for conflict, adding fuel to the flames of disenchantment and frustration.

POVERTY AND INEQUALITY

Inequality in America, although not a manifest intention of our institutions, remains a latent consequence of our economic organization. All societies which contain an inherent stratification system in the way in which economic advantages are distributed must have a bottom rung on the ladder. It is not necessarily the case that the bottom rung, having the least in the way of possessions or income, must be below the subsistence level. The economic history of the United States, however, has never regarded a policy of a minimum standard for all citizens as binding, even if the intentions of most men in politics and industry are good. Lacking a policy structure which guarantees a minimum standard, the best intentions appear to be impotent.

In the thirties Franklin Roosevelt brought a "New Deal" to the American people. The results of the New Deal were to lift a large body of the people out of a depression which had presented the major portion of the country's citizens with an opportunity to taste the effects of poverty. Persons who never lost their commitment of self-improvement and respect for the intrinsic value of work responded favorably to the improved conditions and thereby restored themselves to a respectable status.

But as Miller and Rein remind us, the New Deal lasted only five years, from 1934 to 1938, and ended before improvements could be made for the third of the nation which Roosevelt described as "ill-housed, ill-clad and ill-fed." The New Deal ended without fulfilling its promise to these Americans. It changed the society and the economy in many ways which opened the doors to future advances. It established the principle of concern for the disadvantaged, but it did not solve the problems of unemployment, medical needs, adequate schooling in low income areas, poor housing, and limited social services for the poverty population.[15]

During the next twenty-two years the poor were partially re-

[15] S. M. Miller and M. Rein, "Poverty, Inequality and Policy," in *Social Problems*, ed. H. Becker (New York: John Wiley and Sons, Inc., 1966), pp.427–428.

claimed by society through World War II, with its military service abroad or need for increased labor at home, and partially wished back in by administrations which hoped the vigor of the economy would somehow reach into every pocket and restore every man to some semblance of integration into the economic order. Not until J. F. Kennedy's New Frontier stage was set were good intentions translated into legislative policies. Legislation seeking to remedy inequalities in the social order were enacted and for a time vigorously pursued. Civil rights and economic opportunities legislation was passed and many appendages, pursuing the intent of the original legislation, are still being brought before the Congress. In the mid-sixties the critics of Lyndon Johnson's Vietnam war policies were screaming that the vast expenditures for the war were robbing social legislation of the kind of support that was necessary to fulfill the promises of the New Frontier and the Great Society. The future of social legislation for the poor is still couched in the conditions, largely unchanged, which prompted these movements in the first place. Such conditions or circumstances as unemployment rates, obsolete skills, the Negro revolution, and so on[16] produce the kind of social disruptions which consume the attention of political leaders and reformers.

The notion of inequality is a pervasive concept in our conception of poverty. Inequality defined as differential distributions of income, prestige or power, or as a matter of access to opportunities such as education or jobs, or different treatments before the law or by business is a pervasive fact of every day life of the poor. Across the nation socially conscious citizens are questioning such assumptions as a "jury of one's peers," employment non-discrimination based upon, "race, color or creed," price and quality standardization across different urban communities, and the idea that hard work and good intentions bring just rewards.

The farm worker and independent farmer in America are among the poorest people in the country. They work hard by any standards and they do not prosper.[17] The farmers, like the small business man and many semi-skilled industrial workers, are being shuffled into the poverty ranks by the massive changes that have occurred in the means of production and distribution. Corporate farms, supermarkets and department stores, and technology in industry have ensured the obsolescence of persons of various occupational interests and capacities. This is a fact of social change. To

---

16 For a detailed explanation of the factors that influenced social legislation in the sixties see Miller and Rein, "Poverty, Inequality and Policy," pp.429–432.
17 Bagdikian, *In the Midst of Plenty*, p.75.

talk about inequalities based on differential commitments to the exertion of energy in the pursuit of a decent living is to ignore the fundamental realities of economic change in this country. The Manpower Retraining Act, one attempt to redistribute skills in the quest for equal opportunities of employment, takes as a guiding assumption the notion that while most men will work if they are able, many are not able given the changing requirements of business and industry.

The problem of inequality which most poignantly describes the plight of the poor occurs in the area of equal justice before the law. It is clear that differential treatment affects the poor man in hidden ways in many areas of his life. Discrimination in jobs, in education, and in many areas of public law do not hold that a manifest intention of the organization or the policies of states and nations are to discriminate. This would offend our public, if not our private moralities. Hidden discriminators, on the other hand, feed nicely our desires to advance our own condition at the expense of others without being called on to expand our energies or finances in a public involvement. Two areas in which a latent form of discrimination against the poor has been exercised in the mid-sixties has been in the military draft and in the taxes on commodities such as alcohol and cigarettes. Since there is a clear relationship between economic status and college attendance, for which we will provide evidence in the next section, it is clear that, since most college students are given deferments, a disproportionate amount of drafting must occur in the lower income communities. The poor man, the one who has the least stake in the stability of our system, must pay for it in war with his life more often than those who have a greater investment. Negro leaders have been decrying this fact for several years. In the case of taxes it is clear that, for the little luxury the poor man enjoys, he pays an infinitely greater share of his income than do others. This kind of equality of participation in local, state or national investments is not the kind of equality low income persons desire. An extended graduated income tax might cover the costs equally as well, but the vested interests of high income groups would not be as well served by such a policy. Regardless of the economic arguments for such a policy, it is clear that those who are most politically powerless are the logical victims of discrimination and inequality.

In many areas the low income person is before the law a manifest recipient of discriminatory policies. In March, 1963, the Supreme Court decided in the case of *Gideon* v. *Wainwright* that a state conviction could not be upheld because the government had not provided the defendant with a lawyer as he had requested. For the first time the Supreme Court ruled that the Sixth Amendment guaranteeing a right to counsel was to apply in a state criminal court. But simply guaranteeing the right of a poor man to counsel does not guarantee his equal rights before the law. In the best sense of a fair trial a man must be assured of a competent defense. Counsels who are assigned to cases in federal courts have not, until very recently, been paid for their services. Nor are they reimbursed for the costs that often came out of their own pockets. These attorneys do not receive any investigative or expert help, and their appointment to a case often does not occur until long after arrests are made, leaving time enough for witnesses to disappear and many leads for investigation to be lost. Often these appointed counsels lack the trial experience that is essential for a good defense.

Equal rights for the poor before the law are not a matter of discriminatory laws as much as they are a case of discriminatory execution. Equal protection against illegal treatment cannot be upheld by the poor because of political impotence and ignorance of their rights. The case of integration in the South, even after the 1954 Supreme Court decision, and the rampant violations of the law in substandard housing in the urban ghettoes are two cases in point.

The inequalities which most concern us in this book are the inequality of educational opportunity, the inequality of educational facilities, and the inequality of educational rewards.

THE POOR AS PEOPLE

Before we begin to discuss the educational effects of poverty we should try to get as close as we can to a conception of the poor that is both sociological as defined in terms of income, living arrangements, and so on and meaningful at a visceral level. So long as we know that many poor children do achieve educational success, we can be certain that economic circumstances alone are inadequate to explain differences in rates of success and failure. Sociological factors can come close in predicting these rates but not how they occur. That is, we can speculate on the proportion of slum children who go to college as opposed to the proportion of children from the suburbs and establish significant differences every time. We infer from our data that the different economic circumstances carry the greatest weight in producing these differences, but this does not mean that we know much about the way that the different circumstances operate to advance or retard social mobility.

To understand the mechanics of poverty we have somehow to put ourselves into the world of the poor and to understand the meanings that they attach to the many facets of their lives. At the same time we should not try to abandon our own perspective and values about how mobility is attained because, should we do so, we will not be able to differentiate between barriers of mind and barriers in the social world. If we were to buy the line that many political conservatives offer us, that poverty is a barrier to personal advance only if we let it stand in our way, we are forced to the assumption that all things are possible if only we have the will to achieve them. This naïve conception of the social structure makes two erroneous assumptions: (1) that access to mobility is open to all, and (2) that it is possible to develop attitudes conducive to mobility when everywhere around him the poor man sees failure.

The little prince voluntarily turned pauper in Mark Twain's story of discrepancies in nineteenth-century English economic life speaks to the first assumption.[18] Despite the prince's upper class manners, proper language, and consummate knowledge of the world of the economic elites, he finds himself trapped beyond redemption in the squalor of slum life. He is persecuted more by the distrust and fatalistic attitudes of his comrades in poverty than he is by his former associates who, while possibly well meaning, are as ignorant of the world that he now occupies as he was before his decision to reverse roles. Poverty, to the little prince, was more than economic disadvantage; it was in a very real sense, a circular existence with no exit.

Poverty in America, then, should be conceived as a variation on the same theme. Neither economic conservatives nor radicals could push their doctrinaire conceptions very far in the face of the data that we have on social mobility. If the paths to mobility for the working class are completely closed, then we have no way to account for the effectiveness of labor unions or the increasing number of lower class youths who find their way into college classrooms. If the channels are completely open, on the other hand, we have difficulty explaining the failure of our economic system to produce more than minimal rates of upward mobility for the poor.

The second assumption which we must confront as we move toward a better understanding of the circumstance of poverty is

[18] Mark Twain, *The Prince and the Pauper* (Boston: J. R. Osgood and Co., 1882).

that attitudes which would be conducive of upward mobility can be produced in a vacuum. What many educators believe is that we can somehow implant a set of attitudes that are tactically effective in motivating poor children to aspire to attain a foothold in the legitimate channels toward economic advantage, education, commitment, and occupational responsibility. These attitudes do not spring naturally from the immediate environment of the poor. People living in a pragmatic world are usually forced to socialize their children to the world of the possible. This does not close the door entirely on socialization to the improbable; the rags-to-riches theme is not entirely a dead issue in the environment of poverty, not as long as athletes and entertainers find their paths to quick riches open. Poverty is the kind of environment where the children are taught the routines of the possible. Even though the channels of communication are open across economic lines and the world of success stories is carried into poor children's lives through television and movies, aspirations are not reinforced in the home, neighborhood, or school commensurate with the intense wishes for status. Even if we triple our efforts to convince parents that the paths are open, to develop habits in the young that would promote industrious efforts, the fact that success stories of those like them are glaring exceptions to a felt rule of social life makes our investment of time and money a high risk enterprise.

Developing attitudes conducive to economic striving in a vacuum is the task of Headstart programs in Appalachia, job training in migrant workers' or closed mining camps, poverty programs in urban ghettoes, library programs on Indian reservations, and small loan supports for tenant farmers. Poverty is a life of discrepancy more than of need. It is where the vacuum is, where the circumstances of everyday life cannot support or be supported by our efforts to develop citizenship in the sense of instilling commitments to regard the regular channels to economic stability as available and possible. Persons on the kind of scale that we are considering (a tenth of our population) are not as highly differentiated by the degree to which they aspire to have more as much as they are by their inability to use the institutionalized means to economic rewards.

The poor are those who, although not ignorant of paths to economic stability, are unable to conceive of a reasonable set of actions that will bring *them* this stability. They are those who live in the kind of environment which enforces their predispositions to survive and enjoy a day-to-day existence in any way they can, since planning does not work for them. The poor are those who cannot, with any degree of accuracy, predict the future. Human social activities associated with planning, commitment, and work are usually linked to reasonable predictions about the rewards of effort. The statistics on economic and educational activities that are related to social class point to regularities in this kind of adaptation. Those who try are those who usually succeed. Those who wait are those who see an end to waiting. Those who plan, particularly for long range payoffs, are those who can predict these payoffs. The poor do not plan because they cannot predict. Their lives are filled with disappointments, and the best way to avoid disappointments is not to plan on anything.

Many of the poor are farmers, bound to the uncertainties of the weather and the market. The small farmer hopes for the *status quo*, hopes that he will receive a reasonable return for his investment of time and effort. But he does not expect that things will get much better. He knows about the encroachment of the super-farms and as the small grocery store owner in the city hopes that a supermarket will not move in next door, so too does the small farmer hope that he will not be engulfed by a superfarm. When the encroachment does occur the farm family moves on, either to a life as migrants, or more often to the city where the men take up lives as unskilled or semi-skilled industrial workers. But many of the stationary farmers, unable to accept the feasibility of a new beginning, stay on the farms, either as tenants or as operators of the machinery of the corporate farms. Federal government support for agriculture is almost wholly consumed by the large farm owners and corporate farms. The agricultural worker or small land owner has not benefited. Harrington states:

The surplus foods are scrupulously cared for and controlled; the human beings are not. So these men and women form their culture of poverty in the midst of abundance; they often go hungry while the fields produce more than before in man's history.[19]

Most of the rural poor who are young enough chance a new life in the cities. They begin at the bottom of the industrial complex, establish themselves in urban pockets, and stay at the bottom and in the pocket ever afterward. Mobility within the industrial ranks is infrequent and mobility within the city, except from one slum to another, is restricted by finances. The best outcome of this migration is a steady job; a more typical outcome is a pattern of unemployment. Before long the rural poor become the urban

[19] Harrington, *The Other America*.

poor. A life on welfare becomes for many a way of life, punctuated by checks and excited only by the increase of aid prompted by the appearance of another dependent.

Back on the farm or in the farm communities, life becomes oppressive, hopeless for the older people who remain and for the few young who have to stay and care for their elder relatives. To these people the road out of poverty is symbolized by the roads of their communities, very bad and with no hope for improvement. The major change in the life of the rural poor in Appalachia has occurred with the onset of the industrial migration to the areas of those industries looking for larger profits, such as the textile industry which provides very low pay for labor. In some places in Appalachia the rural farming poor transformed their status to one of a rural industrial poor. The changes were slight.

When Pearl S. Buck extolled "the good earth" and pressed a literary argument for the value of living and working on the land, she must have had something else in mind than the life of the migrant farm worker.[20] Close to three million Americans spend their lives on other peoples' farms. They are not guests nor are they treated as guests. John Steinbeck's classical piece on the life of the migrant farmer described the life of these people as a combination of pathetic deprivation and group hopelessness.[21] The struggle for survival, as the action theme, exposed a kind of unfertile ground in which not only could no hopes grow, but there was neither time nor space to plant any.

Opportunities for life changes do not come easily to the migrant farm worker or his family. Their skills to compete in a competitive economy are beneath consideration, their status within the communities they temporarily inhabit runs off the bottom of the scale. No one at the local level attempts to help them because they are seen as a necessary but temporary blight on the social scene. Working on a piece rate scale, as they do, for perhaps $5.00 for an eight- to ten-hour day the migrant farmer knows little else but hard, long work days. The fatigue of simply surviving puts him beyond considering, since he does not have time for it, ways of producing a significant change in his life. Poverty and hard work side by side with affluence appears to be a paradox that American policymakers have not confronted. The only hope for the migrant workers of the West and Southwest at this time seems to be the activities of the Agricultural Workers Committee and the promises of some politicians. The grape workers of central California, in-

20 Pearl S. Buck, *The Good Earth* (New York: John Day and Co., 1949).
21 John Steinbeck, *The Grapes of Wrath* (New York: The Viking Press, 1939).

spired by charismatic leaders like Cesar Chavez and supported by college youths from Berkeley and Los Angeles and social reformers throughout the state, appear to have a good shot at a living wage and a redemption from indignity.

The near future holds the key to the success or failure of a long struggle to uplift millions of citizens to a place in the social structure. The fact that they are not yet assured a place in the structure is signified by their exemption from federal minimum wage laws, their ineligibility for welfare, their non-voting patterns, and their general exclusion from the major institutions which might safeguard them or their children, the law and the school.

The poor people in the cities and the Negroes in Watts, Los Angeles, have much in common with the migrant farm workers. They live deprived among incredible affluence. The poor are deprived of comforts and, since long range considerations are a luxury, deprived of security. They have time to feel deprived of opportunities only when they become caught up in and consulted on matters of social reform, or when they are swept up in social movements that the majority cannot avoid. These movements are beginning, however, to bring a breath of hope, touching ghetto Negroes and Mexican migrant farm workers in the same way. The feeling people get when they realize that they are not impotent is such that the sentiment shifts from hopes to demands, from doubts to expectancies. The urban poor, crowded in their ghettoes, subjected to high rents for poor housing, high food prices for inferior food, unequal treatment before the law and inadequate educational facilities, are people who today are not only aware of their rights but ready to challenge the system which denies them. The answer to inequalities in the city is a challenge of the poor to the political structure to make things right. The riots in Los Angeles, Detroit, Newark, Philadelphia and elsewhere have accomplished one major victory for the American Negro and for the poor of all races. The poor are no longer invisible. As long as they are a threat to the local *status quo* and a political voice throughout the nation, the poor will have to be seen.

The poor are angry; their resentments of the inequalities of the past have been stirred to the point of action, political and civil. The urban poor have awakened to find that the cities which they associate with their plight have been abandoned to them. The two Americas are produced on a smaller scale within the two cities, the urban and the suburban. More and more mayors, assemblymen, and city councilmen are men and women either from or supported by the people of the poverty ghettoes. If decentralization of political power and civic responsibility is the direction of the future, then the inequalities of social life will undergo a period of adjustment. As of now, the struggle for this kind of adjustment as a way of life is seeping into the attitudes of large segments of the urban poor.

THE EFFECTS OF POVERTY ON EDUCATION

There is no structure in our society so uniquely equipped to assimilate the poor into the main stream of American society as is the school. The school, throughout its long history, has gradually relieved the family of almost all the social responsibility for child rearing that it once had. The school, in terms of its goals as well as its institutional structures, has been designated by the society to make Americans out of all who pass through its classrooms. It has been required by its cultural traditions to socialize all students, regardless of differences, to the expectations of the larger society. This public trust is guaranteed by tradition on the one hand and the overseeing by representatives of this trust on the other. School boards represent the people and the people respond to demands for financial support to the degree that they believe the school executes this public trust.

The school attempts to assimilate the poor by instilling in all students a similar set of values. These values range from interpersonal behavior to job commitments. Assimilation is also intended by way of providing an access for all strata to educational and occupational opportunities. In many ways failure in the latter makes success in the former more unpalatable to the individual. This is simply to say that buying the goals and then being frustrated by the unavailability of the means would have a greater alienative effect than failing at both. The greater part of the following is intended to describe the educational version of equal opportunities.

All children in our society are guaranteed the right to a free education. They are not guaranteed the right to a successful education. This must be earned. It can be earned in two principal ways. One way is achievement at the cognitive level, the other is achievement at the moral level. By the time the average child is one year into his educational career he has been differentiated on these two criteria. This differentiation occurs in terms of the child's display of cognitive ability on the one hand and his ability to demonstrate behaviorally that he has internalized the moral expectations of his school world on the other. These expectations refer to his industriousness, cleanliness, cooperativeness, punctuality, respect for authority, and the demonstration of responsibility.

Children of lower socioeconomic backgrounds do not meet these two criteria in the same way that children of more advantaged backgrounds do. Consequently the children from disadvantaged homes are organizationally separated from their peers. They are assigned to special classes, special reading groups, socially isolated, disproportionately punished, and socially defined by their classmates as educationally inferior. The long range effects of this early placement are usually permanent. When Sheldon and Eleanor Glueck suggested that they could predict educational failure at a very early age they were saying that the predictive effects of early differentiation were powerful.[22] In the same way that persons in a mass society use classifications of persons to simplify an otherwise complex basis for interaction, students are classified as an easy way to teach large classes. Classification of persons and students is a normal and often useful technique for managing one's social relationships. The dysfunctions, however, are considerable, as our literature and experience with prejudice tell us.

THE DYSFUNCTIONS OF CLASSIFICATION

Competitive Antagonisms

In any social system where evaluations of performance are related to rewards, the position of those receiving inferior evaluations is not positively valued by the receivers. People in general, and children in particular, adapt to inferior statuses by developing either an antagonism to those with superior statuses or rationalizing their inferior status by defining it as desirable. Of course many students struggle to move up in the prestige ladder. But as long as it is defined in terms of its association with a given position, the normal ego becomes defensive. The first mode of adaptation, competitive antagonisms toward those who hold superior position and toward those (the teachers) who award the positions, produces an atmosphere for learning which is more social competition than it is a desire to learn. If the position comes to be valued more than the learning, then deviant techniques such as cheating become functional and positively valued. As long as antagonisms control social interactions, barriers to assimilation are raised. Students be-

[22] Sheldon and Eleanor Glueck, "The Home, The School and Delinquency," *Harvard Educational Review* 23 (1953).

gin to attempt to raise their status by diminishing the reputation of others, and this can be observed in the earliest school years. This can be described as the pulley strategy whereby one pulls himself up by pulling others down. Behaviorally this can be observed by such acts as tattling (even making up stories about others to diminish their prestige in the eyes of the evaluator), criticism of each other, stealing the homework of those who do it, and later developing social sanctions against "rate busters" (those who surpass the performance norm of the group).

The second adaptation is one in which the lower status persons defend their ego against inferior definitions by downgrading the importance of the criteria by which they were placed. It is not important to read or to add numbers, for example. If the value of learning is low, the failure is inconsequential. The long range dysfunction of this adaptation is that students begin to develop an ethic for success that is the same as the school's ethic for failure. When Becker asked teachers to describe the characteristics of lower class students, he found that the characteristics mentioned most were the behaviors that teachers punished most.[23] Rather than change to avoid punishment, many lower class students would resolve the problem by upgrading their own evaluation of these behaviors and characteristics so that a sub-culture which orients itself around deviant norms would emerge. It would not be uncommon then, for the student with the most failures on his report card to display proudly his mark of distinction within the deviant group.

Halo and Horn Effects

Students quickly develop in others, particularly teachers, a conception of themselves which becomes hardened into what many teachers refer to as a halo effect, or the opposite, which we could logically call the horn effect. These conceptions follow students through the grades. This is not an indictment of teachers as people. If it is an indictment of anything, it speaks to a form of social typing which invents such slogans as "a leopard does not change his spots." Anyone who has ever taken the time to peruse a large number of cumulative school records (the records which follow a student through his school life) can observe a pattern of teacher descriptions in which one approximates all the others. This, of course, is not to argue that similar definitions cannot be a product of consistent student behavior. At the same time, we cannot help

23 H. Becker, "Social Class Variations in Teacher-Pupil Relationships," *Journal of Educational Sociology* 25 (1952).

but wonder just what effect the possession of these records has on the teacher's definition of the student. Information within the school is not primarily carried by written records. Teachers and administrators converse with each other frequently, and it will come as no surprise to teachers that they talk about students, particularly troublesome students. For many students, particularly the lower class youngster who has not met the moral or cognitive criteria, his reputation follows him throughout the grades.

The Self-fulfilling Prophecy

The self-fulfilling prophecy refers to a process whereby persons, having perceived that they have been typed, structure their behavior to conform to that typing. In the search for a social identity in a complex environment, persons often identify as they are identified. In Bernard Shaw's *Pygmalion*, Eliza Doolittle informs Professor Higgins that people become what they are treated as, meaning that if people treated her like a lady she would quickly identify with that role. With deviant social types the process pursues the same ends, to live up to what people expect. If a child is defined as a juvenile delinquent, through time he usually fulfills that definition. If a poor child learns that, because he has been differentiated, very little in the way of academic excellence is expected of him, he is apt to reduce his motivation and performance in order to be consistent with his social role.

The definition of a person as poor in a society oriented to economic values carries a connotation of inferiority. "If you're so smart, why aren't you rich?" The children of poverty may very quickly assume, once they become sensitive to social differentiation, that there is some kind of relationship between economic inferiority and personal inferiority. Should this occur, the motivation for success becomes dissipated in a concept of the self that finds it hard to believe that one is capable of success.

The differentiation of poverty children into slow learner categories may have this kind of invidious effect. Children define the limits of their performance in terms of this kind of placement. At the same time they may use this self-definition as a rationalization against trying to surmount their present status. If I am not really able, then trying hard is senseless, they rationalize.

Effects of Closed Access to Peers

Contemporary society requires many institutions to socialize the growing child to the expectations of the larger environment. Parents limit their responsibilities, or are limited by the children, to areas that they can legitimately handle. The school advances a number of rules for social behavior and sanctions conformity. But the child, in many areas of his social life, cannot depend on either the school or the home to help him across developmental problems. Problems of dating, of making friends, of joining clubs, of finding acceptable recreational activities, have fallen to the peer group as an important socializing agency. The problem with most friendship groups for children is that they are spontaneously organized along homogeneous lines. It is no surprise to discover that friendship groups form on the basis of common characteristics. It is important, however, to emphasize the fact that the things people have in common correlate highly with their position on the economic ladder. People with like incomes, then, and their children, are typically similar in their styles of life, their preferences for social activity and recreation, their attitudes toward others and particularly toward education.

If mobility for economically disadvantaged youth is a manifest goal of education, then differentiation of the youth sub-culture along achievement criteria inhibits these youths from extending their interaction to those unlike themselves whose attitudes might rub off and influence changes in goals. The predominant socialization effect of peer group interaction is not the goals as much as it is the development of personality characteristics necessary to achieve these goals. Lower-class youths cannot pick up the styles and manners of and insights into the systems they must confront for mobility if their access to others is limited by school organizational routines.

THE INVISIBLE TALENT

Differentiation of students along socioeconomic lines closes channels by which talented lower-class youngsters can be discovered and encouraged. In education the exceptional child is usually one who meets with distinction the cognitive criteria for achievement. However, as we are beginning to realize, talent is often unexpressed because of the undimensional way we look for it. Creativity appears to be a quality which is not an exclusive possession of the economic elite. It is, however, the kind of characteristic which requires an atmosphere of respect and acceptance for it to emerge in classrooms. The kinds of educational opportunities provided for most poverty youngsters is one that focuses heavily on either trying to uplift the traditional cognitive skills or simply to perform a holding operation until the students can drop out and find jobs.

Socio-educational research conducted by David McLelland,[24] Joseph Kahl[25] and others has focused on the problem of differentiating lower-class children who had developed motivations and aspirations for continuing education from those who had not. The results pointed to the fact that certain lower class students, regardless of academic performance, had somehow internalized a motivational quality that pushed them toward mobility goals. Researchers may, in isolated cases, by concentrating money and effort on this kind of discovery, locate talented youngsters in the lower classes. But until a structure devoted to this kind of discovery is a practice in schools, the talented lower-class student is bound to be submerged in the routines of developing minimum communication skills.

EDUCATION AND SOCIAL MOBILITY

One of the characteristics associated with all "advanced" societies is the erosion of all caste systems. In most primitive societies people accept their position as divinely designated and do not challenge the existing structures. Modern society is one in which the old stratification orders are replaced by an open mobility system, at least theoretically. The function of the school in keeping pace with the changing structure of social mobility has been to open channels and keep them open. This is accomplished by providing widespread opportunities to children of all economic statuses to advance their position.

For many years American society was open to mobility from a number of different channels. Rags-to-riches stories were common as persons ascended the social ladder through their inventiveness and mastery of entrepreneurial careers. In the decades following World War II the frontiers of mobility through individualistic initiative were slowly closed and replaced by the bureaucratic mode of adaptation. Society became rapidly bureaucratized so that the regular patterns of contemporary mobility are linked to organizational behavior. The other-directed man in Reisman's typology was one who, sensitive to the expectations of others, developed a social personality acutely tuned to bureaucratic demands.[26] What was and is expected by the organizations through which persons

[24] David McClelland, *The Achieving Society* (New York: D. Van Nostrand & Co., 1961).

[25] Joseph Kahl, "Education and Aspirations of 'Common Man' Boys," *Harvard Educational Review* 23 (1953).

[26] David Reisman, *The Lonely Crowd* (New Haven: Yale University Press, 1950).

hope to rise and stabilize their positions are the prerequisites of an education. These include degrees, knowledges, and manners. In many ways the degree and the style of self-presentation are considered more important than what a person actually knows.

Education is now considered almost exclusively *the* channel for social mobility in our society. When the school differentiates students early in their educational career, it is denying to those who are allocated to inferior status the only opportunity they have for social mobility.

The prospects for social mobility through education are reflected in the following table:[27]

Table 2-1

Percentage of Boys who Expect to Go to College by IQ and Father's Occupation*

IQ Quintile	FATHER'S OCCUPATION					All Boys of Given IQ Level
	High				Low	
	5	4	3	2	1	
(High) 5	89	76	55	40	29	52
4	82	53	29	22	14	30
3	79	47	22	19	10	24
2	72	36	20	15	6	17
1	56	28	12	4	9	11
All Boys of Given Occupational Level	80	52	26	19	12	27

* Based on a sample of 3,348 sophomores and juniors in the public high schools of eight towns that are part of the Boston metropolitan area, 1950.
Source: Kahl, "Educational and Occupational Aspirations of 'Common Man' Boys," p. 188.

The table should be read, as an example, that 80 per cent of students whose fathers were in the top occupational group had aspirations to attend college, and 12 per cent of those whose fathers were in the lowest occupational group had aspirations to attend college.

Even when IQ is controlled; that is, when persons of similar IQ's from different socioeconomic backgrounds are considered, the effects of social status are imposing. The channels for mobility in American society are generally open but they do not appear to be as open for all groups. Those who benefit least from the available opportunities for mobility are those from the lower classes. Even though we can assert, for example, that in one study reported in 1967, 37 per cent of a sample experienced upward mobility of some degree, such a statistic would be misleading if we did not, at the

[27] In Burton Clark, *Educating the Expert Society* (San Francisco: Chandler Publishing Co., 1962), p.64.

same time, evaluate the fact that zero per cent of the sample were mobile, across one generation, from the lower working class to the upper middle class.[28] Only three percent of the lowest stratum were mobile into the lower middle class.

The statistics of social mobility require considerable scrutiny. One should not even surmise from the first table that even 12 percent of "common man" boys who aspired to a college education would attain it. Children of the poverty class may pick up certain cues that lead them to desire a college education and may even speak as if they were seriously considering such an opportunity. But the opportunities are structural and only minimally subject to motivation for these people. The fact is that children of the ghettoes or the migrant farms are not going to be able to take advantage of the opportunities that they believe await them.

Although there are currently in America many voices shouting about how far we have come in improving social discrepancies, the fact is that we have progressed very little. Mobility for the poor today is as doubtful as it was fifty years ago. Only one out of three persons improves his social position from one generation to the next; and of persons in the lower or poverty classes, less than three out of 100, on the average, are able to claw their way to professional status.[29] If it were not for the random fortunes of athletic scholarships, the figure would be even smaller.

ADAPTATION OF POVERTY CHILDREN
TO THE SCHOOL

When poverty children move from an environment characterized by disorder and deprivation to one that reflects order and a number of values that povery children have found to be inefficient in their homes, the result is often confusion and disruption. As one author has expressed it:

Whether a child is receptive or has serious qualms when he enters school, whether he is prone to reject or accept the school authorities, how he reacts to teachers as models of behavior—all, to a great degree are a function of the attitudes and orientations which have been developed in the family setting.[30]

[28] Richard P. Coleman and B. Neugarten, *Social Status in the City* (New York: Atherton Press, 1967), p.18.
[29] S. M. Lipset and R. Bendix, *Social Mobility in Industrial Society* (Berkeley: University of California Press, 1959), p.89.
[30] Frederick Elkin, *The Child and Society* (New York: Random House, Inc., 1960), pp.56–57.

The adaptation of the children of poor families to the school must be evaluated in terms of the two major criteria for selection and allocation—cognitive achievement and moral behavior. The research on this subject heavily emphasizes the former consideration but we have some evidence available supporting assumptions we can make about the latter. Let us first consider the moral behavior of lower class children.

Delinquent behavior in general has been shown to be related to the income of parents and highly associated with poverty residential areas. Reiss and Rhodes studied the delinquent activities of more than 9,000 white boys in Davidson County, Tennessee (1957) and found both kinds of relationships.[31] One important distinction discovered in the data of this study was that not all poverty neighborhoods were associated with delinquency in the same way. The poverty neighborhoods which appeared to have the least delinquency were those that had greater opportunities for cross-class contacts.

This tells us something important about the effects of living in a poverty ghetto as this experience contributes to the child's adaptation to the school. The more entrenched children are in ecological areas which are total communities and are not amenable to cross-class interaction, the more deviant values the child learns. The organization of the city today, where socially mobile groups flee to the suburbs, abandoning the city to depressed peoples, only intensifies the problem of conflicting value systems. Schools in the urban ghettoes present children from these neighborhoods with a vastly different set of life expectations from those which they have learned in their streets and in their homes. The fact that most teachers conceive of their roles in such schools as disciplinarians reveals the dimension of the conflict.

The problems of adaptation to the moral expectations of the schools for poverty children stem from two related sources. On the one hand poverty children do not learn the habits and mannerisms that teachers expect and reward. They do not learn, for example, to express feeling of hostility and conflict through verbal means. These children respond to frustration and conflict with physical aggression. Often when verbal aggressiveness is called forth the manner in which it is communicated is what teachers consider vulgar and disrespectful.

H. S. Becker's study of Chicago school teachers, although

31 A. J. Reiss, Jr., and A. L. Rhodes, "The Distribution of Juvenile Delinquency in the Social Structure," American Sociological Review 26, No. 5 (October 1961): 720–733.

eighteen years old, still accurately represents the attitude of many teachers. When asked to associate to their feelings about the be-havior of lower class children, these teachers reacted strongly to such characteristics of children as being physically unclean, aggres-sive, bad mannered, vulgar and predisposed to sex.[32]

Becker's major point in describing the reaction of middle-class teachers to poverty children is that these teachers classify more than they observe. Reactions to lower class youth are stereotyped reac-tions, and often behaviors which might be ignored in middle-class children are exaggerated in the definitions teachers make of lower-class students.

A second difficulty for poverty children in adapting to the ex-pectations of the school is that they do not stay in one school long enough to adjust their manners and habits to the expectations they find there. The children of the migratory farm families experience most critically the difficulty of adaptation to the moral expectations of the school. They, like many urban migrants, not only do not learn at home the habits that teachers reward, they do not stay in one school long enough to learn them there.

The problem of moral "failure" for poverty children is acute insofar as the evaluation of them as students is heavily influenced by non-cognitive behavior. Students who "misbehave" are subject to sanctions by isolation and "dunce" typing. Most students carry these definitions and their effects with them through the grade levels.

The school deviants are usually the poorest children in the school. Their adaptations are colored by the fact that they are re-jected for their mannerisms by teachers and students alike. If a school should be heterogeneously grouped socio-economically, they are usually in the minority and are socially persecuted. If the poverty children begin to constitute a majority, then the school quickly evolves into an almost total ghetto school since middle-class parents scurry for the suburbs where they can find a "better" education for their children. When the poverty children are in the minority, they are both differentiated by the authorities and they differen-tiate themselves for security and some kind of esteem based upon a reverse criteria. That is, they reverse the values of the school so that they appear to themselves in a more esteemed light. As a group, they became quickly identified as the "bad" or "tough" crowd. Their educational futures are not bright.

---

32 Becker, "Social Class Variations in Teacher-Pupil Relationships."

COGNITIVE ADAPTATIONS OF POVERTY CHILDREN

Research on poverty children shows clearly that over a 5- to 6-year period the IQ's of a sizeable group of children drop significantly. At levels above the fifth grade the disparity between expected and actual achievement becomes increasingly greater.[33]

A survey conducted by the Arizona Migrant Ministry confirms every suspicion regarding the educational development of migrant children. Teachers in seven schools reported that most migrant children were retarded from one to five years in their educational development.[34] Youngsters of migratory families in Florida seldom advance beyond the fourth or fifth grade. The children of New Jersey berry pickers lose on the average of two months' classroom instruction per year and 40 per cent of these are at least one year behind their normal grade level. A similar study conducted on migratory children in Oregon revealed more depressing results. Retardation of these children of at least one year or more reached 75 percent. Better than 40 percent were found to be from two to six years behind. The Oregon data suggested that the greater percentage of migratory children were in school from the ages of eight to eleven, but after this attendance begins to drop sharply.[35]

The literature on social class and educational achievement is voluminous and the conclusions are such that they no longer, in general, need to be cited. The fact that poor children do worse on all manner of standardized achievement tests is at the level of an empirical cliché. The same can be said about intelligence tests. Educators at every level are familiar with the notion of the cultural bias of tests. In effect, since most tests reflect some indication of educational experience and progress, we might further argue that all education contains some form of cultural bias, and that being so, selection and allocation proceed on the basis of this bias.

A general survey of the adaptation of lower-class students to educational experiences must also include a consideration of those who appear to rise above the generalizations. An in-depth study of working-class boys who chose to go to college as contrasted with boys from similar socioeconomic backgrounds who did not was

33 J. Grambs, "The Culturally Deprived School," *Education Digest* 30 (January 1965): 3.
34 H. L. Langer, "Migrants Create School Problems," *Christian Century* 73 (May 1956).
35 Langer, "Migrants Create School Problems."

conducted by Joseph Kahl.[36] The major distinguishing factor between those who chose to aspire to a college experience and those who did not was the pressure and general attitudes of the parents. These attitudes suggested that, for the parents of college-aspiring "common man" boys, the kind of alienation and despondency that often accrue from being situated at the bottom of the social ladder had not taken hold. These parents felt that the social scheme was not bad and that their position was not an unjust differentiation.

The adaptation of "common man" boys to middle-class educational aspirations was seen by the boys as exclusively an economic plot to advance their mobility. Education for the sake of education was not an important concern. In the same way that teachers use early educational performance for differentiation of students, the parents utilized the same criteria to exert or withhold pressure. If the child did not display talent in the early grades, there was little effort to encourage the children to aspire to educational success goals.

In summary it is a simple but unpleasant reality that poor children do not successfully meet either the moral or cognitive criteria of the school. Their achievement scores and grades are lower, their attendance is worst, their removals from class for disciplinary reasons are greater than their counterparts in the middle class. We have looked briefly at the adaptation that these students make to the school. The focus was upon them. Now let us turn to a consideration of the way the school adapts to children of the poor.

MAN YOUR BATTLE STATIONS

Teachers are defensively aware of the difficulties of teaching the poverty child. We do not want to deal in depth with the organization of educational facilites in ghetto schools since we treat this matter in the chapter on race relations. It is sufficient to say at this point that the evidence presented by Becker,[37] Hollingshead[38] and Havighurst and Taba[39] suggests that in economically heterogeneous schools certain students develop reputations which run to stereotypes. Teachers differentiate students evaluatively in terms of achievement criteria, and punitively in terms of moral stereotypes.

---

[36] Kahl, "Education and Aspirations of 'Common Man' Boys."
[37] Becker, "Social Class Variations in Teacher-Pupil Relationships."
[38] Hollingshead, *Elmtown's Youth.*
[39] R. J. Havighurst and H. Taba, *Adolescent Character and Personality* (New York: John Wiley and Sons, Inc., 1949).

Although the Elmtown study is out of date as a description of pupil–school interaction in contemporary society, many of the implications for rural education, in which many poverty students participate, may still be valid. A glaring example of discrepancy in treatment of students based upon class background is represented by an experience reported in the Elmtown study.

The daughter of a prominent class II family did not go to detention. Instead, she kept an appointment with a beauty parlor to have a permanent wave. The next morning the Superintendent walked into the principal's office, diffidently fingered the mail in the teachers' boxes, sauntered over to the windows with his hands in his pockets, looked at the autumn leaves moving across the yard, and in a disinterested way asked, "How is the detention room working?"

The principal answered, "All right, except we are running into the old stall of some students who think they can do as they please!"

(Superintendent) "Yes, I know. The idea is all right, but I do not think it will work in every case. Last evening, Mrs. Newton called Evelyn [the Superintendent's wife] about the church supper next week. She mentioned that Kathy [her daughter and the girl in question] was at the hairdresser's last night!

(Principal) "That is just what I had in mind. Last evening I called Mrs. Newton and told her Kathy was not in detention and I wanted to know where she was. Mrs. Newton told me that she had to have her hair fixed for the dance at the Country Club tonight. When I get Kathy in here, I am going to tell her a thing or two."

(Superintendent) "Now be careful, Alfred. I do not think there is a thing we can do in this case."

The principal sat silently at his desk and shuffled excuses. The Superintendent walked out of the office.

When Kathy came in for her lecture, she was dressed neatly in a brushed wool sweater and tweed skirt. She walked coyly to the principal's desk and he asked in a naïve voice, "Did you forget about detention?"

A pause. "No, I had an appointment at Craig's to have my hair set."

"Did you have to go last night?"

"Yes, tonight I have to go to Mrs. Nettle's to get my dress for the dance."

"All right. Go on to class, but don't let this happen again." After Kathy left the office, the principal threw a pack of excuses on the desk and muttered, "There it goes again! The next time one of these prominent families puts pressure on me, I am going to raise hell!"

Sociologists who are interested in the study of education today are interested in the problems of urban education. Most of the students in America are in urban schools. Moreover, the poor children of America are primarily in homogeneously organized ghetto or semi-ghetto areas within the city. Minority groups in particular are victims of ecological arrangements which are conducive to conflict and disadvantage in education. The adaptation of the schools to the poor in this sense is an urban problem as much as it is a poverty problem and therefore it will be dealt with as such in the chapter on race relations. Our discussion of the culturally deprived child, or educationally disadvanged, or whatever term we employ, can more conveniently be made meaningful in the context of community organization within urban areas.

Insofar as we are concerned with differential treatment of students of different economic backgrounds in the same school the Elmtown model, though exaggerated in some senses, may have its more subtle parallels of differentiation and discrimination in contemporary schools. One teacher in a school that was heterogeneously organized, for example, was obviously on the side of the working class students who, he felt, were constantly getting a "raw deal."[40] "I'll tell you what I do," he said, "to help these kids get along. I teach them to say, I haven't done anything sir, rather than I ain't done nothing! You'd be surprised how many kids get themselves off the hook by sounding like they're not the type to get into trouble."

This same point is further illustrated by the following report:

On other occasions verbal altercations break out between students in the cafeteria or in line and the student hall patrolmen. In one of these that I witnessed, the accused student, a handsome, aggressive-looking young man, defended himself in the informal but explicit language of lower class hostility. This roused the teacher on duty from his former passivity. He walked over to the boy, and silently but with a glare of contempt, beckoned him from the room with a crooked finger and led him along the corridor to the administrative office: the tall boy, rigid in silent protest, the teacher, balding and stoop-shouldered in a wrinkled suit, shambling ahead of him. The youth, I later learned, was suspended for a day.[41]

The attitude of those who enjoy the fruits of the social experience toward those who receive only the peels is very complicated. Anyone who has passed a poor beggar in the streets and has dropped a few coins into a cup does so at least partly, if not en-

---

[40] Reported as part of an interview with teachers while I was assisting in the study on "Dimensions of Teacher Leadership in Classroom Social Systems," by C. W. Gordon, Senior Author, Report of the U. S. Office of Education (Washington D. C.).

[41] Edgar Z. Friedenberg, "The Modern High School: A Profile," in *Readings on the School in Society*, ed. P. Sexton (Englewood Cliffs, N. J.: Prentice-Hall, Inc., 1967), p.218.

tirely, out of guilt. The excessive volunteer work, charity activities mainly, of wealthy women and some men can easily be explained using this concept. We must, of course, not rule out a genuine humanitarian attitude on the part of many but we must also ask the question how much humanitarianism is a rationalization for guilt. If inequality in the distribution of wealth strikes a chord of injustice in many, the typical social adaptation goes beyond the felt injustice. It can go in several directions. Feelings of guilt in many are easily translated into feelings of anger toward those who make them feel guilty. In this way the poor are despised and persecuted for their lowly condition. In a society which for hundreds of years has valued ambition, industriousness, and individual effort, the poor are rejected for their failure to display these qualities. They are scum not only because of the undisciplined course of their lives but becauce of their failure to raise themselves from rags to riches in the true Horatio Alger way. Part of the reason that the rags-to-riches myth still permeates our social conscience so strongly may be because, without the opportunity to blame the poor for their own lack of initiative we may have to place the blame elsewhere, on ourselves, for not ensuring the opportunities which the poor cannot manufacture themselves.

A second adaptation to guilt and to disgust about a way of life that offends our moral perspective is to adopt the out-of-sight, out-of-mind orientation. If we simply move to the suburbs, our guilt and our moral senses are not aroused. This is why, for most people, the poor are invisible.

Then there is the adaptation so common in a society of haves and have-nots, that is, the have-nots must be controlled so they will not take away something from the haves. This kind of social paranoia leads to unilateral resistance to all social legislation which might guarantee a greater portion of America's wealth to those who have none. There are legions who oppose welfare, subsidization of other than corporate agricultural interests, and poverty programs in general. For many years these people have and still do resent the labor movement and labor unions for the organized way they seek a greater share of the profits. The attiude of the grape growers toward the agricultural workers in central California is a current example.

Another adaptation is, of course, an attitude and sometimes an active involvement of persons in the struggle to uplift the poor through any means necessary. The hundreds of college students from the University of California who walked with the grape strikers, who canvassed their communities for food, clothing and money to keep the battle going, is an outstanding example.

Each teacher chooses one of these adaptations or some variation upon these themes. Teaching is a popular occupation for many children of working-class homes. It is a step toward the mobility they seek. The major problem with many of these people is that they really believe that since they have made it themselves, others should also be able to; and if this does not happen, personal rather than social qualities are blamed. The upwardly mobile teacher is a curious phenomenon. In many senses he or she is a marginal person, standing between a working-class heritage and middle-class acceptability. This acceptability requirement often affects such people in a way that forces them to disavow their social source, and this not gently. To the extent that the school behavior of children calls forth the demand characteristics of an upwardly mobile teacher, the response may be more punitive than would be appropriate.

Schools are, in many ways, guardians of the *status quo* in the social order. Teachers are required to accept this responsibility and most of them do. The idea of cultural relativism is not appropriate given this kind of commitment. Students who do not conform to standard expectations are often defined as threats to the stability of the internalized values of the teacher. The values inherent in the poverty class and the frequent rejection of the core values upon which the structure of the school is built make it difficult for teachers to help poverty children. They may be very eager to encouage poor children, but the minimal requirements for this support and encouragement may be an expressed acceptance by the students of the core values and the formal requirements. It is much like saying, "Show me you can stand and I will help you walk." Many poverty children cannot even stand, or walk in the way that is "preferred." This is part of the complexity in the attitudes of persons who are in a position to uplift the disadvantaged. To the extent that teachers cannot sort out differences between abilities and social styles, they will continue to victimize lower class students. How we define poverty children involves a number of complex alternatives and a numerous set of qualifications that must be met before we are really willing to help them overcome the structural barriers to educational progress.

THE SCHOOL AND THE AMELIORATION OF POVERTY

It is hoped that the school can do something about the problem of poverty in the United States, and this theme will be explored in the following pages. In some ways, however, the school has done its share in promoting the condition which it can perhaps remedy. The organization of education has been such that many persons who could have benefited from its content and the degrees or certificates it confers have not been able to so so. Education, as an institution, is more than teachers and subject matter. It is also a privilege and a right that many persons have not been able to secure. Insofar as the school is a selecting and sorting agency we can argue that, as it has sorted to the highest echelons of social life, it has also sorted persons to the lower depths. We do not need to belabor the function of differentiation any further. We wish to consider here only that education has a responsibility not only to provide the knowledge and skills required to eliminate poverty but to bridge the gap between the family and the school, to show the way not only to where the opportunities are but how to use them. The innovations that we must principally consider are linked to a new definition of the role of the school in society, a definition which holds that education in some form and shape is not only available, but for everyone is unavoidable.

In this final section of our discussion of poverty in the United States and its association with educational tasks, we will make a number of statements about possible innovations. Since culture changes so rapidly it is not inappropriate to suggest innovations that do not appear to be currently feasible. Sometimes it is necessary to stretch our imaginations to the bursting point to accomodate the almost overwhelming dimensions of the problem. There are many things that certain schools are already doing to alleviate the difficulty and these will be reported; but there are many things which schools have not tried and cannot because they would represent drastic departure from conventional views, even liberal conventional views. The suggestions and reports included in this discussion are necessarily incomplete. New and exciting programs are springing up over night, and the speculations of a few persons cannot touch all the possible bases. Students of education and society may have within their own experience caught hold of a conception of the school in relation to poverty problems that would be welcomed in classroom discussions, and teachers of poverty children may be operating a situation beneficial to these students which are not reported anywhere. But communication of innovative possibilities is important in all the areas we discuss in this book. What begins as a discussion between a few teachers may eventuate in a district program which then may become a model for other districts. Persons who really care about society's problems have a responsibility to communicate their insights. To a great extent this is what we are attempting to do here.

Many of the experimental innovations which seek to bring the poverty child into the mainstream of educational life have emerged out of a number of federally supported programs for the disadvantaged. Many of these programs have experiences and/or assumptions in common, and we can begin by examining some of these.

EARLY ADMISSION

One assumption of Headstart training programs is that poverty children are already behind non-poverty children when they begin school. For the average American child a number of preschool family and community experiences that help orient him to educational life occur prior to his admission to school. These experiences center around the development of both moral and cognitive skills. These children quickly discover that teachers expect what parents expect and are ready to perform to meet these expectations. Behaviors that were rewarded and punished in the home are rewarded and punished in the classroom.

Presumably given the assumptions of the early experience program, poverty children are socialized inadequately; that is, they do not know what teachers expect because they were not given these performance demands prior to entering school. Therefore educational programs for the disadvantaged seek to provide similar experiences to those which give the advantage to middle-class youngsters. Parents of disadvantaged children are expected to stimulate and encourage their children to participate in activities that help ready them for the school experience. These experiences should be varied and meaningful. They should provide responsibilities and role models. Parents should show, tell, explain, participate, and so on. The home should be a climate in which phenomena are not only experienced, they must be differentiated as well. The assumption here is that the lower-class child is bombarded by experiences, sounds, sights, and feelings but that these are so undifferentiated that they constitute a clamor of sensations. Some recent research by Cynthia Deutsch illustrates this point. Using a sample of poverty children and middle-class children, she provided each group with auditory experiences in which they were to select words covered by a clamor of other noises. Middle-class students appeared to show definite superiority in discriminating words. The relationship between these discriminatory abilities and learning, according to Deutsch, is quite strong, particularly in the area of reading. The author concludes that children from deprived homes are immature in this kind of auditory discrimination but that help in the early years can correct this handicap.[42] This kind of research has been questioned recently, particularly on the grounds that middle-class, rather than lower-class dialects were used for auditory discrimination tests.

Thus for the preschool poverty child, educational programs in cooperation with parents must supply a remedial period of readiness training. In order to start out at least even this child needs similar experiences to those provided in the homes of middle-class preschoolers.

One important kind of readiness activity for preschool disadvantaged children is the structure experience. That is, children need an ordering in their lives so that decisions can be made in a context characterized by regularity and predictability. The regularity that is not experienced in the home becomes an integral part of the early educational experience so that lower-class children can relate to classroom structures in the first grade in the same manner as do middle-class children. They learn the manner and format of asking questions, of answering them, of asking permission, of taking tests, of finding information, of seeking proper recreational or tension-reducing outlets.

If early admission to educational life for poverty children is to become a characteristic of innovative programs, then ultimately educators and experimenters must ask two further questions: (1) How is the character of lower-class life itself to be integrated into the program? and (2) How far can and should we go in changing the early environment of the poverty preschooler?

These questions address themselves to important ethical and educational issues. The first question asks, in effect, whether or not we can make more sense out of educational experiences by relating these to ongoing activities of the preschoolers. The games of young children in poverty areas are not the typical store-bought activities of the middle class. Perhaps we can help to introduce meaningful insights through these game activities. The ethical question involved here is one of denying persons the right of access to middle-class society while still retaining working-class habits. The issue of aggression is relevant as an example. If working-class children define aggression differently from middle-class children (and they do) and only one definition (negative) is rewarded in the school, then we punish children for what they have learned as appropriate behavior. Aggression, generalized to mean the acceptance of exter-

42 Cynthia Deutsch, "Auditory Discrimination and Learning: Social Factors," *Merrill-Palmer Quarterly* 10 (1964): 277–296.

nalizing emotions rather than the repression of them, may be more than a lower-class quality. Speaking evaluatively, it may also be a healthy characteristic and one the school should encourage in patterned ways rather than suppressing. The consideration is that in the interests of securing the kind of conformity that would permit preschoolers to ready themselves for the rigor of the classroom, we may be depriving the poverty child of some of his best qualities.

The second question centers around the assumption that, in order to ready poverty preschoolers, we need to change their environment. This may mean anything from impinging on the normal routines of the family to removing the children from the community entirely. If the assumption that such children live in a detrimental environment is correct, then any changes are potentially an improvement.

If children are to be set on the track of educational success, granting somewhat traditional expectations of school personnel and very gradual change in educational structures, then many activities which must be linked to these structures should be included in their readiness training. That is, for both teachers and students involved, an analysis of the structure of educational success should provide some cues for readiness training.

EXTENDED EDUCATIONAL EXPERIENCES

The middle-class student receives a number of educational experiences simply as a function of his parents' interest in his academic and, ultimately, occupational success. Middle-class parents take their children to plays, concerts, instructive films, and on trips to see historical locales and natural resources; they fill up their homes with educational writings, popular periodicals, and newspapers. In the home parents frequently discuss local and national events and interact frequently with the school to give home assistance in work and guidance in planning. The poverty child does not experience these activities. Many of the non-school activities related to such factors as aspiration and achievement are actually negatively experienced. That is, the poverty child develops loyalties to a set of notions that are alien to educational success. He defines culture as high brow, correct language as pretentious, and non-exciting experiences as a bore.

What appears to be required are experiences which influence the poverty child to make new definitions of the available experiences and to provide him with activities which approximate the educational advantages of the middle-class child. Some programs, emanating from both within and without the school, are already underway. Drama, for example, is being taken to poverty children in many urban areas by dedicated and socially conscious professionals. Many variations on the theme of work-study programs are being tried. Poverty children are being given current events newspapers, such as the weekly reader, without cost; and concerts, films, and other entertaining and educational facilities are being made available. Summer camps for poverty children are supported by philanthropic groups and college student volunteer programs. Vista volunteers set up child care centers and a number of other activities which provide poverty children with creative and educational experiences.

The school and the community must work cooperatively to convince poverty children that educational experiences are not intended to persecute them, but rather to provide them with as much help, materials, and sensory activities as they can handle. The old concept of a rigidly scheduled, nine-to-three educational experience is obviously dysfunctional to the needs of the poor child.

THE RE-SOCIALIZATION OF TEACHERS

We spoke earlier about the difficulty many teachers have in accepting the behavioral patterns and attitudes of children of the lower classes. The attitudes and reactions of these teachers may range anywhere from outright rejection to complete acceptance. Most teachers fall somewhere in the middle of this continuum. At one extreme teachers may feel that they owe both the society and the students their best efforts in making them ladies and gentlemen and good citizens; at another teachers may punish students for behaviors purely out of a personal rejection of a way of life different from their own. Recall that the behaviors which teachers reject are those that involve intensely externalized emotion such as physical aggression, verbal aggression, and vulgarity within the school setting. Many proper persons, of whom school teachers are one stereotype, have difficulty allowing themselves the freedom of this kind of behavior. On the one hand, they define it as wrong; on the other, it disturbs their sense of propriety and arouses anxiety.

Many readiness training programs begin with a number of workshops for teachers. The intention is to make teachers more aware of the behaviors of poverty children and to make the teachers more accepting of this behavior, more able to separate their sense of "rightness" and "wrongness" from their responsibilities to these children.

A teacher of poverty children is defined in the words of one critic as an "alien."[43] This critic's meaning is "someone from another country" who does not understand the habits of the natives and is often intolerant of differences. Another kind of definition which has considerable consequences is that of a negative role model. This is a person who, by definition, influences behavior in the opposite direction of what he says or represents. As a negative role model, a teacher may have serious negative effects while pursuing what she believes to be positive values. This teacher arouses dislike and distrust of classical music because she communicates that she favors it. She may also cause students to define a whole range of educational "virtues," as evils since she is pushing hard for them as "virtues."

The implications of juxtaposing teachers with one set of values against students with a different set are obvious. Therefore most programs seek to prepare these teachers for their task by educating them and in some ways changing them. This task requires certain directions and a few of these may be suggested:

1. Selection criteria are essential. The following characteristics should be included in the development of these criteria —socioeconomic background, cross-cultural experience, capacity for abstract rather than concrete thinking,[44] quality of teaching experience, and history of commitment and involvement in national social issues.

2. Teachers should be resocialized so that invidious definitions of the behavior of others become translated into relative differences which are not evaluated. Resocialization may in- involve a number of techniques, from controlled experiments in which previously rewarded attitudes are criticized or not accepted to basic encounter-type sessions in which persons are forced to examine their own value systems.[45]

---

43 Staten W. Webster, "The Teacher as an Alien," in *Educating the Disadvantaged Learner*, ed. S. Webster (San Francisco: Chandler Publishing Co., 1966), pp.454–466.

44 O. J. Harvey and his associates found that teachers with abstract rather than concrete belief systems had more positive effects (educationally desirable) in cognitive as well as non-cognitive areas of pupil development. O. J. Harvey, J. B. White, M. Prather, R. D. Alter, and J. K. Hoffmeister, "Teachers, Belief Systems and Pre-school Atmospheres," *Journal of Educational Psychology* 57 (December 1966): 373–381.

45 E. Schein and Warren Bennis, *Personal and Organizational Change Through Group Methods* (New York: John Wiley and Sons, Inc., 1965).

3. Teachers must be brought to the point of accepting their responsibility as paramount and be relieved of the temptation to blame the emergence of education barriers on the life circumstance of the child, laying much of the guilt at the feet of the parents.

HOME-SCHOOL INTERACTION

Most readiness training programs see their purposes linked to the integration of parents into the tasks of uplifting disadvantaged students to a level of competitive competence. Program directors with insight involve parents without assuming that the project's responsibility is ever to rehabilitate the parents. Whatever the qualities of families that appear to be interfering with the education of the youth, the educational role is not that of a social worker. The rehabilitation functions of the school may be expressed in terms of adult educational and counseling programs and these indeed may somehow be linked to helping the disadvantaged child. In this context the attempt is to involve the parents in the one goal of helping the child develop attitudes and aspirations which will motivate him to take advantage of educational opportunities.

One of the more important reasons for a coalition of teachers and parents is to secure data for decision making that are not available in the school. Many children from deprived homes do not or cannot communicate the kinds of information that teachers can use to build individual instructional programs. In the search for talent among poverty children educators need all the assistance they can get.

A second reason for seeking parental assistance is to compound the support or reinforcement of skills developed either in the home or in the school. Working-class parents will tend to support those children who appear to have a decent chance for higher education. If the school should extend the range of those children it defines as potential successes and communicate this to their parents, a broader base of support will be established.

A third reason for the coalition between school and home is to assist children in accepting the worth and value of the teacher. The definition of the teacher as a negative role model emerges out of a number of environmental experiences and the home can make a difference in eroding the negative definitions that are made and preventing them before they occur. The old notion of conflicting systems of socialization may also be attacked through the cooperation of parents and children. Specifically, parents and other community resources can provide the school with feedback regarding the educational problems of students. If teachers are receptive to such feedback, a communication network between the school, home, and community can be developed to extend the structural possibilities for educating poverty students.

THE LANGUAGE PROBLEM

The language of poverty children is a disadvantage to educational progress in several ways. First, the child has difficulty in receiving and communicating ideas. Learning is retarded because the information provided is either rejected because it is not meaningful or ineffective because it is not understood. Second, lower class language is a disadvantage because it types the child who employs it. Teachers differentiate students on criteria which are not always related to standardized achievement. Language is one of the more obvious characteristics of students and, regardless of intelligence, can be and is used to type students in categories of high and low success potential. Third, the language of lower-class children is a disadvantage because these children become alienated from the school culture which places heavy emphasis on standard English. The students use this criteria to separate themselves from the culture of the school. They do not feel they belong. They do not talk the same language. Fourth, the language of lower-class children becomes a burden to them insofar as they learn that, since their language is not acceptable, their attempts at communication will be negatively received. Consequently their motivation to communicate in the classroom is depressed.

Standard English is the vehicle by which all school knowledge is communicated. Difficulties with this medium produce frustrations for children even in areas such as mathematics and science. The tendency not to depart from a rigid insistence on developing and reinforcing facility with standard English is based on the school's perceived responsibility to the larger society. The emphasis on standard English is supported, then, by two themes. The first is a concern for "respectability," so that good English is not only efficient; it also becomes a "moral" virtue. The second theme is one of instrumentality. Mastery of standard English is useful for educational and occupational mobility.

Innovative interests in the language problems of the lower classes must confront two, rather than one, major issues. We not only need to worry about how best to develop mastery in poverty students, we must also evaluate the value and function of lower-class language independent of its utility in the middle-class school.

Werner Cohn raises some important considerations in his evaluation of this second issue. His major proposition is that language is deeply linked to the values and orientations of different classes. Lower-class orientations are typically toward family and community, whereas middle-class orientations are toward business or professional obligations. He states, "This difference would suggest that lower-class English, in its more casual grammatical habits, may carry less demanding, less competitive, and possibly more generous modes than the standard language."[46]

Lower-class language seems particularly suitable to the expression of anger and is often more efficient in situations of stress or conflict where rapid communication is necessary, such as in battle.

INNOVATIONS FOR THE MIGRANT CHILD

In recent years various innovations directed toward providing a better educational experience for migrant children have been adopted. These include: (1) the employment of additional teachers during the months when migrants are in the community, (2) the addition of specialists in reading and general communication problems of youth in these communities, (3) establishment of special summer programs for migrant children, (4) college-and Vista-supported programs to train teachers for migrant children, (5) a widespread organization of community involvement programs including basic instruction and vocational guidance.[47] This last includes a program using community support to provide job opportunities, often in a work-study school program.

In relating innovative programs to the educational problems of migrant youth we must consider the course of the future. Technology will eventually signal the death of this kind of occupation. What remains is agriculture and the machines that will make agricultural products available. Long range planning should tell us that the most reasonable careers for the youth who have been tied to agricultural demands would lie in the development and utilization of agricultural machinery.

---

46 Werner Cohn, "On the Language of Lower-Class Children," in *Understanding the Educational Problems of the Disadvantaged Learner*, ed. S. W. Webster (San Francisco: Chandler Publishing Co., 1966), pp.330–331.
47 "Report on Our Migrant Workers," *America* 114 (March 1966): 346.

CONCLUSION

The role of the school in the amelioration of poverty as a social problem resides predominantly in its capacity to become more flexible in its functions and more receptive to innovation than it has been traditionally. Education is the major vehicle through which the generation-to-generation poverty cycle can be broken. The school must provide first the motivation and then the skills, abilities, and knowledge that poverty youngsters require to break free from the demoralizing and debilitating effects of deprivation. The school must also find a way to reverse the trend toward greater and greater pressures to compete for the economic rewards that the successful completion of education can bring. In recent years the upgrading of standards, while pushing bright students harder, has provided what Toynbee has called "excessive challenge" in the environment of the weaker students.[48] This kind of challenge contains such a high predictability of failure that the effort for the students may seem hardly worth it.

Poverty as a social problem is a matter of segregation of persons on the basis of economic differences. Lower-class students, unable to penetrate the social world of the more advantaged students, shut themselves off from most communication. In so doing they preclude the possibility of cross-class socialization and motivation. The school is either unable or unwilling to break down these peer group barriers. It relies heavily on psychometric or academic performance for grouping. It does not face the dysfunctional consequences of these convenient mechanisms for organizing their work.

At this time the school as a social institution is beginning to reevaluate its responsibility to the communities which it services. It is beginning to go out into the community with programs and a sincere desire to convince the poor that it stands ready to accomodate some of its internal patterns to the needs of the community. Progress is slow, but culture changes rapidly; and once the stigma of revolutionary innovations is shoved from the shoulders of society, once fears about drastic change are diluted by an increasing sensitivity to the reality and necessity of change, the school may begin to take the giant steps that are required.

---

[48] In Amitai Etzioni, *Social Change* (New York: Basic Books, 1964), pp.27-39.

3

Problems
of Drug Taking

WE WANT consistently to refer to the problem of drugs as one of "drug taking" rather than drug addiction, not that addiction is not a serious social problem. It is simply that the notion of drug taking is more inclusive and involves other kinds of non-addictive drug-related activities that are as serious, if not more serious, than the problem of addiction. The phenomenon of drug taking is more consequential than actual addictive activity since drug taking in our time is symptomatic of a much greater range of social ills than the fact of addiction itself. The social problem, then, is a set of behaviors involving the ingestion of some kind of internal change agent that produces for the taker some kind of release, at times escape, from the problems associated with normal functioning.

We have said that drug taking is a symptom. It is not, for example, the same kind of social problem as poverty, which may be the source, in some cases, of drug taking. But symptoms are legitimate areas of inquiry, as are broader based social problems. Later, for example, we will be discussing the general problem of alienation which may arise out of many conditions and produce many symptoms which in themselves require scrutiny.

At this time drug taking requires an independent focus because it affects not only a greater number of people than ever before, but also because several institutions, such as the family, government, and schools, have become deeply concerned. Furthermore widespread drug-taking activity is an important social problem because it is illegal. That is, despite the arguments to the effect that many drugs have minimal human consequences, we observe a condition where many persons are blatantly disregarding the law. We are not taking the position here that the laws relative to drugs are or are not good laws; we are simply suggesting that widespread law violation produces a social disruption, a condition that divides a society. The problem, then, is not so much that drugs produce undesirable physiological effects, but that drug taking produces widespread social disruptions.

THE CONTEXT OF DRUG TAKING

Drug taking is no longer a class-related phenomenon. If it were, we probably would not consider the topic for a special chapter in a social problems book. Not many years ago, persons associated drugs with poverty conditions. Nelson Algren's *Man With The Golden Arm* portrayed an excellent literary argument for the association of drug taking with specific kinds of environmental conditions.[1] His main character returned from his rehabilitation to the same environment in which the original need developed. His return to drugs was, therefore, predictable. Sociologically we would have to accept the thesis and the perspective of this description of the etiology of drug taking. We do not want to argue, of course, that everyone from similar disadvantaged environments turns to drugs.

[1] Nelson Algren, *The Man with the Golden Arm* (Garden City, N. Y.: Doubleday & Company, Inc., 1949).

We do, however, suggest that in the past there has been a consistent relationship between being a drug user and coming from a lower-class background and living in a lower-class environment.

Drug taking has also in the past been associated with certain occupations, chief of which was being a musician. Again, sociologically, we can relate a context or an environment to the musician's use of drugs. We can talk about the kind of work, a form of creative expression in which persons believe that they can expand their creative capacities. We can talk about the musician's uncertain and unstable economic life, his isolation from his listeners, his time on the road. Or we can talk about the evolution of a subculture of which drug use is one symbolic component.

Becker's discussion of the deviant patterns associated with career musicianship is instructive as an example of the way in which a drug, in this case marijuana, fulfills a useful function for persons as members of a group, rather than as individuals.[2] The musician, according to Becker's analysis, divides the social world into two groups: himself and others like himself, and the "square."

Feeling their differences strongly, musicians likewise believe that they are under no obligation to imitate the conventional behavior of squares. From the idea that no one can tell a musician how to play, it follows logically that no one can tell a musician how to do anything. Accordingly, behavior which flouts conventional social norms is greatly admired.[3]

Marijuana use by musicians, particularly jazz musicians who are the most removed from the "square", becomes a ritual of definition, as well as a habit for freeing talent. Because many of the most talented jazz musicians had or have a notorious reputation for drug use, younger aspirants have imitated the drug behavior as a way of ingratiating themselves into the culture. The characteristics of leaders of the subculture, as is the case with other sub-cultures, are the most visible and therefore the most logically imitated.

Here we are going from the particular to the general by way of illustrating a point about social contexts. It is preferable to move from the general to the particular, from general propositions about contexts which produce the phenomena to examples of when and how drugs are used. This we will do at greater length as we move into theories and propositions about drug taking and addiction in general.

Every group that wishes to assert its inclusive and exclusive

2 H. Becker, *The Outsiders* (New York: The Free Press, 1963).
3 *Ibid.*

nature does so by developing modes and habits which distinguish it from other groups. These habits and activities come to stand as traits of that particular group and as such differentiate members from outsiders. The requirements of cohesiveness and solidarity for such groups are based on the configuration of these traits. Persons who may wish to participate or identify with such identity groups will, despite personal inclinations to the contrary, conform to the social pressures of the core members of the group. We have often, in commonsense terms, interpreted the fact that young people started smoking or drinking as a case of wanting to belong, to do what the others did. If this kind of pressure is effective on the broadest social level, even when the group is composed simply of other adolescents, we can imagine what the pressures would be in groups such as delinquent gangs, or bands, where intimate and de-limited lines of interaction evist.

DRUG ADDICTION

The World Health Organization defines drug addiction as a

. . . state of periodic and chronic intoxication detrimental to the in-dividual and to society, produced by the repeated consumption of a drug (natural or synthetic). Its characteristics include: (1) an overpowering desire or need (compulsion) to continue taking the drug and to obtain it by any means; (2) a tendency to increase the dosage; (3) a psychic (psychological) and sometimes a physical dependence on the effects of the drug.[4]

The number of actual addicts in the United States is, of course, unknown. Because addiction is a criminal behavior, persons are not likely to report this behavior, even to social scientists. In-formal estimates range from 45,000 to over 100,000 addicts, and these are concentrated in our larger cities—New York, Philadelphia Los Angeles, and the like.

Drug addiction is a problem to society as well as to the indi-vidual. It is a problem in dollars since large sums must be spent to control the drug traffic, to house and attempt to rehabilitate the addict, and, since the cost of a habit can be quite high, the average addict turns to many forms of crime, particularly robbery and prostitution to support these habits. In this way the general public is victimized and police work increases beyond the demands for the control of addiction.

[4] A. R. Lindsmith, *Drug Addiction, Crime or Disease?* (Bloomington; Indiana University Press, 1961), p.23.

Drug addiction begins with the desire of persons to relieve pain, which is often an individual matter, and to belong, which is a social matter. Often these motivations combine in the lives of many. The kind of pain with which the first shot is associated is often physical distress. Many persons become addicted in hospitals where drugs are conventionally used to relieve physical anguish. A second kind of pain is the pain of frustration with social conditions, the pain of poverty and demoralization. In this kind of circumstance an environment which includes many others is usually present so that new addicts join a group of friends or partners in distress. The access to drugs here is part of the normal social environment in the slum.

The notion that drugs can bring a new kind of experience that can carry one above the available euphorias in the routine world attracts a host of disparate types. This kind of addiction cannot be heavily associated with particular economic levels or occupations nor is it associated with one sex predominantly. The road to addiction for many begins simply with the easy access to drugs, in such places as hospitals, military medical facilities, and drug stores. It is predictable, then, that many addicts have had some association with these facilities. Doctors are frequent users, as are Army medical technicians.

Many drug users are adolescents, principally adolescents from low income areas with all the commonly associated characteristics of these areas—low income level and education, high rates of family disorganization, racial and economic discrimination, and high frustration.[5] The adolescent sub-culture, particularly in low income communities, is often the delinquent sub-culture, and certainly many delinquent acts occur in line with drug needs. The channels of communication and the high rate of age-graded interaction assures the "pusher" of a host of salesmen. In many areas the school can be used as the central exchange market for the narcotics traffic.

The treatment for the "hooked" drug addict is varied according to what one can afford. "Kicking" a habit can occur in pleasant medically-supervised environments or it can occur in jail with limited resources. Almost anywhere the treatment is painful and generally unsuccessful. Hospitals at Lexington, Kentucky, and Fort Worth, Texas, receive patients who are forcibly committed by the courts or voluntarily committed. Either way recidivism is high and permanent cures rare.[6]

5 Isidor Chein, "Narcotics Use Among Juveniles," *Social Work* 1 (April 1956): 50–60.
6 P. B. Horton and G. R. Leslie, *The Sociology of Social Problems* (New York: Appleton-Century-Crofts, 1965), pp.564, 568.

The problems with the rehabilitation of drug addicts are large since so much is unknown. Psychiatric rehabilitation on an out-patient basis is hampered by the fact that the patient moves from the doctor's office to the environment which usually is responsible for producing the addiction in the first place. This is also the largest cause of recidivism. After rehabilitation in jail, "cured" patients are sent into the society to make their way. Again, Algren's graphic portrait of the fall of a "rehabilitated" addict rings true. The concept of rehabilitation refers to many practices in many places, and the effects of rehabilitative activities cannot be generalized on the basis of national rates of recidivism. When rehabilitation includes the notion of extended treatment and post-rehabilitative work, such as job counseling and placement, the rates of recidivism can be reduced.

The drug addict has been defined as a criminal and seen as a problem for the law enforcement agencies. In more recent time drug addiction has been perceived as a problem for the medical profession. The rehabilitation of addicts through medical treatment has occupied the interests of persons involved in medical research. The interaction of law enforcement agencies and medical personnel occurs through legislation which requires that physicians file reports to the state departments of public health. Section 3344 of the New York State Public Health Law, which is representative of other states, says "It shall be the duty of every attending or consulting physician to report to the State Department of Public Health, promptly, the name and, if possible, the address of any person under treatment if it appears that such person is a habitual user of any narcotic drug." The problems for many physicians, of course, is that it is never quite clear what constitutes "habitual" use, and of more recent consequence, what constitutes a narcotic. It would be well at this point, before considering some rehabilitative efforts, to summarize some of the important differences that characterize different "drugs."

The Legal Drugs

The legal drugs are different from most others insofar as their administration or absorption is not deemed to constitute a problem to persons who use and may depend on them. These are the barbiturates, tranquilizers, sleeping pills, and the like.

Narcotics

Narcotics are drugs which are considered addictive, and physically and psychologically dangerous to the user. They are prohibited by federal and state statutes. They include mainly heroin, opium, and cocaine. Marijuana, or all parts of the plant *cannabis sativa*, is also covered by these statutes, although the similarity to other narcotics is strongly questioned in some quarters. The most recent terror in the world of narcotics is methodrene ("speed"), the destructive effects of which have already been reported in the literature. Evidence of addiction as well as brain-damaging effects appears to be conclusive so that methodrene can be quickly classified apart from the many popular drugs which we cannot condemn convincingly.

Hallucinogens

Hallucinogens are drugs generally referred to in contemporary literature as psychedelics. The principal drugs in this category are lysergic acid diethalamide (LSD), mescaline, psilocybin and marijuana. Many new chemicals are constantly being developed which would fit in this category. These drugs change the state of consciousness generally to a state of increased awareness or sensitivity which sometimes includes hallucinatory experiences. It is generally accepted that these drugs are not addictive physiologically. There is, however, a continuing discussion about the extent of psychological addiction that occurs with the ingestion of these drugs.

The most frightening drug in this last category, although used far less than marijuana, is LSD. The psychological effects of this drug were first studied in 1943. The attitude among those who were and are experimenting with LSD is that the drug can be highly beneficial in studying the brain and psychotic states. The fear surrounding uncontrolled use of the drug centers around the expectation that the drug will produce a simulated psychotic condition which may not be relieved. Persons aware of this possibility often become frightened that they will not be able to return to a normal state. The actual physiological effects of LSD are minor. The psychological effects vary considerably. Some patterned effects have been the perception of movement in inanimate objects and increased intensity of colors, forms, and figures. Sounds appear to take on form, opposites appear to be equals, time senses become confused or reversed, one's body begins to fuse with the environment, and the limitations of one's physical self become unclear. Particular ideas or things may assume a high meaningfulness. In this sense truth and reality and other abstract conceptions of the universe appear to be vividly understood.[7]

It is the use of hallucinogenic drugs which has produced in-

7 Jerome Levine, "Round Table on LSD." Paper read at the NASPA Drug Education Conference, Washington, D. C., November 1966.

creased public awareness and concern about the problem in the past several years. The amount of confusion that exists in the mind of the public about the relationship between psychedelic drug takers and other addicts, or what we might call hard core addicts, is considerable. It is this confusion that lies at the basis of the extensive controversy that surrounds the law associated with drug taking.

ADDICTION AND THE LAW

The Harrison Anti-Narcotic Act of 1914 prohibited legal access to narcotic drugs, and in 1930 the Federal Bureau of Narcotics was established to enforce the law which had received varying amounts of compliance in the past. The Federal Bureau of Narcotics co-operated with state and local authorities (and in many ways because of this association forced *local* agencies to focus on the problem) to ensure compliance. After World War I, known drug addiction rocketed to an astounding 1 in 400 ratio. After eight years of a functioning Federal Bureau of Narcotics, the ratio had decreased to 1.53 in 10,000. Of course the problem with such statistics is that we know nothing about the increase of unknown addiction between the two periods. Nonetheless since addiction was still illegal in 1918, the figures should provide a gross indicator of the effect of the law in regulating the use of narcotics.[8]

The way in which law enforcement agencies have ignored legal decisions (such as the Lindner case, 1925, in which the Supreme Court decided that medical doctors could use certain discretions in providing drugs to addicts) suggests the attitude that drug addiction is to be viewed as criminal behavior and in no way a physiological disease. Nonetheless inconsistencies in the criminal definition of addiction are reported by Lindsmith[9] in his discussion of experimental practices at Lexington, a hospital established by the Public Health Service. Here, he reports, addicts have been successfully withdrawn and subjected again to drugs by hospital administrators and those carrying on research into this phenomenon. This in itself throws the question of criminality open to dispute. In addition to these practices, the unwillingness of Narcotics Bureau personnel to accept the use of medical attention outside of prison hospitals in aiding withdrawal actually promotes the utilization of the drug peddler to substitute for medical attention. Indirectly, the

8 *Encyclopedia Britannica* 7 (1963): 702–704.
9 A. R. Lindsmith, *The Addict and the Law* (New York: Vintage Books, 1967), p.18.

most serious form of criminality associated with addiction, that of drug peddling, is promoted, but the law enforcement agencies appear to be unaware of this consequence in many cases.

Legislation outlawing the manufacture of heroin was passed in 1924 and marijuana was brought under federal control by the passage of the Marijuana Tax Act of 1937. The Boggs Bill (1951) and the Narcotic Drug Control Act (1956) greatly increased the penalties for traffic in narcotics. In many states the minimum penalties for possession or transfer of narcotics, even without fee and for first offenses, were as much as two years' imprisonment with second offenses calling for five year minimums. In 1956 the state legislature of New Jersey voted to increase the penalties even for first offenses, asking for mandatory ten year sentences. Governor Meyner vetoed the bill, stating that while drugs were a serious problem and to be viewed as undesirable, the penalties were for many individuals excessively punitive; and he cited several examples of persons who, after brief contact with drug use, turned out to be useful and productive citizens.[10]

Laws associated with the use of hallucinogens will be discussed in another context. For the addict the law intrudes in his life in several ways: It classifies him as a criminal because of the use of drugs and thereby subjects him to imprisonment; it restricts his access to drugs to maintain his habit, and he thereby becomes entangled in a compounded set of criminal acts whereby money for drugs can be attained; and it governs the kind of rehabilitation that addicts receive. An example of this last effect of the law can be represented by events of the week of July 1, 1968, in Los Angeles, California. The Synanon Foundation, an organization for the rehabilitation of known as well as unknown addicts, became embroiled with the state regulatory agencies which insisted upon applying medical tests to two residents of Synanon in order to check on whether or not they were "staying clean." With the backing of Synanon, the residents refused to take the tests and were quickly removed by the state and taken to its own hospital-prison for such rehabilitation, where the techniques were considerably different from those of Synanon.

THE CONTEXT OF DRUG ADDICTION

Addicts are usually urbanites from the lower classes. Drugs are almost exclusively available in the city, and places and ways to attain the money to maintain a habit are there. Prostitution, for example,

10 *Ibid.,* pp.25–29.

because of the anonymity of urban life, can more easily flourish in cities than in small towns where control of deviance is simplified by the visibility of most social activity.

Drugs as a marketable commodity appear where the market is right, where most persons who are likely to accede to the pushers' wares are apt to be. Chein[11] conducted a study in New York City which revealed that the areas of highest drug addiction were in the city's most crowded and underprivileged neighborhoods. The addict was usually from a split home, from a home where money problems produced constant aggravations and conflicts. The attitudes of addicts were very similar to the general attitudes of slum dwellers. There were strong anti-police feelings and a belief that people care only for themselves and very little about the welfare of others. The addict also had a general mistrust of most major institutions (church, school, police), a feeling of being lost, helpless, and alienated.

Drugs, then, for most addicts, appear to serve as a means of escape from an uncertain and unproductive life. For many adolescent drug addicts drugs conceivably function as a theme by which members of teenage gangs cohere their organizations. Cloward and Ohlin, in distinguishing several types of such gangs, specify one type that does become characterized by the members' reliance upon drugs.[12]

The prognosis for the rehabilitation of drug addicts is grim.

Treatment for addiction is both unpleasant and not very successful. Withdrawal of the drug must be accomplished whether it be sudden or gradual, with or without the temporary assistance of other drugs. The two Federal narcotics hospitals, one at Lexington, Kentucky, and the other at Fort Worth, Texas, accept both patients forcibly committed by the courts and those who voluntarily apply for treatment. In either case, recidivism is common and the proportion of permanent cures is low.[13]

The problem of rehabilitation is partly linked to public attitude and public policy toward vice in general. Control and cures of addiction would almost certainly be improved if attitudes and, consequently, legal action were not linked to public fear. Rehabilitation through medical treatment could be more effective than other methods, but this would require an act that would permit physicians to provide drugs in small quantities at reduced rates to addicts.

The notion of legalized but regulated drug traffic could have a dramatic effect on the addiction problem, particularly since drugs

---

11 Chein, "Narcotics Use Among Juveniles."
12 R. Cloward and L. Ohlin, *Delinquency and Opportunity: A Theory of Delinquent Gangs* (New York: The Free Press, 1960).
13 Horton and Leslie, *Sociology of Social Problems*, p.568.

would be so cheap that crimes to maintain habits would be reduced. But within the current legal and social structure of drug addiction, the only effective rehabilitation technique appears to be that utilized by the Synanon Foundation. A brief analysis of this technique should provide some insights into the character of addicts and the conditions for effective cure.

SYNANON—THE TOTAL INSTITUTION

If we return briefly to the idea that rehabilitation of chronic deviates cannot be accomplished in a context which presumes a return to the same environment in which the deviance flourished, we can begin to suspect the source of the success of the Synanon Foundation. It appears that the two necessary conditions for rehabilitation are a total institution approach, where all segments of the person's life are guided by that institution, and a commitment to being a member of that institution. If the claim of Synanon that their methods work is correct, and the evidence seems to substantiate their claim,[14] then we can assume that these conditions are met. This is, in fact, the case. Yablonski recounts numerous incidents in which "incorrigible" addicts were turned into useful, productive (in a social as well as an individual sense) persons. The success of the Foundation is indirectly reflected in the kind of support provided by individuals in the society so that it has been able to expand its facilities nationwide and as of June, 1968, has passed the 1,000 mark in resident addicts.

In the same way that a context was seen to be associated with addiction, the construction of another context can be associated with leading a non-addict life. This is not to suggest that there are not personality traits associated with becoming an addict. The simple fact that, granting personality its place in the etiology of addiction, the Synanon Foundation has converted these people into productive human beings suggests the power of social structure in the formation of character.

THE BLACK MUSLIM APPROACH

In the same way that the Synanon Foundation provides addicts with a philosophy of how one should lead his life, the Black Mus-

14 L. Yablonski, *Synanon, The Tunnel Back* (Harmondsworth: Penguin Books, 1967).

lims have replaced drugs with ideology. The description by Malcolm X of the Muslims' rehabilitative effort reveals for us the process by which social meaning and purpose become adequate substitutes for drugs and suggests at the same time the basis on which addiction flourishes.[15] That is, if meaning and purpose can overcome a serious ailment such as drug addiction, we can begin to see how the development of such a life style in the first place could be preventive, or at least could minimize the rates of drug addiction. It has been the ideology of a purposeful life style that has succeeded for Synanon and the Muslims where correctional institutions, unable to capture the loyalty and commitment of the addict, have failed.

HALLUCINOGENS

Social problems emanating from the widespread use of psychedelic drugs are of a different nature from those associated with addicting drugs. They affect different kinds of persons, occur out of a more complex configuration of contexts, and require a different approach to remedial action.

Marijuana has been criminally used by all socioeconomic classes ever since it became illegal in 1937. We can surmise, since statistics can never be completely available on the number and kinds of users, that marijuana is primarily used by the socioeconomic groups exposed to a condition of frustration with their status and lack of opportunities to improve upon it. We can never be certain of this assertion, however, since the likelihood of apprehension of middle-class users is reduced by the secrecy and protection they enjoy in view of their conformist and exemplary postures in American society. Our speculations can be based only upon inferences we make about the contexts in which deviation occurs. We can make inferences from estimates of what persons are risking and from our understanding of the definitions members of different status positions make about the controlling power of the law. We can further make the social psychological argument that the marijuana user, given the decomposing effects of the drug, where persons lose various kinds of personal control, would be infinitely more threatening to those who find it necessary to maintain this control. Those who calculate the consequences of escapades into uncertain psychic domains are less likely to make the voyage. Until very

15 Malcolm X, *Autobiography of Malcolm X* (New York: Grove Press, 1964), pp.259-263.

recent times it is likely that "pot" (marijuana) was principally ingested by those whose contexts led them to other acts of deviance as well, that is, the low income, disenfranchised members of society. Today, without accurate statistics, the tendency is to suspect that the number of "pot" users in the United States runs into the millions.

The users of hallucinogens today appear to be predominantly students, both high school and college. That is not to suggest that the psychedelic or mind-expanding drugs are being ignored by persons in their thirties and forties. The "high" livers, regardless of occupation or social station, appear to have discovered a way to make the daily routines more tolerable and leisure time activity more exciting. The problem, insofar as it represents widespread law violation, is a problem for the whole society. For our purposes the most manageable unit of drug takers and the most relevant to the interests of this book, are the student takers. Before we attack the context of drugs on campus, however, we need to inquire further about the history and nature of the psychedelic drugs.

Marijuana is the mildest of the psychedelics relative to other such drugs. It usually produces a sense of euphoria and a somewhat intensified and altered perception of the environment. Because it has been illegal since 1937, very little medical research has been done to determine the effects of ingestion. What evidence there is does not support the claim of narcotics control authorities that the drug is harmful and dangerous, or at least not more so than alcohol.

Scholarly investigations into the use of marijuana have probed into scattered areas and have produced both inconclusive as well as convincing results.[16] Two studies, for example, pointed to an increased eroticism, particularly in the area of homosexuality,[17] but the Mayor's Committee study in New York argued that there was no direct linkage between marijuana use and erotic stimulation.[18] The research data in the latter study indicated that in only 10 per cent of 150 marijuana administrations was there evidence of eroticism. With respect to dependency or addiction, some research sug-

---

[16] Citations in this section on research on marijuana were taken from W. H. McGlothlin's comprehensive review of the literature in *Hallucinogenic Drugs: A Perspective with Special Reference to Peyote and Cannabis*, Report of the Rand Corporation, p.2937, Santa Monica, California, 1964.

[17] S. Charen and L. Perelman, "Personality Studies of Marijuana Users," *American Journal of Psychiatry* 102 (1946): 674–682; and E. Marcovitz and H. J. Myers, "The Marijuana Addict in the Army," *War Medicine* 6 (1945): 382–391.

[18] *Mayor's Committee on Marijuana, New York City* (Lancaster, Pa.: Cattell Press, 1944).

gests that users experience nervous tensions when supplies are withdrawn.[19] It should be noted, however, that despite reports of tensions and nervousness by hospital patients who served as subjects, doctors and nurses did not observe these changes.

Most investigators agree that physiological addiction from the use of marijuana does not occur. Williams noted that Army prisoners who were permitted to smoke as many marijuana cigarettes as they wished did not increase their usage.[20] In the Mayor's Committee Study observers of marijuana smokers reported that there was no frustration or compulsive seeking of a source of marijuana when it was not available.[21]

Other research on marijuana revealed that persons felt more relaxed, less inhibited, and more self-confident. The lack of inhibition was expressed vocally rather than physically. The effects were estimated to be comparable to the effects of alcohol.[22]

Some cases of psychosis occurring with frequent marijuana use were reported by the Mayor's Committee, but these cases were rare. Freedman and Rockmore, on the other hand, found no history of mental hospitalization in their sample of 310 users who had an average of seven years' usage.[23]

In certain situations where quick reaction time is important to health and safety, such as driving a car or working cutting machinery, there is little question from any quarter that being under the influence of marijuana increases the probability of accident. The arguments against the rigid penalties attached to usage appear to be having an effect, since many state legislatures as well as the Department of Health, Education and Welfare are currently taking a second look at penalties. The likelihood that pot will be legalized in the next decade or two is considerable. But the important problem for the student of education and society is to account for the patterns associated with drug taking, independent of evaluative judgments surrounding its use.

The use of psychedelic drugs such as LSD has increased considerably following the attention given to the experimentation of Timothy Leary and Richard Alpert and to their dismissal from Harvard in 1963 for having conducted experiments with under-

---

[19] E. G. Williams, *et al.*, "Studies on Marijuana and Pyrahexyl Compound," *Public Health Reports* 61 (1946): 1059–1083.

[20] *Ibid.*

[21] *Mayor's Committee on Marijuana.*

[22] *Ibid.*

[23] H. L. Freedman and M. J. Rockmore, "Marijuana, Factor in Personality Evaluation and Army Maladjustment," *Journal of Clinical Psychopathology* 7 and 8 (1946): 765–782 and 221–236.

graduates into the effects and experience of ingesting psilocybin. The two consequently founded the International Foundation for Internal Freedom to proselytize for psychedelics. Having begun in the context of college life, it was logical that experimentation with psychedelics, also conducted in many psychological laboratories across the country, should have taken an informal turn. That is, students decided to explore their inner world out of the same academic and personal motivation with which they had been influenced to explore the world of scholarly ideas.

Leary and Alpert have built a cult around the mind-expanding drugs which they popularized. They and others who support their cause argue that the positive value of psychedelics lies in the insights into and accompanying freedom from social and cultural barriers to understanding that persons attain. This, they suggest, will contribute to a radical transformation of society in the direction of open and honest interaction and a reduction of personal anxiety. They argue that the potential physical dangers can be controlled by careful administration of the drug and careful supervision of the experience.

In 1966 Leary published *The Psychedelic Experience,* in which he talked about the journey to the limits of consciousness. Use of these drugs, he contended (and this has been his contention from his earliest explorations as a respected psychologist), can begin to expand minds beyond the boundaries imposed by language. Our ways of conceiving the world, he argues, appear to be highly structured by the verbal conceptions we use and the space-time dimensions we acknowledge. Drugs are a giant step out of this kind of restraint.[24]

Currently, LSD has been brought under the same severe penalties as marijuana, and as such it constitutes not only a medical but a legal problem.

STUDENT DRUG TAKERS

Time magazine has estimated that about 10,000 students in the University of California have taken LSD.[25] The *Saturday Evening Post* estimated that 30 per cent of Harvard students and 35 per cent of San Francisco State College students have tried LSD.[26]

24 T. Leary, R. Metzner, and R. Alpert, *The Psychedelic Experience: A Manual Based upon the Tibetan Book of the Dead* (New Hyde Park, N. Y.: University Books, 1966).
25 "An Epidemic of Acid Heads," *Time,* March 11, 1966.
26 "Drugs on the Campus," *Saturday Evening Post,* May 21, 1966.

The same article suggested that usage is concentrated in northeast metropolitan and western urban areas. They indicated that in rural areas, particularly in the South and Midwest, drugs are still rare and that alcohol is the standard "high."

What is the circumstance that explains drug taking in two distinctly different contexts—on the streets of the slums and on college and high school campuses? Surely the motivation of delinquents in lower-class communities is not the same as the college boy in his dorm or apartment. What is the same, however, is the climate of association and influence. If some product, in this case drugs, is available, and the climate is such that many people in that environment desire it, then the activity proceeds.

Like the inner city, the college campus is a culture which is in many ways isolated from the wider culture. Within this cultural system there is an ethos, an identification of persons with each other around a set of definitions of the world around them and of the value of certain activities. It is within this group context that the college student is exposed to drugs, be they narcotics or psychedelics. The group exposes or supports members in their activities and even punishes those who through self-isolation refuse to "buy" the ethos. The sub-culture develops a network of communication by which control of members can be maintained, so that "finking" or "squealing" is held to a minimum for deviant acts, and by which drugs can be made available.

The important point to be pressed here is that isolated societies, such as the slum or ghetto and the college campus, are ecologically arranged in such a way that values, strategies, protection, and identification with others in the same situation will ward off any tendencies to internalize the values of the larger society when they are in conflict with the smaller unit. Whereas in the slum values favor immediate gratification, aggression, hostility to law enforcement agencies and the larger society which they represent, and produce a generalized frustration and anger, the campus produces another set of attitudes, equally conducive to drug taking. The youth culture in general in the last dozen years has been taking an increasingly suspicious view of the society which controls its life.

The student rebel who incorporates drug taking into his daily routines does not appear to be the same kind of trivial rebel who characterized the college scene in past decades. Although many adults would prefer to dispute it, since it devalues their own condition, the collegiate rebel would argue that he is not trying to escape through drugs, not running away from anything, but running toward something. If he is rebelling against the old way, it is because he has found, he thinks, a new and better one. As Leary and many of his disciples have argued, the psychedelic movement is more religion than rebellion, meaning that the mind-expanding experience is a religious experience insofar as it is (1) a ritual which binds and coheres the members of the small society, and (2) a way to discover the reality, or truth, or God, that is within the individual.[27]

In general this extreme form of drug taking as part of a radical religious movement does not characterize the average collegiate drug taker any more than the hard-core criminal, thief, prostitute, or junkie characterizes the average pot smoker of the lower classes. The largest segment of drug takers on college campuses do not make drug taking a way of life. But these students do object to the regulations which attempt to restrain them from these experiences. The use of drugs shows their contempt for such regulations. The major criticism of these students, according to a nationwide survey of student leaders, centers around the use of marijuana. These student leaders felt that the sale and distribution of hard narcotics should be illegal but that marijuana was non-addictive and generally less harmful than alcohol. They felt the breaking of the law to be justified insofar as the laws were unjust in the first place.[28] The fact of a large group of people living in proximity with each other and sharing the same beliefs makes it all the more difficult for law enforcement agents to track down secret violations of the law. In this way the campus resembles the ghetto.

DRUGS ON THE COLLEGE CAMPUS

The concern of university administrative personnel about the effects of drug usage began to take shape in the fifties and sixties with the excessive student use of stimulants, particularly dexedrene. The stimulants were used or at least defined by users as instrumental to their achieving the goals desired for them by the institution. As the pressures built and time grew short, students stimulated themselves to more intense and greater efforts to perform.

Tranquilizers hit the campus with greater impact than even the stimulants. The pressures and competition and overload expectations conspired to create conditions of high anxiety that could be alleviated by the new drugs. Still, the rationale for the use of these

27 Leary et al., The Psychedelic Experience.
28 Mathew Wilson, "Students Against the Law: The Power of Negative Thinking." Moderator, November 6, 1967.

drugs was expressed in terms of fulfilling one's obligation to the institution. Not until the illegal drugs entered the college scene did it become necessary to look for reasons of conflict, rather than congruence.

A Princeton report on student drug takers has defined three types of social groupings in which patterns of drug activity emerge. The *social* group uses marijuana like alcohol to reduce the irregular pressures in the environment. This group draws its membership from all sectors of the student body. A second grouping, the *revolutionary isolates*, see themselves as being in open rebellion against the restraints of the campus organization. They argue that they use drugs to symbolize their protest against the system, as a declaration of personal independence. A third group, the *insight* group, takes drugs for mystical and spiritual experience. They are in the world of mind expansion, of exploration of the basic self, and for these persons drugs are simply the tickets for the ride. They are the ones who are most willing and ready to tackle the heavier psychedelics. They do so, however, by using the group and members in it to protect and guide neophytes and to control the behavior of one another. It would appear that group solidarity and protectiveness ward off a number of potentially traumatic effects in the use of such drugs as LSD.[29]

It appears that the major deterrent to increased rates of LSD usage on college campuses is the circulated warnings about the "bad trip," a condition wherein the taker experiences painful psychotic reactions and does not recover after the normal time span has elapsed. Many organizations are attempting to isolate factors associated with the kinds of "trips" that are experienced. One study compared a group of psychiatric patients who had been hospitalized as a result of taking LSD with a group of habitual users who had experienced no adverse effects. The researchers looked for significant differences in race, sex, age, parental deprivation, economic status, residential area, and type and amount of education. Findings were all negative. The only distinguishing factors were social, that is, those who had favorable contact with the drug all belonged to a religious community, religious in the sense of spiritual exploration through LSD, were more often married than the psychiatric patients, and usually ingested the drugs in a context of social solidarity and support.[30]

29 Princeton University Student Committee on Mental Health, Psychedelics and the College Student (Princeton, N. J.: Princeton University Press, 1967).
30 J. T. Ungerleider, D. D. Fisher, M. Fuller, and A. Caldwell, "The Bad Trip: The Etiology of the Adverse LSD Reaction." Paper read at American Psychiatric Association Meetings, Detroit, May 1967.

The principle of solidarity and support helps to account for the presence of wholesale drug taking on college campuses and in slum ghettoes. What specifically is the nature of that solidarity and support? We have already talked about similar values, particularly attitudes toward the forces of control and restraint. We cannot, however, ignore the power of the need to affiliate. This is not expressed as a psychological state but rather as a social condition, a situation in which persons seek together to avoid the alienative effects of their environment. Taking marijuana or using LSD may be defined by many as a way of expressing solidarity with the college sub-culture, in much the same way that this is expressed through the wine ritual in religious ceremonies. For those who honestly believe that they are partaking of something particularly good, who believe that they will derive much enjoyment and satisfaction out of their trips, solidarity becomes a relatively simple state to maintain.

One interesting difference between the slum drug taker and the college drug taker should be mentioned. That is, while the slum taker is usually a person who can be defined as a failure within the legitimate economic status system of his society, the campus taker is frequently among the top students in his class, and the schools at which drug taking is more prominent are the most eminent in the nation (Berkeley, UCLA, Harvard, Wisconsin, Columbia, and the like). One study reported that 67 per cent of all pot smokers at Princeton were on the dean's list.[31] Therefore the standard conceptions of frustration-aggression, an explanation for deviant behavior in the slum, do not apply in the instance of college users. This would support the contention of Leary and others that drug taking does not occur out of frustration and rebellion associated with one's position in the status system but as a means of seeking stimulation that is unrelated to status goals. The use of the hallucinogens, however, may affect one's aspiration to achieve these goals, in which case mobility, or at least the kind of mobility we expect from bright, able students, will be affected.

Most campus drug users attribute mystical and religious experiences to drugs and tend to teach others what to expect, setting in motion the self-fulfilling prophecy. These students equate such experiences with sensitivity and feelings of beauty, often associated with perceived ability to grasp the complex structure of life.[32] In

31 "Potted Ivy, Alienated Students Smoking Marijuana," *Time*, May 19, 1967.
32 R. H. Blum, "Drugs and Personal Values." Paper read at NASPA Drug Education Conference, Washington, November 1966).

a society burdened by computers and depersonalized structures, drug use provides an alternative rationale for living. In this way the effects upon mobility striving can be perceived as a decision against joining the legions of those who never question the regularities of ability and achievement within traditional structures. Continued drug use (and the evidence seems to suggest that marijuana in particular, and even LSD, are not usually one-shot experiences, if the experience is one of mystical and religious insights), may influence people to relinquish economic success goals. If such drug users are the people (and the tendency is to suggest they are), who are the brightest and most able of our youth, then the question of how the drug culture will affect national political and economic leadership becomes important. We cannot at this time begin to answer this question, but the simple fact that a rebellion against our traditional way of life may be substantively supported within the insights of the campus drug society challenges the university to ask about its social role. The university does not, typically, make statements that would reduce motivations of students to explore their inner and outer world and to experiment and innovate in their daily lives. Consequently the university is placed in a position of fulfilling its ideological commitments to truth and inquiry and at the same time meeting its social responsibility. The latter is defined by many politicians and elders statesmen as a moral responsibility, meaning no more or less than maintaining the traditional value structures which are linked to economic goals.

Some colleges have taken steps to demonstrate their eagerness to play an active rather than a passive role in social change and have used the issue of drug taking in a central way. Oberlin College poses an important example. The general faculty of the college has recently adopted a revised policy on student use of drugs. This revision distinguishes between marijuana and other drugs, setting suspension as the upper range of penalties for the use, possession, or sharing of pot. The penalties for use of other drugs remains much more serious, including expulsion from school. At the same time the college was taking a similar position to the exponents of a revisionary policy on marijuana in the larger society. The school makes specific its desire to offer counseling and medical advice and assistance to students who desire to discuss their experience with drugs.[33]

---

[33] "Oberlin's Revised Policy," *School and Society* 96, No. 167 (March 1968).

THE IMPACT OF CAMPUS DRUG TAKING

The statistics on college drug takers suggests that there are con- siderably more non-takers than takers, perhaps ten times more. Then why, we need to ask, are so many journalists and scholars, not to mention politicians, so concerned about this phenomenon? What impact, for example, does college drug taking have upon the use of these drugs on high school campuses? The highest incidence of drug traffic occurs, as we mentioned earlier, in low-income, inner city neighborhoods. Addicts are often high school students on the verge of dropping out of school. They will be most often found in schools with the highest drop-out rates.[34] These drug takers are not the ones who are affected by the behavior of college students. In many middle-class high schools, however, where students are pre- paring for college, the hallucinogens have a popular market. The impact of a style of college living on the minds of students pre- paring for a college life is considerable. High school students imi- tate, as most adolescents imitate heroes, the behavior of those whom they admire in positions they aspire to occupy. These students take on the "it's happening" psychology and attempt to represent them- selves as persons who are already part of the movement. High school students, like (and often because of) college students who provide the example of the style of deviation, find that the ways of the past are no longer useful. Drug use is perceived as a reaction to the outmoded Protestant ethic which guided their parents.[35] The problem for these students is the here and now and not the far- distant future. For many intellectually oriented youngsters a four- year education is a thing of the past. Their sights are set on degrees that may take as much as eight or ten years to attain. In an age stressing the here and now, where the future is clouded by uncer- tainty and war, where barriers to human closeness become more imposing in the form of bureaucratic educational factories, delayed gratification becomes an outmoded ethic. If marches, resistance, pro- tests, and drug taking become the form of expressing new needs for college students, they then become the standard for high school students, and perhaps for many in even lower levels of education. The drama of the disaffected college students has guaranteed that

[34] A. N. Myerstein, "Drug Addiction: A Review," *Journal of School Health* 34 (February 1964).
[35] J. L. Simmons and B. Winograd, *It's Happening, A Portrait of the Youth Scene Today* (Santa Barbara, Calif.: Marclaid Publications, 1967).

their influence over the attitudes and behavior of others, particularly younger students who seek new cues for their behavior, will far outweigh their numbers.

The major impact of the campus drug takers seems to lie in the area of direct and indirect talent loss. Talent loss, as used here, accepts the traditional definitions of what talent is and how it can be put to use in serving the larger society. Mind-expanding experiences through the continued use of hallucinogens appear to move persons away from fulfilling traditional expectations, from becoming committed to and pursuing a career that society values, and into more personally fulfilling uses of time. Many students become so absorbed with self-exploration through drugs that their classwork suffers and they may fall irretrievably behind. Many students do experience disastrous results from their LSD trips and are forced to withdraw from school for varying amounts of time. Indirectly the activities of the campus drug takers influence younger persons into the drug sub-culture, to the point where their experiences with drugs begin to follow similar patterns. The problems are the same for the younger users: The drugs interfere with academic achievement, students often have unpleasant experiences, and many students are apprehended by the law.

The high school campuses will, if they do not already, approximate the college campus as a drug sub-culture. Certainly drug taking on the high school campus is a more serious and difficult problem than on the college campus, since here we are dealing with a double rather than a single phenomenon. When we ask ourselves about remedial programs and educational innovation to combat the problem, it is clear that the same kinds of action programs that would affect drug taking in the slums would require a somewhat different focus when dealing with suburban explorations into inner space.

THE SCHOOL AS THE "FIX" AGENT

In what sense might we suggest that the school has played some part in exaggerating the use of drugs on high school and college campuses? We do not mean to suggest something as obvious as the fact that college chemistry laboratories provided a considerable portion of the LSD supply, as in many instances was the case. What we do want to introduce is the way in which the school, by ignoring certain tendencies and pressures in the informal society of peers, guaranteed that the conditions amenable to the use of drugs would be met. In the final section of this chapter we will make some suggestions about the kinds of activities that might reduce the problematic consequences of drug taking; but first, we need to explore what schools have done, usually in the name of achieving other goals such as control over deviance, which has helped to water the ground in which drugs grow in use.

The Control of Deviance

In order to maintain a desired amount of stability, the school typically routinizes its activities to control the behavior of students. In many areas this behavior is controlled through a rigid organization of punishments and through a process of isolating all the deviants so they will not affect the educational experience of "good" students. This organization ensures two processes, both of which encourage the distribution and extension of drug use. First, it defines the deviant as someone who is expected to misbehave. By isolating him along with other deviants from the large mass of others, these persons begin to develop a sense of group or of family. As a collectivity the group begins to define its own values, usually in opposition to the values of the system which has rejected them. Very often one of these values is the use of drugs. Since the society they reject views drugs as bad, their own position must support the definition of drug use as good.

Second, association as a condition for the transmission not only of deviant values but also of opportunities to participate in deviant activities is relevant to our problem. The school's gross grouping of students in terms of characteristics they may hold in common, appears to be conducive to the sharing of expectations and opportunities.

The defining of students as deviant or as desirable stems from the position of the school as an agency of moral training. Since this conception of the school is part of the unquestioned tradition of education, the fact that schools have not been innovative in developing new ways of integrating deviants into the larger body should come as no surprise. In situations where a large percentage of the student body is seen as requiring strong control methods, the possibilities of integrating these students into the value system of the school is obviated. In the same way that law enforcement agencies drove underground those who were seeking legal access to drugs by refusing to consider any action beyond that of criminal prosecution, the school assumes the same posture. Students in low income or ghetto areas see the school as a punitive institution which they need to subvert in deviant ways in order to live. The drug subculture is a part of that deviant network.

The Effective Outlet

The school has never been thought of as a place to let one's emotions out. For most students school is a place where one regularizes his behavior, restrains any inclinations to express what he feels, and quickly learns to play a role. In this climate the student, at least the middle-class student, learns to be a good citizen, and part of being a good citizen is being in control, particularly in control of normal impulses to react to frustrations. The slum child often finds himself in an intensified version of a non-effective world, since slum children often produce anxiety in school personnel which is reduced by excessive control techniques. We do not need to argue that these children experience greater frustration than children of the middle class. At the same time they are experiencing this frustration, they are impelled to control all improper manifestations of it, such as verbal or physical aggression or even tears.

These children turn to drugs to produce an effect or an outlet for reducing the tension implicit in their educational lives. There is not an adequate substitute within the context of the school itself. In one way or another most students resist temptations to express their feelings because they believe they have something to lose. For children of the middle-class school, the loss is calculated in terms of falling down in grades, in status, in access to college. To the lower-class student, this loss is conceived as punishment, of taking from him his free time, of being sent to discipline schools where survival is hard. As long as the outlet awaits him after school, he will bide his time, and as long as he does not disrupt the *status quo* of the school routines, such students are tolerated and then dismissed to their drug outlets.

THE IDENTITY CRISIS

Most students come to college with the expectation that they will receive something more from their experience than a body of knowledge which they can apply to some career. Coming out of a period of mental and chronological growth often referred to as an identity crisis,[36] students look to the college experience as a place

[36] E. Erikson, *Childhood and Society* (New York: W. W. Norton & Company, Inc., 1950).

for moving toward a less diffuse conception of themselves. In other words, students want to leave college knowing who and what they are better than when they began college. But the American university has gone down the road toward becoming a servant of the occupational world beyond the point of no return. All that the educational factory requires is that students learn how the fit into the world of careers, not who they are as persons. Classes are taught in large, impersonal masses; examinations are scored by computers; advisement is in terms of types rather than individuality. At a time when the multiversity is moving more toward depersonalization, students are becoming passionate about their desire for humanizing experiences. They move to drugs to discover who they are. It is not important at this point to emphasize the fact that universities do not provide self-exploration experiences. This we will suggest later. What *is* important is to see that the way the university has moved toward dehumanizing the education experience, even and perhaps more so in the humanities, has forced students to seek elsewhere some protection against being no more than a punched IBM card. The elsewhere is inward with the aid of a drug.

THE ABSENCE OF POWER

Students on several college campuses have turned to drugs as a statement of their disaffiliation with the institution. The same thing is true in some ways of high school students, although they would not conceive of the dynamics in these terms. When one cannot participate in a system, in terms of helping to shape and guide the organization in seeking system as well as personal goals, he often turns to another system that he has the power to control. By using drugs he can take himself off on an exploration whenever he desires. By omitting students in any meaningful way from participation in its organization, the school forces them into a self-seeking position. These students turn their search into their own minds and find that drugs are tickets to heretofore inaccessible places.

We are really talking about power. Drug taking can be thought of as a way of seeking power over the objects of a fantasy world. Drug takers are typically impotent in the sense of forging their own destinies in any real way. The school perpetuates that impotence insofar as it does not permit the students any control over their institutional life. The college student is just as impotent, in this respect, as the slum student who is rigidly managed in the conduct of his educational life. For both drugs are one form of escape from impotence. It is an unfortunate paradox of our "liberated" culture that we offer students freedom without power. They are, as we define it, given the freedom of choice, but we make it difficult for them to move in the direction of those choices. Our major institutions are still conservative structurally, although they may not be ideologically. Therefore students find themselves in the very unfortunate position of knowing that they are free to make choices which they cannot achieve. They cannot, for example, decide to be independent, to be individualists in an otherwise conformist society. The major institutions of which the student is a member require a certain amount of conformity to guarantee their own stability. Teachers do not feel that they can allow students to do whatever they choose, even if those activities advance the students' development toward independence. Drug taking, then, may be a common phenomenon among students because the only way out of the structural paradox, that is, the pursuance of freedom in a restrained society, is through psychedelic rather than institutional activities.

THE MORALISTIC BACKLASH

Finally we should consider the extent to which the supermoralism of the school has produced a backlash, the use of drugs being one form. It would seem that at a time when social and cultural revolutions have changed our definitions of moral postures, the school, as an agent of society, would assume the responsibility of helping persons adapt to these changes. But institutions in democratic societies change slowly. The culture is ready, for example, to accept the possibility that marijuana is not a product of the arch criminal mind and that it should not be kept out of the reach of citizens through the most punitive regulations possible. We can suspect, however, that the school is not even beginning to prepare students at least to question traditional moral positions. Teachers, despite a constant attempt to modernize the image, still are defined as persons who are the standard bearers of the old morality. And because of this definition, or what we might call a stereotype, the teacher may turn students around, that is, force them to accept opposite positions from the ones taken by the teacher. If the school and the teacher are against drug taking, and if students define both school and teacher as decadent, then drug taking seems to students to be the right thing today. Our problem must be somehow to change the teacher's image if he is to be considered an important component in programs to ameliorate social problems.

THE SCHOOL AS MARKETPLACE

For most adolescents the school is the ecological center of interaction. It is the one place within the community where there exists the possibility of every adolescent interacting with every other adolescent. It is, therefore, the most logical spot to push drugs. It also has the most logical population from which to select pushers. The student himself, interested in making money, sensitive to the needs and interests of his age group, and invisible to the authorities, becomes the criminal simply because the school exists and because it serves the functions that it does. We cannot, of course, contend that the school is responsible for the drug market in this sense anymore than we can blame the structure of government for dirty politics. The problems lies between the structure and the way it is used by different kinds of persons. The senate, for example, can define a code of ethics for the behavior of those who are or want to be senators. But when the prizes for violating this code are high, the ethical code diminishes in importance.

The school also relies upon its ethical code. It is, after all, a socializing agency. The extent to which it fails to win the allegiance of participants to this ethical code tells us something about the way the school fails to provide a meaningful reason for allegiance. That is, persons violate codes when these codes do not have more than an abstract meaning to the individual. Schools, like most families, somehow assume that righteousness is its own reward and that the values of goodness are self-evident. It is not so important, in evaluating ameliorative programs, to consider the disparity between expectations for students and their behavior. It is not even surprising to the school administrator that in some communities his plant is being used as the center of a drug marketplace. What is important is to consider the reasons why students themselves do not have their own good reasons for breaking up such a ring. To do the "right" thing is certainly a weak motivation in our time. We will consider this problem further below.

THE ROLE OF THE SCHOOL

In terms of policy decisions the school does not concern itself with distinctions between the various kinds of illegal drugs. States vary in the way they ask the school to participate in programs to educate students about the use of drugs. Many states hold formal and informal expectations for the role the school should play in this process and are ignored either partly or fully in most places. There is a good reason for this. While there are explicit and implicit expectations for doing something in the school, it is seldom clear what can and should be done.

California, whose narcotics problems are probably as serious as any state given its proximity to Mexico where a long tradition of drug traffic has existed, refers to instruction concerning narcotics in three sections of the state education code:

Section 8553: Instruction shall be given in all grades of school and in all classes during the entire school course, in manners and morals and upon the nature of alcohol and narcotics and their effects upon the human system, as determined by science.

Section 8254: All persons responsible for the preparation or enforcement of courses of study shall provide for instruction on the subjects of alcohol and narcotics.

Section 20456: In all teachers' training colleges, in the State colleges, adequate time and attention shall be given to instruction in the best methods in teaching the nature of alcohol and narcotics and their effects on the human system.

This particular code suggests that the discussion of narcotics should be held in a context of morality on the one hand and scientism on the other. The question then arises, and California school officials have often discussed the issue, of when are students mature enough to comprehend the problem? Implicitly, these persons (and it is certain that school administrators throughout the country ask the same questions) are concerned about several things: (1) the extent to which they can deal with controversial subject matter, that is, what are the dangers of public indignation; (2) the extent to which students can make personal inferences from scientific data; (3) the extent to which the data contradict the moral position of the community and therefore the school; and (4) the extent to which those who are to guide the instruction can be counted on to stress those interpretations which support the moral position of the school.

School districts like to stress consistency in policy decisions, consistency across the broad application. If one set of ideas leads to a decision that children are too immature to discuss drugs before the tenth grade, and another set leads to the conclusion that for slum children the tenth grade is far too late, then we have a typical dilemma. Sometimes the school resolves such dilemmas by ignoring the problem entirely.

The school ignores problems for several reeasons. Some of them, such as fear of arousing the public and the sensitivity of teachers about dealing with controversial matter amidst young minds, have already been discussed. There are several other basic reasons why schools do not educate in problem areas such as sexual deviation, alcoholism, and drugs. Let us consider a few of these in relation to drug taking.

The State of the Knowledge

Because the major drugs that are used by students are illegal, there has been very little research into the short or long range effects. By effects, we mean not only the physiological effects, which may be the prime focus of a high school curriculum, but also the effects on study patterns, on family relationships, on self-acceptance, on social tolerance, and so on. Some areas related to drug taking about which we know very little are:

1. Who is using drugs, which drugs are being used, and how much use occurs?
2. Why do students use drugs and why does society react as it does?
3. Why is drug use more prevalent on particular campuses and what is the relationship between type of campus, type of student, and drug use?
4. How much real opposition to drug use is there?

We know very little and what we do know to now has not yet been translated into a usable format for instruction. When the first study guide for a unit on drug taking appears in the schools, which of the above questions would we suspect will be omitted from the curriculum? There are two ways of being dishonest to students, by commission and by omission, and many school administrators would strongly support both kinds in the interest of stability and control. Therefore a curriculum guide that emphasizes such questions as why students need drugs, decisions about "reasonable" limits, descriptions of the characteristics of campuses and persons who use drugs on campus (the best schools and the brightest students) might be of dubious value.

What, then, do we select as the context of a curriculum unit on drug taking? How do we even begin to answer this question? We might suggest that we would like to achieve the goal of reducing the amount of drug taking as well as reduce the possibility of non-users ever turning to drugs. This would be a good start. From there we might decide, as a good teaching technique, to take the position that we will supply data and let students make their own decisions. Can we chance that? Perhaps we need to build in educated guesses about effects of certain kinds of information and ways of presenting it. One writer has suggested that the school use as many stock techniques as often as possible.[37] What do we know about the value of this technique? The truth is we do not know very much about the value of any technique because the state of our knowledge about what learning should be communicated and how it should be taught is as dismal as the amount we know about the subject.

In a consideration of the kind of knowledge that is available, the way in which that knowledge is and can be organized, and the way in which we would like to use that knowledge, we can begin to see why schools have not really begun the task of educating about drugs.

The Role of the Teacher

The capacity of most teachers to handle a unit on drug taking appears to be about as problematic as the state of the knowledge that needs to be communicated. Perhaps the question of who should do the actual teaching should be left open since a specialist might be required. What is most likely to happen, however, is that if a specialist can be found, he should be utilized to instruct teachers who in turn can carry workshop skills into the classroom.

The major question is, can teachers do the job that is required now? The answer seems to be negative. They are not trained, they are not knowledgeable, and most important, they will not be convincing to many students in slum schools where drug traffic is heavy.

The Availability of Resources

Schools do not typically anticipate future needs. The school is an adaptive institution, shifting its functions and allocating new resources as new responsibilities become present commitments. The role of the school in the amelioration of the problems of drug taking is as yet unclear, and consequently resources are not yet available. The phenomenon of drugs as a serious problem for the schools was as sudden as changing hairstyles or the shift to mini-skirts. These comparisons are not made as frivolous examples but as an

[37] "Straight Talk About the Drug Problem," *School Management* 12 (February 1968): 52–56.

extension of the same problem. In many ways drugs, particularly in middle-class schools, are as much a fad as hairstyles or clothing. That is not to suggest that they are unimportant in the life of the student. The point is that schools are not able to adjust their structures to meet new problems in a rapid and facile way. Committees need to be established, money needs to be allocated, experts must be sought and utilized efficiently, teachers need to be trained, materials must be selected and made available. By the time all this occurs, perhaps students will have shifted from drugs to meditation.

The Problem of Conviction

Finally programs for education in the area of drug taking become retarded because educators are neither clear about, nor committed to a specific position. Educators are as aware as most members of the society that the culture is changing rapidly. They are somewhat anxious about the ground swell emanating from youth, which might appear to be a mounting rebellion against the traditional verities. It may be that, like many adults, educators without confessing it are unwilling to stand in the way of this ground swell, partly because they know they cannot stop it and partly because they are aware that youth at this time are doing what they need to do. The old moralism with its concomitant punishments and its fire and damnation lectures to the sinful may have had its day in education. Although many teachers go through the old motions, simply because they do not know what else to do, they are most certainly ready for a better way. That is, they are beginning to be aware that drug taking is a problem and not a sin and one does not appeal to the old moral techniques to clear up a situation that is not defined by drug users as a moral violation.

For all these reasons educational programs in secondary schools have not been formed around the problem of drugs on any widespread basis. Some activity in this area has been taking place, however, on the college campus.

CONTROL ON THE COLLEGE CAMPUS

College and university administrators are more critically concerned about drug use than most public school administrators because drugs on the campus are construed by many users as part of a higher education. The LSD traffic, along with the widespread use of marijuana, has made such an appreciable dent in college life that legislation seems totally impotent. University administrators, since they do define the student body as more or less adult and consequently responsible for their own behavior, are more apt to consider interpersonal methods of control than public school administrators who take a more "crime and punishment" view of the problem.

The university as an environment in which control of drugs is to be evaluated must not only consider the legal aspects but must also, given its tradition, develop a rational basis for such control. Again, this is not a major problem for the public schools since school administrators do not feel it is necessary to articulate a rationale for control to younger students but simply to enforce the laws and the rules. Nonetheless in the long run the strength of policies regarding control must eventually reside in the commitment of individuals to respect and support the rules. High school students are as ripe for protest against what they consider unrealistic control as are college students, and any viable policy must appeal to the belief systems of the students. The same cultural changes which have produced excessive drug taking among students at many educational levels make it increasingly difficult to regulate the behavior of these students with the old slogan, "We know what is best for you."

The university, which is increasingly being defined as a center for research, cannot easily support a regulatory system which avoids research findings. The university should conduct research to answer important questions about the who, where, and why of drugs. Some universities, as earlier parts of this chapter report, are conducting surveys to find out who uses drugs and where, but this kind of data is always suspect since students, like most of us, will rarely report illegal behavior. From the little evidence that we can gather regarding drug takers, we can begin to accumulate insights about how to reduce the amount of drug use among students. We know, for example, that the greatest amount of drug taking exists in what has been referred to as the "non-conformist" sub-culture.[38] This is the group of students who affiliate least with collegiate activities and are most concerned with personal development independent of classes or formal activities. These students are those who are most in protest against the dehumanizing character of the modern university. Another group, referred to by the Princeton University Committee on Mental Health as the "insight" group, uses drugs to facilitate mystical experiences, a quick trip to the deeper recesses

[38] B. Clark and M. Trow, "The Organizational Context," in *The Study of College Peer Groups*, ed. T. M. Newcomb and E. K. Wilson (Chicago: Aldine Publishing Co., 1966), pp.17-20.

of the mind where the deepest secrets of existence are hidden.[39] From this kind of evidence or at least from the organization of research findings, we can begin to surmise what it is the college lacks that must be made up for by drugs. In the absence of a personalized curriculum and what we might call a humanistic approach to learning, students seek drugs. Students are avid for thrills because their education is not particularly thrilling. Is the answer to find better ways of enforcing the law, or to reconstruct the environment so that such behavior is not necessary?

Through their offices of student deans and counseling centers, many universities, not to mention special committees of a range of experts, are making an honest attempt to evaluate the dimensions of the problem and to come up with some suggestions for policy. Workshops with resident hall advisors, student leaders, and professional psychologists and psychiatrists are operating around the year. On many campuses research committees have been organized and are in the process of gaining data on the depth as well as the effects of drug taking, particularly the effects of LSD. The evidence is by no means all in, but nonetheless policies need to be articulated and facilities and personnel need to be organized to perform a holding operation until more sweeping innovations are instituted.

CONTROL AND RECONSTRUCTION

It has been suggested that there are two logical approaches to the amelioration of drug problems on school and college campuses. One approach is to attack the specific problem head-on, restraining its existence by regulatory controls and by a system of education about the abuses and detrimental effects of drugs. A second approach is to remove from the environment the conditions which drive persons to experiment with drugs or to take them as an escape from their life routines. We can maintain law and order by complete suppression of individual action or by removing the conditions which produce disorder. The former is obviously the easier mode and the school, like law enforcement agencies, prefers easier, more concrete solutions. The role for professional education must be a reconstructionist one as well as a remedial one. We cannot regulate forever against something that students believe they want and need.

[39] Princeton Student Committee, *Psychedelics and the College Student.*

In the area of direct confrontation we have considered two alternatives—regulation through surveillance and punishment, and education via instruction and guidance.

The regulatory function is an essential component of institutions and is served primarily through the mechanism of belief. That is, members of the system must be socialized to believe that the rules are correct and worthy of their support. Most people abstain from committing crimes not because they wish to avoid the penalties for doing so, but because they do not believe in committing crimes. For those who do not hold these beliefs, a system of punishments both formal (such as expulsion or jail) and informal (such as disapproval or withdrawal of affection) can be invoked. When belief fails, as in the case of drug taking on the campus, the formal regulatory process assumes prominence. The challenge for educational administration at this time becomes one of maintaining stability through its regulatory activities while seeking effective ways of encouraging commitment to the values of abstinence from drugs. The success of this kind of task resides in linking the values opposing drug taking to the prominent beliefs of system members in other areas. For example most people value good physical health. If the case can be made strong enough that drug taking is detrimental to health, the amount of deviance and therefore the requirements for regulatory activity are decreeased. This has been the case with LSD since widespread distribution of data taken from psychiatric wards regarding the disastrous consequences of "bad trips" has been disseminated. The case against marijuana is considerably more difficult. Although marijuana is illegal, most users are familiar with the research to date which suggests that the effects of marijuana are no more serious, and in some ways less serious, than the use of alcohol. The one value to which the opponents of student use can link their case is the value that most persons have about obeying the law. For many reasons which can be reviewed in the discussion of the adolescent sub-culture as well as in the Negro culture, the sanctity of the law has been undergoing constant erosion. In general the argument is made by those who find it necessary to deviate that the law can be ignored if it serves neither the needs or the beliefs of the people it protects. Suffice it to say now that the laws regulating the use of drugs and prescribing penalties for such use are considered unrealistic and invalid by large segments of the population. In this situation the consensus of scholars who have turned their attention to the problem is that education is the only real answer. Two representative statements are as follows:

Drugs are neither inherently harmful nor inherently beneficial and one must guard against an overreaction in either direction. The drug abuse problem may be attacked at its roots by transforming education into a consciousness expanding experience with an emphasis on intellectual freedom and creativity. Rather than make new rules, administrators may best take no action except to provide students with help and understanding.[40]

In combating drug use on campus, authorities can defeat their purpose by invalidly condemning drugs or operating with closed minds in attempting to enforce restrictive policies. Educators can be more effective by attempting to communicate with drug users and by pointing out that the narrowness of the drug subculture is a violation of the user's own values.[41]

The second statement opens the door for a consideration of the kind of educational effort that is necessary for uniting a community around a position on this particular issue. We talked earlier about linking proposals for regulation to the prominent values of the members of a system. In the statement given above, Mamlet suggests beginning with an analysis of the value system of the drug sub-culture and making the argument that the use of drugs contradicts this particular belief system or parts of it. If we can make the argument that drugs limit rather than expand self-awareness and reality perception, we can make a more appreciable dent in the use of drug taking for mind expansion reasons than if we talk only about punishments for violation.

EDUCATION ABOUT DRUGS

The school needs to assume a responsibility in helping students come to grips with their feelings about drugs so that they can make intelligent decisions regarding their own actions. As an educational rather than a regulatory function, this tactic is consistent with the guidance approach to educational problems as that approach is currently conceived within guidance and counseling circles. In order to execute this responsibility the school needs to evolve specific activities and programs in several areas.

[40] Joel Fort, "Social Values, American Youth and Drug Use." Paper read at NASPA Drug Education Conference, Washington, D. C., November 1966. Joel Fort is Director, Center for Special Problems, San Francisco Health Department. [41] L. N. Mamlet, "Consciousness Limiting Side Effects of Consciousness Expanding Drugs." Paper read at American Orthopsychiatric Association, Washington, D. C. March 1967.

The Statement of the School's Position

The school must articulate its position to students in such a way that students know where the school authorities stand with respect to violation of drug use regulations. It must also state clearly the stand the school takes regarding its relationship to outside regulatory agencies. Students must know whether or not the school will handle violations as a part of its own jurisdiction or surrender that function totally to the courts. Some universities, such as Columbia, send a letter from the office of the Dean of Students to each student stating the university's policy on drugs and giving a report on the background and current status of the illicit use of non-narcotic drugs. This kind of communication with students can be affected either with a posture of authoritarianism or of advisement. Such a posture may play a part in differentiating the response patterns of the student body.

Clinics and Rehabilitation Centers

Most persons who have considered the drug problem from the position of seeking ameliorative structures agree that the school should establish some agencies where students who are either addicted or confused about their use of drugs can go to discuss openly their problems. In the case of addiction, personnel who are trained to advise as well as refer to appropriate outside or inside agencies should be available. With the majority of cases, which will be "sometimes" users, these agencies can serve a clinical function in which alternative activities to drug taking can be evaluated in the light of individual problems. Offices of deans of students and university counseling centers at the college level and guidance services at the public school level can be asked to evaluate their structures and personnel in the light of requirements for helping drug takers who can be encouraged to consider other adaptations. As a guidance center educated personnel can begin to evolve plans for a variety of activities directed toward the amelioration of the drug problem, both for the present and for the future. School counselors may instruct students as to the academic requirements of a variety of colleges and even consider the interaction of campus and individual personality. A further task which the high school, as a filtering and helping agency, can assume is the preparation of students to deal with the many temptations to engage in drug experiments with college associates.

Student health services on college campuses and their equivalent in the public schools may be asked to play a significant role in the area of drug advisement through education, counseling, and rehabilitation or confidential treatment. The role of such services must, of course, be communicated to students since most students do not understand the relationship of specific segments of university structures to the whole. For example, if secrecy is possible and desirable in student health services, the communication of this fact to students can make a difference in who seeks advice and who doesn't.

The University as Trainer for Drug Education

The university, through its colleges of education, schools of social work and public health, and departments of sociology and/or criminology, can make a collaborative effort to provide educators with the kind of perspective and knowledge to educate and advise students about specific social problems, of which drug use is one type. The American university, despite its posture of accenting pure rather than applied research, is being forced by external as well as internal pressures to focus its resources on the larger social issues of the day. Most of the schools of applied fields of knowledge such as those mentioned above, do recruit and mobilize personnel with this commitment in mind.

The question of what kind of training is necessary for personnel to go out into the schools and handle a variety of social problems connected with drug use confronts professional educators on the heels of a concerted effort to do something about slum or urban education. Some of the strategies employed in the latter area can be converted into principles for an education concerning the drug problem. The notion that a teacher can know what a problem is only by experiencing its effects is useful. In the same way that we place teachers in ghetto schools we can also place them in drug clinics, confront them with college drug takers, expose them to psychiatric and social work personnel who specialize in work with drug takers, and provide them with as much literature on the sociological, psychological, and physiological research on drugs as is available. If we are concerned about prejudices which can interfere with responsibility, we can expose teachers to group discussions and confront individuals with their prejudices and biases. Curricula for a drug education program have not yet been incorporated on any widespread basis in the training of teachers and other educational workers, but committees with the support of foundations and governmental agencies can be organized to develop some experimental programs. It is likely that the embryos of such programs are gestating in the minds of many professional educators, and we should begin to observe the inclusion of such programs in many colleges of education.

Instructing Students about Drugs

After we talk about the horrors of addiction, the dependency, the pain of going without, withdrawal, and crime that are so highly correlated with drugs, what can we say to students that will deter them from seeking experience with drugs? We can talk about a relationship between smoking "pot" and going on to bigger and better highs. But to do this we would have to distort the evidence. We cannot make a causal claim, although we might dishonestly exaggerate the meaning of some relationships. We can cite some evidence regarding the frightening effects of LSD trips, but to be consistent in this posture we would also have to say that some airplanes crash. We know that under controlled experimental conditions bad trips occur infrequently, and our best estimates, which must be very rough considering we do not know how many trips are taken daily, is that bad trips occur less than 1 per cent of the time.

Beyond the very limited amount of data that we have on the physiological effects of drug taking, the main body of a unit on drug education would need to focus on the psychological and sociological consequences of drug taking. We can point students toward the consideration of some important ideas, but we cannot honestly argue that we have supporting data. One of these ideas is that drug taking negatively affects school habits. There is some scattered evidence that students have experienced a diminished interest in school work after drug experiences, but this is far from conclusive.[42] It is, however, the function of exploratory research, such as the kind that revealed this datum, to point to issues which may be important in the study of the effects of drug taking.

It seems that the dominant question which would guide an objective drug education program would be: "Why do people take drugs?" Student drug taking is seldom an outgrowth of an intellectual process, and alternatives to drugs to reach the same goals are seldom considered. If students can answer the question about why drugs are desirable, they might then begin to focus on alternative activities which could provide the same kind of stimulation. Younger students, for example, may not be able to give a better explanation than "getting high feels good." An analysis of what it means to be high may, in a creative classroom with a skilled teacher,

---

[42] J. L. Goddard, "Education Is the Answer to Drug Abuse by Our Young People," *Junior College Journal* 38 (September 1967) : 8–9.

lead to a number of "getting high" experiences which do not involve drugs. These may very well evolve out of the literature of humanistic psychology or even Eastern meditation.

Adolescents often turn to drugs as to cigarettes as a gesture of social solidarity with a particular reference group. An understanding of the social pressures that explain this phenomenon can lead students to an awareness of the irrelevancy of the specific symbol and perhaps lead also to the selection of alternative symbols for group definition and solidarity. Many students may feel, in a time of rejecting a "go along with the crowd" ideology, that the need to express their individuality by idiosyncratic rather than group-induced symbols.

The notion of psychological dependency can be exploited in this context. Although we cannot demonstrate that there is a physiological dependency on marijuana, we can suggest that, as with alcohol, persons avoid confronting barriers to personal development by their reliance on escape stimulants. In this sense marijuana may function much like a tranquilizer, and students may be led to confront the question of the developmental value of avoiding anxiety.

"Should marijuana be legalized?" may not be a popular public education question, but it would be taking the ostrich's way out not to acknowledge the significance of this question. It is a question that the federal government has commissioned a body of experts to discuss and members of Congress are regularly participating on inquiry panels to advance their own knowledge about this issue. Educational activities associated with helping students evolve a position with respect to such a question is consistent with the best intentions of education. That is, the goal of education, taking a page from the expectations of Thomas Jefferson, is to produce an enlightened electorate, a body of people who vote from knowledge rather than prejudice.

THE RECONSTRUCTION OF EDUCATION

The use of drugs can ultimately be described as a turning inward activity. The hard-core addict, like the psychedelic "acid head," is seeking for something from within himself which he cannot discover through his normal participation in the outside world. To the extent that educational structures do not attract students into the meaningfulness of an educational experience, a depersonalized alienation results. Students seek in drugs what they cannot find by way of a meaningful integration within an institution. And to the extent that pressures build to successfully fulfill the obligations of an alienative context, the drug enters as a pressure reducer. If students cannot affect the institution in such a way as to reduce the pressures, they can use drugs to make the pressurizing effects less potent.

The use of psychedelic drugs or hallucinogens is prompted largely by a desire on the part of students to "turn on" their minds, turn them on to what was unobservable or non-perceptible without drugs. Education has become a very dull tool in recent decades, unable to help students utilize their full human potential in the learning endeavor. The use of other than mechanically cognitive facilities has not been appreciated by educators as an important educational tool. The mind has rather been conditioned to fend off any inclinations to utilize the senses in the educational task, that is, to "know" some things because they are felt and the feeling or intuition is trusted. Modern education has convinced us that we can really trust only our heads, and it has encouraged us to rely on our consciences; but it has not released us from the restrictions we have placed on entering the deeper recesses of our sensibilities. Students talk about the wonder of their visions, of marvelous insights, and exciting thought trips. They talk about these things as if only drugs can produce them. They do not even begin to conceive of the possibility of enjoying these experiences as part of one's education.

The paradox is that students are using artificial stimulants to make them able to experience their humanness, because the institutions established to service human needs have reduced man to only a small fragment of himself. The civilized man has evolved to a point where he has traded individuality for respectability; but when too much of the individual goes, modern man reaches wherever he can to retain what he can of himself. Marijuana is seen to be necessary to that end by persons from all social strata; and consequently, since it is not solely a pleasure of the poor, it is bound to be legalized. The question that we need to ask is: "Couldn't we, as educators, find some way to make school the kind of human or turned-on experience that would reduce the need for a chemically-based education?" We may not be able to rely on legal prohibition much longer to buy us some time before the school is forced to compete with drugs for a kind of educational loyalty. We must begin to conceive of the kind of educational reconstruction whose goal it will be to make students able to rely on their own human potential for understanding rather than on the bureaucratic slogans and the knowledge of efficiency which we feel impelled to dispense, even though they kill the spirit and force millions of young people to turn on to drugs to revive what we have killed.

4

Problems
of Family Life

M A N Y   O F   T H E problems of family life accrue from different definitions persons have about what a family is supposed to be. Families differ and members within families differ as to the relative importance that they and others assign to family life. In some senses the simple notion of family life throws shudders into a large segment of the population who believe that a family is a burden as well as a joy. Sometimes the burdensome element gains such pre-eminence that a number of adaptations, the most disruptive of which is divorce, ensue. The traditional conception of the family as a close-knit unit of strength, warmth, and general solidarity has been eroding for a number of years. Today as in all periods of rapid cultural change there are two extreme positions. One is a return to the old values, a rededication to the old challenge of establishing the home as the foundation unit of all social life. The other, a position espoused by many and enacted by some, calls for a redefinition of the family, a conception wherein multiple fathers, mothers, and children develop a sense of interdependence regardless of the actual parental source of children. The psychedelic society espoused and described by Timothy Leary and others requires an abandonment of old ties and the establishment of new ties in which a community emerges as an extended family rather than an association of persons tied by blood.

The largest segment of the American population stands between these extremes. These people are tied to traditional family loyalties by the socialization that they received. They are controlled in their attitudes by the guilt that they experience when they attempt to cut the umbilical cord too drastically. They are reinforced in their inclinations to ward off temptations to be too independent by the traditional character of other institutions, such as the school and the church, which do not reward or encourage radical attitudes or behavior in any sphere. Their attitudes are maintained further by the social approval they receive from members of their communities for participation in "family life" and the disapproval they perceive to be the consequence of a disrupture of this pattern.

At the same time persons who hold roles within a family hold roles in other institutions or groups. Contemporary society is heavily structured around participation in associations other than the family. Many of the motivations aroused through this particular pattern are in conflict with family roles and some variation on the disorganization theme prevails in many homes as a result of these motivations. Fathers who are compulsively involved in some economic activity rationalize the time spent away from their family by the dollars which are accumulated for the family's benefit. Many mothers, aware of the growing disrespect accorded the traditional mother role and at the same time attracted by opportunities for self-fulfillment, find areas outside the family for this kind of expression of self. Children quickly develop deep friendship ties with their peers and begin to live mainly in a world contrived by themselves and kept quite apart from family obligations.

The complexities of modern industrial and technological life require a differentiation of institutional loyalty and responsibility.

Most people find comfortable ways to accommodate their divided energies. But many do not. When the family members begin to choose separate ways in which to function independently of the family unit, problems begin to emerge. They are emerging faster than institutional structures can be developed to cope with them. This is the nature of family life in a world of rapid cultural change.

THE FAMILY IN THE MODERN WORLD

The American family in the second half of the twentieth century is a family which is beginning to redefine its function and its responsibility to individual members. The disruptures that occur within families are often a case of retarded adaptation. Whereas once the family assumed responsibility for education, religious training, production of goods, recreation, medical care, and occupational training, the modern family need not concern itself any longer about any of these matters.

In the past few decades the American family has undergone a period of rapid change, at least rapid in relation to the normal rates of change of major social institutions. Divorce rates have increased considerably, particularly in the middle class where divorce was not long ago a stigma. These rates have continued to increase despite legal efforts to make divorce economically difficult for the husband, despite an increase in marriage counseling, and despite efforts on the part of the courts themselves to bring about reconciliation.

Another change in the American family has been a clear shift in fidelity expectations. Promiscuity and adultery are almost common and for every case that leads to the divorce court, many others are resolved in some kind of "understanding" between marital partners. The major media of entertainment may reflect more of a reality in its risqué dramas than one expects, since popular fiction ordinarily capitalizes on a portrayal of the unusual. Two best sellers, *Peyton Place* and *The Valley of the Dolls,* along with a legion of successful films on the subject of promiscuous marriage, reflect this trend.

For a long time the decline in birth rates, recently halted as a trend, was construed to be a further indication of the weak links of marriage. Other characteristics of family disorganization have been the rapid increase in facilities for child care, the proliferation of early childhood education centers, or nursery schools, and an increase in the number of associations which women join without their husbands, such as the League of Women Voters, Professional Women's Association, Women's Strike for Peace, Congress of Women, and the like.

Parsons evaluated the disorganizing trends perceived in family life as the "disorganization of transition" and suggests that some of the problems are problems of emerging extensions of original family organization and patterns. The fact that there are more divorces, he suggested, is due to the fact that people marry early, before their lives are stabilized economically or socially. He suggested also that the increased rates of divorce reflect disruptions in this segment of the population and among those who are childless.[1] Modern marriage begins for the most part on a different foundation from marriages of an earlier day when persons were ready to have children and settle into standard routines shortly after the marriage.

Parsons argues generally that disorganization within the family as an overriding fact ignores the fact that the concept of marriage as a binding and important institution has not changed in itself. Persons are not disillusioned with marriage because more people marry than ever before and those who divorce almost always remarry. He cites the fact of home buying as an indication that the "family home" concept has not lost its appeal.[2]

Problems of family life are very much a matter of adjusting to new structural patterns within the society and as such may diminish through time as the adjustments occur. Nonetheless in this period of transition sociologists and educators need to describe and evaluate the disruptions which affect the lives of persons within family units. The school as a supportive social institution does serve to accommodate transitions, often assuming some of the responsibilities of other institutions in these periods. The fact that the school at one time or another performs such diverse functions as religious training, recreation, integration of diverse populations, and mental health reflects its pivotal position in the social structure. As new structures emerge to accommodate the emerging functional needs of a society in constant transition, the school's responsibility diminishes, as was the case with religious training and with the integration of foreign populations in the period of high immigration. The role of the school as one of many coordinated institutions at this point in social evolution has been one of reorganizing its own facilities to cope with disjunctions in other institutions. The pur-

---

[1] Talcott Parsons and R. F. Bales, *The Family* (New York: The Free Press, 1955), pp.4–5.
[2] *Ibid.*

pose of the first part of this chapter is to examine the areas of disruption and attempt to describe the problems of family life in such a way as to relate these to the present reordering of educational facilities.

The major dimensions of family problems appear to lie in two broad areas: (1) the physically broken home; and (2) the socially disorganized home. In the second category we will discuss such issues as the modern organization of roles, the effects of leisure for the housewife, the bureaucratic woman, the generation gap, and the "new morality."

THE BROKEN HOME

A broken home will be considered as one in which one or less of the natural parents is living in the home with the children. The kinds of homes we will be discussing are those broken by divorce, desertion, or death, or those characterized by the absence of a father because of non-marriage, or by the absence of both parents where children are raised by foster parents or members of the extended family of one of the parents. We will also speak briefly about homes which contain one stepparent. All of these circumstances in American society carry some social stigma and have been considered in various ways to be associated with maladaptation of children.

Divorce rates vary by age, sex, state, and historical time. Divorce rates have increased considerably in this country since the last part of the nineteenth century, reaching a peak between 1945 and 1950 and then decreasing through 1960. In 1961 the greatest number of divorced persons were females between the ages of forty-five and fifty when approximately five out of every 100 were divorced.[3] Men remarry more often and more quickly, and the reasons are obvious. Their opportunities, in terms of social norms, are greater. Men over forty have three times the age range to choose from, in terms of numbers of available females, than do women. The demographic advantage which accrues to males is somewhat balanced by the legal advantage which women receive in terms of financial settlement and custody of children. Since women lose only a husband and men lose an entire family, the emotional burden for men appears to be more difficult, impelling them to replace the gap in their emotional lives. Since their opportunities are more

3 E. Burgess and H. Locke, *The Family* (New York: American Book Company, 1963), p. 449.

favorable than for women, the stronger motivation is more easily fulfilled.

There have been more than 200,000 divorces each year in the United States since 1945, but these figures cannot adequately represent the actual number of homes being physically broken.[4] There are several other kinds of conditions that are almost identical with divorce although the courts do not have records for them. Many persons break up marriages by separation rather than by divorce. Separation is a convenient disruption for several reasons. Separation is a less disruptive act and thereby more emotionally digestible by people who, while knowing the likelihood of reentering the old relationship to be small, comfort themselves with this possibility. Many separations occur also because persons wish to avoid the scandal of divorce or the expense of it. Another group of persons conclude a union without ever having legally bound it. If there are 200,000 actual divorces each year, the number of disruptions based on separation and desertion probably bring the total of broken homes close to one million.[5] When we add to this figure the sum of the 3,828,000 recipients of aid to dependent children, reflecting deaths and illegitimacy, and the unknown number of non-supported death and illegitimacy homes, the conclusion must be that the one-parent home is a very common phenomenon. The extent to which it is a problem for parents and for schools is the subject of our speculation here.

The fact that most people who undergo a divorce remarry means that the social problems encountered by such people in family life are compounded. On the one hand there is the original disruption, and on the other there is the problem of remaking a family with a new parent. But divorce does not affect all persons unidimensionally. Marriages without children or forced marriages do not end with the same trauma that most others do. A divorce that occurs after a long period of emotional separation does not have the same effect that a divorce has with less separation, even though interaction has been periodically stormy. Goode's analysis of divorced people indicates a continued period of conflict before the divorce, with both parties contemplating such action for several years before the actual move to separate is taken.[6]

The bonds of marriage are held together by several factors: long periods of emotional involvement, community sanctions

4 *Ibid.,* p.448.
5 P. B. Horton and G. R. Leslie, *The Sociology of Social Problems* (New York: Appleton-Century-Crofts, 1965), pp.193–195.
6 William J. Goode, *After Divorce* (New York: The Free Press, 1956).

against divorced persons, religious commitments, and concern for the welfare of children. When all these factors are diluted in some specific environmental context, such as Los Angeles, divorce rates rocket upwards. There are many reasons why a community such as Los Angeles experiences so many disruptions in family life, and we might discuss some of these since other community contexts can be evaluated as variations on similar themes.

First of all, divorce rates are typically higher in Western states than they are in Eastern states.[7] When people leave one part of the country to inhabit another, they often leave behind them the restraints on social behavior that were controlled by the traditions of their earlier location. Extended families, for example, are not as consequential in influencing decisions. A second factor is that divorce rates are higher in urban than in rural areas. This is so for a number of reasons:

1. Individualism is characteristic of urban life, a factor which weakens family bonds.

2. Anonymity is characteristic of the city. This is a situation in which the structures of social control become more diffuse, permitting persons greater latitude in their behavior.

3. People in urban environments have greater independence from family and a greater opportunity to meet new people. Women as well as men experience greater freedom in their non-family activities.

4. Urban families become more differentiated in terms of experience, education, and involvement. Emotional bonds between men and women are weakened by disparate interests.[8]

Third, in comparison with Eastern non-urban areas, the morality of Western urban areas moves drastically in the direction of greater freedom. Where there is greater moral freedom there is greater sexual freedom, a circumstance which is frequently the basis for switching loyalties as well as producing conflict, even when loyalties are not switched. Fourth, and perhaps more superficially, Los Angeles carries an aura of glamour. The whole concept of glamour, and this is certainly generalizable to other communities, makes it more difficult for persons to maintain the illusion of glamour in a marriage which is not typically supportive of a glamorous representation of self.

Finally there is the question of the relationship in urban families between children and parents. The modern urban family is fractionated in terms of responsibilities in the outside community.

---

7 Burgess and Locke, *The Family*, p.450.
8 *Ibid.*, p.71.

Where the bonds of necessity helped to unite the family in the *Gemeinschaft*, or rural, society, the functional interdependence in the *Gesselschaft* community is more abstract, more likely to result in cohesion around other than family activities. Children find their own world of activities and friendships, and loyalties spring up around these associations. Parents who are busy with commitments to their own activites and associations are happy that their responsibilities to children are relieved. So happy, in fact, that a return to traditional dependence would be viewed as an uncommon burden. The success of summer camps, Boy and Girl Scout groupings, after-school clubs, and a host of other child-centered functions speak to the fact that parents are highly supportive of activities that relieve them of the responsibility of occupying their children's time.

These factors describe, in a limited way, the context of the divorce-prone communities in America. At the same time we have described a situation in which divorce is a less conflictual crisis than would be the case in other kinds of communities. An accurate analysis of the context and circumstance of divorce, then, is an important consideration in the formation of remedial programs both for reducing divorce rates and for buffering the impact on family members of the fact of divorce.

Broken Homes and Children

The role of education is usually limited to what we can do for children who are the victims of family disruption. In order to consider this facet of our task later in the chapter, we should now look at some of the evidence that describes the adaptation that children make to conditions of divorce, death, or desertion.

Children are, of course, seriously affected by most divorces. Their parental loyalties are almost always divided, and they lose no matter which parent leaves. They are also affected when either parent remarries. Their role within the family shifts with each reconstitution of it. Since, in our society, children are never really prepared to make drastic adjustments in family roles, the consequences of disorganization are usually serious.

There is considerable evidence that family disruptions, such as divorce, produce problems of maladjustment in children. It is quite true that many similar problems emerge out of homes where there is no ostensible disruption, but this is not the argument. Broken homes are, in a most obvious sense, an indicator of some kind of disorganization in the home. Few divorces occur, as we have stated earlier, without a previous period of conflict. And when the father moves out of the home the child is forced to assume a new role, often in the case with eldest male children as the father surrogate. The child with one parent must begin to adjust to desertion (he often blames himself for the other parent's leaving), increased responsibilities, over-compensation from the mother, intensified rivalry with siblings, social stigma in the outside world of peers and school, and a host of fantasies and regrets.

According to Redl and Wineman, there was little evidence that the aggressive children housed at Pioneer House had even one adult with whom they had built up a warm relationship.[9] Parents in conflict often use children as pawns for their own battles, and the final desertion by the father is easily conceived by the child as a final rejection. Psychiatric literature is replete with cases of child rejection, or perceived rejection, standing as the source of personality difficulties. When and if rejection is assumed as the parental relationship, the child may begin to define the social world as untrustworthy, particularly men in authority positions. The implications of this for education planning are important.

The Broken Home and Delinquency

Physical disorganization of the home and juvenile delinquency have increased at the same rate over the past fifty years.[10] This is not to suggest a causal relationship since both conditions may be symptomatic of other more fundamental problems. The idea of lack of affection or, more sociologically, the lack of control, or both, may represent such causal factors. A distraught mother who must carry the major burden for her family and care for their economic and emotional needs may be too fractionated to dispense qualities of affection or control on her children. Or the kind of reduction of control which is associated with delinquent acts may arise as a contrived way of dealing with male children who have the responsibility of carrying the male load in the family. The function of the father in the home is traditionally one of the authority person who not only regulates behavior within the home but develops in the child an understanding of and respect for the function of authority outside the home. The absence of this socialization is logically related to delinquent patterns.

The conditions under which fathers are absent from the home are relevant to adaptation problems for the children. Related to this circumstance is the way in which the absent father is repre-

9 Fritz Redl and D. Wineman, *Children Who Hate* (New York: The Free Press, 1957), p.51.
10 Charles W. Coulter, "Family Disorganization as a Causal Factor in Delinquency and Crime," in *The Juvenile Offender*, ed. Clyde Vedder (Garden City, N. Y.: Doubleday & Company, Inc., 1954), pp.68–74.

sented to the children by the mother. George Bach conducted an interesting investigation in this area during World War II when many fathers were absent in military service. The children whose fathers were away because of the war displayed significantly less aggression toward their fathers than did children of fathers who were in the home.[11] The soldier father is, of course, an ideal and the conditions of separation were such that an idealized representation of the absent father was almost always presented to the child. The representation of the father in circumstances of divorce or desertion would, given the power of anger and distress, often be quite different. The father-separated child, then, does not suffer only from the objective absence of the father but also from the subjective interpretation of the father, and possibly all men, depending on the mother's ability to accept the husband's behavior as a special, rather than a general, representation of the marital behavior of men.

Sheldon and Eleanor Glueck have investigated many factors associated with juvenile delinquency. In one comparison study of 500 delinquent and 500 non-delinquent boys, they discovered important differences in household composition. Fifty-eight per cent of the delinquent boys were living with their own father as compared to 75 percent of non-delinquent boys. Fifty per cent of the delinquents were living with both parents as compared to 71 percent of the comparison group. Twice as many delinquent boys had at least one stepparent in the home, compared to the non-delinquents (8 percent to 4 percent).[12]

Another large-scale survey revealed similar kinds of relationships with some important qualifications.[13] Monahan, reporting on an analysis of more than 44,000 court records, suggested that although a high percentage of broken homes was apparent in the background of juvenile offenders, the phenomenon was more prevalent with girls and recidivists. Approximately 77 percent of the homes of female delinquents who were recidivists were physically broken.

The sociological findings on the relationship of delinquency and broken homes are often inconclusive and inconsistent. This is always true when we attempt to relate two phenomena which are both so obviously related to other social conditions. However, the

[11] George Bach, "Father Fantasies and Father Typing in Father Separated Children," *Child Development* 17 (1946): 63–80.
[12] Sheldon and Eleanor Glueck, *Unraveling Juvenile Delinquency* (New York: The Commonwealth Fund, 1950), pp.87–104.
[13] Thomas Monahan, "Family Status and the Delinquent Child," *Social Forces* 35 (1957): 250–258.

fact that many persons have inquired about this relationship, perhaps to discover certain common elements, indicates that an association or tendencies are often observed. The fact that many youngsters from broken homes do not become delinquents argues that we need a more comprehensive theory to explain delinquency itself. But this is a chapter on family disorganization, and we do suspect that family circumstances are intimately associated with the adaptations that children make to the outside world. When one parent can fulfill the support (financial and emotional) and control requirements that produce stability in the home and consequently out of it, the broken home is not a factor and we should look to other causes for deviant behavior of children. Too often, however, regardless of intentions, when money is not adequate and when the remaining parent does not have the emotional strength to go it alone, problems with children are predictable.[14]

Illegitimacy

Having a child out of marriage is not illegal in most places. But society, in order to strengthen its attitudes toward the sanctity and value of marriage, has ensured that violations do not go totally unpunished. The stigma attached to illegitimate children and mothers who have them is our way of controlling this kind of deviance. The stigma in many ways leads to feelings of guilt, and this guilt can lead to punishment of the symbol of guilt, the undesired offspring. The problem of adaptation that many illegitimate children experience stems, of course, only partly from the social stigma. It is loaded with problems similar to those experienced by children of divorced or separated parents. That is, illegitimate children do not experience the controls and effective interaction of a "normal" social unit. Illegitimate boys do not learn the male role in traditional ways and are often required to assume many of the functions of the male without benefit of a model. Illegitimacy presents problems in another way. Approximately one out of five marriages is preceded by conception.[15] Therefore the whole notion of the forced marriage and its ramifications in subsequent interaction between parents become a relevant concern. It seems clear that if the social stigmata associated with illegitimacy were weakened by the gradual acceptance within society of this fact, then marriages founded on guilt and necessity would be less frequent.

[14] A. K. Cohen and J. F. Short, Jr., "Juvenile Delinquency," in *Contemporary Social Problems*, ed. R. K. Merton and R. Nisbet (New York: Harcourt, Brace and World, Inc., 1961), p.111.
[15] Goode, *After Divorce*.

The problem of illegitimacy can be expanded to a consideration of what happens to the child if it is unwanted by the mother. If the child is kept by the mother, the difficulties mentioned above are likely to be encountered. If it is not kept, the fact of adoption becomes the focal concern. A foster home can be found for most white children. For children of non-white minority groups (Negroes, Mexicans, Indians) the solution is often a home where no real parents are available, such as an orphanage.

The limited literature on the adaptation and adjustment of foster home children to social institutions seems to suggest that no significant relationship is to be found between foster home placement and subsequent delinquent behavior. In a survey of relevant literature Williams[16] concluded that most delinquents had made a satisfactory adjustment after foster home placement, a finding which was corroborated in a later study by Theis,[17] who found that 77 percent of 797 subjects had made a good adjustment to society.

The literature on the association of broken homes to delinquent adaptations is, in some ways, out of date. This is not because sociologists and others have not kept their literature current. It is simply a matter of their having moved on to more productive areas of inquiry. The consequences of physical disorganization, or for that matter any kind of family disorganization, are complex and require a more comprehensive approach beyond that which single factors, such as broken homes or low income, can provide. The concepts of control and peer group association appear to be the most penetrating themes in the overall explanation of delinquent patterns. Control, insofar as it involves the availability of suitable role models as well as consistent patterns of interaction and responsibility, is a more encompassing concept than the fact of brokenness. At the same time a modern conception of influence toward adaptive and maladaptive patterns in youth must focus upon the prominent place of peers in the life of youth. Only in the sense of the family possibly mediating the expectations of the youth culture can we make a convincing theoretical argument for the effect of broken homes. To consider this argument independent of the overall associations of the children from broken and non-broken homes, however, would be to ignore the vitality of the movement toward explanation from social science rather than from association. When we begin to explain, for example, why broken homes are associated

16 H. D. Williams, "Foster Homes for Juvenile Delinquents," in *The Juvenile Offender*, ed. Vedder, pp.74–81.
17 S. V. Theis, "How Foster Children Turn Out," in *Longitudinal Studies of Child Personality*, ed. A. A. Stone (Cambridge: Harvard University Press, 1959), pp.272–273.

with maladjustment, we begin to encounter the kinds of issues that can also account for the adjustment in non-broken homes. This is the kind of approach that we shall take in the next section.

THE SOCIALLY DISORGANIZED HOME

The socially disorganized home is one in which a pattern of conflict exists. This is not to suggest that any home that has a series of arguments between the role occupants is disorganized. Actually, a home with no arguments whatever is more suspect than one that has them. Although this may be a perfectly adequate survival technique for some marriages, generally one could expect a normal amount of squabbles.

A socially disorganized home, as we think about it here, is one that is predictably detrimental to the persons living in the home environment. The conflict of which we speak is almost institutionalized in and reflected by the patterns of interaction between members. The behavior within the home is marked by constant aggression or withdrawal, inappropriate antagonism toward children, divided interests, sexual problems, drinking, and absence of consistent affection. Outside the home the behavior reflects the need to compensate, to seek affection and positive interaction elsewhere, to replace the home with organizations, love affairs, and bars. The actual cases are ordinarily variations of some sort, usually more limited in terms of actual destructive action, but nonetheless a variation on the prototype described above and ordinarily associated with disturbed children.

Disorganization of families is often a function of a transition from one stage of marital order to another. Many persons who marry and begin a family while still in school undergo this kind of disruption but settle their family life in life after college. Other forms of disorganization emerge out of the sheer absence of parental supervision due to the fact that both parents work. The conflict in this situation centers around the conflicting expectations for the behavior of the mother, and we will discuss this as a separate problem later in the chapter. We mention this particular dynamic to suggest that many problems of social disorganization are structural, that is, not always a matter of an interpersonal conflict between husbands and wives. At the same time, by way of broadening the perspective for looking at problems of disorganization of families, we need to suggest that a typical structural disruption is one in which children divide their loyalties between friendship groups and parents. Should conflict occur despite a history of non-conflict between parents, or between parents and children, peer groups will exact strong loyalty, causing strain both in the person and in the family.

Family disorganization is often a result of the unclear lines of authority and responsibility that are characteristic of many contemporary family situations. In an age when women are expected to compete successfully with men in both the professional and family worlds, traditional role postures become distorted and diffused to the point where responsibility is either random or highly inconsistent. Disorganization and conflict, in this case, are functions of clouded and anxiety-surrounded expectations for the behavior of others in the home. Neglect, for example, or even simple lack of supervision of children as a price of too much general involvement in the world, takes its toll on those who require structure and control—the children.

THE INDUSTRIAL FAMILY

From its inception industry has had a way of diluting and disrupting traditional family organization. In its progress from an institution where all functions are serviced to one which gropes for consistency, the family has never clearly settled on a set of responsibities which could replace those it surrendered by becoming a part of the industrial revolution. Now, in the latter stages of industrialization, the family has surrendered many of the cohering conditions it developed in the early states of industrialization. We need to focus chiefly upon the concept of the extended family and the concept of the community. The typical urban family until recently was an extended family, a family with low rates of physical or social mobility, and a family with ethnic community identification. The neighborhood characteristics were as influential in motivating the way families related to each other as were the sex, age, or occupational characteristics of members. That is, the family unit was extended even beyond the confines of the weakest blood ties to include a loyalty to its community and its neighbors. In many ways the community took on the posture of a family insofar as it began to service the need dispositions of family members for support, recreation, socialization, and identification.

It is interesting that through time the adaptations to a new situation, in this case the formation of an urban family structure, come to be defined as the traditional culture which becomes disrupted as one moves on to other adaptations to changes in the industrial movement. The solidarity of the extended family in a new living arrangement, which occurred either in the same home or within the same neighborhood in different homes, was a convenient buffer to the disruption of the traditional structures of the home. The city was not all *Gesselschaft*, not so long as the communities evolved as they did. The contemporary adaptation to changes in the economic structure of society sees families taking the next to last step toward the abolition of the traditional concept of family solidarity. The final step would be, of course, the complete dissolution of the concept of the family unit. The modern family is loosely tied to extended relationships and to the idea of community. The surburban society does not generate the kind of familial patterns that characterized the homogeneous communities of the more than half century following the industrial revolution. Physical and social distance has been put between family members and most friends. The consanguine family is now conjugal and the attachments of persons to their communities are limited by the effects of constant motion up the economic ladder or across the state or nation.

As families move into new relationships to society, new and different forms of disorganization emerge. The current form appears to be one of fluid loyalties, inconsistent identifications, and confused role models for the children. The status-oriented family is still capable for the most part of developing in their children an achievement motivation that will maintain a consistent pattern of upward or stable mobility for the family. But in many cases the failure of the family to ward off the inclination of children to negate these values of the middle-class ethic in which they were reared suggests that the family does not have the power to exercise control once the children leave home, and often not before that.

The modern family may be seen as a number of independent individuals maneuevering for fulfillment in systems outside the family orbit. These systems are influenced in their structure by the way in which they form to socialize persons about interactions in the larger society rather than in the immediate one, such as home or neighborhood. The present day is a period of institutional rather than personal role models. The role models for the youth of today are often the ideal types of institutional life: school, politics, entertainment, sports, and for some, the church. For a small but highly publicized group, the role model concept is reintroduced on the same basic level as the traditional rural family. The hippie family, extended and solid in their dependence and affection, find that their role models have been dead many years and need to be reincarnated. These are the land squatters and the ante-reservation Indian. The psychedelic leaders, in their emphasis upon family organization and rural ritual (new forms), serve as the dominant role model for the youths who wish to "drop out."

Contemporary industrial family disorganization, then, appears to be one of confusion and disillusionment rather than manifest conflict. Persons fight and argue, not out of any real differences or vested interests, but as a way of expressing frustration and leveling blame at one another for not being able to accommodate stability and change at the same time. Fathers and mothers appear to be having some difficulty stabilizing the home, routinizing the activities, disciplining and supervising the children, while at the same time maintaining an active professional and social life outside the home. When the realization that each has gone beyond the limits of his capacity to integrate his roles in the different institutions, other problems such as heavy social drinking which produce other serious disruptions, may emerge.

The parents of today's youth are being accused of being irresponsible in their relationships with their young, and being inconsiderate of each other despite the fact that there has been a considerable increase in the kinds of things family members concretely do for each other. All members of the family have been relieved of a large number of domestic responsibilities, such as washing clothes, washing dishes, much cooking, carrying out garbage, and the like. We can all relate to the number of devices we all supply to each other to make our work easier. Another index of the increase of new kinds of family concern about one another is demonstrated by the contrast in possession of protective life insurance between 1900, when 13 percent of the population owned insurance, and 1960, when 67 percent of the population owned life insurance.[18]

It appears that one of the major new functions of families is to be bigger and better consumers. In a time of affluence the major daily decisions for a family may revolve around the allocation of consumer power throughout the family. It is unlikely that the basic alienation and isolation that emerge in families with consuming status drives can be resolved in this way. And it is also unlikely that stability within families can be advanced by insuring everyone and everything against the possibilities of the unpredictable. The earlier form of protection of family, symbolized by the primitive man in his loin cloth stringing his bow while his family hunched

18 *Life Insurance Fact Book* (New York: Institute of Life Insurance, 1966).

behind him, seems to represent a more stable interdependency than the family strung together by insurance policies.

We can now move from the general context of family disruptions to specific behaviors, or circumstances which would tend to aggravate the equilibrium of the family unit. We are continuing to consider the family unit as intact and are suggesting areas which strain this wholeness. The situations we want to consider briefly are: (1) drinking and/or alcoholism, (2) working mothers, (3) problems of family size, and (4) problems with extended family.

ALCOHOLISM IN THE HOME

Most adults drink. Most drink in their home, in front of their children, and believe that they are not endangering the mental health of the children or disorienting the family. There are some facts about drinking and family life, however, that influence us to speculate more precisely about the drinking that we observe in most homes. For example in a study by Bacon it was discovered that of persons arrested for drunkenness, twelve times as many were divorced and six times as many separated as expected of persons of similar ages. Kephart later concluded that drinking was a causal factor in over 20 percent of American divorces. Alcoholism has been correlated with family financial problems, high geographic mobility, downward social mobility, and legal entanglements.[19] It is not always clear, however, whether drinking is the cause or the effect.

The alcoholic in the home is a person who demands and drains from others and returns little if anything to those from whom he exacts his care. In addition to draining the family emotionally, the alcoholic drains the family economically, compounding the disorganization and distress. Not only does the alcoholic father disrupt the family's budget for food and other needs, he also manages to create a relatively unstable work pattern which further contributes to the disorganization pattern. And finally, by way of summarizing this category of disorganized family life, the evidence suggests that children of alcoholic parents show relatively high rate of physical, emotional, and psychosomatic ailments.[20]

Alcoholism may be defined as an illness in the same way we

---

[19] See R. G. McCarthy, ed., *Alcohol Education for Classroom and Community* (New York: McGraw-Hill Book Company, 1964) for a complete discussion of the association of alcoholism with other problems.

[20] J. K. Jackson, "Drinking, Drunkeness, and the Family," in McCarthy, ed., *Alcohol Education for Classroom and Community*, pp.162–163.

may view drug addiction. As such, the family problem is one of illness and can be viewed in the same way we would consider the effects of any prolonged illness. While it is true that prolonged illness does produce strains on the family, particularly economic strains, the normal physical ailments, because of the way they are socially defined, usually help to unite the family. The effects of alcoholism tend to be disruptive; few families can look upon the behavior associated with an alcoholic state and forgive its disruptive effects on the grounds of sickness. Society has not yet advanced that far.

THE WORKING MOTHER

The image of the American woman has changed—as a statistic, in terms of her actual behavior, and as a magazine-like advertisement for herself. That is, the portrait that advertising executives lean on to convince the American woman about what she needs is one of marginal domesticity and major urbanity.

Between 1940 and 1960 the increase in the proportion of all women working was from 25.6 percent (1940) to 34.8 percent in 1960. The increase of married women in the labor force during the same period jumped from 14.7 percent to 30.5 percent. The proportion of mothers with children under six jumped from 8.6 percent to 18.6 percent and to 39 percent for those with children six or older.[21]

The kinds of problems associated with working mothers can be differentiated in terms of a number of important factors such as: (1) need to work, (2) status of job, (3) enjoyment of work, (4) on-the-job relationships (particularly with men), and (5) length of time employed. It is no longer possible to take the position that mothers' working is associated with the family's need for additional income. Certainly many, if not most, people like to have more than they do; but as we look at the number of middle-class mothers in the labor force (about 30 percent, we must begin to look for other explanations. The simplest explanation is that today's middle-class wife is bored, has had more education than her earlier counterpart and therefore is more qualified to work and, abstractly, wants to be more self-fulfilled than she can be in the home.

Hoffman, in discussing the decision of women to work, empha-

21 F. Ivan Nye, ed., *The Employed Mother in America* (Chicago: Rand McNally & Co., 1963), pp.7–8.

sizes the absence of creativity in the housekeeping task. Cooking, formerly the most creative of the housewife jobs, seems to be as unimaginative today as the other routines, such as washing, vacuuming, ironing, and so on. Packaged goods and standardized recipes have, for most women, taken all the creativity out of cooking.[22] Fancy cooking for guests, however, is another story. Frozen foods are adequate for family, but good recipes are needed for company.

If there is one major factor that we need to consider here, since the effect on children is our principal focus, it is the definition of the role of mother that working mothers make. In an investigation of the motivations of working mothers, it was found that job experiences were mentioned as often as home experiences as giving these mothers a feeling of worth, and that the value attached to the role of mother diminished after the child entered school.[23] The value of the mother role as a star-spangled concept seems to be diminishing in importance. Many mothers, if they stay off the job long enough to care for the children until they are ready for school, feel they have earned the right to go to work. Many women, of course, do not feel that they even need to make that much of a sacrifice.

The consequences for the children and for the family as a cohesive unit of a mother's working are not certain. Some evidence suggests that the children of working mothers are more maladjusted, more delinquent, and have more sexual identification problems than children of non-working mothers. A recent survey of these studies, however, has suggested that when race and socioeconomic status are held constant, there do not appear to be any differences between working and non-working mothers in their attitudes toward child rearing, family life, and domestic responsibilities. Nor does there appear to be any evidence that suggests that working mothers feel less parental love and responsibility to their family than non-working mothers.[24]

The mere fact, however, that the mother does work creates a set of problems that can be directly linked to her physical absence. If she is not in the home at the time the children are there, for

22 W. W. Hoffman, "The Decision to Work," in Nye, ed., *The Employed Mother*, pp.26–27.
23 R. S. Weiss and N. M. Samuelson, "Social Roles of American Women: Their Contribution to a Sense of Usefulness and Importance," *Marriage and Family Living* 20 (November 1958): 358–366.
24 E. Herzog, "Children of Working Mothers," Children's Bureau Publication, U. S. Department of Health, Education and Welfare (Washington, D. C.: Government Printing Office, 1960).

whatever reason, she is not available to handle requests or conflicts. Often the child will be required to resolve his own dilemmas since he may be unwilling to seek help from a baby sitter or even from an older sister or a grandmother. A mother who is absent from the home during periods when the child is at home may be able to routinize the behavior of the children and manifestly state the rules and regulations, but she is not present to enforce them.

The school child is obviously less able to call on the mother for assistance in after-school homework or school-related activities in the same way the child of a non-working mother can. We might infer further that the amount of attention the working mother gives the child, even after working hours, cannot be as considerable as the attention given by a non-working mother. The reason for this assertion is that the number of things the working mother needs to do in the home must be squeezed into the period of time she has left after work, whereas the non-working mother can get most of the chores out of the way while the child is in school and free herself for interaction with the child when he arrives home.

The times when a working mother becomes a clear problem for the family are when she needs to work to maintain the family, when she dislikes her job and becomes fatigued by it, and when her working hours make it impossible for her to be with the children when they start their day or when they arrive home. It is also a problem when she cannot make adequate arrangements for overseeing and caring for the children. It can be a problem when the parents use their separate occupations as a means of competing with each other for status or achievement. A problem may be created when her occupational role in some way causes the woman to define her relationship with her husband in such a way that children have difficulty with their sexual role identifications. The only sense in which education can aid the child or the family is through the isolation of the specific form of the problem that is created by the mother's working. Some suggestions will be advanced later in the chapter.

FAMILY SIZE

The literature on large families has declined as rapidly as the phenomenon of large families has declined. The only sense in which family size is really important to our discussion is when there are more children in the home than can be taken care of by the parents. In this view of large families the problem may be more one of income or ethnicity than it is of the family. There is, however, some literature bearing on the subect and as long as the phenomenon is one that may contribute to family disorganization we should consider some of the dynamics.

Most persons seem to be easily able to romanticize the large family. Large families have amused and endeared audiences on the stage, in films, and in literature. Even in recent years, when the mode has been toward small families, two of the most popular films ("The Sound of Music," "Yours, Mine and Ours") have been about large families.

In opposition to this portrait of large family harmony there is some evidence that suggests that children of large families have more personality problems,[25] more school problems, less social mobility, and greater participation in voluntary, non-family-oriented activities.[26]

Bossard's overall contention, (earlier mentioned evidence notwithstanding) from an extensive study of large families, is that growing up in a large family is more conducive to being able to handle the realities of life than would be the case with small families. He concludes that the child's adustment in group situations, such as the school, is advanced by participation in a large family.[27]

Children of large families may experience some difficulty in school because of a lack of personal determination to seek the kind of status that school offers. It seems that they expect less attention and consideration than children who are used to attention and use techniques to produce it. We also assume that the child of a large family would have less opportunity for undistracted schoolwork in the home. Distractions will be more frequent, opportunities for recreation and entertainment more available, and space limited. Further it would seem that the advantage of parental assistance, if this can be utilized, would be diluted by the number of children to whom the parent feels responsible.

A final sense in which a large family can produce a situation of domestic strain is in the area of parental feelings of being overburdened. For some the responsibility of raising a large family may be more difficult than they had anticipated during the early years of child begetting. Parents often blame each other for having let the other fall into that kind of bind.

25 Glenn R. Hawkes, L. Burchinal, and B. Gardner, "Size of Family and Adjustment of Children," *Marriage and Family Living* 29 (1958): 65–68; and Dora Damrin, "Family Size and Sibling Age, Sex and Position, Related to Factors of Adjustment," *Journal of Social Psychology* 29 (1949): 93–102.
26 P. H. Landis, "Teenage Adjustments in Large and Small Families," *National Association of Deans of Women* 18 (1953): 60–63.
27 James Bossard, *The Large Family System* (Philadelphia: University of Pennsylvania Press, 1956).

The only child is another story. He is a demographic phenomenon that appears to be static over time. Whereas the percentage of all families with four or more children declined from 32.8 per cent in 1900 to 12.6 per cent in 1960, families with only one child increased over the sixty-year period only 3 per cent, from 18.5 per cent to 21.6 per cent, decreasing only 1 per cent from 1930 to 1960.[28]

Only children are forced to interact predominantly with adults since siblings do not exist. They are more socialized to the language and knowledge of the adult world than children with siblings. The potential problem for the homelife of a family with an only child is that all the expectations for the progeny are focused on the single child. If parents fail to shape the child to want and to achieve what the parents want for him, the parents do not get another chance.

The only child is often overprotected and showered with excessive quantities of love, affection, and goods which represent the affective domain. In many ways the only child, although well prepared to meet the normal expectations for class-room performance, may not be able to develop a separateness and independence from the institutions which encapsulate him. He will do what it takes to please his parents and teachers, because he perceives well their requirements, but there may develop uncertainty in areas where social conditioning has not been so effective.

An only-child family is one in which both parents must agree on the desirable goals and behaviors for the child. One parent cannot, as often happens in larger families, accept the decisions of the other parent for child A and by so doing reserve the final say to himself for child B. Only children, according to an early study by Cutts and Mosely, are usually born after long waits or many miscarriages, and are of births that were so difficult that no other children could be born.[29] Conflicts between parents over the goals for this singular investment, if such conflicts should occur, are bound to cut deeper than arguments most parents have about their children.

THE EXTENDED FAMILY

Problems of the extended family are many and varied. They are problems which ordinarily affect newlyweds, but they often intrude

---

[28] Burgess and Locke, *The Family*, p.345.
[29] N. Cutts and N. Moseley, *The Only Child* (New York: G. P. Putnam's Sons, 1954).

so deeply into the marriage that permanent strains and defenses are highly charged in the marriage. Relationships between married persons and their parents can usually be predicted from the kind of relationships the married couple had with their parents prior to marriage. An overly protective, highly solicitous parent is not likely to relinquish his burden to her or his child's spouse. Adjustment in marriage is closely related to the approval of the mate by the parents, and related to this is the extent to which the child is able to detach himself or herself from the expectations of the parents with respect to the choice of a mate. Dependence on the approval of the parents can interfere with the marriage in several ways. It can restrict the physical mobility of the family, intensify the demands made on the new member to conform to the expectations of the parents, intrude on privacy, influence the goals of the marriage, produce strains in raising the grandchildren, and confound relationships with friends. Many parents, believing that they have invested so much of themselves in child rearing, believe that they have the right to control and regulate the lives of the children well into marriage. Many of them succeed in doing so since many children do not know how to separate themselves from the entrapment of an extended dependency. Children frequently marry the kinds of persons the parent expects him or her to marry, and the resultant problems are often resolved by punishing the spouse for not being the kind of person that could make the other happy. For the most part the parents, regardless of their protestations and cries of anguish, usually escape the center of the conflict as husbands and wives tear each other up in pain and disillusionment.

Parents are particularly apt to cause problems when they attempt to apply to contemporary life situations traditional expectations with which the children find it difficult to comply. Children interacting in a heterogeneous racial and ethnic society and subjected to a liberalizing education may find it hard to accept the expectations of finding a mate with similar ethnic and racial characteristics. For many parents the list reads much more extensively, including such expected properties as education, income, age, ambition, respectable parents, and a career of high respectability. To many, being divorced constitutes an immoral quality.

Another sense in which the extended family produces an additional degree of disorganization in a family is when parents either expect to or must live with the children, particularly in their older age. This problem may be seriously compounded if the care given by the children also requires financial support. Retirement systems were not common to today's grandparents who grew up in an age characterized by small business, individual enterprise, and weak unions. The grandparents of tomorrow are not likely to produce the same problem, except in the sense of intruding into the privacy of the family.

CROSS GENERATIONAL DIFFERENCES

The gap between parents and children increases drastically every generation. The geometrically increasing quantity of events and interactions that shape attitudes and values has currently produced a generation of young adults who, almost literally, have nothing in common with their parents. More than anything else they have a different conception of valuable ways of using time. Many parents have genuinely sacrificed to provide their children with experiences that would make it impossible for them ever to communicate with each other again, at least in the way that their parents were able to communicate with their grandparents. Parents who believe that their children owe them the kind of loyalty that requires the children to interact frequently often mistake the childrens' need to avoid feeling guilty for a desire to share the parents' lives. This in turn builds up a resentment on the part of the children that may persist for many years.

The significant difference between parent and adult relationships of this and past generations can be attributed to the explosion of knowledge, the technological revolution, increased and almost compulsory educational experiences, extensive physical mobility, the disappearance of tradition-bound communities, and a host of idiosyncratic experiences, many of them deviant, such as drugs and sex. Another significant factor is that the whole culture today restrains the growth process so that the thirty-year-old, a very mature man or woman a generation ago, finds it rather difficult to pass on into adulthood. Affluence and the availability of "youthful" activities are retarding circumstances, so much so that tomorrow's children may complain that their parents are too young, rather than too old, to understand them.

THE HOME AND THE SCHOOL

The most common sense approach to the analysis of student problems is to assume first that the problem resides in the home. Teachers are home-oriented creatures, convinced that the source of every deviant act can be traced to some disrupture in the home. Researchers and directors of applied programs also operate out of the same basic consideration. Most Headstart programs begin with the principle that remedial efforts need to start with the kinds of interactions that occur in the family and to supplement or subvert some of the effects of home life. The general argument breaks down into a two-pronged focus, one centering on a conflict of cultural commitments, the other on problems associated with motivating people to learn when such motivations have not been internalized into the home. These assumptions lead us to conclude that some repair work on the home background will have concomitant effects on students. This may or may not be true, depending on such factors as the longevity of the problem, the role of the child in the home, and the degree of commitment the child has made to other affiliations (church, school, peer group).

The background of the phenomenon of teachers' associating student problems with home experiences can probably be traced to the widespread popularity of Freudian principles of psychology. Freud's contribution to education in the first part of the twentieth century was the circulation of a set of ideas which attempted to explain problem behavior in the light of early childhood experiences with the family. Today these ideas are part of the conventional wisdom of education and for the most part go unchallenged. Most of the research conducted on the interaction of family characteristics and educational behavior has looked at easily observable factors such as broken homes or the economic status of the family. Little research has been generated which attacks the crucial issue of the way in which conditions of physical disorganization, such as death or divorce, or social disorganization, such as marital conflict or various estrangements of the family members, actually contribute to the problem behavior of children. The absence of such studies can be attributed partly to the difficulty researchers have in gaining access to data about the intimate aspects of family life. At the same time the problem of deriving causal effects in social research is considerable, since it is not easy to control either the effects we want to introduce or the people we want to observe.

The way in which the economic status of families affects the behavior of family members was discussed in Chapter Two. In the first part of this chapter we began to analyze the kinds of problems that families experience and to speculate about the potential effects upon children. What little evidence there is on these effects suggests relationships but not causes.[30] The best we can say at this

30 C. Weinberg, "Family Background and Deviance or Conformity to School Expectations," *Marriage and the Family* 26 (February 1964): 89–91.

point is that problem-causing conditions in the family manifest themselves in student deviance or difficulty in some cases but not in others. We know, for example, that some children of working mothers do well in school and others do poorly.[31] The same kind of conclusion can be drawn from research on the effects of divorce, separation, physical mobility, and the like. What we now need is a better explanation of why some children do and some do not have school problems as a result of the same family disruptions. Some of the explanations might be obvious but difficult to measure, such as the effects of divorce. It would seem safe to speculate, for example, that children who find that the conflict in the home is reduced when the parents separate and who receive more love and attention from the mother after the father is out of the house will improve their school habits. Others experiencing the same kind of disruption may react with feelings of being rejected by the leaving parent and anger toward the mother whom they may perceive as inciting the separation. We cannot possibly cover all the possible other conditions which could influence the direction of the adaptation of the child. But we can discuss the way educational systems can aggravate family problems and the way in which they can help children and parents either avoid or reconcile difficulties.

The school does make the assumption that it has some responsibility in the area of acquainting students with and often helping them to understand the nature of the home and family and their role in it. Many first grade classes utilize the home as a point of departure for learning, and interestingly enough, high schools have in recent years included a course in the senior year which focuses on home adjustment. Many school districts vary these patterns somewhat, but it is generally true that the home becomes a center of focus in the beginning and the end of a public education.

The school aggravates as well as ameliorates certain family problems by the same activities. The school has in contemporary society assumed many of the earlier responsibilities of the family. Furthermore the school takes the position that it is available to assume additional functions as families wish to abandon them. In many cases the school relieves the family or a parent of responsibilities it cannot assume; in other cases, by the school taking over these functions, parents may become motivated to decrease the amount of responsibility they take in the raising of their children. The modern elementary and secondary school is an agency for socialization, recreation, entertainment, and baby sitting, as well as education. Its activities range from cuddling and grooming to super-

---

31 See *Effects of Maternal Employment on Children,* Social Security Administration (Washington, D. C.: Government Printing Office, 1960).

vising hobbies, from inducing manners to organizing dating functions.

Until now, except by invited contact, the school has attempted to pursue its full range of functions without interfering with the student's homelife. There have been times when parents have been asked to participate in conferences about student progress or attend meetings or teas to understand, if this is possible in this way, what is going on in the school. With the advent of Headstart and other ameliorative programs, the school program is beginning to involve parents in a less superficial manner. The larger educational scheme for children of the disadvantaged is to consider the parents an important part of the child's education. As this kind of involvement increases across class and community lines, the school's absorption of the family's functions become even greater, perhaps to the point of displacing the parent as the primary source of influence in the child's life. In a moral sense this may be healthy for some children and unhealthy for others. It may salvage those who would be washed away in the wake of family disorder, but it may also encourage even greater abandonment of family cohesion and responsibility on the part of parents who do not appreciate the task of child rearing.

In the United States there is currently an attitude, satirized often in daily papers, which views the child as an intruder upon the peace and tranquility of family life. This attitude views the end of summer vacation as an ecstatic moment, a signal that relief in the form of a seven- to eight-hour-per-day baby-sitting institution is ready to emerge. Some teachers' unions have learned that the best way to ensure the support of the community is to call a strike at the beginning of the fall term after the parents have had the children for two and one-half months.

This cynical view is presented to suggest the double effect that the school has on family life. For many one-parent families and when mothers need to work, the school as a baby-sitting agency serves a very practical function; but when neither is the case, the effect may be one of increasing even further the gaps in family cohesion that are so characteristic of modern industrial society.

If we accept the fact that many families, because of problems of physical or social disorganization, have neither the time nor the emotional climate for the adequate socialization of the child, then the role of the school may be crucial. If on the other hand we view the mechanics of school socialization in the light of ever increasing control over the lives of children, and if we also question the adequacy of the job the school can do, we may want to argue that the school should reduce its responsibility in marginally educational areas. What we may ultimately be forced to desire, by way of a compromise, is that the school should assume certain "family" responsibilities for certain children but only in special ways with special personnel. We can illustrate this highly general suggestion in the following way: Let us assume that our case records tell us a second grade boy comes from a broken home. He lives with a mother, a grandmother, and an older sister. Our intuition at this point suggests that, in the absence of a male role model, the student should be assigned to a male teacher. If this is as far as our thinking carries us, the child may be just as well off with a female teacher. The point is that if we are going to make such a decision, we must also be ready to assess the kinds of male models we have available, the way in which the mother has been playing the mother role since the home became broken, and the specific kind of attention or counseling the child needs. This can be done only with professional personnel. The problem with most schools is that they attempt to solve emotional difficulties stemming from problems of family life armed only with intuition and perhaps a little concern. The best thing that educational personnel can do if they wish to enter into the arena of reducing the effects of family disorganization is either to prepare themselves professionally for the task or to avoid playing that role.

The problem that educators face in attempting to play a knowledgeable role in reducing the negative educational effect of family problems is that they are not experts in emotional problems nor are they skilled in the rehabilitation of social deviants. The most obvious recommendation we can make is that educators begin to think about staffing the schools with experts in both areas. Such experts not only interact with individuals in a therapeutic task but more essentially prescribe structural changes to facilitate programs devoted to making family life more meaningful and perhaps less detrimental to children.

THE PARENT SURROGATE

In organizing her school for young children Anna Freud worked on the assumption that preschool teachers or primary grade teachers were not mothers of the children and would be harmful to the children if they acted like mothers.[32]

---

[32] Anna Freud and D. Burlingham, *Infants without Families* (New York: International Press, 1944).

The whole conception of the primary school teacher as a mother surrogate is alien to our modern ideas of the importance of early learning. We do recognize that achievement of children in the first years of school is highly predictive of their future achievement patterns. Failure to develop learning skills at this time can be disastrous to an educational career. For this reason it would seem that our best teachers should be located in the early grades, not further along on the educational ladder after students have already evolved a pattern of motivation and achievement. That we do not operate under this assumption is evidenced by the low degree of status attached to primary teaching as opposed to other levels. We might also argue that educational requirements for teachers at this level are less stringent than requirements for teachers at other levels. For some reason educational decision makers assume that mistakes in the early years are not so damaging as those made later on. The consequences of employing this rationale can only be surmised, but an educated guess would suggest that they are seriously detrimental.

THE SOCIAL CLIMATE

As a social system, the school and the classroom provide opportunities for students alienated in the home to become integrated into another institution. Often the alienation in the home carries over into the school and barriers to educational progress appear. The system being more flexible and possessing more facilities than the family can act to confront such barriers. The major ways that the institution accomplishes this on a widespread basis is to provide a climate for identification and to provide a number of role models to facilitate identification with role areas that may not be available in the family. Some of these areas can encompass large identifications, such as career orientations, scholarships or athletics, or very special socialization skills that assist persons in their mobility from one style of identification to another. These would occur in the areas of manners and morals. The school may also serve as a climate of aspiration, inspiring many children who do not receive such a supportive attitude in the home to attain goals supported by the school. Or it may simply provide opportunities for the expression of abilities, such as leadership or organization, that did not emerge in a family frought with conflict or disorder.

As a social climate, the school presents to many children a portrait of order and stability which may be missing in the home.

Order and stability may be reflected in the meaningfulness and sanity of communication, or simply in having a place to work, paint, or study without constant distractions, perhaps without the apparent violence in the voices of arguing parents. As an agency of social integration, the school presents students from diverse backgrounds with a model of social expectations. As such, it helps to identify for migrant children, or children of immigrant parents, the core American culture from which most life choices must be made. The school in this way may be seen as helping children in ways that families with certain limitations cannot. But overall the major ameliorative action must come through the mechanism that distinctly characterizes the school, that is, education.

EDUCATION FOR FAMILY LIVING

The central concern of education, when its function appears to be solidifying diverse groups or cultures as in periods of high immigration or racial integration, must be with people's differences as well as their similarities. The whole idea of integration of persons into a system or society involves structures which allow people to interact despite differences of function or status. The success of a military venture often depends on the cooperation of several different ranks. Although competition between students for grades or honors may cause some to harbor ill feelings against their classmates, the school still produces a system of people working toward the same ends regardless of their formal or informal status within the school. The school moves in a state of equilibrium toward chosen goals when members know their roles and the responsibilities associated with these and understand the interrelationship between roles. Conflict or disequilibrium appears when communication breaks down to the point where persons do not understand these relationships or when the commitment to uphold them disappears.

The family can be analyzed in the same way, and the lesson that educators can learn from this kind of analysis is that a family, like a school, has its best chance for equilibrium when people understand their roles and their relationship to other roles, and when they have the commitment to uphold what they understand. The question then becomes: What can the school do to clarify these relationships and to solidify the commitment of students to maintain the system in equilibrium? This is a structural rather than a substantive argument. That is, it is not necessary to accept the kind of family or the kind of school, for that matter, that exists. We may desire change, innovation, or even radical reconstitution. Whatever the form, however, its viability hinges upon the notions of understanding and commitment.

ALTERNATIVE FAMILY SYSTEMS

Education for family life can well begin with an extensive discussion on the part of students about the possible forms of family life. The subject can be treated historically, contemporaneously, and futuristically. Students may be able to suggest forms of family life which those who organized the curriculum did not conceive.

The discussion of alternative forms of family life will introduce students to a cultural perspective that can help them define all forms as linked to a particular time and a particular place. In this way no single form will be perceived as intrinsically superior or inferior. The study of anthropological systems usually has such an effect on students in any area. The effect of this may be such that persons suffering from the discomfort of difference (when a father or mother is not in the home or when grandparents share their home, for example) can begin to grasp the perspective that their situation, while different, is not inferior simply because it is different.

Literature describing almost every permutation of family structure and pattern of authority, from the father to the uncle to the children, can be culled from anthropological studies, and such a book can be used effectively at almost any level of educational progress. We can even introduce, through this medium, the idea of international political perspectives when we begin to talk about the state family and the idea of control and ownership of children such as the situation described by observers in Red China. Hersey's *The Child Buyers* can be used as a point of departure to extend this perspective into future Western technological society where parental decisions for their children may be mediated by considerations of the values of scientific exploration and progress.[33]

From this perspective we can conveniently shift to an analysis of the *anarchical family system* of which American society provides many a model. Students can discuss the advantages and disadvantages of defining and achieving separate goals and attempt to stipulate the conditions under which this form of family life can work and the conditions which make it impossible. From here we

[33] John Hersey, *The Child Buyers* (New York: Alfred A. Knopf, Inc., 1960).

enter conveniently into a consideration of the *democratic family model* versus the *authoritarian model* and look at the pros and cons of each of these.

The hippie family provides us with the most obvious portrait, since it already exists, of a future possibility, and by focusing upon this structure we can open the door to an analysis of important forces which lie at the base of many patterns of family disorganization today. The hippie family can be characterized as a loose structure, loose in the sense that any combination of persons, ages, and sex variations is legitimate. All traditional roles undergo a literal stretching in the sense of incorporating a number of persons, several fathers for each child and several children for each adult male. Each of several women constitutes a single wife to many husbands and vice versa. The family interconnections can be extended astronomically and often are. The traditional notion of possession of either persons or material goods by others disappears in this communal identity. In this way old family conflicts produced by "unfairness" in the distribution of anything or by jealousy in interpersonal relationships is reduced. There is the possibility, however, that the communal family might begin to act like a single unit in defining other units as off limits to the family husbands or family wives.

The educational interest inherent in a discussion of this kind of family structure must lie in an examination of the source of frustration or conflict in present forms that would cause persons to turn to such a radical departure as the hippie family.

WHY THE SEARCH FOR ALTERNATIVES?

The contemporary family operates on the economic principle of single and collective ownership, of goods in common, but more significantly, of each other. That is, the children "belong" to the parents, and the wife belongs to the husband, and vice versa. This is not only sexually but in almost every way not related to earning a living. Jealousy, which disrupts many families, is a jealousy of activities as much as it is of other persons. The hippie family places great faith in the slogan "every person should do his own thing" but the modern family, while highly permissive structurally, is highly dependent interpersonally. If the school is to play a role in helping students adjust to current forms of family life, it must be able to communicate the way in which the advantages of the hippie community can be introduced into the core family.

If independence within institutional boundaries is to be encouraged, perhaps the school can begin by introducing students to experiences in which they can perceive that the whole institution does not need to topple in order to gain certain kinds of freedom. Allowing the child freedom of movement within his own building would be a beginning.

The industrial or technological family rarely provides children with the experiences of work, responsibility, independence (what we might call maturing or transitional experiences) that were so common in the rural family. Despite a very limited set of alternatives, the rural child moved much more smoothly into the role of the adult than does the urban child. Both Mead and Benedict have commented on the disjunctures apparent in the growth process of "civilized" youth, particularly in the United States.[34] Their argument was that experience within the family was such that children did not typically relate to normal human functions and growth processes. The industrial child is protected against birth, death, sexuality, adult work, and responsibility in ways that are guaranteed to make him anxious and curious. The hippie family integrates the child, often in ways the civilized society finds distasteful, into the styles and functions of the adult members of the group. This, too, may have its problems. But our concern is with the reasons why today's youth are in constant conflict with their parents and the kinds of activities that the school can provide to reduce this dissension. In this area the school may need to integrate both parents and children into an educational program which discusses such fundamental questions as how to handle a death in the family, or a separation or divorce. The point is that children react with so much difficulty to family disruptions because such disruptions are never made, in any sense, a part of their lives prior to the occurrence. They experience these things only through shock; they are protected from maturing by the fragmented lives all the members lead.

Freedom (they may call it independence) is for most children something they must capture on their own, if and when they can. It is something that the hippie family worships, because it is such a precious and usually unattainable commodity in the non-hippie family. The educational task may be one of clarifying the way in which freedom and independence for children can be made part of normal family functioning. The average female today (the male's

34 Margaret Mead, *Coming of Age in Samoa* (New York: William Morrow & Co., Inc., 1928); and Ruth Benedict, *Patterns of Culture* (Boston: Houghton Mifflin Company, 1934).

case is somewhat different because of military service) moves from one circumstance of structural dependency to another. She moves from family, to school, to her own family, a husband, and then children. Problems are inevitable when the mutual dependency in the marriage is threatened by the innumerable opportunities each spouse has to do things on his or her own. In this sense the problems of the second generation family can be attributed to the limitations imposed by the first. The school may be the only agency by which the generation-to-generation dependency cycle may be broken. Males, of course, despite military service, follow a similar pattern, particularly the large number of males who go on to higher education. The dependency battle of these males is often fought on the grounds of the campus when colleges play the same role as the restrictive and controlling parent.

When persons seek an alternative structure, it is because the one that has been arranged to serve them is inadequate, at least inadequate to the pressing requirements of adult functioning in a stressful society. The school's role, if the school is to play any kind of role in ameliorating problems through the vehicle of innovative programs, is to operate as a change agent. In the area of family life problems the school can organize activities which either supplant the deficiencies of the family, or it can educate the family to include in their own activities experiences which will unite the members. This by no means suggests that we return to the bromide of "the family that plays together stays together." From the standpoint of intensifying dependency on other members of the family, this suggestion can have dysfunctional consequences. The school's role is to communicate an understanding of the dynamics of family life through the application of sociological and anthropological literature and thinking, so that today's students, vis-à-vis their parents and later on vis-à-vis their own children, can understand the circumstances which produce conflict.

Following are brief discussions about some kinds of problems that may be viewed as themes around which to focus educational experiences.

Roles in the Family

A discussion of family roles introduces students to the notion that families are divided functionally, another form of division of labor. Its divisions can be considered in some cases as obsolete, given the current stage of social and cultural evolution. Parents and their children can discuss together the areas where traditional division of labor should yield to new conceptions of the functions and responsibilities of each member. The role of the mother as housekeeper, for example, can undergo scrutiny in the light of time-saving devices and opportunities for the mother to utilize her new found time creatively. As such, her working or participation in activities outside the family is not viewed jealously as retreating from a posture of on-call dependency.

Sociodrama is a sociotherapeutic technique to clarify problems by giving persons the opportunity to observe typical roles within a social situation interacting with other roles. It is one kind of activity that can be translated into an educational experience. Students can be asked to play one role and then another so that they learn the many juxtaposed positions that are possible in family life. This kind of learning experience can then be translated into more negotiable possibilities for ameliorating family conflicts.

In educational situations where families can be asked to participate in the educational experience of the child, the school can function to improve perceptions of parents as well as of the children. Role-playing techniques can be efficiently employed toward this end.

The whole notion of roles involves the perception and internalization of expectations. Communication breakdown, leading to externalized conflict, occurs because these expectations are unclear. They are not necessarily unclear because parents have difficulty in communicating what they expect of their children. The main problem is that they do not really know what they expect. The same is true for the children. The inefficiency of a family unit when disorganization takes place arises out of the diffusion of expectations that exists in the family. Industries roll merrily along because the expectations are clear and manifest. The same is true with schools, churches, and government agencies. The family, however, is one institution which never develops a set of manifest rules to guide the interaction of its members, never articulates its specific goals, and consequently never plans specifically for attaining them. Families do maintain a set of roles which are traditional and like a tribal community, recognizes the taboos it will enforce and the behavior it will reward. But because of the orientation of the contemporary family outside of the home, there is considerable difficulty in integrating people, given their separate outside orientations. Educators can begin to ask about and relate these external orientations to family life by having students talk about how what they do outside of school contributes to or conflicts with the dominant patterns and goals within the family. This will not always be clear or obvious, and consequently the educational task may be one of discovering with students what these goals, plans, and patterns might be. If a conflict exists, it becomes an excellent clue to discovering or making manifest the core orientation of the family, since without conflict we cannot always be aware that there is a pattern that can be disrupted. Institutional patterns are usually most apparent when forces conspire to disrupt them. Educators can use these conflicts as the mechanism by which they and students can describe and understand the family patterns.

Family Problems

This topic simply covers a range of family problems in a cross-cultural way so that the student can explore without anxiety a number of circumstances which may occur in his life, if they have not already occurred. The student can be given reading material and challenged to discuss ameliorative programs. Discussions can be held about why certain disorganizing ruptures occur and the range of possible consequences. If education is to be made real, then the notion of protecting the child, which is the prominent cultural mode, must undergo scrutiny. Divorce and separation have serious effects on children because of their ignorance about what such disruptions actually mean. Children are often left to their own limited experience and perception to make sense out of the events which intrude into their routine lives.

The school assumes an important role in preparing children for adult functioning, and this can only be accomplished by exposing children to experiences which will help them know what disruptions in social living really mean. Occupational allocation is a very limited conception of the school's participation in this process. Family problems are human problems, the problems of people in institutional life, and as such the school, if it has any educational function at all, needs to be considered as a place where humanizing takes place. Exposure to experiences and discussions about family problems are ways of humanizing students.

The Changing Family

Most children today cannot conceive of a world without television. They can learn that there was a time when television did not exist and also learn about what people used to do for recreation. But this is usually a lesson in history that has very little meaning for the child. Many of the problems of family life—such as working mothers, high rates of divorce, a split between adult and youth cultures, and others—are products of rapid transitions from one conception of a family to another. At a time when family loyalties were deep and extended to distant as well as close relatives, it was not necessary to conceptualize a role for parents after their children grew up. Not many years ago parents conceived of their older years as centering around the lives and activities of their children. Even today many parents still hold to this expectation. Frequent and extensive social as well as physical mobility, however, have eroded this kind of traditional family dependency. High rates of divorce and frequent remarriages intrude further into the traditional ties. Family roles must be understood within an evolutionary framework. That is, what it meant to be a father yesterday must be compared to what it means to be a father today. Speculations about the meaning of the evolution of family roles for the future are also necessary if an educational experience pointed toward helping persons develop skills and interests which will allow them to adjust to new family patterns (which we might think of as disruptive only insofar as we don't know how to cope with them) is to be meaningful.

Many of the problems which grow out of the relationship between parents and adult children can be linked to changing conceptions of family life. For the most part neither the parents nor the children understand these changes, and consequently they are not prepared to make mutually adjustive changes themselves. The need, for example, of women to work is not solely an individual psychological need. If we treat it as this educationally, we weaken considerably the generalizability as well as the heuristic value of the problem. If we define this need as a product of social and cultural change, however, and analyze the social forces which produce the need on a widespread basis, we come close to conceiving our educational function. Women feel the need to work because they have had more education, because technology has made it possible to dispense with household chores quickly, because other agencies such as schools and playgrounds perform a convenient baby-sitting function, and because the prejudices regarding the role of women in the labor force are disappearing. Understanding this changing social pattern makes the absence of a mother much less than a desertion to the child.

The role of the male and female child has also undergone some changing conceptions. Even in the last quarter of a century we have seen a widespread shift in expectations for the education of the female. What does it mean for a woman to be pointed toward a college education rather than marriage or a temporary vocational task? What does it mean for a son to know that his life is his own and his role in the support of the family is not necessary? Most students cannot understand a world where dependencies were functionally as well as psychologically necessary any more than small children can understand a world without television.

New Roles for the Family

There are many abstract things that parents do with and for children that are never conceived of concretely as new and important functions. One of these is the education of children for creativity; another is the use of the family as a therapeutic unit; a third might be the development of social responsibility. For most of our cultural history parents have contributed more to making children dependent than making them independent. Most children have developed their parents' prejudices, their economic aspirations, their voting habits, their religious convictions, their attitudes toward school, their moral beliefs, and their ideas about happiness. For most young adults happiness is wall-to-wall carpeting, a color TV, and a houseful of appliances. For some young adults happiness is duty to mankind. For many there is no happiness, only confusion. The school does not appear to be taking a position. Educators approve of creativity although they often seem to be stifling it; they talk vaguely about the healthy personality but are inadequately trained or motivated to produce it; and they believe in humanity but cannot translate this meaningfully into an educational goal. For the most part creativity, mental health, and social conscience and devotion do not vary according to the schools our children attend. These qualities emerge because some parents work hard at producing them, because in the absence of traditional family responsibilities the social and psychological development of the child is in the front of their minds. The family that is at all aware of the depersonalizing effects of intensified industry through technology is a family that thinks about what it can do to develop the unique and creative qualities of the child.

If the school is primarily devoted to the task of staffing the technological factories, then the encouragement and watering that educators do to promote individual creativity would work against the efficiency demanded by the larger society. How then can the school evolve structures to aid parents in playing their new roles in their relationship with their children? This can only occur cooperatively, and the only structure that can accomplish this is a resource structure, a set of available classes, workshops, materials, and hopefully experts who can aid parents play these roles efficiently. Up to now, for example, guidance counselors have performed as trouble-shooters, bringing parents into the situation in order mutually to conceive some remedial techniques. A new definition of the counselor's role is to learn from parents the kinds of goals they have for their children and the kinds of educational tasks they are attempting to undertake, so that the counselor may provide advice or resources to parents to aid their efforts.

CONCLUSION

Problems of family life become problems of educational life in two ways. One, these problems often impede the educational progress of the child, and to the extent that the problems are manifested in disruptive behavior, the distraction of the teacher's energies has an effect on all the children in the classroom. Two, problems of family life call forth the school's commitment to help the child develop as a functioning and contributing social and human being. The school is in partnership with the family in this enterprise and in the same way that parents can and have assisted the school to do its job better, the school can and does reciprocate. Often, however, the school's efforts are intuitive, unplanned, and unskilled. It is not necessary for every teacher to be an expert in these matters. It is necessary, however, to develop a structure of expertise which may consist of special classes with expertly conceived curricula, minimal training of educational personnel to understand and advise students or counselors, and a set of activities specifically conceived to educate students about the structures of family life. In this way disruptions that affect children can be accepted as less than extraordinary and although irregular, amenable to the kinds of family reorganization that make continuity in the other areas of children's life possible.

5

Problems
of Sexual Behavior

No aspect of human life seethes with so many unexorcised demons as does sex. No human activity is so hexed by superstition, so haunted by residual tribal lore and so harassed by socially-induced fear. Within the breast of urban secular man, a toe-to-toe struggle still rages between his savage and his bourgeois forbears. Like everything else, the images of sex which informed tribal and town society are expiring along with the eras in which they arose. The erosion of traditional values and the disappearance of accepted modes of behavior have left contemporary man free, but somewhat rudderless. Abhorring a vacuum, the mass media have rushed in to supply a new code and a new set of behavioral stereotypes.[1]

T H I S rather frightening and challenging view of the human social condition, in a state of transition between organized inhibition and disorganized freedom, sets an accurate stage for our discussion of the problems of sexual life. It is unfortunate that society, usually protective of its stable interests through the organization of complicated social institutions, has been unable to plan for this transition. Cohesive institutional intervention has not protected society's interests, and thus the forces of economic determinism have found a rich ground for profit—namely, sexual attitudes and suggestibility. In order to insure profit private enterprise has created a sex industry which seeks to circumscribe all definitions and meanings of sexual life held by contemporary society. For enormous profits the sexual fantasy life of Americans is graphically served up on paper and celluloid. The cost to Americans in terms of psychological comfort, marital stability, and rampant deviance may be as great as that which they have had to pay for that other familiar demon—puritan morality.

In the discussion that follows our interest centers on the two major social dysfunctions caused by this unnatural buying and selling: rigidly structured inhibition and the diffuse freedom associated with the revolutionary developments in our sexual morality.

The problem of sexual values, despite its relatively minor position in social problems literature, has been included in this book for several reasons. First, it has become apparent in recent years that the most obvious single item that reflects change in cultural values is the change in attitudes toward what had previously been regarded as "deviant" sex. Second, the sexual revolution makes the adaptive problems for school-attending youth serious in the light of what they are exposed to outside the school and uneducated to inside the school. Third, the knowledge of mysteries surrounding sexual behavior has expanded into a monumental literature, much of which is either erroneous or misleading. Finally, the problem will be examined because psychiatrists, college counselors, and other social agents and agencies report that the most frequent cause for seeking professional aid centers around sexual problems, both in and out of marriage.

Obviously the whole realm of sexual behavior is opened to modern readers through very profitable businesses. The reams of

[1] Harvey Cox, *The Secular City* (New York: The Macmillan Company, 1966) p.167.

pornographic and sexually stimulating literature, including nudist magazines and *Playboy*-type periodicals, must be regarded not only as a result of profit-seeking, but also as a symptom of change. Whether or not the sheer incidence of such literature is a problem cannot be assessed without confronting the question: "What does it mean?" It is unlikely that, as some uninformed politicians have suggested, the mass reading of such material will signal an increase in sex crimes. It is equally unlikely that the touched-up photographs of spectacular females will prompt married men to dispense with their wives. It is even possible that the availability of vicarious sexual experience decreases the likelihood of irrational actions. Freud made the same point years before—that the function of many social activities is to help spin off or create an outlet for libidinal instinct energy that might otherwise necessitate socially deviant patterns of release[2] These are referred to in psychoanalytic terms as sublimations or displacements. The availability of vicarious sexual outlets in books, magazines, and films probably means only that society is ready to accept in the open what it has in the past been able to accept only in secret. In what sense, then, is this a problem?

It is a problem in the same way that leisure time, for example, is a problem. It signals the onset of a phenomenon that most of our citizens, particularly youthful ones, do not know how to handle. Inability to cope with or adjust to changes in sexual norms is represented by increased student pregnancy, sexual anxiety leading to frigidity and impotence, sexual incompatibility between married partners, extra-marital relations, premarital relations, and a host of other unconventional phenomena, such as incest, wife-swapping, and the hippie family, a situation within which several women and men live intimately together. There is no evaluative or judgmental import to these conditions. They are social problems insofar as they affect the participants, their families, and the moral sensibilities of many citizens.

Homosexuality and nymphomania were not listed among the other problem areas, because any increase in the incidence of such tendencies is not a likely consequence of shifting sexual norms. Nonetheless the openness with which sexual aberration is being presented to members of our society could influence many homosexuals, for example, to recognize actively their tendencies and participate in homosexual acts from which they would have restrained themselves in the past. One of the problems with homosexual behavior which compounds the original concern is that in most states

[2] In C. Hall and G. Lindzey, *Theories of Personality* (New York: John Wiley & Sons, Inc., 1957), pp.46–47.

homosexuality is illegal. In a later section we will consider the problem of homosexuality in some detail.

For those who have always viewed the secrecy surrounding sexual relations dysfunctional to mature sexual development, the sexual revolution, or what has been so named, may appear as a breath of freedom in what had always been an unfree sexual world. To view it as such may be premature. We might also say that anything that makes so much money for so many people should be viewed circumspectly. The economic value of open sex may not be a legitimate basis for mistrust, but we must mistrust it because it is not primarily and genuinely concerned with freeing the society of its sexual hang-ups. Sexual images and the resulting dependence on fantasy life can hardly be viewed as a legitimate vehicle for social change. It is no more useful to the average person vicariously to view sex through a love affair between two movie idols than it is to expose him to the world of work by presenting him with the life story of Howard Hughes. Of course, people do not pay money to see plain people make love or plain Jane in the nude, yet a major problem of a beauty culture such as our own has always been that without love intimate partners soon lose their beauty. Beauty in the nude may be equally defeating if this causes us constantly to revise our physical standards upward. In other words the current brand of sexual revolution may be retarding the real revolution many years, because it orients us to fantasy sex rather than genuine sex. If we are satisfied that the current trends signify important changes, it is unlikely that we can mount a movement seeking to understand the true basis of sexual love. But much of this is speculation and cannot be considered a scientific analysis of the source of a particular social problem. We need to begin with what we know about sexual deviation.

THE QUESTION OF SEXUAL DEVIANCE

Any discussion of deviance requires the statement of an acceptable standard so that we can define deviance as aberrations from that standard. In establishing a standard, however, we are faced with the dilemma that sexual norms have been in great flux since World War II. The most general statement we can make that will suffice for most of our discussion is that the acceptable standard for sexual behavior is what does not make people socially uncomfortable—specifically, that there should be no sexual behavior prior to engagement and very little prior to marriage and that all sexual behavior should be heterosexual and legal. The war obviously extended the range of permissible sexual activity beyond this general standard. Since "the standard" as expressed above always refers to the establishment of permanent relationships, the war obviously challenged these regulations of human behavior, for the difficulty of establishing permanent relationships during war time and the threat that relationships might never be stabilized due to the possible death of the man, forced necessity to take precedence over tradition.

Another challenge to establishing any "standard" for sexual behavior is the fact that rates of change in permissiveness affect some members of the society more rapidly than others. The disparity in the rate of change between generations, for example, is partly responsible for the generation gap that is discussed in more detail in the section on adolescence in our chapter on alienation.

When the adolescent's biological development brings the opposite sex into sharp focus and sexuality becomes one of the adolescent's most serious areas of distress, his needs influence him to posit a more flexible position on sexual behavior than the adults who influence him. Although most adults disapproved of the standards held by the youth culture, many were shocked to discover in 1948 with the publication of Kinsey's *Sexual Behavior in the Human Male,* that the professed sexual norms were not reflected in actual behavior.[3] Nevertheless the majority of the adult society while they questioned the value of these principles in their own lives continued to offer to youth the same basic sex norms, including premarital chastity, the sanctity of marriage, and the necessity of a love commitment. In contrast the norms of the competitive dating phase of adolescent life often emphasized lack of affectional commitment, mutual exploitation, and heavy petting.[4]

A recent survey provides evidence of the differing attitudes toward premarital sexual permissiveness held by youth and adults. Using a sample of 1,500 adults and 900 students under the age of twenty-one, Reiss found that 61 per cent of the adults as opposed to 85 per cent of the youths thought petting for the engaged male was permissible. For the female the percentages were 56 as opposed to 82. These findings are typical of others reported in the

[3] A. C. Kinsey *et al., Sexual Behavior in the Human Male* (Philadelphia: W. B. Saunders Co., 1948).
[4] E. A. Smith, *The American Youth Cultures* (New York: The Free Press, 1964), p. 8.

survey, suggesting that while adults have shifted in their permissiveness to a more accepting position, the youth group has moved even further ahead, maintaining a still significant generational gap.[5]

Other studies reflect the same pattern. In a survey of attitudes towards virginity, both mothers and daughters were asked to respond to the question, "How important do you think it is that a girl be a virgin when she marries?" Of the mothers, 88 per cent thought it "very wrong" not to be a virgin, 12 per cent thought it "generally wrong" and none "right in many situations," compared to 55 per cent, 34 per cent and 13 per cent of the daughters. Both the mothers and the daughter were also asked, "Do you think sexual intercourse during engagement is very wrong, generally wrong, right in many situations?" The percentages in each response category were 83, 15 and 2 per cent for the mothers and 35, 48 and 17 per cent for the daughters.[6]

In 1956 Kinsey revealed evidence about the sex life of women, as he had earlier about men.[7] According to Kinsey, the stated norms did not reflect actual behavior. It is to be expected that a change in male attitudes will be accompanied by similar changes in female attitudes, since both are influenced by the same cultural changes. One important factor which may have contributed to greater flexibility in sexual standards among females is the development and popularization of the birth control pill. The certainty made possible by this contraception method has reduced much of the fear that was at the root of moral stands regarding sexual activity. With the elimination of the fears over pregnancy, the incidence of premarital sex is rapidly rising.[8]

The Context of Permissiveness

Permissiveness has been associated with the expansion of some large social values, such as freedom and individuality, and the erosion of others, such as the post-war conceptions of marriage and love. Brought down to its more structural components, permissiveness in sexual attitudes can be linked to institutional affiliations. As adolescents reduce their loyalties to their families and replace them with corresponding loyalties to peers, the area of restrictive-

---

5 Ira Reiss, *The Social Context of Premarital Sexual Permissiveness* (New York: Holt, Rinehart & Winston, Inc., 1967).
6 R. R. Bell, *Premarital Sex in a Changing Society* (Englewood Cliffs, N.J.: Prentice-Hall, Inc., 1966).
7 A. C. Kinsey *et al., Sexual Behavior in the Human Female* (Philadelphia: W. B. Saunders Co., 1953).
8 "The Pill—How It Is Affecting U.S. Morals," *U.S. News and World Report* 61 (1966).

ness is reduced and the support for developing more permissive sexual activities increases. Since sex is not part of the dialogue in families, the sexual reference group becomes the group of peers. Persons who are strongly integrated into their family units, such as youths who must assume the responsibility for younger brothers and sisters, do not develop permissive attitudes as readily as those who are more integrated into a friendship group.[9]

Family integration is indicated not only by the amount of responsibility assumed by the adolescent but also by the nature of interpersonal contacts. The amount of individual freedom permitted to adolescents is not only a reflection of the greater range of permissiveness extant in the family but an indication that parents expect their adolescent children to take the responsibility for and meet the consequences of their own decisions. In such cases sexual permissiveness in adolescents is likely to reflect the trend toward general permissiveness in the family. This view accounts for permissiveness as a function of family socialization. Children raised under such conditions have more liberal attitudes toward a whole range of social acts.

Another view of permissiveness is based on the idea that parents who are restrictive of freedom encourage deviant behavior as part of a process of the children's asserting necessary independence. Children who participate in rebellious sexual behavior, violating the expectations of family to the extent that we can deduce that they are rejecting parental views, are more likely to suffer psychological effects from their aberrations than those who reflect a permissive attitude as a result of socialization.

Those children who feel integrated into religious institutions are likely to make the same adaptation as those who are integrated in a dependent way into family structures. The morality of the church as an institution that communicates a morality set and institutionalizes sanctions against sexual violations can affect the sexual adaptation of young people, whereas adolescents who do not develop loyalties to such control institutions are often free to make their own choices.

The institutional condition that would appear to be most closely linked to diffuse and ambivalent attitudes about sexual behavior is one which removes sexuality from the broad base of interactions. Since sexual matters are not usually openly discussed with children in families, churches, or schools, we may infer that children are left to their own speculations and consequent anxieties about sexual roles.

---

9 Reiss, *Social Context of Premarital Sexual Permissiveness.*

Even in the movement toward liberalizing the permissive base of institutional interaction, the first step is usually away from a dogmatic and manifest set of restrictive rules. Children who are exposed to this transition phase of institutional posture often react with ambivalence and anxiety because the ambiguous attitude change has not been a complete one. Young men and women attempting to account for differences in their sexual behavior are often referred to family experiences by psychiatrists and psychologists. Frequently the young people cannot say with conviction that their parents were negative in their sexual attitudes or even not permissive. At the same time they cannot say the opposite. The social reality is that we are in a period of transition when institutions are able to surrender the old dogmas, but we are not yet in a period where the same institutions are able to affirm a new value set. The instability of many social and sexual relationships between males and females can be associated with this transition, where clues for behavior are frequently absent, or at least not definitive.

Problems of Greater Permissiveness

The rapid liberalization of sexual attitudes has had disorganizing side effects on many persons. As in any change of values, the knowledge of what needs to be done to avoid problems lags far behind the instrumentation of attitudes into behavior. The rapid rise in rates of venereal disease, illegitimate pregnancies, and illegal abortions, many of which have had fatal or near fatal consequences, are the more prominent side effects.

Based on available evidence, illegitimate births involving teen-age mothers doubled during the period 1940 to 1961.[10] In Philadelphia in 1966 junior and senior high school girls constituted 40 per cent of unwed-mother petitions for support.[11] The fact that large numbers of illegitimate births are not reported allows us to assume that the increase is probably even greater. It is also possible that a sizable percentage of children born to married teenage mothers were conceived prior to marriage.

The extent of illegitimacy in births to adolescent girls is usually viewed as a function of careless, irresponsible behavior on the part of lower-class persons who are assumed to be highly indiscriminate in the choice of sexual partners. Many lower-class mothers have the unfortunate experience of raising several children, no two

10 W. Thompson, *et al.*, "Sex Education, A Ball Nobody Carries," *The Clearing House* (February 1965).
11 Sylvia Sacks, "Widening the Perspectives on Adolescent Sex Problems," *Adolescence* 1 (Spring 1966): 79–90.

of whom have had the same father. Middle-class moralists, in their desire to support their prejudices, would rather think that such an example was more the rule than the exception, but evidence points otherwise. One study, choosing a representative sample of 68 per cent Negro unwed mothers and 32 per cent white, found that the illegitimate child was not usually the issue of random sexual behavior. Most of the mothers in this sample had more than temporary association with the fathers, were going with the fathers for an average of six months, felt love for them at the time of impregnation, and often believed that the relationship would culminate in marriage. Only 13 per cent of the sample were impregnated by married men.[12]

Abortion, the third possible consequence of unwed conception (illegitimacy and marriage being the first two), is of serious concern to the society at large and to public health centers in particular. A report in *Good Housekeeping Magazine* stated that approximately 180,000 abortions were performed on teenage girls in 1964. Again we can assume that not all cases have been recorded, and some estimates run to over 1,000,000.[13]

In the United States abortions are not only dangerous to physical and mental conditions, but they are usually also illegal. Some states have loosened their laws to permit legal abortions to be performed in cases where the health of the mother is in serious danger, or in cases of rape or incest. The future of abortion laws is a problem which we shall consider in our discussion of sex education. Unfortunately, even within extra-legal structures, the lower-class person, in this case the female, suffers inequities in the kind of treatment she receives when having to abort a child. She is not only more likely to be impregnated due to looser parental control, she is also more likely to experience an untrained "quack" who will perform the abortion for what she can afford.

ABORTIONS AND VENEREAL DISEASE

In the same sense that legal codes have pushed drug traffic underground, thus creating a deviant mode (producing criminals), the sanctions against abortion have produced a group of persons (abortionists) who themselves fall into the criminal category. These facts

[12] H. Pope, "Unwed Mothers and Their Sex Partners," *Journal of Marriage and the Family* 29, No. 3 (1967): 555–567.
[13] J. Robbins and J. Robbins, "Growing Need for Sex Education in Our Schools," *Good Housekeeping Magazine* (November 1965): 94–95.

cannot be dismissed on the absurd grounds that if all laws were abolished there would be no criminals, for there are serious arguments which take the position that legalizing both drugs and abortion would have a salutary rather than a disorganizing social effect. The question, "Should abortion be legalized?" can usefully be raised as part of a program in sex education.

The Kinsey survey suggested that 85 per cent of the abortions performed were done by licensed physicians. Since this is probably true and since abortions are very costly, it seems to be indicated that abortion is in some way a social class advantage. The abortion structure is usually well organized. Abortionists receive referrals from regular doctors and often establish a set of links to guarantee their own protection. The laws regulating against the practice of abortion appear to be highly unenforceable since estimates indicate over 300,000 abortions are performed annually. It is not certain why the law is not enforced. Perhaps it is a result of the secrecy of the operation, perhaps a result of police corruption and/or police tolerance.[14]

The aftereffects of abortion on the woman is another significant factor. Some evidence suggests that American women who have had an abortion experience more psychiatric disorders, involving guilt and shame, than do women in Scandinavian countries where abortion has been legalized. It has not been established how much psychological disturbance actually does occur in women in the United States as the data are usually derived from reports of psychologists and psychiatrists who speak about the biased sample of those women who seek professional help.[15] If it can be proved by further empirical study that the negative psychological effects of abortion in Scandinavian countries is less pervasive than in the United States, the logical inference can be that guilt and shame are socialized in an inhibiting culture such as that of the United States and serve to control the amount of deviance that might otherwise exist.

Thus it has become a real problem for the school to make a stand in helping students to adjust to abnormal as well as normal responses to social pressures. If students are taught that there is little reason to feel guilt over an abortion, one of the socializing mechanisms of education breaks down; if we perpetuate the attitudes regarding deviance, not considering the deleterious effects abortion (when committed in spite of prohibition) is going to have

14 E. M. Schurr, *Crimes Without Victims* (Englewood Cliffs, N. J.: Prentice-Hall, Inc., 1965), pp.30–35.
15 *Ibid.*, pp.42–44.

on the young people, we do little to help students protect themselves against psychic discomfort. Perhaps it is possible to find a
way of simultaneously serving two apparently conflicting goals, but
serious dialogue in the area must be opened before any progress
can be made.

Venereal disease is another social problem controlled and affected by similar social pressures as those which are attached to
illegitimate pregnancy. In California alone 53,000 cases of venereal
disease were reported in 1965.[16] During 1967 and part of 1968 the
problem in San Francisco became so chronic (primarily due to the
hippie concentration) that organized educational programs were
conducted on the streets of Haight-Ashbury. The problems of
venereal disease, more than any single consequence of sexual permissiveness, could be alleviated by a health education program in
the schools; resistance continues to exist even to so fundamental
a solution.

THE SEXUAL "HANG-UP"

Probably more insidious than venereal disease and illegitimate
births are the psychological difficulties produced by anxiety about
the sexual experience itself. One of the major causes of divorce in
the United States is sexual incompatibility.[17] And even though
sexual incompatibility does not always lead to divorce, the problem
often presents marital partners with a heavy psychological burden.
Frigidity in women, impotence in men, and many other related
sexual "hang-ups" provide psychiatrists with more patients than
probably any other symptom of social maladjustment.[18]

Contrary to the way in which deviant sexual behavior is often
described as symptomatic of a lack of sexual outlet, evidence indicates most rapists and "Peeping Toms" are, more often than not,
married men. One clue to a more accurate perspective of the problem of sexual deviancy or the sexual hang-up can be found in data
provided by Kanin.[19] In a study of the sexual responses of a group
of college males, he discovered that those males who were most

[16] *VD Information for Students,* State of California, Department of Public
Health, 1966.
[17] W. J. Goode, "Family Disorganization," in *Contemporary Social Problems,*
eds. R. Merton and R. Nisbet (New York: Harcourt, Brace & World, Inc.,
1961), pp.431–432.
[18] This is so almost by definition, because Freudian and neo-Freudian theories
which provide the foundations of therapy are based on a sexual model.
[19] E. J. Kanin, "An Examination of Sexual Aggression as a Response to Sexual
Frustration," *Journal of Marriage and the Family* 29, No. 3 (1967): 428–433.

aggressive in the approach to females were more successful, but more sexually dissatisfied, than non-aggressive males. This suggests that sexual outlet is not necessarily a prerequisite to sexual adjustment.

The psychiatric assessment of the successful "wolf" or in a more contemporary term, the playboy, is one in which the male is seen as seeking a rich supply of sexual outlets in order to avoid intimacy with any single female. A variation on the same theme is revealed in a study by Kuhendall where he found that almost half of the males surveyed (131) were unable psychologically to take advantage of sexual opportunities, that is, in situations where the female was willing to participate. More than half of the group who reported no sexual intercourse whatever were those who backed away from relationships which could have culminated in sexual intercourse.[20]

The foregoing discussion leads us to a reformulation of some traditional views regarding sexual problems, for certain patterns in contemporary social organization have produced a set of inhibitions at the same time that we are experiencing an expansion of sexual opportunities. Perhaps the answer lies in the way in which we currently view the relationship between love (or intimacy) and sex.

In a technological, bureaucratized society, such as the United States, all elements of traditional romantic behavior are reduced to functional, instrumental techniques. The classical romantic love stories, such as *Romeo and Juliet, Wuthering Heights,* Abelard and Heloise, Guinevere and Lancelot, and many others, could not in their original form be popular today. The profit merchants recognize better than anyone that people want to read about sex, not love; the separation of sex from love is a logical consequence of depersonalization. Sex is possible without feeling, but love, by definition, is not. The sexual "hang-up" is intricately associated with the process of dehumanization necessarily concomitant with the stabilization of a technological society. In order to make the kinds of work-culture advances we have observed in modern times, romantic or spiritual tendencies which might conflict with technological efficiency have been extinguished. If the average man today were to protest the fact that there is no romantic or spiritual reality to his work, our culture of industrialized efficiency might be shattered.

The theme of work, of efficiency, is even carried into the literature of marriage—a "how-to" literature. An evaluation of fifteen major marriage manuals reveals that sexual behavior is typically

[20] L. A. Kuhendall, "Characteristics of Sexual Decision Making," *Journal of Sex Research* 3, No. 3 (1967): 201–11.

treated as a process of inducing orgasm through a set of instrumental "strategies" and techniques. In such manuals sex play is treated as work,[21] just as there are frequent allusions to work in our everyday, informal conversation about sex—for example, the phrases "you have to work up to it," "I'm working on her," "she gave me a work out." Many books and pamphlets on the "Art of Love," and the "Techniques of Love Making," treat the subject of sex only as "technique," and this does not contradict the contemporary social conception of what love is. The whole idea that a woman should not give her body easily often implies that the man has to earn it, in the same way he would earn a house or a car. Again the association of elements of the Protestant ethic, such as industriousness and ambition, with the winning of a sexual offering is only another variation on the theme that a person cannot appreciate what he has not earned.

The only sense in which we can make an argument that this adaptation to sexual interaction is dysfunctional is to hypothesize that sexual satisfaction cannot be complete without the introduction of human elements which have almost become obsolescent in a dehumanizing society. It appears that one of the most dehumanizing experiences, from the surging ground-swell of student protests and the kinds of problems that college students have, is the experience of education. In the final section on recommendations for education, the point will be argued that sexual freedom will be advanced in the process of humanizing education.

HOMOSEXUALITY

Homosexuality may be thought of in two ways: first, as a pattern of deviant sexual activities within which persons act out their sexual impulses with members of the same sex; or, in contrast, it may be thought of as an aspect of personality, a tendency, which describes the sexual character of the individual independent of his behavior. In the first instance homosexuality denotes social deviance; in the latter, a simple inversion of normative characteristics. Because society expects persons to relate sexually to members of the opposite sex, those who do not necessarily make normal persons in society uncomfortable. In order to prevent discomfort society invokes special regulations to prevent the externalization of perverse inclinations. Even though the regulations are generally ineffective,

[21] L. S. Lewis and D. Bussett, "Sex as Work: A Study of Avocational Counseling," *Social Problems* 15, No. 1 (1967): 8–18.

normal members of the society are content insofar as their disapproval dispatches the limited amount of control it can over such an uncontrollable phenomenon as homosexuality. Thus it becomes a case of "I don't care what people do in private, so long as I don't have to know about it." Regulations protect most individuals from being exposed to expressions of a sexual mode they do not like to think about. Generally the mechanism of social control which most effectively regulates sexual deviance is the internalized desire on the part of most citizens to maintain the *status quo* of the society in which they have invested their lives. Any real change in the society's norms deprives the individual who is not prepared to make the transition himself of the opportunity to say, "This is my world." The resistance of most adults to changing sexual values can be partly explained in this way.

Goffman argues that the most useful sociological conception of homosexuality is one that views homosexuality as a theme which guides the organization of a group. As in any other cohesive group, homosexuals have certain standards and norms in common.[22] The organization of homosexual groups supports the single homosexual in his willingness to rebel from traditional restrictions in the same way that the peer group of adolescents protects and socializes members to patterns which bring them into conflict with the adult world. It cannot be argued that the homosexual community has any legal or political influence to change laws or norms relating to their group. Yet as the problem increases, the regulatory mechanisms appear to become more and more impotent. If many people are doing it and it is not a crime against person or property, then perhaps it is not worth too much worry.

It should at least seem plausible that society creates homosexuals in the same way it produces most deviant types. The theory that homosexuality is genetically produced has very little evidence to support it, but the maintenance of this belief is a useful way for members of the normal community to avoid their responsibility for the discomfiture and punishment of homosexuals.[23]

The homosexual who has himself internalized the norms and rules of the society and does not wish to commit a crime finds himself without an acceptable sexual outlet, even though Americans, for the most part, do not believe persons should be punished for a condition about which they can do nothing. If we place homosexuality in this perspective and give an evaluation of the short and

---

22 E. Goffman, *Stigma: Notes on the Management of Spoiled Identity* (Engle wood Cliffs, N. J.: Prentice-Hall, Inc., 1963), pp.143–144.
23 Schurr, *Crimes Without Victims*, pp.70–71.

long range consequences of not regulating against homosexual acts, students should be able to come to some objective conclusion about their particular position.

Homosexuality as a non-genetically produced behavior can, like any sexual behavior, be produced structurally. In other words people can be influenced to behave homosexually if the norms of an institution or a society are conducive to such behavior. The high incidence of homosexuality in prisons and detention homes is a case in point. Another structural aspect of behavior-learning views deviant adaptation as a mode produced by the differential access persons have to both opportunities and role models. A rejection of heterosexuality may occur both for those who do not feel adequate to the social challenge of heterosexuality, or for those who have existed in an environment in which the role of the male is perceived as undesirable. When more is known about the homosexual as a social type, it is likely that sociologists will be able to outline a theoretic programmed social construction which will produce only heterosexuals.

A model of socially produced homosexuality can be constructed in terms of a study which has been done of homosexual behavior in a correctional institution for adolescent girls. The girls studied were between the ages of twelve and eighteen and on the average had been in the institution for approximately ten months. This last point is emphasized to suggest that some old notions (*i.e.*, that only many years of deprivation, as in the case of long-term prisoners, leads to radical departures from original standards and self-conceptions) are false. If homosexuality can be produced in very temporary living situations, its difficult nature should be of more serious concern to the larger society. Extraordinary conditions are not required to produce homosexual behavior.

In this particular institution the notion of "going steady" was common and popular. The "steady" couples usually consisted of a female role and a male role. The latter were called "butches." The butch would dress and wear her hair in a boyish manner and would compete with other butches in a vigorous and sometimes violent manner for the possession of the most attractive girls. Physical contact was common but limited usually to holding hands, dancing, and some kissing. As in most institutions of this nature, control generally prevented further intimacy. Intense anxiety or guilt was rarely observed. New girls at first were anxious and concerned about becoming perverts, but after indoctrination they became fascinated by the new experience.

Findings based upon fifty-seven cases reported that 69 per cent of the girls participated in "going steady," 71 per cent had experienced kissing other girls, 11 per cent had done some sexual caressing, and 5 per cent had participated in stimulation of the genitals. Of the 69 per cent who developed temporary homosexual attachments, only 9 per cent had had similar experiences prior to entering the institution. Of the girls who, previous to institutionalization, had had no homosexual experience, only 9 per cent expressed an intention to continue homosexual practices upon being released from the institution.[24]

The authors of the study pointed to several dynamic factors in past social relationships which are of interest to our problem. Most of the girls who had experienced homosexual relations had also had sexual relations with men. These were, according to the reports of the girls, seldom enjoyed. Sex was used only to establish some relationship with a person of the opposite sex. Acceptance was somehow defined as requiring sexual activity. The girls felt degraded and abused by the men, and 20 per cent of the sexual experiences had been with fathers, brothers or stepfathers. Because the girls' greatest anxiety appeared to relate to desertion, sexual behavior seemed to them a way of preserving a relationship .

The study and some of its implications suggest valuable insights into the dynamics of sexual relationships in a repressive society. Homosexuality for men as well as women may be an adaptation to the degrading way in which sex is viewed by many adults, particularly parents. It is likely that many men consider sexual behavior as a way of angrily defying the normative system in which they are imprisoned. In such a relationship the female is bound to react adversely to the man's instrumental rather than loving use of her body.

Homosexuality is organized ecologically. If its existence rather than its cause is defined as the problem, we must consider as the source of the problem the structures which maintain and promote its occurrence. Both New York and Los Angeles contain areas where homosexuality flourishes. Most other cities contain at least one or two "gay bars." The law cannot contain the problem by arresting persons who frequent the homosexual spots, for it is not a crime to be a homosexual. It is only a crime to engage in homosexual activities, and this, for the most part, occurs in private. Yet the number of homosexual night spots seems to be on the increase, and we must ask ourselves why. Perhaps it is a reaction against the "sexual revo-

---

[24] Seymore L. Halleck and M. Hersko, "Homosexual Behavior in a Correctional Institution for Adolescent Girls," *American Journal of Orthopsychiatry* 32, No. 5 (1962): 911–17.

lution." As more persons become anxiety-ridden due to expectations for their sexual performance, the homosexual condition is more easily acceptable, less demanding. If homosexuality is defined as a social problem, then the increased permissiveness apparent in all sexual areas must be in some way accountable for the increase in rates of homosexuality.

The social norms regarding such behavior as homosexuality and incest accurately reflect the repulsion most persons experience when thinking of such acts, so it may be assumed that these behavior patterns violate the sensibilities of most members of the society. Homosexuality and incest are, for most persons, the most seriously repressed of all sexual feelings. Nevertheless, it must be recognized that persons who do participate in acts of homosexuality and incest are products of the same society which produces those persons who repress such feelings. Persons who participate in such acts violate some basic social laws and are likely to be suffering the anxieties and guilt called forth by the shattering of basic and deep beliefs. In the same way that a young girl may suffer when she breaks the social-sexual contract she has had since childhood, and which is represented in her own belief system, those who violate more serious canons are bound to suffer more.

NYMPHOMANIA

Nymphomania is a condition of women who have a compulsive need for sexual experience and have no control over the extent to which they participate in sexual acts. It is a condition which not only brings pain to the person but can produce disruptions in normal social arrangements such as marriage. Nymphomaniacs, unlike the stereotype of "loose" women, are usually not outside of the normative order. As have most normal members of the society, they have internalized most of the control values as well as most of the emotional needs of that society (such as the need to be successful, the need to be loved, the need to be virtuous). And because of this, the nymphomaniac suffers greatly from acting out her sexual needs.[25] Thus nymphomania is a social problem in the same sense in which other sexual "hang-ups" are a social problem.

There is, perhaps, in the minds of many women a thin line between normal sexual needs and nymphomania, and often in such cases the woman will rely upon the latter explanation (her imagined

[25] Albert Ellis and Edward Sagarin, *Nymphomania: A Study of the Oversexed Woman* (New York: Gilbert Press, 1964).

nymphomania) for sexual permissiveness rather than face up to a conception of herself as a loose woman. Relaxation of sexual morality can have positive consequences for both types, since the nymphomaniac can, conceptually, be relieved of the weight of guilt for behavior she cannot avoid. The more normal drives can be accepted as being less than pathological.

COMMUNAL SEX—THE "EXTENDED" FAMILY

One of the by-products of the hippie revolution has been the frequent establishment of communal living arrangements which lead to, and are often based upon, extended sexual arrangements. In their rejection of the society which they feel has imposed too many restrictions, these people are eager to attack through behavior the family, the most fundamental institutional complex in our society. There is not enough evidence, since the developments are so recent and the population involved so small, as to the consequences of this new sexual arrangement. The only fact we are certain of is that venereal disease reached epidemic proportions in the major community where this arrangement was practiced. The main question for future investigators to answer is how such arrangements, in the light of the tradition that the participants are violating, actually affect the members. We will also be interested to see if the experiment produces converts at a rate that will disturb the equilibrium of the family structure itself.

THE "SWING" CULTURE

Suburban sex, as described in the Chapman report and elsewhere,[26] and portrayed fictionally in such books and films as *Valley of the Dolls*[27] and *Bob and Carol and Ted and Alice,* must be viewed as a symptom of another major disruption in the sexual habits of Americans. Like homosexuality, wife-swapping is also beginning to experience some social organization. "Swingers," the term adopted to describe wife-swapping activities, are able to regulate their deviant wishes through the availability of establishments. The Swing Club in Los Angeles, not only willing but eager to advertise its

[26] Irving Wallace, *The Chapman Report* (New York: Simon and Schuster, Inc., 1960); and J. T. Warren, *Age of the Wife Swappers* (New York: Lancer Books, 1968).
[27] J. Susann, *Valley of the Dolls* (New York: Random House, Inc., 1966).

attraction, thrives on the business of providing a meeting place for those who wish to trade spouses. The *Los Angeles Free Press, The Village Voice,* and *The Berkeley Barb* run dozens of advertisements weekly where persons attempt to contact other couples with similar predilections. The extent of such activity, like other forms of sexual deviation, can never be fully known. The publicity surrounding such activities is always more readily available in urban centers where anonymity is something of a protection and interpersonal relationships are more impersonal. But if these tendencies reflect something besides urban possibilities, the structure of our sexual standards is indeed uncertain.

SEXUAL DEVIANCE AND SOCIAL CLASS

The greatest amount of sexual deviancy has been attributed to the very affluent and the very poor—the very affluent because they are above the norms and the very poor because they are outside of the normative system. The great masses that are referred to as the middle and working classes are subject to the restraints of standards because they have the greatest stake in protecting themselves against social disruptions. The social psychology of the masses is one of maintaining or improving upon social position. Disapproval from those who are depended on to validate status can dislodge one from the security of social acceptance. Conformity in all areas of social behavior is the characteristic adaptive mode of the middle class and those who seek entrance to it. The core standards of the middle class become the beacons for those who are upwardly mobile and produce almost a super-conformism in their approach to social relations. The most "moral" are usually those who are in transition upward on the class ladder. The phenomenon is a familiar one in the sociological literature. Frazier's description of the black bourgeosie[28] is a portrait of what Merton has referred to as anticipatory socialization.[29] This idea describes the upwardly mobile as persons who seek not only to adhere to the standards of the core American class but to so internalize and reflect them that there cannot be the slightest doubt about their social character. Upwardly mobile Negroes, according to Frazier's description, represent just such an adaptive posture.

For those at the bottom of the class ladder we can put together

[28] Franklin Frazier, *Black Bourgeosie* (New York: The Free Press, 1957).
[29] R. K. Merton, *Social Theory and Social Structure* (New York: The Free Press, 1957).

a better picture. It does not surprise us to discover that most crimes are committed by inhabitants of the poverty culture. We know the majority of those convicted of crimes of almost every category, except embezzlement and tax evasion, are the economically disenfranchised. It is hard to accept a set of standards of conformity when these prevent persons from gaining any part of the national wealth. It is also hard to subscribe to moralistic beliefs when one has little to lose from social disapproval.

The majority of prostitutes, pimps, purveyors of dirty pictures, rapists, and strip-teasers emerge from the lower classes. Except for rape, the other activities are simply viewed as innovative techniques for attaining the rewards of the economic system.[30]

Another type of behavior which reflects the adaptation of the lower classes to the normative system is reflected in the number of children born out of wedlock. Members of the lower classes are more likely to live together out of wedlock than persons of other social statuses. There are often instrumental reasons for such behavior. An illegitimate child is no disgrace to a woman who has nothing to lose by way of status or respect. On the other hand she may have something to gain. Most states have a welfare program that ensure that children without fathers are cared for and supported. Women can count upon various states for support in this area for which they surrender little. Some may argue that she gives away her self-respect, but what respect is possible in poverty is not clear. Many women who have internalized the sexual standards of the core culture, who are either middle class or aspiring, would rather hide their illegitimacy or make some adaptation to it, such as marrying someone they do not love, than live with the stigma of capitalizing upon a violation of sexual norms. Pregnancies of teenage girls in schools in low-income areas are reported far more frequently than pregnancies in middle- or working-class communities.

The whole psychology of having nothing to lose produces socially, for members of the lower class, a context whereby sexual deviation is not defined as immoral. Social and political leaders do not seem to understand that the best way to ensure conformity to social standards is to parlay the mechanisms that work so effectively in the middle classes into a program for the lower classes. That is, if persons have a stake in the system they will internalize the values by which this stake is maintained. The punitive approach can do

---

30 "Innovative" is used here in the sense of innovating upon the institutionalized means of attaining economic goals. See Merton, *Social Theory and Social Structure*, pp. 141–142.

little more than intervene a set of punishments and pose these as alternatives to beliefs. Social history has taught us that this is a very poor substitute for normative control of deviant acts.

To look at racial characteristics independent of socioeconomic factors as correlates of sexual permissiveness would be to ignore the more significant factor. The association of some kind of exaggerated sexuality with being Negro has evolved as a common stereotype in contemporary thinking. There is evidence to suggest that middle-class Negroes are less permissive in their sexual attitudes than whites of comparable socioeconomic status.[31]

The sexual behavior of Negroes as a social type follows very closely the patterns associated with disenfranchised persons of every ethnic group. The fact that more Negroes are disenfranchised economically than any other single group impresses prejudicial associations upon the usual (common sense) mentality, but other conclusions, such as the effects of poverty, occur more readily to the analytical mind.

THE SOCIAL CONTEXT OF SEXUAL INADEQUACY

The problem for most men and women growing up in a society which refuses them legitimate access to sexual experience without benefit of a marriage license is that they are largely unprepared to deal comfortably with such an experience. This does not mean that the sexual act requires some kind ·of psychological preparation for man any more than it does for animals. The problem is that for man the sexual experience is conducted within a framework of sexual socialization that makes the sexual act a loaded one. It is loaded with associations, particularly those which define sex as something dirty, sinful, and inappropriate. Conferring a piece of paper which certifies that a couple is legally married and therefore eligible for the sexual rights appertaining thereto seems to be an absurd condition at best. Anyone who understands the power of social conditioning recognizes that attitudes and fears become internalized often as taboos and cannot arbitrarily be exorcised when the moment becomes appropriate.

For most children reared in a society still heavily influenced by puritanical attitudes, there is no provision for exposure to sex as a normal human function. Anthropologists have discovered many

[31] J. S. Himes, "Some Reactions to a Hypothetical Pre-Marital Pregnancy by 100 Negro College Women," *Journal of Marriage and the Family* 26, No. 3 (1964): 344–347.

primitive societies where preparation for sexual adulthood begins early in the child's development.[32] When some knowledge about the human sexual experience is kept from children and they are aware that it is being hidden from them, even though the parents may not wish the child to believe that sex is wrong or sinful, he is bound to define it as such. Why else, he will reason, must it be kept such a secret? A child will further reason that should he violate the taboos regarding sex he will be punished. Therefore any attempt to express himself sexually carries the internalized threat of punishment. Most social restraints operate on a deviate-punish basis. Why should sexual behavior be an exception? The family, the church, and the school appear to the child to be collaborators in the effort to restrain him from sexual activity. In the presence of such an overwhelming institutional mandate, it is not surprising that most children, and later adolescents, and even later, adults, define their sexual behavior as deviant.

Society not only punishes latently by working through the guilt mechanisms and socialized fears, but it also through its regulatory institutions seeks to punish persons who deviate from normal sexual routines. It attempts to prosecute persons involved in rape, peeping Tom-ism, pornography, transporting minors across state borders for the purpose of sexual relations, prostitution, homosexuality, exhibitionism (which can run the gamut from indecent exposure on city streets to too much exposure on the burlesque stage), and contributing to the delinquency of a minor, even if the minor is willing. Even if the hidden persuaders were less effective, the manifest ones would serve to make a telling point to members of society that, in dealing with sexual feelings, one needs to be cognizant of the dangers inherent in stepping beyond the bounds of normal sexual expression. There are even laws on the books, seldom enforced, which make illegal such sexual behaviors as adultery, fornication between unmarried partners, and "abnormal" sexual acts, even between marital partners.

Widespread violation of both the laws and the standards signifies that the flexibility of both are not adequate to accommodate the needs inherent in the society for greater sexual expression. By greater, we refer to a more extensive base of sexual activity. This is not to suggest at all that the disruptive behaviors should be defined as healthy in the context of a society which is sexually repressed or whose laws and standards are unrealistic. It is only to

---

32 Ruth Benedict, "Continuities and Discontinuities in Cultural Conditioning," in *Personality*, ed. C. Kluckhohn and H. Murray (New York: Alfred A. Knopf, Inc., 1955), p. 528.

press the point that social problems are usually socially organized and take the forms, almost by definition, of aberrations from the standards. It is impossible, for example, to develop drives for exhibitionism in a nudist colony, and prostitution could not be a career in a free love society.

The pressure for sexual variety is another symptom of a society which cannot come to terms with the basic needs of its members. This felt need is expressed in extra-marital relations, or even voyeurism if the guilt of extra-marital relations is too much to bear or if the possibilities are unavailable. Such activities are problems to society insofar as their consequences cannot be absorbed within the normal patterns. Marital partners usually demand fidelity of the other, even when participating in extra-marital relations themselves. Although illogical on some grounds, sexual feelings intrude into relationships in the form of possessive needs, and the double standard does not, according to the thinking of those who hold it, need to be rationalized on a logical basis.

Another sense in which society molds the form of sexual problems is through its reliance on culture heroes and heroines. It may be this phenomenon that creates the psychological necessity for sexual variety, both before and during marriage. The culture hero is the ideal male role model. He is strong, protective, muscular, tall, handsome and, above all, potent. He is in many ways the modern day counterpart of the cave man lover. His way of approaching the female is to be aggressive, demanding, beyond rejection. He is capable of overwhelming any verbal or physical protestation. He never fails. Not long ago a young writer received his manuscript back from the fiction editor of a contemporary successful sex periodical. On the little rejection slip which accompanied the manuscript was written one sentence: "I'm sorry, but our heroes are never impotent." It does not much matter how well a story is written. If it does not sell the culture hero, in the form of aggressive potent men, it does not normally come to the attention of the general public. The culture hero, like James Bond, is the master of the physical and cognitive worlds. He can do practically anything, and audiences applaud loudly when he accomplishes an implausible feat. For boys who grew up during and after World War II, this image is the standard against which many measure their own capacities. The war hero displayed so often on the screen, particularly in the period during and immediately following the second, as well as subsequent wars, represents in another costume the same fearless figure. How could a man, undaunted by death, be daunted by a woman?

The current heroine is not, above all, the mother type. She is never seen in a kitchen or a laundry room. She is, rather, vivacious, beautiful, unworried, buxom, desirable and desiring, and thoroughly physical. She is a Marilyn Monroe, a Jayne Mansfield, and a Raquel Welch. She is poured down the throat of the American male by the bucketful. On the screen or in glossy print she is eminently available for a small fee. To many males she is in reality a terrifying threat. When one combines the culture hero with the heroine as filmmakers like to do, we then have the image of the heroic combination: a conception of love and lovemaking between two such personifications that the average person must, if he has any doubt about how he measures up to the image, experience the kind of anxiety that produces impotence in men, frigidity in women, and a search for the sexual partner that will make it all happen. Consequently we observe the extra-marital treadmill.

THE IMAGE OF THE FEMALE

Despite the influence of the playboy conception of the feminine sex object as someone who can be bought and persuaded with style and tasteful gifts, the definition of the female in contemporary society has more significant roots. For most of contemporary history the male–female relationship has been one of dominance–submission. Even the playboy style is simply another variation on the dominance theme. The woman is still treated instrumentally, dominated by the male. The particular form of domination in this instance is one of control through affluence, an expected direction in an affluent society. But because women could not always be dominated, the male defensively began to propagate a set of myths which would remove the burden of failure from himself and place it on the character of the female. Women were defined as scheming, evil, dangerous, treacherous, cold and often, if the woman was highly inaccessible, as a *femme fatale*.[33] The separateness of the sexes in almost all institutional life made it almost impossible for the female to assert her own image beyond that which was accorded her by the male. Because of a number of stereotypes about the woman, she was prohibited access to occupations in the same way she was refused equal participation in politics or normal conversation. The notion that many seamen had about a woman being bad luck on a boat is but a specific instance of the woman-as-albatross idea that

[33] H. R. Hays, *The Dangerous Sex: The Myth of Feminine Evil* (New York: G.P. Putnam's Sons, 1964).

has carried into much of contemporary thinking. For every cliché about a woman standing behind every man, there are ten on the theme of a woman being a man's undoing. The role of Eve in the garden has provided man with the prototype for many of his self-protective conceptions of woman.

A male adolescent sexual experience is seldom viewed as an act of love but rather as an act of conquest. Male peer reference groups devalue virginity, a concept that is possible only in a view of cross-sex relationships as one of dominance over some kind of foe. That is not to say that individual women are viewed as combatants, which may sometimes be the case, but that the universal woman with her configuration of adversary characteristics is a legitimate object for conquest. This says a great deal about the character of inter-personal relations between the sexes. And in a time when the woman is asserting her own achievement orientation, the gap may increase even further. Many men are afraid of women, and that is a significant social problem. The fact that access to sexual experience is available forces these frightened men to make some kind of adaptation, and the two most unsatisfactory of these are aggression (viewed as a vigorous conquest) or withdrawal. Impotence in many men may be a convenient strategy for avoiding facing their lion.

BASIC NEEDS

Other than the need for some kind of sexual outlet there are no needs related to forms of sexual expression which are basic. The rationales that are presented to defend extra-marital relationships center around the view that man is basically polygamous. We are often told, from street corner conversation, to cocktail parties, to social criticism, that we are all being crucified on the cross of monogamous marriage in order for society conveniently to manage the care and feeding of children. The fact that so many persons feel that sexual variety or communal sex is a more honest or basic expression of needs is only a result of social restraints. Most social restraints have the power of producing in persons the need to violate the restraints. We know from child rearing that the child always seeks most after that which is prohibited him. Adults, those who are not completely debilitated by anxiety and are willing to face their own desires, will recognize this tendency. To a great extent this is what sex in contemporary society has evolved into— the need to see, touch, experience areas of the body which have been prohibited to us unless we can display a legal document that tells us the restraints are legally cancelled.

The dynamics of socially produced sexual forms, forms of normal as well as deviant acts, are processes which are important for young people to understand. There are hundreds of millions of sexually deviant acts in a potential state that can be avoided through some kind of educational experience. But instead the school plays a role in guaranteeing that these deviant acts will be played out some time in the future, creating problems for the society and for the many persons involved. In the next section the role the school plays in being affected by, as well as affecting, sexual deviation will be considered.

SEX AND THE SCHOOLS

Many of the problems that we have discussed can be attributed to the wholesale ignorance surrounding sexual behavior. Children are not only not taught about sex, they are not even exposed to it. And through hundreds of little protective devices, the adult communicates to the child that sex in any form is a closed door. Parents usually take care not to expose their bodies to their children, the genital areas are guarded from birth on, the hands of babies are slapped when they engage in masturbative play, children are censored when they repeat a word referring to some sexual organ or sexual behavior, and social leaders try to exert a protective censorship over the mass media so sex and nudity will not be revealed to children.

When the time comes and children attain a sexual maturity physically, the subject remains a secret. In a survey of over 25,000 teenagers, William Blaisdell, a Washington, D.C. public health specialist, found that only one in fourteen teenagers received information about sex from his parents prior to learning it from other, usually misinformed, teenagers.[34] This is not to suggest that had these teenagers received the information from their parents they would have been better informed. The parents who do not broach the subject with their teenage sons and daughters are usually those who carry with them a host of misconceptions and neurotic anxieties about sex themselves. Many parents may want to communicate with their children on the subject of sex but find it too difficult, too

[34] L. Gross, "Sex Education Comes of Age," *Look*, March 8, 1966.

awkward, too confusing, and consequently resign themselves to the fact that their children will have to learn about sex in the same way that they did, from their peers.

By the time the generation gap has opened wide and adolescents have chosen a community of peers to serve as their significant reference group, it is generally too late to improve communication with the child. The parent is now defined, in some matters like sexual behavior, to be too old-fashioned and patronizing to present the facts honestly. Usually by this time the anxieties the child has already developed over the subject make it impossible for him to use the parent as an educative agent. The interaction on this topic is, it appears, too loaded for both of them. The best the child can expect, and he knows this, are platitudes which his own experience belies. It is both easier and more appropriate to learn about sex from his peers.

Responsibility for sex education has been abdicated as a function of the American family. Accordingly the school has in a minimal way been charged with some responsibility in this area. Unprepared as it is, the school has made weak gestures in this direction.

Most sex education activites that have appeared in the curriculum in the past decade or so have defined sex as a health matter and assigned instruction to health specialists, principally the physical education teachers. This usually occurs after the sixth grade and involves a separation of the sexes. Again the old definitions are made cogent. Sex is perceived as something that boys and girls cannot learn about together. The treatment of sex as an academic subject, either in physical education or biology classes, evolves into a discourse on cold biological facts. The ideas of sex as a psychological condition, as a problem in human relations, as a segment of social values, ordinarily go untouched. What, then, do the students really learn to help them overcome the anxieties related to sex that they have? For the overwhelming majority of students, the answer is, up to the present, nothing.

A HISTORY OF SEX IN THE CLASSROOM

The most stereotypical characteristic of the traditional school teacher is her moralism. Waller referred to the school as a "museum of virtue" and has characterized the teachers he observed as women who would have difficulty finding places to live because adults were unwilling to conduct themselves in a manner that they felt would be required by this person.[35] Nonetheless if this moralistic posture was not presented in the classroom, the same parents would desire her dismissal. The expectation for the moral behavior of teacher was considerably higher than most persons had for themselves.

In describing the way in which young female teachers were excluded from most of the social events of the community, Warner and his colleagues, who were doing a status study in a small mid Western town, wrote:

There is a feeling among people of the middle class position and higher that a teacher is a straight-laced person and is likely to put constraint upon a party or other informal gathering. We hear in Old City such statements as 'Of course his sister is out there a lot of the time now and she is a terrible stick. She is a school teacher and doesn't drink and they can't have much fun when she is around.'[36]

Follow-up interviews with teachers regarding their "ultra conservative" behavior seemed to show a portrait of conformity to expectations which were not necessarily those of the teachers themselves. Teachers seemed to suggest that they would readily participate in such discouraged practices as smoking and drinking if there were not such a threat of disapproval surrounding them.[37]

It would seem that a vicious cycle is set in motion without a clear beginning or end. The expectations for the behavior of teachers impinge upon them from sources which they, not as individuals but as a professional group, have produced. It also seems to be the case, from this kind of evidence as well as from the inferences we can make about the kind of teachers that emerge from liberal institutions in a permissive cultural period, that citizens do not want to be as restrained or inhibited as they are, that teachers do not want to produce this kind of person, and that teachers would prefer more personal autonomy and to see dispelled the traditional image of the teacher as a supermoralist. It is not yet clear at what point the cycle can be broken. As long as the mastodons of the past hold a kind of moral investment in the maintenance of traditional roles, the cycle will continue, gradually weakening until the time when these public leaders relinquish their hold on the public morality through the schools. The only other alternative

[35] Willard Waller, *The Sociology of Teaching* (New York: John Wiley and Sons, Inc., 1932).
[36] W. Lloyd Warner, R. Havighurst, and M. Loeb, *Who Shall Be Educated* (New York: Harper and Row, 1944), p. 104.
[37] *Ibid.*, pp.104–105.

is a kind of social–educational revolution from within, and rumblings in this direction seem to be currently centered in professional organizations, since teachers seem to have discovered that their image, as well as their salary, suffers when control of their profession is out of their hands.

As a result of community expectations, teachers to survive in their chosen occupation have had to include a moralistic image in their conception of their role. It is still the case that the hard-core prescriptions for the behavior of teachers can be traced to the expectations of the community, particularly the most outspoken members of the community who typically happen to be the most conservative members with respect to social and moral issues.

Because sex in all its ramifications has been considered a subject of utmost delicacy, teachers have been prone to avoid any mention of it in the classroom, for several reasons. First, sex is and always has been a controversial subject, and any attempts to confront this kind of controversy would be met with the anxiety that always accompanies dealing with such issues in the classroom. The anxiety is born, most specifically, out of the concern that teachers feel for the security of their jobs. A second reason is that women have traditionally been more conservative in their moral attitudes than men, and probably have held the same view as the representatives of the community who were most concerned with maintaining the *status quo* in the school. Third, as women, and often as unmarried women, the average teacher has been personally anxious about sex and would have been psychologically disturbed by any reference to it in the classroom.

When Becker asked the school teachers he interviewed about the behaviors they disliked in lower-class students, a frequent comment was that they were vulgar and too oriented to sex.[38] The role of teacher is a middle-class role, and one of the primary characteristics of persons occupying such roles is their reliance on control. Since the expectations of others constitute the principal cue for behavior, persons need to guard against their own inclinations and tendencies so that others should not be offended. Lower-class students, as most teachers recognize, often provide teachers with their most serious control problems, because these children do not want to control their own feelings. If they are thinking about sex, they are apt as not to say something about it. And like most highly controlled persons, teachers become very tense in the presence of interactional elements which threaten to go beyond their capacities for

[38] H. Becker, "Social Class Variation in Teacher-Pupil Relationships," *Journal of Educational Sociology* 25 (1952): 451.

control. If sex is never mentioned, is kept completely out of the environment of the classroom, there is less chance of losing control over the behavior of the students. Teachers like to feel that they have control at all times, but since they do not know what to do about a sexual reference, even if it comes up as a sincere question from a concerned student, they are likely to sidestep any attempt to turn it into an educating moment.

For many generations students of English have been reading Chaucer's *Canterbury Tales* in English classrooms, but almost never were they permitted to read *The Miller's Tale*. Any reference to parts of the sexual anatomy in romantic or even Shakespearean literature were quickly skipped. Censorship of children's literature operated as intensively thirty years ago as it does today. The criteria for the inclusion or exclusion of books are more often than not the degree to which it avoids any controversial issue. Many a librarian, without having any effect, has made mention of the fact that if the criteria for censorship were strictly employed, the Bible would have to be removed from the schools. Many educational leaders today acknowledge their responsibility for keeping children out of harm's way by ensuring that nothing that the children read will be detrimental to their mental health. The possibility that total ignorance about issues that are or will be significant in their lives can have detrimental effects is too complex a concept to influence directly most educational decisions.

Even though the development of artistic ability requires some understanding of the human anatomy, students are discouraged from ever painting nudes. Even in most colleges and universities, art classes are not permitted to have nude models.

It is clear that sex in the classroom has been institutionally absent. It is not surprising that enlightened educators and citizens have difficulty in convincing parents or administrators that a sex education program can be a valuable addition to the curriculum.

Effects on Students

The orientation of the school toward sex has, for many students, dysfunctional consequences. It may be functional in the mainenance of the school in a stable form to categorically deny the relevance of sexual feelings, but for many students the result is that they do not develop ways of dealing adequately with their own sexual urges.

IDENTITY DIFFUSION. The pre-adolescent and the adolescent exist in a developmental period that requires them to discover some kind of identity in relation to their beginning orientations toward the adult world. Identity for the adolescent centers around two major factors: (1) his occupational identity, and (2) his sexual identity. The school makes a serious effort to help the student orient himself to a career. It may do this too zealously and too early since students may not be ready to make as strong a commitment as the school requires. In the area of sexual identity the school makes no effort. And by so doing the school, like the home, contributes to the serious disjuncture that American adolescents experience. The adolescent's concern about his sexual identity is reflected in the desperation that seems to accompany heterosexual relationships. Many young women seem to think their sexual identity is defined by the way they can catch and hold a man. A number of misfortunes, as we have reported, befall these adolescents on their way to discovering their sexual identity.

INTERPERSONAL DISTRUST. Most schools are coeducational but schools do not offer students any rationale for being that way. The assumption is that males and females live in the same world together, and therefore it is perfectly natural that they should occupy seats together in the same classroom. But males do not necessarily understand females or vice versa. The classroom is a group of persons forced to interact with each other, often for educational benefits, but a large segment of each class is generally ignorant about the motives and feelings of the other segment. When sexual drives begin to appear, the already unclear relationship between the sexes becomes more confusing. The most common strategy for reducing tension under such conditions is to develop a posture of distance, often accompanied by distrust. Furthermore under such circumstances persons unable to confront some basic questions about members of the opposite sex evolve stereotypes. A common stereotype of the male is that of a person who wants to use a female for his own "dirty" purposes. To many males the stereotype of the female is of a person completely controlled by the moral standards of her society, and any attempts to approach her with his own sexual feelings arouses her anxiety. Students do not learn to trust their own feelings, and consequently they project this distrust upon others, intensifying the stereotype. Playing the sex game in all its stereotyped and anxiety-producing ways reduces the possibility of achieving a more honest form of interpersonal relationships with members of the opposite sex.

THE ORGANIZATION OF DISTRACTION. The surest way to guarantee that students will concentrate more on their sexual rituals than they will on their studies is to keep them worried and confused about the world of sex. A convenient way out of being obsessed with one's inhibitions is to employ fantasy to drain off the tension. In the average classroom there is extensive material for sexual fantasies, and students use it whenever possible. By repressing any form of sexual context, including the most innocent hand-holding, students quickly resort to devices which teachers cannot observe. An obsession with sexual sensations, which is common in pre-adolescence and adolescence, is a function of the inabiilty of educational programs to discover a way to reduce sexual tensions and inhibitions.

THE PUNITIVE APPROACH TO SEXUAL BEHAVIOR. Students do not usually emphasize their sexuality, as in the way girls dress or wear their hair, or express their curiosity, as small boys might do, or become pregnant as teenage girls might, deliberately, to disrupt the routines of the school. Nonetheless the same punitive measures that are used to retard disruptive actions are brought to bear upon students who engage in some form of sex-related behavior. Female students are sent home if their skirts are too short, and small boys are punished for looking in the girl's bathroom, and pregnant girls are expelled. And junior high school boys are given detentions for reading "dirty" books. Even if it is all they are motivated to read, the school would rather see them illiterate than "immoral." The problem is not so much with the punishment. It is that control measures, which are not accompanied by honest explanations of why they need to be employed, serve only to alienate students from the school. Punishment accompanied by some realistic explanation of the necessity for it can be an integrative education experience for the student. But to be told that this is something he simply does not do because it is wrong is not very helpful. The same argument can be applied to the punishments that boys receive when they are caught with pornographic literature in their pocket. Rather than make this occasion the basis of an educational discipline, it simply becomes an extension of the old policy of denying the necessity that children feel to explore the sexual world.

THE NEGATIVE ROLE MODEL. Students who feel that teachers do not have an honest interest in their needs and problems will classify such teachers as persons not to be respected or believed. The dishonesty that students recognize in most teachers when teachers attempt to hide from them, usually by omission, the secrets of the adult world, specifically the sexual world, removes the teachers from the possibility of being accepted as a role model.

Moreover for many if not for most students the dishonesty and social and personal distance which teachers maintain in their relations with students forces students to define the teachers as a negative role model. In the assessment of the child such a teacher is a person who not only is not to be believed or imitated, but one who actually provides cues to the child to perform in opposite ways. For this reason students who are given recommendations for a reading list, since the teacher has never assigned or permitted books dealing with sex and perhaps other areas the student is curious about, will be certain to avoid the books on that list.

Teachers are expected to introduce students to the value of reading, but many adults never read anything but books characterized by sensational sex. If teachers could teach students to appreciate books dealing with basic feelings about sex, as well as some sordid sides to everyday life which teachers avoid, then the likelihood of advancing the status of reading as an important activity would be increased.

EDUCATION AS SUBLIMATION. Psychiatric literature is replete with incidents of persons turning their sexual energy into culturally acceptable and even desirable activities. For many middle-class students, anxious about their sexuality, the academic arena provides a uniquely favorable environment. It is perfect grounds for sublimation since both parents and teachers, who seem to value sex least, value studying most. The school, of course, rewards such behavior and by doing so encourages the extension of sublimation.

THE ACCENTUATION OF THE GENERATION GAP. The school continues the job that the parents have started of separating the child from the adult. In the area of sex the student is put quite as much on his own as he is in the home. This helps to tie him even closer to the peer group as a source of influence. For many students the school, in its insistence on defining the student's goals and behavior for him, structures for him a power relationship. And the only power he may have rests in his ability to disrupt the activities of the school. The generation gap is a gap in values, and many of these values focus around the child's conception of his sexual role. If this cannot be accepted and dealt with honestly and openly by adults, then the adolescent conceives of few other strategies to bring him closer to the adult world. The adults, on the other side of the challenge, as the limited changes in the schools indicate, ignore the challenge almost exclusively.

These are some of the direct and indirect ways that the school influences the adaptation that children make to sex. In general the most condemning statement we can make about the school is that, despite its posture as an enlightening institution, it keeps children in the dark about sex. The consequences of this failure to assume a critical responsibility can be observed in the number of mistakes young people make in pursuing their sexual roles. To extend the condemnation further we can suggest that the school, in its desire to serve the social needs of America, reaffirms its partnership with the most conservative ideologies in the system. The far reaching effects of maintaining and promoting sexual inhibitions unfortunately carry over into the personal lives of the people the school presumes to help to grow to a more effective and affective maturity.

Sex Education Programs

There have been some successful experimental programs in sex education in the United States. Being as they are experimental programs, the resistance to them is not as serious as it might be were the school to announce a sex education program of its own. In January, 1965, an organization entitled the Sex Information and Education Council of the United States was formed. Since then the organization has actively sponsored talks and programs in schools and has made efforts to reach parents throughout the United States. Its intention is to develop honest and even blunt confrontations with students and teachers on the subject of sex problems and sex education. The organization has also evolved a clearing house function where literature on sex education programs and methods of teaching about sex are being stored.[39] The fact that the programs are being sponsored and promoted by a national group rather than a local district may account for the success and survival of its programs.

We have made reference twice to the advantage of introducing programs in such a way as to avoid the anxiety of school leaders over the evaluation of their participation in such problems. It is not a secret that school administrators are sensitive to the attitudes of the public and typically attempt, when they can, to avoid any confrontation with community leaders over controversial issues.

Although the treatment of specific facts about sexual behavior would advance the level of intelligence that students would use in their participation in sexual activities, the major treatment depends on creating the kind of educational experience that makes students both knowledgeable about and accepting of sexual interaction.

[39] Mary Calderone, "Planning for Sex Education," *NEA Journal* (January 1967): 26–28.

THE FUTURE ROLE OF THE SCHOOL
IN SEX EDUCATION

Schools are currently caught in the same dilemma that has always plagued them. They stand on the one hand as the guardian of public morality, and on the other they are expected to develop innovative structures to protect society from the evils that ravage it. Advancing one cause usually retards progress toward the other. Parents do expect teachers to take a serious responsibility in the area of developing and maintaining a moral code of behavior. But morality, in many instances, when translated from universal codes to norms which are highly particular to a society at one point in its social history, becomes no more than a process of regulating the *status quo*. Parents would be quite willing to raise the level of their children's comprehension about sexual life, if only this could be accomplished through avoiding any moral implications. And because this cannot be done, given all the special cultural meanings that any discussion of sex evokes, the role of the school becomes one of passivity and impotence.

Any progress, if it is to be made, must be couched in the most legitimate and intelligent framework and articulated to members of the community in this way. Parents must be made to understand that sexual problems are problems of ignorance of sexual facts as well as the consequence of unsatisfactory interpersonal relations. The success of any realistic sex education program depends in large measure on the ability of those responsible for such a program to communicate to and convince parents that the program is both sound and desirable. And this must be stated in terms of both cognitive and affective experiences. The cognitive experiences are those dealing with the many facts of sexual life. The affective experiences are those which make it psychologically and socially possible to relate in a positive manner to a sexual partner.

The success of any sex education program further depends on the personnel and the curriculum that are to be involved. We have to answer such questions as "who should teach it," "what should the training of such personnel be like," "what topics or content are to be considered" and "what are the best methods or experiences by which the content can be learned."

Who Should Teach Sex Education Programs?

Persons who are selected to become involved in a sex education program must be those who can dispel the image of the teacher as a virtuous moral guardian. Whether the program is to take the form of specific courses or is to be integrated into many courses that already exist, the first handicap of communication is the fact that adolescents in particular, as well as younger children, do not bestow their honest attention and belief upon those who teach them about social and ethical matters. What we have called the generation gap and what we have referred to as negative role models, peer socialization, and the image of the teacher, are all factors which need to be confronted as a first step in developing the kind of program we envisage. This requires the education, socialization, and humanizing of teachers. The product of this preparation must be a teacher who:

1. is honest, frank, and direct in his communication with students;
2. is willing and capable of opening himself to an exploration of his own concerns and anxieties;
3. is knowledgeable about the effects on personality of economic position, age, family organization, and a host of other social variables;
4. is able to understand peer group norms and can work within such a framework. That is, he needs to understand the definitions that peer groups make of sexual and social relationships and avoid an intergroup conflict by presenting expectations that are antithetical to those of the student's reference group;
5. is able to offer individual counseling when necessary, as well as being knowledgeable about referral agencies when some problems seem to require the assistance of outside personnel;
6. is familiar with the kinds of experts who can advance the task of sex education, and is knowledgable about the access routes to such experts;
7. is familiar with techniques of group dynamics and sensitivity training so that the learning group will not be retarded by their own inter-personal restraints and inhibitions;
8. is able to differentiate between morality and normative traditions, so that his own role should not be defined as protector of such traditions for their own sake; and
9. is able to teach about the function of moral principles in the larger social context so that rules or standards can be discussed independently of their "sacred" social connotations.

The teacher who possesses these qualities will be one who can dispel the images which have been built up over the years which would retard the success of even the best planned program of sex education.

What Should Be Taught?

The topics which should be taught in sex education programs are those which constitute the basic physiological components of sexual functioning, as well as those which are known to constitute the basis of sexual malfunctioning, or what we might call sexual deviance. The latter area is, of course, the most likely to cause problems since sexual feelings are associated with many feelings and sexual problems are not always problems to the persons involved. A distinction does need to be made between problems for the person and problems for the society. Both of these perspectives need to be discussed. Premarital pregnancy, for example, can be discussed in terms of the girl's suffering social rejection, her assuming an unwanted and often impossible responsibility, the effects of forced marriage, the retardation of her educational or career goals, the inhibition of her social life, and the effects upon the child of being raised without a father. From the second standpoint premarital pregnancy can be discussed in the context of the effects of widespread sexual permissiveness, from the perspective of the function of the family structure, and possibly from the point of view of the effect on families and the potential for marital stress should the mother wed.

While this example reveals some of the logical socio-psychological consequences of one form of sexual deviation in the present social context, the student may want to consider the possibility that, given other social structures, the same effects may not be forthcoming. Some societies, such as Sweden, have managed to absorb the dysfunctional affects of extended sexual permissiveness by creating, through their major institutions, a new set of structures. These new structures have caused a reduction in the amount of social rejection for sexual deviation, protecting persons through legalized sterilization and abortion and providing contraceptive devices for all females above the age of fifteen. Through special agencies the society ensures that all children born out of wedlock will be well received and cared for.[40]

Students should be taught about sexual problems, or if "problems" is deemed too loaded and too biased a word, then about departures from normative accepted sexual behavior. Such topics

---

[40] William E. Mann, "Sexual Standards and Trends in Sweden," *Journal of Sex Research* 3, No. 3 (1967): 191–200.

as premarital sex and extra-marital sex can be linked to a discussion of the traditional meaning and function of marriage. An objective assessment of the functional rather than the traditional conception of marriage will lead students away from inclinations to attack established institutions simply because they were conceived by others than themselves.

Homosexuality can be described, *in a non-normative sense,* as a variation on, rather than a deviation from, established sexual modes. It is useful, in bringing about understanding in children, to think about variations within a category such as sexual behavior rather than to consider one form of behavior as standard and all the rest as deviations. Like nymphomania, homosexuality can be conceptualized as a psychological state, that assumes invidious evaluative connotations only when superimposed upon a set of specific cultural meanings. Incest can be discussed in the same way, pointing students to a kind of cultural relativism that would remove the witch-hunt framework from one's assessment of such behavior.

Another useful topic area can be the love versus sex dichotomy under which such subemphases as pornography, commercialized sex, sexual unrealities, and expression of masculinity through sexual performance and conquest can be treated. Paralleling this focus the whole notion of inter-personal relations can be discussed in an attempt to explore the way in which unsatisfactory sexual life can be linked to our conceptions of interpersonal and particularly cross-sex, relationships.

Such topics as abortion, homosexuality and prostitution can be discussed within the framework of the desirability of legalization, and secondary school students can develop a set of debates or discussions to present each perspective.

How and When Shall Sex Education Be Taught?

Many of the controversial topics discussed in the preceding section cannot be made particularly meaningful to elementary school students, but secondary school students should be able to deal cognitively with such sensitive areas if the subjects are introduced in an intelligent and humane way. Sex education can begin, however, with a bowl of guppies on the first-grade windowsill. Children can be taught, as often they are, how baby animals are born, but the relevance of such instruction becomes insignificant without planned, developmental programs carrying into the later years. The main point that should be stressed and experience provided to make it meaningful is that birth is a natural human function. It is not one that is frightening or even dirty, but only becomes so if children are separated early from their human experiences.

In the early grades children can be exposed to the growth processes of nature. Children can be introduced to the fourth R, reproduction, and the organs which are functional to this process. Prenatal development can be treated at this time. In the later elementary years sex education should begin to take on a more meaningful, extra-school set of associations. The correct language of sexual life should be imparted and related to peer group colloquialisms.

The next stage can involve a useful separation of the sexes where problems unique to the sexual maturation of each sex can be discussed. At times the groups can be integrated and shown such films as Walt Disney's *The Story of Menstruation*. Males might be encouraged to ask questions about the unique sexual development of the opposite sex and vice versa. This approach can help to dispel the illusions, ignorance, and unreal perceptions that conspire to make members of the opposite sex threatening to each other.

During the high school years sexual discussion in mixed groups can begin to confront sensitive and controversial areas where again ignorance has provided so many students with the foundations of later sexual problems. Sexual desires can be treated as human feelings rather than the urgings of demonic tendencies which must be repressed because they are wrong and evil. If there is to be control of sexual inclinations, the functional reasons for such control should be outlined and discussed.

What has been suggested, in brief, is a comprehensive program, threading its way throughout the educational experience. Given the support of the community and the availability of personnel, the curriculum can be developed and executed. Its success however, depends on the strategies teachers use to make students open to the educational values inherent in such a program. This requires establishing a frame of mind on the part of students that will force them to extinguish tendencies evolved in family and peer groups to treat such a program in a suspicious, defensive manner.

If a sex education program is to be a meaningful educational experience, one that will ultimately help adolescents bridge the gap to adulthood, these adolescents need to be treated like adults— that is, trusted to develop in ways that are healthy and functional rather than suspiciously expected to develop in ways that will be disruptive to the system and consequently led by rules which communicate distrust.

One cannot, as Margaret Mead has recently pointed out, look to other societies for answers. Despite the progress that Sweden has made in transforming itself from a puritanical to an enlightened culture, Sweden has a population and a cultural tradition which are different from our own. Theirs is homogenous, ours is heterogeneous, and the task of transforming a diverse population into a cohesive one is most easily facilitated by establishing rigid rules and norms for all. This causes us certain problems which are unique to our society.[41] The task will not be easy and progress will be slow, but the schools, with their enormous influence and diversity of visual material, must begin the task. As Mead suggests:

I think we have no choice but to teach our basic knowledge about sex in the schools. This is the only situation in which we can be certain of reaching every child and adolescent. In this rapidly moving and uncertain world, the risks involved in ignorance are much too serious for the individual and for our society.[42]

[41] Margaret Mead, "What We Can Learn from Sex Education in Sweden," *Redbook* (October, 1968): 34.
[42] *Ibid.*, p. 166.

6

Problems
of Mental Illness

MENTAL ILLNESS is of interest to sociologists and should be of interest to educators, because this condition reflects something about the society. For educators in particular the types and extent of mental problems can reveal social conditions which affect the behavior of students. At the same time an analysis of this area helps to illuminate the contexts within which we teach and perhaps reveal some areas in which the school can work as an agency of intervention. If our analysis should reveal, for example, that many students are by their own conception alone and lonely and contemplate self-destructive acts as their only way of reducing their anguish, then educators have a clue to the kind of classroom environment which might alleviate such pressures.

There can be no certain estimates of the magnitude of the problem of mental illness because, if we use figures of persons hospitalized, we know something only about the availability of care facilities. We do not know how many persons walk the streets daily in a state of chronic anxiety or even episodic neurotic anxiety who either will not enter care centers or who cannot because of the lack of facilities. A number of surveys of the incidence of mental illness have revealed estimates of from 10 to 25 per cent of the population.[1]

When we speak of mental illness in this chapter we refer to a wide range of psychological difficulties, from mildly disabling neurotic states to clearly psychotic behavior. The latter can be assigned the status of insanity by legal agencies who rely on the expert opinions of consulting professionals, primarily psychiatrists. Emotional illness is often defined on the basis of the degree of disability the illness causes. When persons cannot function normally in their routine tasks of job and home, we say that they have emotional problems. We can further add that mental illness takes on a socially deviant character. Simply put, if persons cannot or choose not to perform their responsibilities in ways expected by society, they are often designated as social misfits. They are diagnosed by society at large as "sick." If persons withdraw entirely from their social responsibilities, we conclude that they rightly belong outside society's normal environment, in some kind of home or hospital.

If we admit that mental illness is defined normatively we will need constantly to shift our criteria as social norms expand and contract. In a depression, for example, when jobs are scarce for most people and unavailable for many, persons may exist in a state of unemployment for a long period of time. Such persons will not be defined as emotionally disturbed because the normal values toward work change to accommodate to the problems of the economic cycle. When work is plentiful, when an economy is booming, and persons decide not to work, they are described as maladjusted. As our particular society at this point in time moves toward an all-consuming other directedness, where every act is conceived in terms of the expectations of others, then individualism, once

---

[1] P. Horton and G. Leslie, *The Sociology of Social Problems* (New York: Appleton-Century-Crofts, 1965), p.545.

highly regarded, is defined as deviant. Persons who take this route are seen as out of touch with reality. In this sense many individuals who might have functioned normally in other contexts are perceived as having emotional difficulty.

In general then and for the purposes of this chapter, we will define mental illness as an internal condition which prevents persons from functioning more or less comfortably within normal social contexts. As we shift to a consideration of emotional problems of the young, we will consider mental illness to be a condition which hampers the growth or development of the child in cognitive as well as social areas. As we focus more precisely on educational growth, we will be talking of mental illness as an internal state which retards the educational development of the child as student.

CARE AND TREATMENT OF THE MENTALLY ILL

Because the concept of mental illness emerged out of a number of models of human pathology evolving through periods of growth in medical knowledge and theory, the province of the mentally ill has been traditionally associated with the medical speciality we call psychiatry. Our knowledge of the incidence as well as categories of mental illness, as these have been formally designated, come from the records of mental hospitals and psychiatric clinics. When people are mentally ill they go to some kind of a doctor, usually a medical doctor. Over one million go every year to hospitals and clinics[2] and many more go to private practitioners. The kind of care they receive varies according to a number of factors. Obviously quality of care is related to facilities available for such care. Overcrowding of hospitals and insufficient staffing resulting from inadequate support are imposing barriers to adequate care. Mental patients constitute more than 50 per cent of all hospital patients, but despite this imposing statistic, the average expenditure for the care of mental patients is almost one-tenth of the expenditure for the care of other kinds of patients.[3] Part of the rationale for this inequity resides in the assumption that although mental illness is a legitimate medical problem, the treatment of these patients can be handled by persons of less training than medical specialists. One of the characteristics of what we might think of as a poor care condition is the fact that the doctor-patient ratio is so

[2] L. Duhl and R. Leopold, "Mental Illness," in *Social Problems*, ed. H. Becker (New York: John Wiley & Sons, Inc., 1966).
[3] *New York Times*, 18 April 1954, p.10.

low that the care must often be left to untrained personnel.[4] Conditions have certainly improved since Deutsch wrote his revealing account of conditions in state mental hospitals, but the complaints of state hospital administrators and concerned citizens still resound.

The kind of medical care that is available for emotionally disturbed patients is further influenced by the patient's or his family's ability to provide expensive treatment. The average fee of psychiatrists is gradually moving above the thirty-dollar-per-hour rate. The cost of private mental hospitals is considerably more than the average citizen can afford. One important factor that extends the possibility of relief for persons who cannot afford individual treatment is the rapid increment in our knowledge about and use of the psychiatric drugs. The effects of such drugs have been indicated by the reduced numbers of persons who are institutionalized.[5] This does not necessarily suggest that the new drugs have affected any kind of permanent cure. It does appear to mean that such products as tranquilizers make it posible for persons to survive the tensions and pressures which previously had rendered them incapacitated.

The greatest hope for the treatment of the mentally ill is the changing attitude of the general public toward mental illness. This is reflected by the extensive network of child guidance centers that parents and schools support throughout the country. It is often easier to awaken an apathetic or even hostile community to the serious problems of our society by appealing to their concern for children rather than other adults. The great disparity in treatment facilities and attention according to a person's social and economic status as revealed by Hollingshead and others will probably decrease as part of the overall national effort to reduce the inequities in American social life.[6] Making the poor of America visible, as a phenomenon of the second half of the twentieth century, may have such an effect if a reaction against this conception of social justice does not retard our social progress. If equal care for the mentally disturbed (and in fact any care at all for large numbers of persons who would not have received it without the events of the past decade) is to emerge as a viable public policy, it is most likely to survive as a force dedicated to saving the man by saving the child. The school is likely to maintain and increase its association with agencies devoted to helping children and consequently ensure

---

4 Albert Deutsch, *The Shame of the States* (New York: Harcourt, Brace and World, Inc., 1948).
5 Horton and Leslie, *Sociology of Social Problems.*
6 A. B. Hollingshead and F. C. Redlich, *Social Class and Mental Illness* (New York: John Wiley and Sons, Inc., 1958).

greater support for mental health facilities than could emerge from the institutional associations of adults.

In many industrial areas the same remedial tendencies can be seen. One of the most certain ways of ensuring the initiation and support of altruistic programs, such as mental health plans, is to convince industry that there is a logical economic gain to be derived out of the support of rehabilitative programs for their disturbed workers. Many industrial organizations have already taken steps in this direction, a further symptom of a growing awareness of the need for increased care for the mentally ill.

CAUSES OF RESISTANCE

We have suggested that our concern with mental illness emerged out of an interest in the way in which social and cultural conditions produce individual problems. From another perspective we might suggest that the deplorable conditions surrounding the treatment as well as the lack of acceptance of the mentally ill has its roots in certain social circumstances. That is, social forces contribute to the emergence of mental illness in the same way they contribute to what is being done about the problem.

We can begin by suggesting some simplistic ideas, all of which explain in some degree part of the resistance of persons to acknowledging that psychological aberrations are illnesses and that society owes the mentally ill some kind of effort to alleviate their anguish and to seek preventative measures. First, there is the idea that we fear what we do not understand, and that we seek to reduce the fear by conjuring up the most convenient rationale to explain what it is that is making us fearful. In many primitive cultures mental illness is defined as a supernatural possession by some spirit which inhabits the body of an ill person. Many not-so-primitive societies have experienced variations on the same theme. The Salem witch trials, which sought to reveal the presence of the devil in the bodies of deranged men and women, demonstrated such a process.

Another less than supernatural but equally invalid approach was the view, supported by much religious doctrine, that mentally aberrant persons were basically evil and that their deviant acts revealed these basic predilections. At a time when persons were acutely sensitive to signs which would define them as destined to be saved for heaven or designated for hell, the mark of a good man was that he did not behave in any deviant manner.

A second notion which influenced the way persons defined

mental illness was the association persons made between mental illness and deviant acts. It is still difficult to convince a jury that a person should be treated with leniency because he is not responsible for his behavior. Although legally insanity can be considered a factor which mediates criminal punishment, the average person does not ordinarily separate the insane act from the actor. Crazy people do crazy things, and to avoid the effects of this behavior the person should be punished severely. The difficulty that supporters of the abolition of capital punishment have encountered reflects just such a view. Most persons take a very short view of techniques for protecting themselves from being potential victims of deviant acts. Therefore if mentally ill people are likely threats to one's own safety, persons believe they can best protect their safety by ignoring the rehabilitative possibilities and focusing on ways to keep such people out of contact with themselves and their families. In a very real sense the American parent, like his counterparts in most of Western civilization, protects his children and himself by refusing to consider policies of making visible what he would like to keep invisible. The more we can sweep the mentally ill under the carpet, the less we have to be concerned about threats to our stability.

A third reason for lack of interest in or acceptance of the mentally ill is tied up in the history of our conception of the human mind. The development of psychiatric knowledge has lagged far behind developments in other branches of medicine, primarily because of the nature of the mind itself. Unlike the brain, its physical dimension, the mind is not easily subjected to scientific measurement. Nor is it easily acknowledged that the mind should lie within the legitimate domain of medical inquiry. For many years the mind was felt to be the object of philosophical and religious inquiry, that it was more closely linked to the spirit than to the body. When Freud began turning his scientific training to the study of the mind, he met with strong resistance within his own body of colleagues. If professional scientists were unwilling to face up to the task of considering the mind and particularly its pathology a legitimate domain for attention, one can imagine the attitude of the average layman.

Finally we can turn to a brief consideration of the social nature of contemporary Western man. He is the man who almost categorically will avoid any involvement with the irregular aspects of social life. He does not wish to acknowledge, much less understand, the anguish in the world around him. This is why the poor have remained invisible, why involved social protesters are viewed as peculiar, and why murderers face the gas chamber. Modern man, faced with a complexity of social patterns, must reduce whatever phenomena he can to manageable, simple units. It is simpler to view the mentally ill as bad than as ill. It is simpler to treat ignorance as a convenient mode of adaptation rather than to confront the necessity of understanding a problem.

THE SOCIAL CONTEXT OF MENTAL ILLNESS

It is very difficult to speak of individual factors as accounting for emotional disorders. It is both easier and more meaningful to talk in terms of contexts or cultural strains, or themes, which can help explain the dynamics of mental stress. The individual experiences a condition such as a traumatic sexual experience, an authoritarian father, incarceration, or economic failure, which has meaning only within a social and cultural context. Sexual attack, for example, is bound to have less serious effects in a sexually permissive society than one that is highly puritanical. More importantly, the latter social context is more likely to produce such actions than the other. The value of understanding important cultural conditions is that we can then explain variations in rates of mental illness even though we cannot make special predictions about individual cases, or even explain these in individual terms. The topics which are discussed in the following pages are the socio-cultural forces, or contextual conditions, which influence psychological adaptations on a society-wide basis.

Cultural Disjuncture

Ruth Benedict[7] and Margaret Mead[8] have exposed differences between primitive and civilized child-rearing practices with specific references to the kinds of experiences which have helped primitive children evolve into maturity with a minimum amount of difficulty. This was logically counterposed against American techniques which have almost always guaranteed that youth would reach a disjunctive impasse between childhood and adulthood. This disjuncture occurs as a result of the failure of American parents to expose children to the kinds of experiences which reduce the anxiety associated with performing adult roles. We associate mental breaks with pressure

[7] Ruth Benedict, *Patterns of Culture* (Boston: Houghton Mifflin Company, 1934).
[8] Margaret Mead, *Coming of Age in Samoa* (New York: William Morrow & Co., Inc., 1928).

situations. Persons experience a great deal of tension when faced with such pressureful situations as job performance, sexual performance, and marital performance. The perceived pressure can be viewed in the context of role difficulty. It is not always that the task that produces the tension is so imposing. From this view the more relevant factor is that the person is not psychologically ready to perform the task at all.

In many modern societies the personality of the child, as developed through the mechanisms of cultural growth, does not meet with a continuous cultural experience. There occurs a discontinuity between early and late cultural conditioning which can be observed in the disparity between the roles of the child and those of the adult.

The child is sexless, the adult estimates his virility by his sexual activities; the child must be protected from the ugly facts of life, the adult must meet them without psychic catastrophe; the child must obey, the adult must command this obedience. These are all dogmas of our culture, dogmas which other cultures do not share. In spite of the physiological contrasts between child and adult, these are cultural accretions.[9]

Benedict talks about areas of development which are important to the maturing child, important in the sense of familiarizing the child with the phenomena that he will be required to face as an adult.

The Rate of Cultural Change

It is quite possible to describe radical departures in attitudes towards important social functions from the last generation to the present one. What this means essentially is that many of today's youth have rejected the socialization that was imposed upon them by their parents. If we look only at statements and behaviors, we might easily conclude the existence of such radical changes. These changes have occurred in such areas as sexual behavior, occupational goals and activities, political behavior, and ways of relating to others. But behavior in terms of a current code does not mean that the participants can fully accept the consequences of their behavior in the light of their earlier training. Nor does it mean that what they have to do can be done without tremendous anxiety produced out of the unfamiliarity of behaving in ways they cognitively recognize as necessary. Many student teachers today, for

9 Ruth Benedict, "Continuities and Discontinuities in Cultural Conditioning," in *Personality*, ed. C. Kluckhohn and H. Murray (New York: Alfred A. Knopf, Inc., (1955), p.523.

example, are compelled to ask for assignments in ghetto communities. They are asked to interact intimately, and they believe that it is right to do so, with others whom they do not know. And because many of today's youth believe that the time has come to give unselfishly to improve the human condition, they expose themselves to situations which often produce more anxiety than they can handle. Many of these student teachers, and often regularly assigned teachers, retreat from the task in anguish, acknowledging that they cannot handle what they have asked themselves to do. They were psychologically unprepared. The same is true with sexual behavior, with assuming an occupational role, with being a parent and a spouse. The cultural definitions of what one needs to do and be have not caught up with the psychological states required to perform the tasks. Today's woman, fully conscious of the contemporary conception of a woman as a functioning contributing human being, cannot reconcile the demands put upon her by children and husband to fulfill the role of mother and housewife in the light of all that women are currently expected to be. She cannot accept a passive or a submissive role in the marriage, and in forcing herself to forsake what she believes to be her necessary identity, she suffers the anguish and anxiety that accompany functioning in a role about which she is ambivalent. Other areas in which the speed of cultural change produces psychological difficulty occur frequently in the occupational world. The man who sees his task being assumed by a machine or threatened by automation suffers not only the insecurity of economic uncertainty but the anxiety of a loss of occupational identity. The man who is retired at a time when he still feels capable of performing a useful function is another case in point. With the disintegration of extended family ties and inexperienced at recreation, the retiree is set adrift in a world he does not want to inhabit.

Learning to cope in a society that moves too fast to condition its members to adequate coping mechanisms is a problem for everyone. For those who have to develop these coping mechanisms behind a strong internalized loyalty to the teachings of parents and clergy, the problem is critical. When mental illness occurs, it may be because the present cannot be accommodated to the self which has its roots in the past. More importantly, the mental illness may be a function of the inability of society, acting through its major agencies of socialization, to produce the kind of flexibility and confidence that is required to cope with a rapidly changing environment.

Another interesting feature of rapid cultural change is that, with the circulation of psychiatric attitudes and language, normal nervousness is quickly translated by the person experiencing the sensation into an anxiety attack. One is never quite certain whether or not the bulging hordes seeking entré to the psychiatrist's couch were not, in a sense, produced by the psychiatric profession itself. In this view of the increased incidence of neurotic symptoms we might argue that the supply of patients increases to meet the expanding availability of practitioners. Unfortunately the effects of the rapid introduction of a psychiatric conception of one's world has produced a greater supply of patients than the doctors can handle. Looking at minor mental illness in this way we can further argue that, independent of the specific ailments produced by specific social conditions, we have reached a point in social history where new definitions of old feelings have contributed to the awareness that many behaviors which were normal in the past are now "sick." This point will be elaborated further in the discussion of the diagnosis of student problems.

Pressures in the System

Persons have always occupied social roles, and to the extent that these roles were incompatible with their conception of self, stress would follow. Incompatibility is not only a matter of conflict between two sets of expectations. It may also be a matter of role overload. This describes a situation where persons are expected to perform in their several role capacities or even within a single role more than they believe they are able. When the expectations are seen as excessive, or when the expectations are incongruent with what a person feels he wants to or should do, a condition of pressure results. The counterpart psychological condition is tension and in more serious cases is neurotic anxiety or perhaps phychotic episodes. Pressure then is the condition resulting from the interaction of the environment and the personality. It should not be considered, however, that pressure is purely a function of a person's perception. We know that there are structural pressures, pressures inherent in the patterns of specific social conditions. We know that regardless of the sample of persons we choose to look at there will be a greater number of psychotic incidents among a group of men engaged in war action than a group of men who sell insurance, for example.

We can report evidence that greater rates of mental illness are discovered in specific ecological areas and social positions than other areas and positions. We further have evidence that men are treated for mental disorders more frequently than women. Unless we wish to argue exclusively on the basis that men are intrinsically less stable emotionally than women, and that this is physiologically based, we would have to accept the probability that the kinds of roles men perform are generally more stressful than the roles of women. There are structural pressures in occupations, as there are in ecological living areas and in positions in the social structure. Studies have shown that men are more likely to be committed to mental hospitals than women, single persons are more likely to be committed than married persons, urban persons more often than rural persons. Commitments decrease as one moves further away from the center of the city, and commitments are higher among Negroes and foreign born than among whites and native born.[10]

We mentioned earlier that the rates of commitment differ for persons of differing social positions, and we can represent our structural argument through a consideration of this phenomenon. Very simply, in a society founded on economic principles, where the typical mode of aspiration is toward possessions, the greatest pressure is on those who are unfavorably located in the economic order to compete for these rewards. The pressures to succeed are realistically greater since the opportunities are less for persons of little skill and education. This is not to suggest that persons with one million dollars do not feel intense pressure to attain two million dollars. Many do. The point is that the pressures for the disadvantaged are linked to the conditions in the economic order. The pressures for the millionaire are almost entirely internal.

Poverty itself, as a disenfranchised position in the system, contains many of the ingredients which push people into escape channels, such as insanity, which they never wish to use.

Poverty does not appear to bear a particular relationship to suicide, although it may to other kinds of emotional strain. The

[10] Horton and Leslie, *Sociology of Social Problems*, pp.548–549.

Table 6-1

Suicide Rates*

Country	Suicide Rate per 100,000 population	Year
Japan	25.3	1955
West Germany	19.3	1955
United States	10.2	1955
Ireland	2.3	1955
Mexico	1.3	1955
Egypt	0.1	1954

* Only a few of the thirty-seven countries in the original list are presented to illustrate differences between industrial and non-industrial societies.
Source: United Nations, *Demographic Yearbook*, 1957.

poorest state in the Union, in terms of industrial activity, Mississippi, has a considerably lower suicide rate than California, which
has experienced enormous industrial growth.[11] The same pattern
can be observed for suicide rate differences between highly industrialized and non-industrialized nations.

Economic striving, and the cyclical frustrations inherent in
most mobility patterns appear to be more closely related to mental
anguish than the sheer fact of poverty itself. Persons can become
accustomed to almost any static condition, including poverty, even
if they do not like it; but one does not become accustomed to a
process of economic competition with its normal ups and downs so
readily. Patterns further reveal that periods of economic disruptions, particularly the early years of the depression, witness accelera-
tion in suicide rates.[12]

Suicide as a symptom of mental illness is particularly relevant
to our problem of student disorders because we later in this chapter
devote a special section to the consideration of student suicide. The
sociological principle, suggested in the early writing of Émile Durkheim, is that pressures in the system are felt differentially by persons in different social arrangements.[13] His point was that some
persons are more able to absorb stress than others, depending on
their affiliations. Catholics, for example, because of their association
with the church and because of the cohesive nature of their family
life, have greater supports against the disabling quality of much
social pressure. The same argument can be advanced for married
persons as against single persons. It may be that increased rates of
neurosis in Americans, as this relates to family disorganization, is
not so much a function of the trauma of dislocation as it is of the
loss of supports against the imposing pressures of normal social
functioning.

The Social Organization of Introspection

When middle-class mothers decide to breast-feed their young
instead of bottle-feeding them, it is usually because they have
learned or have come to believe that it is important to give the
child a sense of warmth, to communicate to the child in the most
intimate way that he is loved. Neo-Freudian principles have had
their impact on the interpersonal behavior of persons who are
sensitive to and consequently influenced by intellectual ideas. Liter-

---

[11] J. Gibbs, "Suicide," in *Contemporary Social Problems*, ed. R. K. Merton
and R. Nisbet (New York: Harcourt, Brace and World, Inc., 1961), p. 239.
[12] *Ibid.*, p.249–250.
[13] Émile Durkheim, *Suicide: A Study in Sociology* (New York: The Free
Press, 1951).

ature and the mass media have had a strong impact on a society which has time, interest, and access to vehicles of entertainment and instruction. The prominent American fiction of the nineteenth century was adventure literature. Mark Twain, Jack London, Robert Louis Stevenson and Bret Harte were representative. Novels were produced in which people did things, rather than sit around and introspect about who they were. Even as late as the nineteen-twenties the most popular books were about people in action with their environment. Horatio Alger stories were still popular and Ernest Hemingway and Scott Fitzgerald delighted reading audiences with stories about war and far-away living. Fitzgerald in particular captured his readers by delineating the life styles of persons with whom few could identify. Although Hemingway and Fitzgerald were producing social commentary, of a nature which was later intensified by the writers of the thirties of whom John Steinbeck was the most representative, there was still not a compelling focus upon motives. Readers did not ask why persons behaved in certain ways. They were led to the conclusion that given the times and circumstances in which they lived, there was really no alternative.

John Osborne's play, *Look Back in Anger* (1957) had a great success on the American stage. His characters talked about the end of battles to fight, the end of adventures to have. This signified the beginning of a time to turn inward, to think about oneself, one's motives, the direction through which one could become fulfilled. Such ideas as fulfillment, actualization, and self-realization became popular.

In the sixties a variety of Eastern philosophies stressing introspection began to attract the attention of college youth.

As guidance functions increase in the schools, students are frequently asked by both counselors and teachers to think about themselves, who they are, what they want to do in life. And they are often led down the garden path of introspection to a style of self-orientation which eventually leads many to seek the kinds of experiences, such as wildcat experimentation with psychedelics, which they believe will help them to penetrate more deeply into the mysteries they are committed to uncover in themselves. This is being said descriptively, not evaluatively. We should not conclude that because introspection, of necessity, brings a great deal of concern, strain, and confusion with it it is an undesirable activity. We have simply suggested that society has evolved a different kind of cognitive orientation than was characteristic of most periods of the past and out of which a number of structures have evolved to accommodate this phenomenon. All clinical functions, which could be stretched to include even such expressive activities as art, music, and dancing, conspire to ensure that this adaptive cognitive mode will be perpetuated. The kinds of problems inherent in this direction can be represented by the following story.

A teacher decided, influenced by a course in educational psychology, to get at student problems through the use of art. She had the students paint for her a picture to represent anything they wished. When they were finished, she collected all the paintings and took them home that night to analyze them. One painting, done by a very small boy, was painted all in black. The people were black, the streets were black, the houses and trees were black. This she immediately took to be an indication of some problem of adjustment. The following day she called the boy to the front of the class and spoke privately with him. She asked him about his family, his feelings about the other students, and his feelings about school. Then she finally asked him about the painting. "Why did you feel you wanted to make everything black?"

"It was the only color I had in my paintbox."

The point is that we have reached a time in social history, given the influence of Freud and his disciples, when even our most simple definitions and conceptions of others are structured by this influence. The one color in the paintbox is surely a more obvious answer than it is a symptom of pathology. But the major institutions have all been infused with psychiatric notions out of which routines are built. The assumption is, then, that the more we think about psychological pathology, the more likely we are to perceive it in ourselves and others.

Bureaucratization

The age of Reisman's other-directed man is the age of bureaucratization. Reisman's conception of the social mechanism which maintained an other-directed or bureaucratic orientation to life was anxiety. The inner-directed man of the past who took his cues for behavior from an internalized set of beliefs instilled permanently upon a fixed ego is becoming obsolescent in a period of flexible and shifting social norms. The dominant cue of our time is the expectations of others, and bureaucratic man has his antennas alerted perpetually for signals about how to behave. If he does not behave in the way expected of him, anxiety arises so that in order to reduce the tension he shifts to a more conforming mode.[14]

Because anxiety is the dominant mechanism of social control,

14 David Reisman, *The Lonely Crowd* (New Haven: Yale University Press, 1950).

bureaucratic man lives in a constant state of anxiety. More than ever before in history man works for others, in a context where pleasing others is his principal means of mobility in the organization. Rather than conceiving of pleasing others as making others happy, it is more accurate to think of a process of avoiding offending others. This kind of offense is reflected in any kind of aberrant or deviant behavior. Nonconformity occurs more often as a process of not picking up the correct cues for behavior than from wilful violation of the norms. The latter behavior usually characterizes either a person whose ego is so strong that he feels he can absorb the disapproval occurring as a result of violating norms, or a person with psychopathic tendencies, a person in whom social controls are not internalized. In the process of always inspecting oneself in relation to the expectations of others, considerable inner tension arises. Neurotics who are constantly afraid of being rejected are often those who have lost the capacity to pick up cues easily or who cannot handle what they perceive to be conflicting expectations.

Bureaucratic man lives in a climate of conflicting expectations, and whereas most conflicts can be resolved on the strength of the situation or the weighing of expectations, many cannot. The demands of home, family, friends, voluntary associations, public service, and church are often incompatible. Bureaucratic man plays many roles both within a single institution like the family where he is a father, husband, and the economic mainstay, and within several other institutions. If he is constantly pushing himself to accommodate the needs of all persons in his role configuration, the pressures become intense.

In his work role man is caricatured (although the exaggeration in individual cases is not always correct) as either consumed by ulcers or driven to the cocktail lounge as the only means of getting through the day.[15] The organization man is the dominant occupational type in contemporary society, and this mode is likely to incorporate even more people as the small business as an occupational form disappears into economic history.

The Impersonal Role Model

American society is characterized by being vastly susceptible to the propaganda inherent in its media of entertainment and advertising. The Madison Avenue view is that the American people will believe anything they are asked to believe if they are presented with the appropriate visual and cognitive cues. The average husband

[15] W. A. White, *The Organization Man* (New York: Simon and Schuster, Inc., 1956).

is bombarded, for example, by a number of images of housewives greeting them at the end of a work day, bright, sparkling, and beautiful. All that is necessary is that they bathe in the right bubblebath and a metamorphosis is ensured. In the face of this expectation the average male comes home from a stressful day at the office and is immediately confronted by a wife who shows the wear and tear of her own stressful day. He is then brought into that domestic world, and his tensions multiply. Movies and television have oriented us to the belief that life can be beautiful, usually in highly unrealistic ways, so that we are often groping for ways of making it so which are destined to failure. The reorganization of the family in industrial urban life has had the effect of so diffusing identity models that these are sought from the larger society, often from the images sent forth from the entertainment industry. What a man should be and how he should relate to a woman is diagrammed much more convincingly by John Wayne types or athletic hero types than by fathers. Neurotic anxieties are the logical consequence of a failure to be able to imitate the culture hero. Mental illness in general can often be the consequence of experiencing constant failures in attempting to attain the image of an ideal husband, wife, mother, lover, or worker.

THE EMOTIONALLY DISTURBED STUDENT

For many years the only way in which emotional problems came to the attention of educators was through the behavioral deviance of the child himself. The principle of looking for or anticipating such behaviors through understanding the contexts in which emotional problems develop is a recent innovation. Educators do understand something about the effects of family disorganization and poverty, but many well-to-do families with apparently good relationships experience the same psychological disorders as others. The context within which these problems grow and ultimately strike in the form of a breakdown or a suicide attempt are vastly more complex than we yet understand. The discussion which follows will attempt to describe several symptoms of emotional disorders and analyze the possible sources from which they are produced.

Physiological Symptoms

One day's observation in an average classroom will reveal a host of physical acts which can be suggestive of underlying emotional disturbance. Some of these are excessive nervous motions such as head scratching, foot tapping, pencil biting, and the like. Other forms are symptoms of withdrawal such as sleeping or drows-ing, or hiding motions such as crouching behind others or slouching in the seat. More blatant acts are aggressive behavior, such as pushing or hitting, crying, or taking frequent trips to the bathroom. It should be noted immediately that all of these behaviors can have perfectly normal explanations: a dull class, lack of sleep, a physical ailment, or having drunk excessive liquids the previous day. If such behavior remains constant and patterned through time, however, it should provide important diagnostic data and bear exploration.

The way in which mental problems emerge from physiological conditions can be illustrated by obesity. Obesity *can* be purely a physiological development consistent with gene structure and influenced by hereditary factors; but if such factors are not evident, the possibility of obesity's being a neurotic adaptation to life circumstances has to be considered. This, like other unsatisfactory physiological adaptations, can be considered within the framework of a social problems approach. A special program entitled "The Overweight American" was recently produced on national television. We are all familiar with the legion of techniques, from planned diets to body slimming salons, which have economically capitalized on this phenomenon. The current rage is jogging, and people of all ages can be observed trotting around the parks and city streets. What are some of the social forces which have contributed to this adaptation by millions of Americans? Let us pursue a consideration of obesity as an example of physiological symptoms of psychological conditions produced in a social context.

First of all we can suggest that being overweight does not need to be a problem, and many persons live happily in this condition. But they are the ones who have not bought the values of the beauty culture. Americans are by any standard obsessed with beauty. This is not true of all cultures. Latin cultures, as well as many Pacific Island cultures, have few emotional "hang-ups" in connection with obesity. But we do, and consequently children who are fat receive many taunts and expressions of disapproval. And contrary to some myths about the happy fat man, there is evidence that corpulent children are unhappy and have many adjustment problems. "Timid and retiring, clumsy and slow, they are not capable of holding a secure place among other children."[16]

Interestingly enough, overweight can be attributed to both

[16] Hilda Bruch, "Obesity in Childhood and Personality Development," *American Journal of Orthopsychiatry* 11 (1941): 467–74.

abundance and poverty. The average American can afford any kind of food he wants, and children who make demands that their affluent parents do not wish to ignore, perhaps because it is too difficult, will request foods that taste good. This often means special sauces or rich desserts. At the same time the poor American who must budget his money buys foods which are filling and inexpensive. These are usually the starch-based foods. The problem for some ethnic groups, such as Italian-Americans and Mexican-Americans, is that they are loyal to their food traditions in a culture which disparages the effects of eating such fattening food.

Another social force which can account for overweight is the large number of sedentary jobs which characterize a bureaucratic economic organization. A third is the explosion of the restaurant culture and the dinner party culture. Affluence has made it possible to eat out on more than special occasions, and the dinner party round has become a prominent social mode in suburban America.

With children the dynamics are somewhat different. Most of us are familiar with the association that many mothers draw between eating and love. The prototype is, of course, the Jewish mother. But in the sense that middle-class parents in general treat love, rather than external manipulation such as punishment, as the binding force of their relationship with their children, the emphasis on eating to give and receive love in return can be a variation on the same theme.

More than intake of calories, the problems of obesity in children can be associated with the decreasing rates of calorie output. For this no single factor can be blamed more than television. The streets of suburbia on a Saturday morning, unlike the streets of urban areas and those of suburbia formerly, are usually desolate. The children are hunched before the tube absorbing all the special programs designed to sell toys and cereal to Mom through the pleadings of the children. The schools cannot possibly compensate for the decreased calorie output in the at-home activities.

As a symptom of emotional disorder obesity can and usually does reflect a state of unresolved conflict in the child. Spock makes the basic point that unhappiness in children produces the need to overeat and consequently leads to obesity.[17] The social forces which contribute to unhappiness in children need to be evaluated from this perspective. We can only generally suggest that problems of children are as closely associated with the development of social competence as are the problems of adults. If a child can understand

17 B. Spock, "Problems of the School Child as Encountered by the Pediatrician," *American Journal of Orthopsychiatry* 11 (1941): 434.

and accept the cues provided for him by persons in his significant reference units, such as the home, the school and the peer group, his adaptation is not likely to take the form of psycho-physiological irregularities.

Pressure and Emotional Stress in Youth

Emotional problems of youth are not necessarily on the increase. They are simply increasingly being diagnosed. Administrators, counselors, and teachers are more acutely attuned to the presence of mental disturbances than ever before. Based on this kind of assessment, Bower concluded that over 40 per cent of school-attending youth had mental problems and poor emotional adjustment.[18] Even if we grant that the most inclusive criteria are being used in such designations of maladjustment, the problem of personality adjustment of youth is imposing.

The consensus among authors who are concerned with the emotional problems of today's youth is that young people are being subjected to more pressure than they can integrate into their lives. Parents, particularly middle-class parents, exert extensive, unnecessary pressure on the child, keeping him on the move, and constantly trying to get him to achieve standards which are too high, not permitting him to relax and absorb his experiences.[19] The struggle of the middle class to maintain or even increase status, perhaps to validate it through the successes of the children, is paralleled and perhaps exaggerated in the working class where the channels for mobility provide more limited access. The struggle and sacrifice that accompany sending a child to college is, for the working-class person, a justification for putting the pressure on the child and keeping it on.

Pressure does not emanate exclusively from the home. The school as an agency of the public organizes its facilities in such a way as to expect and coerce students to achieve commensurate with the expectations of the parents.

When the combined pressure of the home and school cannot be absorbed into the daily routines of the child, the result may be a series of disastrous failures. These are not so much failures of ability as they are failures of the psyche to maintain stable patterns in the face of intense pressures to achieve.

Breakdowns in functioning capacity may be directly linked to the context in which the expectations are being applied. Many stu-

[18] Eli M. Bower, *Early Identification of Emotionally Disturbed Children in School* (Chicago: Charles C. Thomas, Publisher, 1960).
[19] G. Goldenson, "Who's Pressuring Johnny?," *PTA Magazine* 60 (1960).

dents undergo academic failure because they are not happy or comfortable in the context in which they are asked to work. Schools,
like people, do have personalities, and the comixture of incongruent personality styles can lead to the kind of emotional disorders
that plague hosts of children as well as college students. Nasatir's
position, that academic failure is as much a function of the context
of study as it is the ability of students, is an important conception
of the problem.[20] The fact that American schools for the most
part are homogeneous in approach and style suggests that if that
context fails, few others are available to alleviate the stress situation.

Adolescent and College Suicide

One of the most serious ways in which children communicate
their distress that too much is being demanded from them is the
suicide or the suicide attempt. By considering this symptom we
should be able to shed light upon some of the sources and manifestations of pressure.

From our perspective suicide is not in itself a serious social
problem. It is, of course, serious for the persons and their families,
but the incidence of suicide among young people is not so excessive
as to provoke a major exploration of the phenomenon itself. However if suicide is conceived of as an end point in a continuum of
distress, our consideration of it may illuminate the factors associated
with it and thus shed light upon less critical adaptations that are
eminently worth our consideration.

In the United States approximately thirty boys and girls under
the ages of ten take their lives each year; between ages ten and
fourteen the figure is fifty. In the fifteen to nineteen age group the
figure rises to close to 300, and in colleges and universities one
study has set the figure as thirteen for every one hundred thousand
students. These figures do not include "hidden suicides." New
York health officials have estimated that about 10 per cent of all
fatal car accidents and 15 per cent of home accidents, such as those
involving poison, can be attributed to successful suicide attempts.[21]

Most suicide attempts are expressions of a severe depression,
which in turn is considered to be a turning of anger inward toward oneself, the person being unable to handle the more appropriate manifestations of the anger. Sometimes the attempt is considered

---

[20] D. Nasatir, "The Social Context of Academic Failure," in *Social Foundations of Educational Guidance*, ed. C. Weinberg (New York: The Free Press,
1968).
[21] M. Clark, "Children in the Dark," *PTA Magazine* 55 (1961): 10–13.

to be a spiteful attempt to punish parents for having angered the child.[22]

Research on adolescent suicides has been increasing in the past decade. Some findings of studies conducted at the Los Angeles Suicide Center are helping to break down the myths about suicide that have evolved in the absence of serious inquiry. A sample of these findings are:

1. Children who threaten to take their lives are more likely to do so than those who do not.
2. Suicide is not a function of insanity. An analysis of 3,000 suicides of all ages indicates that the majority were emotionally disturbed but not insane.
3. Suicide does not happen suddenly, without warning. Most potential suicides have a pattern of warners which sensitive observers can perceive.
4. The tendency to commit suicide is not inherited.[23]

Depression appears to be a consuming characteristic of the young. They are angry about their lives and they find it increasingly difficult to handle this anger through normal sublimative techniques. The depression itself is seldom related to a particular history of academic achievement, according to studies conducted by the Cambridge Samaritans, a society concerned about the welfare of Cambridge University students. The major cause for despair in incidents reported to the society was loneliness rather than academic difficulties.[24] The suicides and suicide attempts at Cambridge and Oxford have raised for English educators the question of whether or not the academic environment can afford to be ignorant of techniques to improve social relationships.

Loneliness and isolation may be more positively associated with good scholarship than bad, since it is the allegiance to academic commitments, often in a competitive sense, that cuts the student off from his peers. The serious question raised by this possibility is: How can educators focus more attention on the personal problems of good students when it is precisely those students who, because they do not disrupt the class, go unnoticed?

The view that suicides are highly related to feelings of loneliness and isolation is consonant with the early view propounded by Durkheim who suggested that social cohesion would mediate the

[22] "Child Suicide Attempts," *Science Newsletter*, May 20, 1961.
[23] Clark, "Children in the Dark."
[24] E. Maycock, "Depression, Despair and Suicide," *New York Times Ed. Supp.* 2647:47 (Fall, 1966).

effects of frustration.[25] On the other hand an undesirable cohesion, for example, one in which children are absorbed almost wholly by dependent parents wishing to extend their own dependence to the children, can lead to suicidal attempts as a gesture of flight. Suicide in this sense is seen as a cry for freedom.[26] These two views suggest the necessity of considering the kinds of educational experiences which can be both supportive in an interpersonal sense and permit a degree of independence and autonomy at the same time. Some suggestions along this line will be offered in the concluding section of this chapter on the role of the school.

College suicides also appear to be as associated with pressure as do suicides at other ages. In Japan the suicide rate seems to go up with the taking of examinations, a period when the pressure is felt most sharply.[27] The suicide rates at Cambridge and Oxford are several times that of institutions where the competitive pressures are less acute.[28] In the total educational community college suicide rates appear to outweigh those at other education levels. We can make the argument that the age group is more prone to suicide, but that is not as convincing as is the idea of the effects of academic competition on the college campus. Philip Wendell, editor of *Moderator* magazine, foresees, basing his predictions on his investigation of the causes of college suicides, that college suicides will rise above the 1,000 per year mark, with suicide attempts rising to 9,000 per year. His further assessment, which is consonant with our more general concerns, is that over 10 per cent of America's 6½ million college students in 1965 had emotional problems sufficient to warrant professional help.[29]

What are the principal sources of stress in college life? The first period of difficulty for many students is the period of entrance when the student must develop for himself a set of independent routines. It is usually his first away-from-home living arrangement and his first major competitive effort. Although in retrospect many students may argue that high school work was harder, the actual academic challenge for these students was probably considerably less. A second source of stress, once the first critical academic tests have been passed, may be to define for himself a collegiate role

25 Durkheim, *Suicide.*
26 M. Clark, "Suicide in Childhood and Adolescence," *NEA Journal* 53 (November 1964): 32–33.
27 "Examination Hell: Japan's Student Suicides," *New York Times Ed. Supp* 2475:533 (October 26, 1962).
28 "Student Suicides Cause Concern in England," *Science Newsletter,* March 21 1959.
29 P. Wendell, "Suicide and Student Stress," *Moderator* 5 (October 1966): 8–15

and to establish associations in which this role can be played. If he wishes to choose the role of an independent scholar, he must be able to pay the price in loneliness. If he wants a more typically collegiate role, he must face up to making social contacts and striving to be accepted by other collegiate types. A third source of stress comes if a student is forced to face up to his occupational identity. The real crisis may come when he decides that he does not wish to pursue the career that he has chosen. The sacrifice in time and money that went before, the difficulties of deciding on something more appropriate, and the problems associated with confronting anger toward parents as well as facing parental disapproval of a possible career change are inherent. A fourth source of stress is academic expectations in areas or even courses where the relevance of the subject matter is unclear and often unrelated to individual needs or interests. A fifth source of stress is coming to grips with the impersonality of the bureaucratic monolith that many an American university now is. When we add to this list the innumerable stress situations produced by unclear expectations for academic performance and the overloads associated with additional responsibilities, such as outside work and/or the family, the case for pressure is convincing.

THE SCHOOL'S CONTRIBUTION TO EMOTIONAL DISORDERS

We have already suggested that the school plays a significant role in producing the stress situations which affect the mental health of students. It would be useful to examine in more detail the precise way that the school performs this disorganizing role.

Competition

One of the principal ways the school produces disruptive consequences for children is through its techniques for motivating students. One such prominent technique is competition. Students are constantly being comparatively graded for all performance. They are also asked to compete for honors, for favorable positions in the class, for teacher approval, and for places in esteemed activities such as teams, bands, newspaper or yearbook, drama groups, and student government.[30] The rationale for such activities, although a rationale is never required, is that society at large is organized

---

[30] See C. Weinberg, "The Price of Competition," *Teachers' College Record* (November 1965).

on just such a model. Therefore students are being sensitized to the adaptive modes which are most conducive of normal social functioning. In this capacity the school performs as a completely passive agent of social and cultural change. To argue that the school should take an innovative role which may in the long run influence normative patterns on a society-wide basis would be to ask the school to perform in ways that would be radical departures from its tradition.

The effects of a social world of competition are, of course, that there are more losers than winners. To counter with the slogan that winning is not important but how one plays the game, or some such strategy for rationalizing failure, is to perpetuate a set of meaningless myths. They are meaningless in the sense that while persons may articulate such slogans, the slogans do not appreciably affect the adjustment people make to failure. We can further extend the argument to suggest that even the winners are losers. They lose insofar as they suffer considerable stress in the winning, and also because in later periods, such as college life where the stress is considerably greater, they must accommodate themselves to a society of winners. The loneliness and isolation that can follow from a pattern of competitive academic pursuits is a major ingredient in the stress associated with suicidal attempts and, more generally, emotional disorders at the college level.

Standards

Another area in which schools impose structures which are dysfunctional to many students is in the area of standards. If we view the drop-out or the academic failure as a person who does not meet the minimum standards of performance, then any raising of such standards predictably increases the ranks of those who turn to other standards to satisfy their ego needs which are so devastatingly mutilated in the academic arena. In order to protect their self-esteem, many students who cannot meet the standards of the academic area turn to deviant patterns which they then rationalize as a competitive mode to that of academic success. In this way the patterns of what are viewed as neurotic adaptations are socially produced. If our concern is with keeping most students within the ranks of normative adapters, it would seem that the standards should be flexible enough to define more performances as acceptable. This would require a multidimensional conception of standards rather than the unidimensional one which currently characterizes academic expectations. There are many cases in which deviant behavior is a socialized mode, when students are raised in an environment and within a family which pays no allegiance to the values of the Protestant ethic. But in many other cases deviance is an unfamiliar and in many ways painful mode for those who have to reject their family socialization in order to take on the social habits which are antithetical to those values. This does occur with students who have been taught to value the traditional modes but fail in their efforts to succeed in terms of them. Middle-class delinquency is not a comfortable posture for the participants; it is rather the only adaptation they can make given the inflexibility of the standards imposed against their inability to meet them.

To most students meeting standards means achieving status within the system which conceives the status positions. This is not so much a matter of competition as it is of demonstrating minimal abilities. When students cannot meet the minimal levels of status in the society that is important to them, the esteem of their peers eludes them. This kind of failure produces the kind of depression that is associated with irrational and often desperate behaviors. The school needs to conceive of status systems that are likely to offer a wide range of success channels to students with different levels of ability and different kinds of skills.

Control Patterns

A third way that the school serves to frustrate and disorganize some students is through its reliance on a punitive model for control. Students are forced to function always in the shadow of punishment and restrain themselves from acting spontaneously for fear of invoking these punitive sanctions. This kind of repressive environment acts on students in the same way that a police state would act upon citizens. There is almost always the assumption on the part of educators that if the punishment system were removed, students would act in ways that would totally disorganize the system. This kind of environment leads inevitably to the conception of the school as a repressive and hostile institution which does little to reduce the anxiety that young people experience in much of their institutional life.

Affective Experiences

A fourth way that the school serves to perpetuate disorganizing conditions is through its failure to institutionalize affective experiences. The educational mode is typically one which encourages the absence of affect. Feelings, which can be as important to learning as they are to mental health, are restrained to such an extent that temporary aberrations, be they expressions of anger or delight, are treated as deviant acts.

The human condition is one of feeling as well as cognition.

For reasons that are tied to the need for control, the application of techniques to bring feelings to bear on cognitive material is considered unrealistic, if not potentially destructive to the academic process. This policy too, like some others which have been discussed, is adopted from the routines of bureaucratic life. The consequences of the repression of feelings may be ulcers for bureaucrats. For children the consequence may be observed in a number of neurotic acts. For those children whose self-control mechanisms will not even permit minor outbursts of affect, the consequences may be even more serious later in their academic careers.

Conformity

A fifth contribution which the school makes toward the production of psychological disorders is its reliance on a conformity rather than an individualistic model in the routinization of its activities. In this way the school joins other social institutions in helping to convince students that the best way to survive in a complex and sometimes confusing world is to do what everyone else is doing. The problem with this manner of conducting institutional affairs is that although it preserves the system in a state of equilibrium, it helps to bury for individual members a number of individualistic inclinations which may emerge to haunt them in other ways another day. The conformist model also contributes to the development of an elaborate anxiety network which overruns its normal boundaries when conformity is difficult or when the expectations are unclear. It is for this reason that students who have not been socialized to middle-class values find it very difficult to survive in an environment which rewards compliance to these values and expectations. It may also be why the rates of foreign student suicides on college campuses are appreciably greater than the rate among American students. Conformity and routinization of tasks are obviously deterrents to creative and independent activity. Students who repress their inclinations to be creative, those who are most sensitive to begin with, are the most likely candidates for psychological disorders. The whole concept of individualized instruction as it presently exists in educational systems is recognized as a farce by the entire educational community. It is practically impossible to develop a system of individualized instruction within the framework of the kind of conformity model that has been described.

A counterpart to conformity and routinization processes is the time-consuming nature of the child's schedule. Between the school and the home the child does not want for activities. The problem is that the child never has much to say about the way his day is scheduled. In a society where time is money and where few people have the capacity to entertain themselves, the school prepares the child to submit to an overscheduled life, where free time (and ultimately leisure time, for the adult) must be filled from external sources. Many persons undergo their periods of most serious stress when they are not busy. The creative use of leisure time has not yet become a compelling issue for educators. The school in this way does its part in conditioning in children a need to be scheduled. The future of labor appears to be heading toward shorter work weeks and earlier retirement ages. The despair and depression that so many workers undergo when they are forced to retire is understandable in the light of their past histories of highly scheduled routines. We have often heard persons in different circumstances remark that they go crazy when they have nothing to do. The dynamics of boredom make the remark more literal than is usually intended. The inability of educational systems to develop self-initiated activities on the part of students is a failure to prepare students for circumstances in which self-initiated and creative activities can be a potent force in the battle against mental breakdowns.

Divide and Weaken

Another major way that the school has failed in the past and is failing in the present is in helping students develop strengths which would serve to dissipate the debilitating effects of pressureful experiences. That is, the school might recognize its own defeating power and give students psychological exercises to help them bear up under the strain. The school provides the pressure but does little to help students emotionally cope with it. Rather than take preventive measures and institutionalize activities to build emotional strength, the school, in its latest strategy to play a role in the amelioration of emotional problems, takes a rehabilitative posture. The direction of the school's commitment in this area is easily inferred from the fact that it initiates counseling services on an extensive basis at grade levels (junior and senior high) where problems are beginning to appear, and almost totally ignores the guidance function in the elementary grades where the strengths to deal with the pressures to come can most fruitfully be developed.

Very early in the child's educational career the school latently employs a divide-and-weaken strategy to capture the loyalties and commitment of students, and to ward off as long as possible the cohesion of students. This cohesion could very well be the one factor which, if channeled and directed, might reinforce individual students as they work through pressureful experiences. The whole process of commanding the child's loyalty through presenting and withdrawing mother surrogate rewards, and then the institutionalization of competition, and finally the classification of students into educational types according to several differentiating categories (i.e., curriculum major), does its work to prevent students from relying upon a community of others for support. The school is not defined by students as such a community. Other students, teachers, and administrators are not conceived of by children as peers or partners in a human journey, but as a network of largely impersonal roles, from which little warmth or support against psychological hazards can be gathered.

THE SPECIAL CLASS—A CORRAL FOR MISFITS

The school has asserted its recognition of responsibility in the area of emotional problems by organizing a special class devoted to the education of emotionally handicapped children. The principal aim of the special class is to provide a continuity in the learning process while focusing on the special problems of individual students. Ultimately the success of the class is to be measured by the return of the students to their regular classes. In part the special class is intended to service the regular classes by removing students who retard the progress of the other students. The manifest purposes are to provide greater individualization of instruction, a reduction of the normal pressures, alleviation of conflict experiences with other students, and release from a pattern of unsuccessful school experiences.

Many dysfunctions of well intentioned programs, however, can be observed. The students assigned to special classes are forced to recognize, if they did not before, that they are being treated as special cases, and they recognize that there is a considerable stigma attached to the assignment. Students often view the placement, since they have been socialized within a punishment model as has been suggested earlier, as simply another form of punitive control over their behavior. The child in the special class is in fact isolated from his peers in other classes. Special class children are often not integrated with the rest of the student body in any activities, including lunch and recreation. Furthermore despite the reduction of class size the child is forced to interact exclusively with other children who are experiencing emotional difficulty. Despite the questionable value of exposing the child to the realization that he is not alone in his state, the major consequence may be to intensify the disorders as children encourage each other to act out their own tendencies.

It may be that given the inability of educators to evolve a planning structure through which preventive functions rather than rehabilitative functions can be instituted, the special class is the only stop-gap situation available. It would be unfortunate if a greater effort geared toward preventing emotional crisis than has been attempted in the past was not forthcoming.

THE PREVENTIVE ROLE OF THE SCHOOL

The role of the school in ameliorating the social and psychological consequences of mental disorders must take its cues from models of development and growth, rather than from the perspectives of a pathology model. If we begin with the principle that some children are sick and we have a responsibility to help them overcome these psychological barriers to learning, our only course is rehabilitative techniques. If we begin, rather, with the view that there are conditions within the institution which can have adverse effects on the student participants, we take a reconstructionist view. Our central concern in the latter case is with organizing the kind of educational structure that does not contain the septic characteristics that affect children so adversely. A growth model is one that conceives of the student as evolving through a number of experiences toward an emotional as well as a cognitive maturity. If the mental health of citizens in general is defined as a social problem that is within the jurisdiction of the school, then significant structures, rather than temporary strategies, are required.

Many students who have fallen into states of depression and despair have done so because they were lonely or isolated. Suicidal students are less likely to belong to a cohesive group than non-suicidal students. How can we evolve supportive structures within educational systems? What does it mean to have a supportive structure? A supportive structure is one that organizationally provides for the kind of student interaction that reduces feelings of isolation. It organizes students around common interests or even common concerns or problems. It often makes a reference group out of an occupational group. On the college level or on the high school level, occupation can be used as a superficial basis for the organization of small groups. In this context students can share what it is they think they are getting into. In a therapeutic way anxieties are laid on the floor in the center of the group. They become group problems and as such cohere the members in their desire to seek solutions. Reference groups are often impersonal groups, particularly when persons begin to formulate career plans. When academic emphasis prevents persons from formulating close-knit friendship groups, the reference group of mathematicians or educators is a wholly inadequate substitute, that is, unless such groups are expected to meet frequently in small units.

The principal need in educational systems to reduce depersonalization is the development of the small group as the primary unit rather than the individual and rather than the class or the large group. At the same time there needs to be interaction between these small group units and the teaching, counseling, and administrative personnel. This suggests reduction of social distance. The functional attributes of social distance, which are more rationalizations for maintaining status and privacy than anything else, need to be evaluated in the light of the kind of impersonalizing of student lives that such a posture helps to create.

Society is acutely aware of the impersonal nature of social interaction. As a result, some units are attempting to do something about it. Industry in particular is supporting programs such as sensitivity training and basic encounter groups to bring about more intimate kinds of social relationships. It is something of a mystery why schools are always lagging behind business and industry as programs highly relevant to educational goals undergo innovative reorganization.

Many incidents of mental disorders can be associated with the frustration people experience in attempting to attain the goals in which they believe. Frustration is ordinarily followed by anger which can be translated into patterns of aggression or, if the anger is intolerable and consequently repressed, into depression states. Widespread neurotic aggression which produces interpersonal difficulties at one level can also lead to serious conflicts on a social level. Intergroup hostility, excessive prejudice, and sometimes maddening war-like orientations can be attributed to the projection of internal frustration onto larger groups or even countries. This kind of latent hostility may be useful when national leaders want to promote conflict, but it is not a characteristic of a healthy society.

The school can play a major role in developing strategies for dealing with frustration by structuring its programs around the concept of multidimensional successes. Education has to become a game in which everybody wins. How can this be effected given the fact that the rules of the game are such that only part of the players can win? The answer resides in the intelligent manipulation of the values which do exist so that different values can be applied to different activities. For example we talked earlier about the schools' meek atttempt to socialize students to the belief that "it is not so important whether or not one wins or loses, but how he plays the game." The weakness of the alternative to winning is that how one plays the game is seldom rewarded. Many students, for example, are given C's or average grades, depending on the marking system, if they try hard but do not perform well. Those who do perform well are given A's. As long as the evaluation system differentiates as it does, the minimal rewards associated with trying hard are overshadowed by the rewards for performance. This will continue to be the evaluative mode as long as we grade on the basis of a single criterion for success. Some schools have minimized this problem by doing away with comparative grading entirely. This is the first step. The second is to develop activities in which the minor criteria (showing interest, working hard, being imaginative) are made more important to the students.

Continuity of Growth Experiences

Modern society is not organized around many of the patterns associated with rural or primitive life. This does not mean, however, despite the transition from one form of society to another, that important child rearing foci were not lost in the passing. Several of these foci were mentioned earlier in the discussion of the cultural disjuncture between childhood and adulthood. Although the specific goals of child rearing systems are different, the general problems are the same. We must still ask the question about the kinds of experiences, in our society, that children require to become healthy adults. What kinds of experiences do adults have that the school can help children anticipate realistically and without anxiety? The answers are relatively simple.

Adults take responsibility for others, they love and make love, they work, they face tragedy, they budget, they bear children and raise a family, and they make friends and interact with strangers. Many adults do not do these things very well, and many suffer mental disorders because they cannot involve themselves with these experiences comfortably. The direction for a curriculum based on experiences devoted to making young people less frightened of becoming adults is embodied in an understanding of the activities and experiences of adults. But the school, for the most part, treats children as if they were always to remain children. The world of the adult is a secretive and often mysterious world to children, and the school plays a role in maintaining the mystery. For many adults who are unable to help children cross the bridge between childhood and adulthood the excuse is ignorance. They do not know how. They do not know how to do this any more than they know how to teach children to read or do mathematical computations. The institutional division of labor in our society is responsible for this. The school applies an occupational emphasis in conceiving strategies to help children grow cognitively. The commitment of the schools to play a professional role in the psychological growth of children is still diffuse.

The only suggestion that can be made at this point is that if the problem is mystery, the role of the school is to make the adult world less mysterious. If the adult world is frightening, educators must discover ways of making it less frightening. Structurally, the answer must lie somewhere in the domain of exposure. Our common sense tells us that people overcome fear when they become familiar with the phenomena that frighten them. This suggests an experiential education. Children learn what it means to take responsibility for others by taking it, and they learn how to relate to strangers not only by reading *Our Neighbors* but by being given the task of meeting and discovering a stranger. The reduction of the psychological disorders of adolescents is the goal of this approach.

Institutionalized Effect

Among the several remnants of early puritan values that structure the activities of the school, institutionalized repression of feelings may be the most serious deterrent to the release from emotional stress. One characteristic way of solving the problem is by encouraging students to do what they are told, thus obviating the conflict. But this is only external conflict. Internal conflict is a product of a person's inability to be comfortable simply doing what is expected of him.

Society at large is organized around a system of designating appropriate and inappropriate areas for the expression of feelings. It is quite acceptable to yell and scream at a ball game or to cry at a funeral or to express ecstasy at a wedding. But normal social interaction is kept free from the honest expression of feelings. In this way affect is socially organized. And since we can assess the way it is socially organized, we can produce it almost anywhere we wish, given some control over the system. The school is currently organized around proprieties, and these proprieties are arbitrary. It is not acceptable to demonstrate anger toward a teacher or in most cases at any time in the classroom. It is highly inappropriate to give vent to feelings of joy if this might involve dancing or shouting in the classroom. It is appropriate to restrain one's feelings. This norm is maintained as much through the kinds of educational experiences that are conducted as it is through the routine sanctions that are applied when deviations occur. For the most part the learner is a passive observer of knowledge. He develops his cognitive skills quite apart from any feelings he has about the material he is learning. If he is interested in the subject, that is acceptable; but the typical kind of interest that is desired is, again, a passive posture toward knowledge. For the most part students are not subjectively involved with learning. They act cognitively, but they do not participate very often in the learning experience. Too much subjective participation is often felt to be potentially disruptive to classroom order.

The Reduction of Pressures

The school needs to assess seriously the functional versus the dysfunctional attributes of activities which produce pressure for the student. Pressure, like competition, is functional in the sense of maintaining motivation and mobility for many students. Some pressure, like some anxiety, is useful in bringing out the kind of awareness and sensitivity that may be required for certain difficult tasks. We know, for example, that students perform better in tasks that they believe will count for or against them than when all the pressure is off and they are asked to perform the tasks for their own benefit.[31]

The problem that produces many psychological difficulties among students appears when the pressure is too much and the anxiety is too high. How, then, are we to assess the degree of pressure that we can apply and still remain within the bounds of predictable safety. There is no specific answer to this kind of question, but once educators begin to ask the question, we have begun to move toward a more therapeutic view of education. The best way to proceed in this task is to ask about the specific structures that produce pressure and then ask if there may not be alternatives which fulfill the same function but do not produce the same amount of pressure.

What are these pressure structures? We can list them as follows:

1. Grading or evaluation
2. Conformity

[31] For a survey of anxiety reaction to pressure, see H. Klausmeir, *Learning and Human Abilities* (New York: Harper and Row, 1961), pp.300–302.

3. Parental aspirations
4. Overscheduling
5. Work overload
6. Lack of clarity of expectations
7. Conflicting expectations
8. Competition
9. Lack of affective outlets
10. Career decisions
11. Need to affiliate

We have discussed all these points in other parts of the chapter, and there is no need to review our analysis here. However since the plight of many college students is becoming increasingly evident, we might take the time and space here to consider a model academic environment in which efforts have been made to reduce the pressure on students.

The entrance requirements of the model institution are evaluated on an individual basis. The goal of the admission office is to select a student body that is heterogeneous in its performance ability, its potential, its interests, its racial and socioeconomic characteristics, its non-academic talents, and its political and social attitudes. Once the students are admitted they are oriented to the expectations of the institution. They are told that no one will be dropped for academic performance at any time since it is not possible to fail a course. It is only possible not to pass a course, but the course or the examinations may be taken as many times as the student wishes. The student will be oriented to the view that the university is a community which he may leave and return to at will. He may take courses for credit or not for credit. He will be further oriented to the availability and activities of the counseling center whose major purpose is the purposeful integration of students as persons rather than academic types. He will be invited to attend perpetual basic encounter groups. He will be told that the government of the university operates through a coalition of administration, faculty, and students; and the means by which students can participate will be described.

He will be further informed that degree requirements remain flexible to allow for courses which students may request and help organize. In the course of his academic career he will be advised to seek out experiences which might help to solidify his understanding. If he can demonstrate that his level of understanding of different phenomena has been raised, he can be given credit toward his degree, even though the experience may have taken him away from the campus. He will learn through the behavior of others that there is no necessity to complete a degree in any specific period of time. And with this pressure off he may find it easier to shift career programs in mid-stream.

These are but a few of the ideal possibilities for the organization of a university environment which does not challenge the individual student to hold on to his sanity. The American university, of all the educational levels, has done the most in the past to promote social and cultural change. If change is necessary, as most of us agree that it is, and if problems of mental health are to be affected by such change, then the challenge to the university to develop theory and to provide an example must be accepted.

7

Problems of Race Relationships

PROBLEMS of race relationships are problems of prejudice and discrimination, past and present. They are problems of injustice, of poverty, of segregation, of racist distinctions, and of past, present, and future conflict. Race relations in America are only a problem when such relations are bad. They have never been good in the past, but structurally they have not been so bad as to threaten the society with major disruptions. They are that bad now.

Problems of race relations are problems of the city, and form the foundation for much of the difficulty underlying urban education. Non-white races are moving rapidly to replace the whites as the urban majority.

Between 1940 and 1960 the Negro population doubled in New York and Philadelphia, tripled in Detroit and Chicago, and multiplied five times in Los Angeles. Projections for the future see similar increase patterns.[1] In many major cities the Negro public school population is well over 50 per cent; it is over 75 per cent in Philadelphia and Washington, D.C. Most urban specialists are convinced that the non-white population will constitute the majority in such cities as Washington, Detroit, Chicago, Philadelphia, Baltimore, Cleveland and St. Louis within the next two decades. Given present trends and patterns—that is, whites with children moving to the suburbs—the white student in the public schools in the city will be a rarity. There is then little sense in talking about problems of urban education independent of the problems associated with membership in a disadvantaged minority group. For this reason this chapter will treat problems of urban life in the context of problems of race relations. Those urban circumstances that are unrelated to race, such as pollution and congestion, will not be considered.

In the United States there are no problems associated with being Oriental or Semitic that are sufficiently generalizable to warrant treatment here. There is certainly and probably always will be a degree of prejudice and discrimination associated with being different. Certain critical historical periods, such as World War II and the years immediately following, witnessed socially organized discrimination against the Japanese. But in the usual sense we do not hear very much talk about an Oriental "problem," or a Semitic "problem," or a Jewish "problem." We do hear references to the Negro "problem" and the Puerto Rican "problem" in Eastern metropolitan centers, and the Mexican-American "problem" in the West and Southwest. We also hear at times about the Indian "problem" and we shall make brief mention of this. Obviously because of the relative size of the Negro population and because of the events of the past decade and a half, our main focus will be on the black man in America.

Sometimes we will use the term Negro, other times we will talk about the black man or the black American. The difference will be only in context. When we are making some historical or demographic point, such as number of crimes or arrests, size of population, education level, or aspiration characteristics, we shall use the term Negro, a designation of racial type. When we talk

[1] P. Horton and G. Leslie, *The Sociology of Social Problems* (New York: Appleton-Century-Crofts, 1965), pp.474–475.

about the black man, we refer specifically to the participants, known or unknown, militant or non-violent, in the contemporary struggle for civil rights. The Negro is a social type, characterized only by racial characteristics. The black man is a participant in a movement, and although his racial characteristics are Negroid, according to our anthropological classification system this is unrelated to our concern with action or movement as the unit of analysis. Although the distinction may not be analytically useful, it is prompted by the emphasis of the times. Black men themselves like to employ a distinction between black and Negro that has other connotations, such as the distinction between a man who wants to be black and one who, though disaffiliation with his ethnic group, seeks entrance into the middle-class white society.

There is another relevant distinction that needs to be made out of the same concern that has prompted the distinction between black and Negro. And this is the meaning of the phrase "problem of race relations." In the summer of 1965, when Watts started burning, it became eminently clear to most observers that here was the point at which the problems of race relations ceased being exclusively the black man's problem and commenced being a problem for the total society. It is not fruitful then to conceive of the history of the Negro "problem" as beginning with the white slave traders, and running through slavery and lawful segregation. In this context, although it was the white man's shame, it was not the white man's problem, except perhaps as social conscience performed its work. Relationships with the black society became a contemporary problem of race relations when the first seeds of what was to be a policy of confrontation were planted in Birmingham, Alabama. The Birmingham bus boycott, by definition, meant confrontation. In this case it was an economic confrontation and whites were affected. The historical *Brown* v. *Topeka Board of Education* decision of the Supreme Court in 1954 became another point at which race relations began to take on a different meaning from the past. Our specific focus then in the majority of pages which follow will treat race relations in the context of the contemporary confrontation of the black society with the white, and the relevance of that confrontation for educational policy.

THE PHENOMENON OF PREJUDICE

The complexities of social functioning brought down to an individual level force persons to make definitions of others by categories. The most simple and basic differentiation is made between *those like me* and *those different from me*. Color difference is one convenient mechanism for making such distinctions. Another is the status one holds within a delimited social community. A third is the historical definitions that children learn early in their socialization process. Once distinctions between others are made, the process of evolving a set of evaluative beliefs about persons in different categories occurs. These beliefs are soon treated by the believer as facts, and as such, these "facts" structure interaction.

The soil of prejudice is the social experience. Since persons incline to participate almost exclusively with people like themselves, they learn or extend their knowledge of other group or types by internalizing the definitions made by members of their reference group. The social experience as the basis of prejudice is evidenced by the fact that racial attitudes are not apparent in very young children. It is only after the formation of social cliques and the evolution of normative and value systems that prejudices appear.[2]

Prejudice becomes intensified by the process of selective perception and the utilization of the rule of exceptions.

Circular reinforcement enables a person to find in Negroes or Jews whatever traits his prejudice prompts him to look for, and having thus found them, his prejudice is reinforced. To one who thinks Negroes stupid, a cloddish Negro confirms his prejudice. An intelligent Negro, however, is an "exception" who also confirms the prejudice, for, if he is an "exception," then all the rest must be stupid. Thus, the "exception" proves the rule, confirms the prejudice, and the prejudice becomes totally divorced from the reality it supposedly describes.[3]

Once prejudice develops, however, what are the mechanisms that maintain it? Several factors seem to be apparent, the most obvious of which is that persons do not interact often with groups or individuals toward whom they hold unfavorable prejudices. If they do interact, it is usually on an economic basis, where persons either employ or exploit others, or in situations of confrontation. In both cases the prejudice serves the person holding it by allowing him to justify the exploitation or to rationalize the antagonism. Another mechanism is centered around the facts of social position. Rather than conceive of different social positioning as a function of differential opportunity structures, persons incline to interpret failure to achieve position as a function of basic characteristics of the

---

[2] Bruno Lasker, *Race Attitudes in Children* (New York: Holt, Rinehart and Winston, Inc., 1929).
[3] Horton and Leslie, *Sociology of Social Problems*, p. 407.

individual or type. This notion is eroding somewhat as more people, through higher education, are being exposed to the dynamics of economic organization. But it is still a popular view in many places. When economic positions are the same, however, the mechanisms which maintain the prejudice, as with the white lower class in the South, are to appeal to social distinctions. If prestige is important to the individual, as it almost always is, then it becomes psychologically necessary to discover and believe that personalized qualities raise him above others in similar economic positions.

A further and perhaps most fundamental mechanism in modern times is the association of minority groups with deviant behavior. After the burning and rioting that have occurred in many major cities in the past few years, the form of prejudice toward blacks turned from a conception of them as lazy to one of being violent. The fact that more Negroes than any other racial group are involved in criminal activities and crimes of violence leads many prejudiced people to conclude that deviant tendencies are a basic component of the Negro's character. Again these persons find no motivation to seek for alternative explanations, which can easily be found in an analysis of the social structure.

The concept of the Negro as violent, despite earlier inclinations to characterize him as lazy and shiftless, also has its source in some earlier conceptions which were seldom articulated in this way. The quality of untamed violence has always struck the civilized person as being associated with primitivism, and many people have believed that Negroes are intrinsically primitive. These people's ignorance about Africa, and indeed their psychological tendency to associate black with some form of primitive evil, has made easy the transition from earlier to current definitions of the black man.

The maintenance of prejudice has been effected often in such subtle ways that the average person could not begin to observe the way in which he has been influenced. We have, for example, mentioned the association of black with evil. Davis, in an analysis of *Roget's Thesaurus,* has looked at words associated with whiteness and blackness. His conclusion is that of the 134 words associated with whiteness, forty-four are favorable and pleasing, such as purity, cleanliness, immaculateness, bright, shining, and fair. Blackness, on the other hand, has 120 associated words, none of which is favorable. Among the sixty words which he found to be distinctly unfavorable were such terms as blot, blotch, smut, sully, and the like. In addition, he found twenty words directly referring to race, such as Negro, nigger, darky, blackamoor, and so on.[4]

4 Ossie Davis, "Conference on Racism in Education," *Civic Leader* 36, No. 14 (1967): 2.

THE NEGRO CULTURE

One of the mechanisms which maintains social distance and prejudice is the conception of others as different. One way to augment this difference is to conceive of others as having a culture distinctly different from one's own. To conceive of Negroes as having had a cultural "experience" which was or is in some way distinct from the American experience is a totally erroneous conception. Not until recent Black programs, often militant, has it occurred to the American Negro to associate his experience with that of the African.

The most critical "experience" in defining through time the character of most Americans has been their training as Christians. The Christian "experience" was one of unifying persons around certain ethical standards and beliefs, chief among which is non-violence, brotherly love, honesty, and charity. For several reasons, most of them economic, the Negro has not been able, like his white counterpart, completely to practice what he was preached to about, but the main thrust of the civil rights movement, through the dominant role played by Martin Luther King, Jr. and his partisans in the Southern Christian Leadership Conference, demonstrates clearly that the lessons were learned. Even in the more violent and disorganized centers of Negro urban life the church has played a significant role. As Emerson, the black hero of Julius Horowitz's powerful comment on black-white relationships, says to his white friend, "If there weren't a church in Harlem, your throat would have been cut long ago."[5] Or as Malcolm X said, "The black man needs to reflect that he has been America's most fervent Christian—and where has it gotten him?"[6]

Unlike the culture of the Puerto Rican and the Mexican-American, which we will discuss later, the Negro experience is profoundly American. It is more accurately described as a culture, if the word is necessary, as part of the culture of poverty with its concomitant adaptations; and poverty is not unique to any national culture. Any claim to the distinguishing features of a plantation society as producing relevant cultural configurations in the black man of today is to ignore the prominent problems of a contemporary conception of race relationships.

To associate Negroes with a rural economy and consequently

---

[5] Julius Horowitz, *The Wasp* (New York: Bantam, 1965), p.5.
[6] Malcolm X, *Autobiography of Malcolm X* (New York: Grove Press, 1964), p. 369.

to characterize their adaptations as that of the rural poor would be to further mislead. The fact is that proportionately more Negroes are urban dwellers than are whites, and furthermore, even by 1950 63 per cent of all Negroes lived in urban areas outside the South. The figure is probably currently much higher.[7]

The most distinguishing characteristic of the Negro's urban experience is that he lives in a ghetto. A ghetto is characterized as a homogeneous concentration of persons with similar ethnic backgrounds. The concept of a ghetto, and such has usually been assumed in the definition of it, is usually associated with slum living. It is possible to talk about Golden Ghettos where only rich Jews or Italians dwell, but these are uncommon as a form of ecological organization. By the time persons have acquired sufficient income to purchase expensive homes, they have usually been adequately integrated into the mainstream of society. For most persons the system makes it almost impossible to attain wealth without a degree of integration.

The Negro ghettos of the urban North are portraits of plight and despair. The following description is representative.

The rent's $70 a month and the whole building's crawling with rats. The plaster is falling down. It ain't fit for dogs. But what can you do? My wife's always trying to get into one of those projects, but they won't let us in until I find a steady job. So we're always finding ourselves right where we started, nowhere.[8]

Emerson lived on West 125th Street off Lenox. His building had an elevator but it wasn't running. We had to walk up six flights. . . . His building looked like it had been gutted by a fire. The mailboxes were smashed. The lock on the front door was pulled out. The telephone in the hallway was pulled out of the wall. There was a huge mirror in the lobby. I saw Emerson reflected in eight pieces in the broken mirror. The walls of the lobby were smeared with chalk writing. Children seemed to be running out of the walls. I expected rats to be crawling on the ceiling. The marble on the stairway was worn away. The windows on the stairway landings were broken, covered with chicken wire, the soot piled up. The walls on the stairway landing were scribbled with chalk, the chalk dug into the walls. The scribbling was hysterical, the names of children, the monsters, the half-dozen curse words known to everyone. The building felt wet, as though it had sunk into a cave. . . .

Emerson's voice came back on the tape, "I've heard of babies being

7 Ray Mack, "Race Relations," in *Social Problems*, ed. H. Becker (New York: John Wiley & Sons, Inc., 1966).
8 *Life*, March 8, 1968.

found in furnaces, garbage cans, the gutter, on stoops, and I've heard of babies being thrown off roofs. Now I've seen one."[9]

The quality of housing does not describe more than one segment of a black ghetto, and dramatic incidents like babies being thrown off roofs are not representative. One cannot find a paragraph, or even two or three that can communicate even the barest essentials of what it feels like to live in a black ghetto, which in many ways is what it feels like to be black. Claude Brown's exceptionally communicative portrait of Harlem, may come as close as any description now available.[10] But this is and can only be a description through feelings and experiences, not through the observation of the landscape. And it requires the whole experience, since no part is quite adequate to describe the way the ghetto has shaped the psychology of the black man. As Brown reveals, this is not a unidimensional social psychology. For the same ghetto which produced despair and anger and a life of street fighting has also produced a strung-out, addict generation, and recently a generation of radical activists. The modern black ghetto as a physical and social entity is a place where, for many, "All this crying and needing and wanting is about to drive me crazy."[11] It is this state, rather than a need to integrate the black man into a white community, that has produced the "up against the wall-ism" that has forced him to come out fighting. It is to this recent development in black history that we will return in a later section.

As one might surmise, Negroes do not extract a proportional share of income from the economy in relation to their numbers. Almost half of all Negro families have a yearly income of less than $3,000 and 23 per cent of these have family incomes of less than $2,000.[12] Negroes are highly overrepresented in unemployment rates, on welfare roles, in menial service jobs, and in prisons.

Economically as well as socially the relationship between Caucasians and Negroes has been one of superiority and inferiority. This is determined and maintained by a process of defining social positions. First, the major society defines the value of certain characteristics such as manners, honesty, industriousness, and the like. Then institutional forces are set in motion which reward, differentially, the degree of behavioral conformity to the standards. Then

[9] Horowitz, *The Wasp*, pp. 78–79.
[10] Claude Brown, *Manchild in the Promised Land* (New York: Signet Books, 1965).
[11] *Life*, March 8, 1968.
[12] L. H. Keyserling, "Progress or Poverty." Paper read at the Washington Conference on Economic Progress December, 1964.

status groups began to form around a general evaluation of one's conformity to the standards. Since positions cannot have meaning without a stratification system, a system evolves which determines not only one's position but one's probable access to higher positions. The Negro in most cases occupies the lower rung of the stratification order. Often ascriptive factors, such as skin color, become linked to the designation of a person's social position. If access to opportunities is to be accorded to Negroes within traditionally white organizations, it is more likely to fall to a light-skinned Negro than a black-skinned one.

The psychological state of the black man in America is one of frustration and anger. He has been deprived of his basic right as a human being to live with decent housing, adequate food, and opportunities to work. He has been deprived of his dignity, and deprived of his tradition, of his identity.

We shall have our manhood. We shall have it or the earth will be leveled by our attempts to gain it.[13]

THE AMERICAN INDIAN

The American Indian today constitutes less than one-half of 1 per cent of the population of the United States, not really enough people to consider as a social problem within the general framework of this chapter.[14] It seems somewhat within the tradition of American inhumanity to the Indian to say to him now that we cannot be concerned about his problems, since his problems do not have much of an impact on the rest of us. But the case of the American Indian does provide us with a prototype of race relations in the United States and must be mentioned as part of the general analysis of American patterns of racial interaction.

We do not need to recount here the history of white warfare against the Indian which in one way or another caused the near extinction of his race. We do need to emphasize the patterns by which white racial guilt was rationalized. The formation of the Bureau of Indian Affairs was intended as a statement of national commitment to guarantee that the rights and health of the Indians would be supervised. In some ways the federal programs over-

---

13 Eldridge Cleaver, *Soul on Ice* (New York: McGraw-Hill Book Company, 1968), p.61.
14 J. E. Roucek, "The Most Oppressed Race in the United States: The Indian," *Educational Forum* 29 (May 1965): 477–485.

shadowed the structures that had produced poverty and isolation for the Indian in the first place. The whole concept of a reservation for Americans, the first Americans, in the second half of the twentieth century, is a stain on our national pride. But mechanisms for rationalizing and ignoring our history are common in circumstances where a society does not wish to make a commitment to real change, but rather a token commitment to guarantee that further injustices are retarded.

Sixty or more per cent of American Indian students do not complete high school. This can be partly explained by the fact that the responsibility for the education of Indian students is left in the hands of the states, and these particular states, largely in the Southwest, are in areas where the most intense prejudice toward Indians resides. The national government does grant subsidies, but these do not make the important difference.[15] The fact that Indians in these states are not assimilated, not integrated, and do develop attitudes of alienation and hopelessness tells us what the outcome of such programs is. Racial prejudice toward non-white minorities is always more intense and rampant in areas where these groups congregate. After a trip to the United States in 1904, Max Weber, a German sociologist, talked about the relative lack of prejudice he observed being exhibited toward Indians as compared to that shown to Negroes.[16] He based this evaluation on the fact that persons respected Indians for their unwillingness to submit to slavery, as the Negro submitted. On an abstract level attitudes toward non-white minorities can be generated which really have little to do with the fact that most white Americans cannot live harmoniously with non-whites.

The fact is that everywhere that American Indians reside they are defined as being outside the social structure, and consequently they do not fit into the mobility pattern that the school supports. And so long as these people, because of their small size and relative passivity, do not pose a potential threat either to the political or economic interests of their larger communities, the plight of the Indian is likely to be ignored. When only the conscience of the advantaged majority can work in their favor, it is no wonder that their hopes for the future are so pathetically low.

---

15 "U.S. Indians," *New York Times*, May 31, 1964.
16 Peter I. Rose, *The Subject Is Race* (New York: Oxford University Press, Inc., 1968), p.52.

THE PUERTO RICAN

Puerto Ricans, if distributed geographically throughout the country as are Negroes or even Orientals, would not constitute a "problem." But like Mexican-Americans, the problem of and for Puerto Ricans results as a function of their being concentrated solidly in a limited geographical area. Over 550,000 Puerto Ricans had migrated to New York City by 1956.[17] Like Mexican-Americans, they are true immigrants in the sense that they come to the United States speaking a different language and have previously been socialized primarily in a rural society.

Immigration from Puerto Rico, a small commonwealth, is large because there are no migration bans. Immigrants come because their condition in Puerto Rico is one of poverty and because, in the same cycle that characterized early European immigrants, they have family and friends in the United States. Puerto Ricans migrate to the locales where they have family. This is not exclusively because of ties but because they know that their language barrier will be less of a problem in already established Puerto Rican communities.

We need to ask why a group of people would leave a warm homeland where they are the dominant ethnic group to come to a cold climate where they are a different-speaking, dark-skinned, minority group and where, since communication between the United States and Puerto Rico is considerable, they know that their people experience serious discrimination. The answer lies partly in the role the United States has played in Puerto Rican affairs. Since we began to exert considerable influence over the affairs of Puerto Rico, life on the island has changed. Infant mortality rates which were 113 per 1,000 births in 1940 decreased to 41 per 1,000 births in 1961. Life expectancy at birth changed from thirty-eight years in 1910 to seventy years in 1960.[18] Consequently the population has been increasing rapidly, but the available living space has not been. The occupational structure, likewise, cannot accommodate the available work force.

The cost of transportation between San Juan, the capital, and New York City has fallen to a point where many Puerto Ricans can afford the fare. They arrive in New York and are met by a host of family and friends. The cohesiveness of the friendship group

17 Mack, "Race Relations," p.323.
18 *A Summary of Facts and Figures*, Commonwealth of Puerto Rico, 1963, pp. 4–5.

and the fact that they do not have return fare makes them more tolerant of their early experiences with the climate and the pace of life. They locate immediately close to their friends in four major areas—Morrisania (in the Bronx), Spanish Harlem, the Lower East Side, or the Upper West Side of Manhattan.[19]

The characteristics of the Puerto Rican immigrants are: (1) there is a greater proportion of women here than there on the island, (2) non-whites are represented in a slightly higher proportion than whites, (3) they are older than the island's general population because they do not usually bring children, (4) there are more who are legally married than in the island population, (5) they are seldom single, (6) they are more literate than the general population of the Island, and (7) there are more skilled and semi-skilled workers and fewer agricultural workers than would be represented by the distributions of these occupational categories in the general population.[20]

The new arrivals usually reside with their families until they can find work. Here they experience the same discriminatory policies as Negroes. The advantage that they have over Negroes, however, is that they have skills which are desirable in some New York industries, particularly the garment trade where they comprise 20 per cent of the Ladies Garment Workers Union. The Puerto Rican worker may also find work in rubber plants, aquarium supply houses, and corrugated box factories, or in the many New York restaurants as bus boys and dishwashers. If jobs are difficult to find, he has available to him a special office established by the Puerto Rican government, which aids him in this effort.[21] This is a particularly unique feature in migration history.

Some of the adaptation problems that the Puerto Rican migrant experiences are a function of his color (more blacks than whites emigrate), his language (Spanish), his religious rituals (many believe in spirits although they often classify themselves as Catholics to avoid integration difficulties), and their marital status. Between one-fourth and one-third of Puerto Rican marriages are informally joined (consensual) and in New York such marriages may prevent persons from gaining access to public housing developments.[22] This represents for the Puerto Rican an additional handi-

---

19 Dan Wakefield, *Island in the Sun* (New York: Corinth Book Co., Inc., 1961), pp.4–5.
20 C. Wright Mills, *et al.*, *The Puerto Rican Journey* (New York: Harper and Row, 1950), p.25.
21 Christopher Rand, *The Puerto Ricans* (New York: Oxford University Press, Inc., 1958), p.9.
22 *Ibid.*, p.84.

cap in establishing a more suitable standard of living than he maintains.

Most Puerto Ricans have dark skin, but this is not as predictable as with Negroes. As a result, they suffer similar patterns of racial discrimination as Negroes. This is most evident in the kinds of jobs they are offered and the areas in which they are permitted to live. But unlike the Negro the Puerto Rican has not had adequate time to develop a sense of relative deprivation. The average Puerto Rican takes a job that pays considerably more than he was making a short time before on the island, and as bad as his residence is, it is likely that his most recent one was worse.

The Puerto Rican has developed an antagonism to Negroes as a result of the proximity of their living circumstances. Such antagonisms were not characteristics of interaction between the two groups in Puerto Rico. But the feature of culture conflict and oppressive living circumstances make it difficult for the two groups to live together harmoniously. On the "turf" or local level the struggle is purely one of holding and maintaining dominance in a geographical area. On another level, entering the United States in a period of intense racial antagonism, the Puerto Rican may feel that the discrimination he receives would not have been so serious if the Negro had not paved the way. As a result, the Puerto Rican does what he can to avoid being identified as a Negro. One study has indicated that among Puerto Ricans there is a definite association between darkness of skin color and the retention of the Spanish tongue.[23]

THE MEXICAN-AMERICAN

The Mexican-American presents American society with the same kind of problem as do Negroes. They are in the society, but in few cases are they actually part of it. The effect of their presence on American society occurs as a result of population concentration. Like the Puerto Rican, the Mexican-American has migrated to one major geographical area, the American Southwest. The main urban concentration is in the Los Angeles area where more than $1\frac{1}{2}$ million Mexican-Americans dwell.[24] The Mexican-American in Los Angeles is part of the urban poor. He is characterized specifically,

23 C. Senior, "Research on the Puerto Rican Family in the United States," *Marriage and Family Living* 19 (February 1957).
24 Walter Fogel, "Education and Income," in *Mexican-Americans, Advance Report* (Los Angeles: University of California at Los Angeles, 1965).

as part of his Los Angeles experience, as being socially and culturally isolated. He lives either in his own ghetto or one that he
shares with other disenfranchised minority groups. Approximately
one-fourth are functionally illiterate, and like many Negroes, are
designated by certain standards as educationally retarded. Of the
three major minority problem groups (Negroes, Puerto Ricans, and
Mexican-Americans), Mexican-Americans have the highest rates of
school drop-outs. Because of the migratory life that many Mexican-
American families follow, Mexican-American children have the
largest rates of transfer from school to school.[25]

The average family income for Mexican-Americans is less than
$5,000 a year, with more than one-third of the group earning less
than $3,000 a year.[26] Employment is irregular and generally of the
lowest level. In many parts of the Southwest Mexican-Americans
experience the same discrimination as that experienced by Puerto
Ricans in the Northeast.

The Mexican-American does not want to contribute to the
current mainstream of American society. He has been improperly
socialized to want to, primarily because he does not feel that he
has any stake in the American society. He has not been integrated
in any real sense, nor has he been influenced to want to move toward integration. At the University of California at Los Angeles,
the largest university in the urban area populated by the majority
of Mexican-Americans, only a handful of Mexican-American students are currently officially enrolled. The effort of those who
actively seek to broaden the educational possibilities for students
of Mexican-American descent is a new phenomenon in the area,
paralleling the activities of black students throughout the country.
The majority of Mexican-American residents, because of their position on the social and economic scales in the areas in which they
reside, have become, as is the typical pattern, a source of social
disorganization.

Mexican Immigration

Like the ancestors of the American Negro, many Mexican-
Americans (those who were not here prior to the white man) were
first brought to the United States as a source of farm labor. In the
ten-year period, 1920–1930, when immigration laws were loosely
supervised, the majority of original Mexican immigrants entered
the Southwest. Approximately half a million Mexicans entered at

25 R. Singleton and P. Bullock, "Some Problems in Minority Group Education
in Los Angeles Public Schools," *Journal of Negro Education* 33 (1963): 139.
26 Fogel, "Education and Income," p.4.

this time. After 1930 when immigration laws were strictly enforced, the immigration figures dropped considerably. More than 22,000 entered between 1931 and 1940, and 60,000 between 1941 and 1950. The enforcement of the laws caused a considerable increase in illegal entry, and the figures began to rise again in the fifties.[27]

Most of the immigrants came from agricultural environments in Mexico. They came without skills, without money, and with a folklore tradition; and because of their characteristics they settled in geographical areas that were suitable to their rural traditions. Often those who entered legally found that the competition for work in rural areas was considerable, and they drifted into the cities, settling in low income, slum or semi-slum areas and often creating ethnic ghettos. Their competition came mainly from people of their own origins, the illegal "wetback" (a name associated with swimming the Rio Grande to avoid border checks), and the contract labor groups that were imported by wealthy land owners. The urban Mexican-American holds a similar status to that of his rural counterpart. In San Antonio, Chicago, and primarily Los Angeles, the urban poor, the ghetto poor, have changed their life chances little from that which had in Mexico. The connection between the urban Mexican-American and the rural Mexican-American is only one of abstract social position. Until very recently the struggle for equal opportunities was an individual matter and usually a lost cause. Only in the wake of recent efforts to organize migratory workers in northern California, and attempts by some urban Mexican-American leaders to influence the major social institutions by pressing their plight and their cause, has the Mexican-American attained some ethnic solidarity, in some ways similar to but not as far advanced as the cohesion of the black society behind critical social issues.

Like the American Negro, the Mexican-American has experienced discrimination and segregation. Restaurants often refuse to serve him, graveyard owners refuse to bury him, and real estate agents conspire to keep him out of Anglo areas. The prejudice and discrimination that he experiences cause him to seek the psychological sanctuary of his own community, leaving only when forced to seek work. Because of his language and the color of his skin, the Mexican-American has fallen victim to social stereotyping. This leads to isolation and the concomitant ethnocentrism that arise when persons are unable to become integrated into the larger society. Ethnic identity for the Mexican-American is an identity of shame as well as pride. He is aware of his inferior status but has not yet discovered the mechanisms to advance the cause of his pride above that of his social shame. Isolation has also retarded the motivation of Mexican-Americans to abandon their language and cultural style. Family relationships, leisure time activities, and the Catholic church are valued and rituals associated with religious or national holidays as they were celebrated in Mexico are retained.

The major resocialization force in the life of the modern Mexican-American is the school, in interaction with first generation Mexican-Americans, the sons and daughters of the immigrants. The adult has much less contact with the Anglo society than does his child. The pattern of problems, however, as is the case with Negroes and Puerto Ricans, is that of *de facto* segregation. Educational officials hold dearly to the concept of the neighborhood school, since officials are often more concerned about budget than any other factor. When a neighborhood is a ghetto, the school is a ghetto school. The specific way in which an ethnic population influences the adaptation of the school is the subject for a later section of this chapter. It is important now only to emphasize that segregated schools restrict the kind of interaction across racial and class lines that is so necessary for the kind of interchange of socialization patterns that might reduce the disorganization that emerges from culture conflict.

Social Status of Mexican-Americans

Most Mexican-Americans are poor; according to any scale of social class they fall at the bottom. One of the problems associated with this status which intensifies the disillusionment and frustration of the Mexican-American is that he is more class conscious than is the average American.[28] As such, the Mexican-American is influenced to develop a class system within his own cultural group. The lowest groups within this stratified order are the migratory farm workers and the laborers with little, if any, education. The middle class of the Mexican-Americans is composed of railroad workers, semi-skilled industrial workers, small business men and skilled workers. The upper class consists of those who belong to the professions. The status evaluations are based on occupation and educational background. The majority of Mexican-Americans, like Latins everywhere in the Spanish-American world, belong to the lower class. Those who do achieve status within the Anglo-Saxon world usually leave the community, creating a void of role models for the Mexican-American child.[29]

28 J. H. Burma, *Spanish Speaking Groups in the United States* (Durham, N. C.: Duke University Press, 1954), p.94.
29 *Ibid.,* pp.94–98.

One of the reasons why the Mexican-American has attained only limited mobility in Anglo society is because of his unfamiliarity with and consequent unwillingness to use the vehicle of organization. As the case of the labor movement reveals, organizations have been the single most significant force in achieving social mobility for depressed social groups. Few Mexican-Americans belong to political organizations, few belong to labor unions. They belong to fewer organizations than Caucasians of similar economic backgrounds. The two most prominent characteristics of Mexican-American participation in organizations, which reduces their progress toward social mobility, are that (1) membership is usually limited to those who already have achieved mobility (the Mexican-American middle class), and (2) participation usually occurs around church-based local organizations which do not appear to have more than an expressive function, and such participation is not conceived in terms of wide-scale political action.[30]

As black militants have argued for the Negro, the only means by which the generation-to-generation poverty cycle can be broken by Mexican-Americans is through a rejection of the Anglo definition of mobility, up the white ladder toward membership in the majority society. As long as the majority of poor ethnic groups are convinced that the mobility system is open and are driven to compete for the few rewards available to dark-skinned people, the majority of non-white ethnic groups will remain poor, given the unequal access to the reward systems. The fact that Mexican-Americans, despite their inferior position in the Anglo society, desire a kind of class mobility, means that the problem for the radical leadership is almost overwhelming. Unlike the black society, which has had better than a century to conceptualize its problem, the Mexican-American sub-culture is only beginning to conceive of a political route to freedom. But with the lessons of the new black man before him and the opportunities for a coalition of the disenfranchised, the brown American is likely to move up from institutionalized poverty in a far shorter time than his black counterpart.

THIS GENERATION OF BLACK MEN

The sense of urgency, of desperate need to do it now and to capitalize on the momentum that has become a force in American society, has become a premise to the struggle for Black Power.

[30] C. F. Marden, *Minorities in American Society* (New York: American Book Company, 1952), pp.128–155.

The whole question of race is one that America would much rather not face honestly and squarely. To some, it is embarrassing; to others, it is inconvenient; to still others, it is confusing. But for black Americans, to know it and tell it like it is and then to act on that knowledge should be neither embarrassing nor inconvenient nor confusing. Those responses are luxuries for people with time to spare, who feel no particular urgency about the need to solve certain serious social problems. Black people in America have no time to play nice, polite parlor games—especially when the lives of their children are at stake.[31]

Despite the anxiety-ridden protestation of a witch hunting class in American society, few if any intellectuals support the view that riots in the major cities over the past few years are "Communist inspired." Those who do not wish to accept the conclusions of the Kerner report, (about which we will say more later) that America as a basically racist society has produced a set of conditions which provide the soil for riot, can excuse themselves from guilt or responsibility.[32] This soil (conditions of poverty, deprivation and humiliation) is adequate in itself, given the spontaneous defiance of a new generation of angry black men, to spur outbursts of fire and violence. Anyone prone to believe that everything in America is fine and the *status quo* would be maintained without the intervention of Soviet or Maoist agents has never walked through the black ghetto with an open mind and inquiring eye.

It takes no one to stir up the sociological dynamite that stems from unemployment, bad housing, inferior education already in the ghettoes. This explosively criminal condition has existed for so long it needs no fuse; it fuses itself; it spontaneously combusts from within itself.[33]

In no area that would be considered an appropriate topic for this book is it less possible to ensure currency than in the discussion of the black revolution. The best that it seems possible to accomplish is to state some of the principles and guiding principles which characterize the black man's position. The elaborations and ramifications stemming from such premises or positions are constantly emerging from the pens of a new generation of black writers. Perhaps we can begin to anticipate some of the directions that these extensions might take. If one understands the framework within which the new directions will be couched, he should be able to

---

[31] Stokely Carmichael and Charles V. Hamilton, *Black Power* (New York: Vintage Books, 1967), pp.viii–ix.
[32] *Report of the National Advisory Commission on Civil Disorders* (Washington, D. C.: U. S. Government Printing Office, 1968).
[33] Malcolm X, *Autobiography*, p.366.

make sense of them in context. Unfortunately too often the uninformed reader understands concepts and propositions used by members of other ethnic groups only within the framework of his own associations. Black power is the most vivid example in recent times. Communicated in a period of riots, the concept of black power was originally perceived by the white society, particularly white liberals who might have known better, as a black commitment to a militant confrontation with the white society, and the riots were perceived as the operational arm of the black power philosophy. Now that the articulation of black power has reached a wider audience and a conception of black power as political and economic power has been at least partially comprehended, the defensiveness of the white society has decreased.

This book attempts to freeze a dynamic process as if change itself were static. This is fraught with problems. In areas such as race relations where events move rapidly, we sometimes need to lead our reader much as a quarterback leads his end, or as a torpedo is fired ahead of the ship it is trying to strike. If the end falls or reverses position, or if the ship stops, then we have missed our mark. This is the chance that needs to be taken. Many American Negroes today do not like the expression "black man"; they prefer to imitate the style of the middle-class white. Perhaps the precursors of change in the black community are a small minority. A survey conducted for CBS for incorporation in a TV series aired in the fall of 1968 asked black youth to cite their racial heroes. Less than 10 per cent mentioned Rap Brown, Huey Newton, or Stokely Carmichael. The heroes were still Martin Luther King, Jr. and other non-militant black men. In this chapter the works of Malcolm X and Carmichael and Hamilton are emphasized to the point where they may appear to be most representative of black thought today. This may not be the case at the time of this writing. It is predicted that it will be the case at the time this book is being read.

In discussing the black revolution we often refer to the posture of modern militancy. Again this is not to argue that at this moment the militant mode of adaptation predominates over the non-violent mode representative of King, Abernathy and their followers. Nor is it to suggest that militancy among blacks is new. Marcus Garvey, the black separationist of the twenties had as many loyal adherents as any black leader today. Militancy is not new, and it may not even be militant, although most blacks in the movement for equality and justice may wish to retain the term if it functions to present an image of confrontation, even when one does not exist. The black man in America, now as in the near future, does not possess any real military power and may not be able to stand behind his threats to provoke guerilla warfare. The majority of black people may be for integration and non-violent progress, but it is not nor is it likely to be fashionable to admit this. Much of the power of the black man resides in his ability to make a convincing argument that if his needs and demands are not met he will disrupt the institutional *status quo*. He has proved in isolated situations that disruption is possible. The black man needs an evolution out of the present, and he knows that the only way to secure this evolution is to talk revolution. This is likely to be the posture for at least the next decade, and consequently a large segment of the remainder of this chapter concerns itself with the developing ideology of the black revolution.

The discussion which follows will attempt to set in some realistic perspective the connotations of the most frequently used phrases and concepts of the revolution. Like most revolutionary programs, the slogan-like quality of many of these phrases should be seen as necessary instruments of that movement. Scholars, as well as most laymen, often grow weary of political slogans. After many repetitions slogans almost cease to be meaningful and those who use them are defined as parrots and devoid of any sensible intensity. The function of slogans, and we have witnessed many of the Marxian ideas depersonalized by such a process, is simply a way of uniting a group of persons who bear a similiar unique relationship to the social structure. Given a common set of articulated ideas, articulated in ways that are memorable and that provide spokesmen with common frames of reference slogans are as cohering as would be a common language. "Religion is the opiate of the people," and "Workers of the world unite, you've nothing to lose but your chains," have maintained their functional viability long after the issues appear to be irrelevant in Western industrial society. Similarly the slogans of the black revolution, the concepts which we hear reiterated, serve such a latent function. Our purpose in the following pages will be to attempt to comprehend the special meaning in the special context of such concepts.

The context of the black revolution is a context of reaction, a response to patterns of discrimination and exploitation that touch the majority of Negroes in some way during most days of their life. The ideas that are to follow can be comprehended only in the social context of action and reaction. The specific form of this context can best be represented from the Kerner report previously mentioned. The following list of Negro grievances represents the most general configuration of social disruptions experienced by the

Negro in America. The specifics can be discovered only in the accumulated history of every black man, and this would require a number of pages that no library shelf could contain.

CHART M-1
PERVASIVENESS OF GRIEVANCES

Grievances Found and Number of Cities
Where Mentioned as Significant

1. Employment and Unemployment
   (found in at least one of the following forms in 20 cities)

Unemployment and underemployment (General lack of full-time jobs)	19
Union discrimination	13
Discrimination in hiring by local and state government	9
Discrimination in placement by state employment service	6
Discrimination in placement by private employment agencies	3

2. Police Practices
   (found in at least one of the following forms in 19 cities)

Physical abuse	15
Verbal abuse	15
Nonexistent or inadequate channels for the redress of grievances against police	13
Discrimination in employment and promotion of Negroes	13
General lack of respect for Negroes, *i.e.*, using derogatory language short of threats	11
Abuse of Negroes in police custody	10
Failure to answer ghetto calls promptly where Negro is a victim of unlawful act	8

3. Inadequate Housing
   (found in at least one of the following forms in 18 cities)

Poor housing code enforcement	13
Discrimination in sales and rentals	12
Overcrowding	12

4. Inadequate Education
   (found in at least one of the following forms in 17 cities)

De facto segregation	15
Poor quality of instruction and facilities	12
Inadequacy of curriculum (*e.g.*, no Negro history)	10

Inadequate Negro representation on school board   10
Poor vocational education or none at all   9

5. Political Structure and Grievance Mechanism
(found in at least one of the following forms in 16 cities)

Lack of adequate Negro representation   15
Lack of response to legitimate grievances of Negroes   13
Grievance mechanism nonexistent or inadequately publicized   11

6. Inadequate Programs
(found in at least one of the following forms in 16 cities)

Poverty program (OEO) (*e.g.*, insufficient participation of the poor in project planning; lack of continuity in programs; inadequate funding; and unfulfilled promises)   12
Urban renewal (HUD) (*e.g.*, too little community participation in planning and decision-making; programs are not urban renewal but "Negro removal")   9
Employment training (Labor-HEW) (*e.g.*, persons are trained for jobs that are not available in the community)   7

7. Discriminatory Administration of Justice
(found in at least one of the following forms in 15 cities)

Discriminatory treatment in the courts   15
Lower courts act as arm of police department rather than as an objective arbiter in truly adversary proceedings   10
Presumption of guilt when policeman testifies against Negro   8

8. Poor Recreation Facilities and Programs
(found in at least one of the following forms in 15 cities)

Inadequate facilities (parks, playgrounds, athletic fields, gymnasiums, and pools)   15
Lack of organized programs   10

9. Racist and Other Disrespectful White Attitudes
(found in at least one of the following forms in 15 cities)

Racism and lack of respect for dignity of Negroes   15
General animosity toward Negroes   10

0. Inadequate and Poorly Administered Welfare Programs
(found in at least one of the following forms in 14 cities)

Unfair qualification regulations (*e.g.*, "man in the house" rule)   6

Attitude of welfare workers toward recipients (*e.g.*, manifestations of hostility and contempt for persons on welfare)   6

11. Inadequate Municipal Services
(found in at least one of the following forms in 11 cities)

Inadequate sanitation and garbage removal   9
Inadequate health and hospital facilities   6
Inadequate street paving and lighting   6

12. Discriminatory consumer and Credit Practices
(found in at least one of the following forms in 11 cities)

Inferior quality goods (especially meats and produce)   11
Overpricing (especially on days welfare checks issued)   8
Exorbitant interest rates (particularly in connection with furniture and appliance sales)   7
Fraudulent practices[34]   6

BLACK IDENTITY

. . . we must first redefine ourselves. Our basic need is to reclaim our history and our identity from what must be called cultural terrorism, from the depreciation of self-justifying white guilt. We shall have to struggle for the right to create our own terms through which to define ourselves and our own relationship to the society, and to have those terms recognized. . . .[35]
My point of view is certainly formed by my history and it is probably that only a creature despised by history finds history a questionable matter. On the other hand, people who imagine that history flatters them (as it does, indeed, since they wrote it) are impaled on their history like a butterfly on a pin. . . .[36]

A man's identity is laid upon him like a cloak at the moment of his birth, especially in a society which emphasizes not only differences but invidious comparisons in these differences. The white American society has given to the Negro every characteristic which it then uses to discriminate against him, to mock him, and to ignore him in his struggle for dignity. As Malcolm X so emphatically proclaimed, the greatest crime committed by the white man against the black was to rob him of his identity and teach him to hate the identity that was given him. For many blacks in America, there

---

[34] *Report of the National Advisory Commission.*
[35] Carmichael and Hamilton, *Black Power*, pp.34–35.
[36] James Baldwin, "Unnameable Objects, Unspeakable Crimes," in *Black on Black*, ed. A. Adorf (New York: The Macmillan Company, 1968), p.95.

has been a tendency not only to resent his black qualities but to blame these, rather than the white man's abuse of them, for producing his sorrow.[37] The theoreticians of the black struggle for equality and justice conceive of identity as a matter of differentiating the black man from the image imposed upon him as part of his American experience. So long as this image is maintained, the black man's ability to attain some power over his own life is retarded. The selection of African loyalties, of a Muslim religion and sometimes names, of Swahili as the relevant language, and of an emphasis on reconstructing the conception of blackness as beautiful rather than sinister or ugly are the most obvious forms of the identity transformations. The evolution of a militant rather than a passive posture is a less obvious but perhaps more significant shift in identity. It is significant because it expresses not so much an attitude of frustration at being restrained from access to the white man's opportunity structure, although this is important, but because it expresses the black man's desire to detach himself from the whole spectrum of white values. Black anger is directed as much toward the upwardly mobile Negro and the Uncle Tom, as it is toward the white society which the middle-class Negro wishes to join.

The black man feels more than anything else that he must detach himself from the tradition and long-range consequences of his slave role, which in many ways he still feels—not only the bitterness of this early humiliation, but the stigma that he has been forced to retain in order to survive as a "free man," since only the literal chains were removed after the Civil War. The real chains were forged in "a system designed to destroy ambition, prevent independence, and erode intelligence for the past three and a half centuries."[38]

Identity is heritage, and if a cultural group exists over a long enough period of time, they can be selective about the heritage they wish to identify as significantly their own. Few blacks wish to relate to their heritage as slaves. They can find, however, in both African life and history a heritage of which to be proud, complete with heroes and beauty. But this heritage, the spokesmen cry, was ever denied to the people who needed it so much.

For many Negroes the result of the American experience is perceived as a journey to obliteration, to the complete and final death of an identity. This can be seen as one function of integra-

---

37 W. H. Grier and P. M. Cobbs, *Black Rage* (New York: Bantam, 1968), p.23.
38 Charles E. Silberman, *Crisis in Black and White* (New York: Vintage Books, 1964), p.77.

tion. The integrative process, as analogized by the Muslims in the story of Yacub, is one of ultimate assimilation through marriage and birth, to the point where dark skins are ultimately to be replaced by varying stages of white and finally white altogether. To this end, the Muslims teach, the black man must be wary and teach his brothers who do not approve of the mating of two dark skins.[39]

It is to protect against this kind of ultimate cooptation of the black American that Coptics, Muslims, and ultimately other black men seek to reemphasize another tradition, that of the African, and to exaggerate the positive values inherent in some parts of the American experience. Two of these forms occur in the slogans, "Black is beautiful," and "The black man has soul."

It is not important to understand what soul means to a black man, although perhaps some whites can come close to understanding. It is more useful to understand that the emphasis on soul is a prideful kind of ethnocentrism that designates one form of black superiority which whites can never attain. Soul is in the food and the way it is prepared, it is in the style of dress and the walk, it is in the music the black man plays and loves, it is in his language and his relationships with his friends and family. It is so intrinsically indigenous, produced out of an unreplicable experience, that no white can ever really understand much less develop it. And if it is emphasized enough, black people, who need to be cohered in their identification, will come to believe that there is no reason to emulate the white gods.

Identity is, of course, cohesion. It is a process of making brothers and sisters out of all black men. Identity is a cohering mechanism, a process of seeking in the black experience a set of desirable traditions, the components of the soulful past, which will hold black people together in the face of temptations to continue to buy the white man's economy and the white man's identity. The threat of the Muslim movements throughout the country, to the black power structure in the black community, signified the failure of this leadership to cohere the black man behind a common identity. Today blacks do appear, on the crest of black nationalism, to be establishing that identity which is the prelude to any kind of meaningful integration. To integrate prior to discovering that identity would be to join together out of the unidimensional tradition of superior–inferior relationships. An identity separate from that imposed by the white society means to the black man moving toward integration that a coalition is possible based on respect for

39 Malcolm X, *Autobiography*, pp.165–166.

differences rather than upon invidious distinctions based upon positions in some order to which both racial groups owe allegiance. Without identity, integration only means more of the same, except with a little more politeness.

BLACK POWER

Once the identity of the black man is revived, so that he perceives a coherence around certain basic definitions of himself and others, he has established the basic condition for acting together, for constituting a force in American life. Politically cohesion can mean a voting bloc, and given the fact that in voting white society splits pretty much down the middle, 10 million black votes, as a bloc, can mean a significant difference for the black man's welfare.

One of the most important foundations for the understanding of Black Power lies in our conception of its emergence in time. That is, why now? And if we can understand why now, we can perhaps better understand its significance in American social life. In one sense the meaning of the Black Power movement can be found in the fact that not a half decade ago black leaders were willing to go to jail to pay this price for the necessity of keeping the movement active. On April 16, 1963, Martin Luther King, Jr. wrote, in his "Letter from Birmingham Jail:"

I cannot sit idly by in Atlanta and not be concerned about what happens in Birmingham. Injustice anywhere is a threat to justice everywhere. . . . My friends, I must say to you that we have not made a single gain in civil rights without determined legal and nonviolent pressure. . . . We know, through painful experience, that freedom is never voluntarily given by the oppressor; it must be demanded by the oppressed. Frankly, I have yet to engage in a direct-action that was "well timed" in the view of those who have not suffered unduly from the disease of segregation. For years now I have heard the word "Wait!" It rings in the ear of every Negro with piercing familiarity. This "Wait!" has almost always meant "Never." We must come to see, with one of our distinguished jurists, that "justice too long delayed is justice denied."[40]

King goes on in this same letter to speak about the revolutions of oppressed peoples around the world, of non-white peoples in Asia and Africa crying out for political independence. He talks further about the moral right to defy and even break unjust laws, of the history and historical respect accorded to other traditions of

[40] In Adorf, *Black on Black*, pp.174–192.

civil disobedience. He reminds us that it was "illegal to aid and comfort a Jew in Hitler's Germany," that laws are a function of the human groups which create them and have no eternal moral significance. He closes this letter with a reminder that even in nonviolence his people were treated brutally as reminders that their efforts for freedom were not yet acceptable.

Martin Luther King, Jr., and others like him put the movement on the road from which there was no turning back. The fact of the early civil rights movement itself was a fact of Black Power; the demonstrations, imprisonments, and boycotts had their effect. The contemporary conception of Black Power, however, must be viewed as the next step in the struggle, impelled, perhaps, because the early strategies were having only minimal consequences.[41] In order to keep the momentum going, new strategies needed to be conceived.

The goals of Black Power as a political force require the society to inspect carefully its values and institutions, to find new structures to solve political and economic problems and to broaden the base for political participation.[42] It is clear that the expectations of black liberation leaders for the white society to put its own house in order, to solve the black man's problems for him, are out of the realm of structural possibility. At the beginning of the movement and even as late as 1965, as Malcolm X observed, there was little structural possibility that the black man either would be in a position to put the national house in order.

Negroes—Afro-Americans—showed no inclination to rush to the United Nations and demand justice for themselves here in America. I really had known in advance that he wouldn't. The American white man has so thoroughly brainwashed the black man to see himself as only a domestic "civil rights" problem that it will probably take longer than I live before the Negro sees that the struggle of the American black man is international.[43]

Without being able to resort to the white society, without faith in the white liberal, and without any recourse to international collaboration, the black leader saw that he must first put his own house together. This means identification, and then cohesion, and then economic and ultimately political power.

---

41 For example, twelve years after the Desegregation Act (1966), 94 per cent of southern Negro children attended segregated schools. See E. W. Brooke, "Blueprint for an Open Society," *Negro Digest* 26 (December 1966): 7.
42 Carmicahel and Hamilton, *Black Power*, p.39.
43 Malcolm X, *Autobiography*, p.364.

Black Power is essentially community power. It is the power that one achieves within his own community to help restructure or modernize the institutions in that community, and it is the power that communities exert on other communities as a function of solidarity. The process by which this power is achieved takes many forms, and these will be considered as separate topics. The goals are something else. They are goals of self-determination and internal leadership, of economic survival and social opportunity. The ultimate goal of Black Power as a national movement can be envisioned as a cumulative product growing out of localized control of one's environment.

Black Power means, for example, that in Lowndes County, Alabama, a black sheriff can end police brutality. A black tax assessor and tax collector and county board of revenue can lay, collect and channel tax monies for the building of better roads and schools serving black people. . . . When black people lack a majority, Black Power means proper representation and sharing of control. It means the creation of power bases, of strength, from which black people can press to change local or nationwide patterns of oppression—instead of from weakness.[44]

More than anything else Black Power holds as a goal something that has always been a part of the American democratic tradition —the participation of a man in the decisions which affect his life. It is simply a matter of gaining rights which are clearly the property of black men as established by the Constitution. The anger that is so often associated with the advocates of Black Power is the anger of a man who must fight and die for the enjoyment of rights that have already been granted him.

There are undoubtedly many persons who would prefer to conceive of Black Power as a militant challenge to the white society in order to justify their own blind wish that some force, paramilitary, or police state, would wipe from the face of his earth the black grimace, the black anger, which seems to be threatening his placid existence. Many white liberals may still be trying to reduce their own dissonance with the Black Power movement by conceiving of black "disruption" as temporary, perhaps misguided, and expecting a return to the safe programs of gradual integration.

But rather than view the Black Power movement as a step toward armed confrontation, which the black leaders view as suicidal or pregnant with implications for riot and civil disorder, the viewer of the black position might begin at least to attempt to understand

[44] Carmichael and Hamilton, *Black Power*, p.46.

Black Power in the sense in which Carmichael and Hamilton would like to have their book, *Black Power,* read:

This book presents a political framework and ideology which represents the last reasonable opportunity for this society to work out its racial problems short of prolonged destructive guerrilla warfare. That such warfare may be unavoidable is not herein denied. But if there is the slightest chance to avoid it, the politics of Black Power as described in this book is seen as the only viable hope.[45]

The main thrust of the Black Power movement is to achieve political influence at a community level. In the light of this goal it becomes irrelevant to the black movement that some black people are handed political office, and it is particularly this phenomenon which confuses the relationship between white liberals and black reformers. Many whites believe that as more Negroes receive political appointments or are even voted into office by the white majority, as was Senator Brooke of Massachusetts, things are changing in the right direction. These liberals do not understand that the structure of power must be guaranteed, and must not be merely the vague visibility of it in many political offices. The structure of power means that the black community can influence elections and voting patterns of elected officials; it does not mean that it can demand a form of tokenism based on the white man's conscience.

INSTITUTIONALIZED RACISM

. . . until the fact of white racism is admitted, it cannot conceivably be expunged; and until it is far more nearly eliminated than this Commission—or any fair man—could find today, how can that great commitment of money and effort here recommended even be approached, much less made?[46]

When blacks, or whites for that matter, scream out about racial discrimination, finally sloganized as "institutional racism," they do not refer to the overt acts of bigotry that are so vividly illustrated in the activities of either the KKK as an extreme example or the closed shops of many unions as a more moderate one. The racism that so clearly motivated the early slave traders to subjugate human beings to misery and indignity, and to rationalize any feelings of guilt by the sole consideration of profit, is not from the contemporary white man's viewpoint his guilt or responsibility. This can

---

45 *Ibid.,* back cover.
46 T. Wicker, "Introduction," *Report of the National Advisory Commission.*

be illustrated from the following speech, reported by Kozol, in which a prominent member of the Boston school committee attempts to defend the white man, or Bostonian in this case, from any indictments of racism or discrimination.

No young or old Negro-American today has been a slave. Besides almost the whole population of Boston is made up of persons of Irish, Italian, Polish, Canadian and Jewish background, who were miles away from America at the time of slavery. If a few Yankees still live in Boston, their grandsires atoned for the sin of their race by shedding their blood in the four-year horror of civil war battlefields.[47]

The difficulty that most people have in understanding the angry cry of institutionalized racism lies in the fact that they do not understand institutionalization. They assume, since most of the people they know or speak to do not appear to be overtly prejudiced, that the institutions they live and work in do not contain racist functions. They do not consider that because black people have inadequate work situations, poor housing, little education, segregated schools, and little political power, there must be something inherently discriminating in the larger institutions that regulate social life. The structure of racism is infinitely more potent than the accumulated prejudices of the citizens who conduct the routine affairs of social organizations. Most individuals, for that matter, cannot even conceive of ways of restructuring these institutions given the most humane set of motivations.

The Christian church is frequently cited as the first and last bastion of institutionalized racism. The church throughout history has been either the advance guard, or the mopping up and consolidating arm of conversion of the non-white, often of the exploitation of the non-white. The true Christian with the conviction that Christ "is the way" can, when viewed in the most favorable light, be described as intending to do the black man a favor by providing him a way toward salvation which he might never have discovered himself. The black rage erupts out of reflection upon the consequences, and a new set of definitions about the role of Christian faith in the American Negro's life emerges. This is most intensively represented in the conception of Christianity put forth by the followers of the Nation of Islam, the Muslims.

The Christian church became infected with racism when it entered white Europe. The Christian church returned to Africa under the ban-

[47] J. Kozol, *Death at an Early Age* (Boston: Houghton Mifflin Company, 1967), p.105.

ner of the cross—conquering, killing, exploiting, pillaging, raping, bullying, beating—and teaching white supremacy. This is how the white man thrust himself into the position of leadership in the world.[48]

Or, brought up to date in the language of the Harlem street-Muslim described in Claude Brown's fictional representation:

Yeah, there's a lot more to it. This whole religion is foreign to a black man. A black man's got no business kneeling down and praying to some old crazy figurines and talking that old "Our Father," "Jesus," and that kind of business. This Christianity thing is the worst thing that ever happened to Negroes. If it wasn't for Christianity, Negroes would have stopped praying a long time ago. They would've started raising a whole lot of hell. They would've known. There would've been thousands of Nat Turners and Denmark Vesseys. But most of the Negroes were too damn busy looking up in the sky and praying to some blond-haired, blue-eyed Jesus and some white God who nobody was supposed to ever see or know anything about. You look at it around here. The Negro's got a whole lot of religion, the so-called Negro, the black man. He's got more religion than anything else.

But he's still poor; he's still being abused. So why the hell don't the white man take some of that religion he's been preaching to us all the time and give us some of the money? Why don't he take some of that religion and use it himself, to make himself less mean and stop killing all those people, lynching all those people down there in Georgia, Mississippi, and Alabama? If there was anything to this white man's religion, he wouldn't be so damn wicked. How can he be so righteous, if it's going to let him come in here and take a whole country from the Indians, kill off most of them, and put the remainder of them on reservations?[49]

The culture of American society is a culture of status values, of loyalties to traditions, and a belief in the inevitability of social justice. In combination these values maintain the important institutions in a relative equilibrium. Persons do not change their roles because they live by the expectations of tradition and are often restrained by inadequate money or lack of ideas. Most Americans are at present either unwilling or socially incapable of bringing about institutional change. They cannot conceive of new forms of police regulation, penal systems, distribution of economic power, politcal organization, or education. And until they can, the cry of institutionalized racism will continue to resound. What is it then that the black man wants the white man to do to end this

---

[48] Malcolm X, *Autobiography*, p.368.
[49] Brown, *Manchild in the Promised Land*, p.332.

form of racism? From the white man's point of view he asks a great deal.

I tell sincere white people, "Work in conjunction with us—each of us working among our own kind." Let sincere white individuals find all other white people they can who feel as they do—and let them form their all-white groups, to work trying to convert other white people who are thinking and acting so racist. Let sincere whites go and teach non-violence to white people.[50]

The difficulty inherent in this expectation is that the white man does not know how to work with his white brothers. The well meaning white attempts to show his concern and his commitment by interacting with blacks on some friendship or ameliorative level. But when he is told to remove himself from black ranks and work among his own, as SNCC told its white supporters, the white liberal or even radical often finds the challenge beyond him.

This is because the black man is asking the white man's help in changing the system that has for so many years enslaved and discriminated against blacks. He is asking the white man for radical action, since he believes only radical action can produce the social disruptions that will change institutions. And most whites are not radicals. Psychologically it is the most difficult thing in the world to behave as a radical after being socialized in a climate of comfort and advantage. The black man's radicalism is motivated by the human stake he has in reducing racism. He has been and is still a victim. He knows he has nothing to lose and much to gain. This is more than ideology, the only motivational support that the white man has. Until the white reformer who wishes to do something to advance the cause of racial equality is willing to put his life and career or whatever on the line, as many whites did in Mississippi or in Chicago during the Democratic National Convention of 1968, then the black man will have to go it alone. And he will go it alone, if he must, with the ultimate consequence of warfare on the streets, black concentration camps, or the institutional capitulation to the black man's needs.

"BURN, BABY, BURN"

Although the civil disorders which flared in many Northern cities between 1965 and 1968 can easily be traced to a history of racist discrimination in the United States, the important focus of the

[50] Malcolm X, *Autobiography*, p.377.

commission assigned by the president to investigate these disorders was to begin with an attempt to explain the new mood of the black man. Why was it happening now, what made it finally occur when the conditions which produced it had been present for over a hundred years? The description provided by the commission of the initial events which precipitated the Los Angeles (Watts) riots, as well as those in other Northern cities, presents a portrait of spontaneity. A black man will be stopped by the police, an angry interchange will occur, a shot will ring out, a black man or woman will lie bleeding, onlookers will throw rocks, more will come, cars will be turned over, and then the burning and looting will start.

By the end of World War II over 1 million Negroes were in uniform, thousands of others saw service in Korea, and a disproportionate number of blacks went to fight yellow people in Viet Nam. Many were decorated; they felt they had done something for their country. The return to civilian life brought a return to normal, a denial of opportunity for education and for jobs, and present again was the racist discrimination everywhere. Black men were angry and pressed for governmental action. The black mood was becoming apparent. Men who had marched in Germany and in the South Seas and in Korea started to march in Birmingham, Selma, and toward Washington. Civil rights legislation began to flow, slowly, moderately, but at least forward. School desegregation became a legal reality, but whites were not ready to accept it as a physical reality. The example of the struggle to integrate black students in Little Rock evolved into a pattern throughout the South. But the federal government was committed to making a show of support for its own laws. Integration as policy was accomplished. The black man in America, through the vehicle of television, saw the frightened yet courageous faces of black children making a giant step toward freedom. He saw them jostled, forced to cry. And later he read about four little black girls bombed to death in Birmingham, watched his brothers being chewed by vicious police dogs and beaten by police night sticks in Selma, Alabama. He began to see again and again his brothers pounded and dragged from lunch counters and from the steps of city halls where they had peacefully walked to protest their pitiful condition. By 1963 with the Birmingham boycott and the bloody riot which led to the death of the four girls, the black man had been fired into a functional loss of fear.

At the same time that it became apparent that the black man was no longer willing to sit passively back and allow white racism to plow him under, it was also apparent to whites as well as to blacks that there was a large disparity in advantages and opportunities between blacks and whites. As the nation moved toward the reduction of this disparity at governmental levels, the blacks became more angry at the disparities they observed, angry that laws had to be enacted to give them the rights they deserved by being citizens of their country and fighting for it in three wars. What was probably a spontaneous eruption in Watts had far-reaching social psychological consequences in the rest of the country. The black man witnessed that he could do something with his accumulated rage—he could strike out and terrorize the "master race." He discovered that his anger was now a weapon, a source of potential violence, and he learned that to be pacified, to surrender his anger, would be to surrender perhaps his last opportunity for equality. His anger was kept alive and is very much alive today. At times it finds outlets in civil disorder, and that, too, keeps the anger burning. The white society knows that it cannot make many mistakes. It has learned that the death of one man, a culture hero who represented non-violence, could set off violence in dozens of cities.

Thirty-four black men are reported as having died in Watts. In the minds of many if not most other blacks these men are martyrs, heroes. The greatest weapon the black man has now evolved out of his anger, and his experience is the fact that he is not afraid to die in the struggle he has carved out for himself. And he knows that every time he follows the cry "burn, baby, burn" he might very well die. But hundreds of thousands of black men knew as much when they took up arms in Germany, the South Pacific, Korea and Viet Nam.

"Burn, baby, burn" is a cry of glee. The black man utters the expression with a smile, the kind of smile that is possible only to a man who has been forced into a position to enjoy someone else's loss. It is the smile of the "field negro" slave watching the master's house burning while "house negroes" scurry in an effort to help the master save his property. It is clearly symbolic of the division that has always characterized the attitude of the haves toward the have-nots, particularly when the haves, having has evolved out of the toil of the have-nots.

Considering conditions rather than mental attitudes, the report of the Advisory Commission on Civil Disorders summarized the "causes" of the riots. The causes have been discussed in several ways to this point, and therefore it is not necessary to elaborate upon them. They are the specific forms of racism in America.

1. Pervasive discrimination and segregation.
2. Black migration and white exodus.
3. Black ghettos.
4. Frustrated hopes.
5. Legitimation of violence.
6. Powerlessness.
7. The police.[51]

People can come to know intuitively what political leaders learn from experience: One is most likely to get what he wants when he is able to demonstrate visibly the consequences of human or economic investment. It is much easier to secure a multimillion dollar allocation for space exploration when millions of viewers can watch on television the flight of the astronauts than it is to secure allocations for the invisible poor, whom the mass of Americans do not want to see. Burning buildings are dramatically visible and hard to ignore. Most Americans, judging from the current politcal climate, want visible restraint to protect them against visible conflagration. It is clear from the recommendations of the Commission, however, that the simple-minded approach that sees the solution as one of firemen with rifles and increased police supervision (it should be remembered that the Commission cited police incidents as prominent in starting riots) will not, in the short or long run, solve the problem. Only through a comprehensive and dedicated effort to restructure the social, educational, and political institutions can the flames of anger be extinguished.

BLACK MOBILIZATION—THE UNITED FRONT

Black radicals, like their white counterparts, disagree as to the most effective methods for achieving social justice. SNCC (Student Non-Violent Coordinating Committee), will disagree with the NAACP and with the Southern Christian Leadership Conference. These, in turn, may disagree forcibly with the Black Panther Party, a group of black militants who adhere to the philosophy of self-defense by "whatever means necessary." White leaders realize the violent potential in this kind of confrontation, and perhaps one form of power is thus achieved. The point is that black leaders of almost all organized groups hold to the important principle that differences must not be aired before the white man. This is "family talk" and

[51] *Report of the National Advisory Commission,* pp.203–205.

must be so regarded by all black brothers and sisters, be they Muslims or Christians, militants or advocates of non-violence. A united front is crucial to the achievement of the goals of the Black Power movement. To this end black organizations, at least in this stage of the movement, recognize the value of non-coalition and non-assimilation. Whites are not welcome in any of the leadership capacities. This does not mean that whites, all whites, are to be defined as the enemy. Those who care can find ways to aid the movement, and this assistance is welcomed.

There is a definite, much-needed role that whites can play. . . . Given the pervasive nature of racism in the society and the extent to which attitudes of white superiority and black inferiority have become embedded, it is very necessary that white people begin to disabuse themselves of such notions. Black people, as we stated earlier, will lead the challenge to old values and norms, but whites who do recognize the need must also work in this sphere. Whites have access to groups in the society never reached by black people. They must get within those groups and help perform this essential educative function.[52]

The mobilization of blacks seems to have gained impetus when blacks realized they would not have to coalesce with whites to gain their ends. This kind of coalition, either with or between organizations, posed too much of a threat to the viability of the drive for mobilization. Even in the one seemingly significant coalition that black militant groups were interested in effecting, between the Black Panthers and the Peace and Freedom Party in California, the ground rules still remained that each organization was to do its own work in its separate spheres of potential influence.

Where the really sincere white people have got to do their "proving" of themselves is not among the black "victims" but out on the battle lines of where America's racism really is—and that's in their own home communities; America's racism is among their own fellow whites. That's where the sincere whites who really mean to accomplish something have got to work.[53]

Black unity, the closing of ranks, has required the black man to listen to the "take care of our business" philosophy espoused by many and juxtapose this against his current or planned participation in national events and programs. Things have moved rapidly in the direction of unity. They have moved from a temporary

[52] Carmichael and Hamilton, *Black Power*, p.81.
[53] Malcolm X, *Autobiography*, pp.376–377.

emphasis of the role of the black man in history and the way this has been carefully excluded from the white man's texts, to a criticism of such black "heroes" as Crispus Attucks, who was one of the first to fall in the American Revolution. The line is now that Attucks should have been taking care of business, the business of helping his own people rather than fighting to the death for the survival of a slave-holding and racist society. Brought up to date, the black man's role in Viet Nam has been shifted from an emphasis on participation to achieve greater rights to a devastating attack on black men who want to fight for this country's defense of freedom in Southeast Asia when it is felt they should be fighting for the freedom of their own people in America. Black mobilization is dependent on the success of the "take care of our business" principle, and the success of this anti-establishment position cannot yet be evaluated. The ranks of those who are members of most black organizations is a statistic only known to the leadership of those organizations. It is clear, however, that black radicals do not wish to divide their people by asserting the impossibility of a coalition between blacks of various ideological persuasions or even social class position. A closing of ranks means that all efforts are being made to make the movement a necessary alternative to that of separate groups working in separate ways. The number of defections of the black bourgeosie to the radical movement is also not an available statistic but we might infer that, in the era of the black revolution, even the most solidly entrenched middle class Negro has at least to be aware that he is needed by his people.

THE WHITE PROBLEM IN AMERICA

Many whites, particularly liberal whites, have withdrawn their support from the civil rights movement because they see the trends in the black position becoming "racist"-oriented, the condition they had hoped to alleviate. Racism as a popular contemporary notion does not have any meaning apart from discriminatory practices, injustices, economic and social deprivation, and inequality of power or opportunity. To argue that black militants wish to develop or intensify an about-face in the superiority-inferiority status of blacks and whites is a rather unrealistic expectation. Black separatism, or even black militant confrontation, can be meaningfully interpreted only as a program of liberation, but hardly as a struggle for domination of the white society. The goals of the civil rights movement have never changed, only the means by which the cause might be pressed home to those who need to be convinced.

Gunnar Myrdal, the Swedish sociologist who came to America to study the Negro, recognized early in his investigations that the Negro, as a problem or as a social adaptation, was a creation of the white American and could be explained only by explaining the white mind in relation to the Negro.[54] The black problem in America, we can assume, is a combination of the problems Negroes suffer as part of their American experience, and the problems inherent in the nature of the Negro's relationship to the white man. In the most contemporary sense the Negro problem seems to mean: How much damage can we expect the Negro to do to and in our cities this or next year? It seems in a sociological sense that the black problem is a function of the white problem. The black man's adaptation in the United States can be easily plotted on a chart of white policies of discrimination and exploitation. And these policies can be traced to the white man's conception of the Negro and his definition of their mutual relationship to the world in which they both live. The problem, for example, is not so much that the Negro lives a marginal existence in a ghetto but that his place of residence is predetermined by his inability to live in the same community as whites, even if he has the necessary money. He may physically inhabit a house in a white community, but the experience of most blacks is that psychological survival depends on being with their own.

The premise of this special issue is that America can no longer afford the luxury of ignoring its real problem: the white problem. To be sure, Negroes are not blameless. It takes two to tango and the Negro, at the very least, is responsible for accepting the grapes of degradation. But that, you see, has nothing to do with the man who is responsible for the degradation. The prisoner is always free to try to escape. What the jailer must decide is whether he will help escaping prisoners over the wall or shoot them in the back. And the lesson of American life is that no Negro —no matter how much money he accumulated, no matter how many degrees he earned—has ever crossed completely the wall of color caste, except by adopting the expedient of passing. Let us come to the point and stand on it: Negroes are condemned in America, not because they are poor, not because they are uneducated, not because they are brown or black—Negroes are condemned in America because they are Negroes, *i.e.*, because of an idea of the Negro and the Negro's place in the white American mind.[55]

The "white problem" in America can be designated as an attitude, a fixed and concrete habit of mind about the way inter-racial

[54] Gunnar Myrdal, *An American Dilemma* (New York: Harper and Row, 1944).
[55] Lerone Bennett, Jr., "The White Problem in America," in Adorf, *Black on Black*, p.105.

relationships should be. Over and beyond this conception is one that challenges our skill and intelligence beyond the point where we might expect it to function. It is the notion that racial hatred is over three hundred years old, impressed deeply on our collective mind by the accumulated injustices and institutionalized provision to maintain these injustices, even after the inter-personal hostility has disappeared. To continue waiting for the traditions to erode, given their strength and their implicit inclusion in our social and moral law, could easily mean that no human being living today could see the end of racism. This may well be the view of many, but this kind of delayed gratification is not any longer a typical mode of thinking in the arena of moral injustice. The white man's most serious problem, as an extension of his traditional definition of the Negro, is that he is utterly unprepared to understand the evolution of the modern black man. He is confused about militancy, does not understand riots, and honestly thinks that white men of good will will in time give the Negro all he wants and needs. The white man who openly admits his prejudice, or even his willingness to permit racist discrimination to go unchecked, has another kind of problem. He must live with irreconcilable beliefs, for just as he is a product of a culture loaded with rationales for the exploitation and degradation of the black man, he also has a feeling for the democratic tradition. He knows this tradition in his country's history. There is too much dialogue in this country today for him to bury his contradiction. He must live with his rationalizations and be increasingly aware of them. They are becoming harder to believe. And if he expresses disbelief, he must change as a person. This is not easy for him. He will go on creating more contemporary rationalizations. In his desperate search for comfort, he even frequently ascribes to the black revolution the probability of its being dominated by Soviet or Red Chinese agents. The white problem in America is then a combination of racist traditions and a consuming ignorance of process, particularly of revolutionary process. This is only to suggest that the white and black problem in America is to learn how to avoid in the years to come a series of bloody confrontations between the races. In order to survive for three hundred years it has been necessary for the black man to understand the white man. The black man today is no longer interested in this kind of marginal survival. The choice is placed squarely on the shoulders of the white man in America. He must accept his problem, try to understand it, and work harder than most whites are currently willing to work to make possible the evolution of equality in America.

MINORITIES AND THE SCHOOLS

> The goals of assuring equality of educational opportunity and provid-
> ing the most effective education for every child are inherent imperatives
> of American education in this latter half of the twentieth century.
>
> Any society which is to remain visible and dynamic must raise the
> educational standards for all of its people and must exploit and use
> constructively high intellectual potential wherever it is to be found.
> The argument in support of this is no longer sentimental.[56]

Clark's point is essentially that the pressure for stimulating and
rapid efforts to provide equal educational opportunities for students of all races comes not from our conscience but from our concern about our internal as well as international social health.

Negroes, Mexican-Americans, and Puerto Ricans generally do
not do well in any of the categories by which educational attainment is gauged. They do not achieve well, they do not become well
socialized to the values of the Protestant ethic, they do not come
to aspire to extended educational opportunities, they do not become integrated human beings, either in the sense of racial integration or social integration. By social integration we mean coming to believe that one's student role is meaningful in the light of
the overall school program. They do not feel they belong and
consequently do not want to belong.

For the last decade educational and social reformers have been
calling for and sometimes receiving support for programs to increase the educational opportunities of these minority group students. Bureaucratically sponsored programs of this sort require
some kind of verbal designation of those to be helped, and such
people have been variously referred to as deprived, culturally disadvantaged, educationally disadvantaged, culturally or socially different, and the like. Once given a program and a set of labels to
specify the recipients of special attention, the reformist activities
received nationwide publicity. Sometimes it backfired, as in the case
of the Slater school in New York where angry parents struck and
picketed the school to protest a special and what they considered
invidious distinction made between their children and others.[57]

The concern with educational opportunities of minority groups

---

[56] Kenneth Clark, "Educational Stimulation of Racially Disadvantaged Children," in *Education in Depressed Areas*, ed. Harry Passow (New York: Teachers
College Press, Columbia University, 1963).
[57] Estelle Fuchs, *Pickets at the Gates* (New York: The Free Press, 1966).

has been ballooning in educational and political circles for a number of years, and consequently there have been many sociological and educational treatises on the subject. It is not necessary graphically to represent the findings here. We knew what they would be, in general, before the studies were undertaken. The Coleman Report, for example, the last in a long series of investigations attacking the dimensions of differential success rates between students of different economic and racial characteristics, should put to rest, at least for the present, the need to validate the fact that Negroes do not do as well in schools as whites. Even in racially integrated schools, for example, the black student suffers a worsened self-image as a result of his own invidious comparison between himself and the white students around him.[58]

We know, convincingly, what the outcome of the black and brown student's educational experience is. We do not know so much about how it happens. Rates of success are much easier to portray than the way these rates are produced.

PRODUCT AND PROCESS

The following table taken from Coleman's survey of the distribution of educational advantages represents a statement of a relationship between a characteristic of a group of persons, in this case race, and an educational outcome, or what we might think of as the product of the interaction of students and schools.[59]

Table 7-1 describes the end product of an educational experience. It tells us, for example, that of all native born whites whose parents were also born in the United States who began high school, 75 per cent of both males and females graduated. The figure is even higher for native born whites whose parents were foreign born. For native born Negroes only 52 per cent of the males and 56 per cent of the females who began a high school career managed to complete the experience. The data reveal that the outcome of an educational career is different for whites than it is for blacks and browns. It does not, however, tell us how these differences were produced. This is what we mean by *process*.

58 James Coleman, *Equality of Educational Opportunities*, U. S. Office of Health, Education, and Welfare (Washington, D. C.: U. S. Government Printing Office, 1966).
59 Coleman's results must be evaluated in the light of the fact that many large urban areas did not participate in the study. Many weak findings regarding differential opportunities were possibly influenced by this fact. It is the assumption of the Kerner report (Report of the National Advisory Commission, p.428) that larger and more revealing discrepancies in Negro-white human and material facilities would have appeared had the cities participated.

Table 7-1

Selected Measures of School Retention for Persons Twenty to Twenty-four Years of Age by Sex and Ethnic Status, U.S., 1960*

ETHNIC STATUS	PERCENTAGE FINISHING FIFTH GRADE WHO COMPLETED SOME HIGH SCHOOL		PERCENTAGE COMPLETING SOME HIGH SCHOOL WHO GRADUATED	
	Male	Female	Male	Female
United States	86.5	89.8	73.6	73.9
Native white of native parentage	87.8	91.2	75.3	75.4
Native white of foreign or mixed parentage	90.9	93.7	78.3	81.0
Foreign born	75.9	76.9	75.5	71.0
Negro	74.5	80.8	52.7	56.1
American Indian	67.3	68.8	50.4	49.0
Japanese	96.5	96.1	88.5	87.4
Chinese	92.7	92.9	85.2	84.9
Puerto Rican	61.4	63.3	40.9	47.0
Spanish surname (Mexican-Americans in Southwest U.S.)	68.3	69.2	55.8	58.4

* Taken from Coleman, *Equality of Educational Opportunities,* p. 450.

Specifically the kind of process that needs to be emphasized here is the process of institutional failure to provide for blacks and browns, as well as for whites, the opportunity to utilize the educational experience to one's full advantage. In analyzing this process it is not useful even to consider the way in which the individual characteristics of those who "fail" or are "failed" conspire to produce this failure. That is, for example, we cannot advance our knowledge of what happens to Negro, Puerto Rican, and Mexican-American students by concentrating on what it means to be one of these categories independent of how society defines these persons and how they are treated in the schools. Whatever the black or brown man is in the United States, he is this only in the context of historical or institutional definitions of him. Let us turn our attention then to the structural implementations of those definitions.

SEGREGATION IN THE SCHOOL

The prominent process by which social mobility is attained by those who are at the bottom of the social class ladder is through some kind of exposure to the values and to the experiences of those whose status is higher. Social institutions are able to provide this kind of exposure but historically this has not been the case. Racial segregation is found in churches, in ecological living arrangements, and in schools. Through a process of personal as well as institutional organization of schools and schooling, the dark skinned people of the United States have been largely unexposed to their white counterparts. In the Southern part of the United States we observe a tradition of segregation by fiat, of segregation stemming from the manifestly planned separation of the races. In other sections of the United States, the conception of the "neighborhood" school has had much the same consequences. What we now call *de facto* segregation is a process of utilizing a racist model of ecological organization in order to ensure racial homogeneity in the school. Such an arrangement has been defended and is still defended on the grounds of making the school experience a link to the home experience, that children who play together should go to school together. It is also the most economically efficient arrangement for the district and often for the persons who might otherwise be required to pay for transportation out of their neighborhood.

In 1954 the Supreme Court in a historic decision (*Brown* vs. *Topeka Board of Education*) ruled that the principle of "separate but equal" was a continuation of racist definitions of school organization and that schools should be desegregated. Yet as late as April, 1964, only 15 per cent of Negro children were in bi-racial schools. In Arkansas only 13 of 415 school districts desegregated and less than one per cent of the state's 112,012 Negro school children attended white schools.[60] School boards have found many a loophole by which the Court's decision could be circumvented. They have been able to gerrymander a district in order to invoke the neighborhood school concept and maintain segregation by decree. Presently there are several cases pending before state and federal supreme courts to hasten compliance with the 1954 decision and to close some of the loopholes.

In the North the flight to the suburbs of white families and the subsequent *de facto* racial segregation of living facilities has hampered most efforts to develop more racially balanced schools. To compensate for such a trend the Economic Opportunities Act of 1964 has provided funds for the upgrading of education programs in the schools which have been largely abandoned to Negro and Puerto Rican students.

What are the effects of racial isolation? It might be useful to attempt to answer this question in the context of an assessment of

60 *The New Republic*, March 28, 1964, p.5.

the effects of integration. Many urban school districts, unable to solve the problem of integration, have attempted to emphasize compensatory programs in the belief that these programs, rather than the sheer fact of integration, will be meeting their responsibility to the students. The thinking or perhaps rationalization takes the form of arguing that the problem for disadvantaged children is a lack of motivation and preparation to learn, not the fact of their racial isolation. If compensatory activities can make learning possible, then the integration problem is another kind of consideration, social rather than educational. And since the school's responsibility in the social arena is ambiguous, the educational problem takes priority. Can we argue that integration is an educational as well as a social problem? To do this we need to consider the effects of integration above and beyond compensatory efforts. Some research is available. The Madison Area project, (Syracuse, New York) a program of compensatory education in predominantly Negro schools, conducted a massive effort to upgrade the learning skills of Negro students over a three-year period. At the end of this time students who had participated in the Madison Area project were compared with Negro students who had been integrated in schools with no compensatory programs. The comparison showed that Negro students in predominantly white schools were achieving at approximately a quarter-grade level above those in project schools. The Syracuse public schools conducted their own study in this area and found similar results. The integration program had better effects for Negro children than the compensatory programs. The Berkeley school district made a similar analysis. When comparing the achievement scores for a group of Negro children who had been bused to predominantly all-white schools with students in Negro schools who had received compensatory assistance, the bused children showed a more rapid rate of progress.[61]

The U. S. Commission on Civil Rights, exploring the question of integration versus compensatory programs, concluded that from the evidence they analyzed in many cities the integration of Negro children was of more significant educational advantage than the compensatory programs.[62]

The point is that integration of racial minorities appears to have important educational effects and, if the school admits its legal and moral responsibility to educate all children equally, the neces-

[61] *Racial Isolation in the Public Schools: A Report of the Commission on Civil Rights* (Washington, D. C.: U. S. Government Printing Office, 1967), pp.128–131.
[62] *Ibid.,* pp.128–137.

sity for reducing racial isolation in the schools is clear. Anyone who has made a personal visit to the ghetto and the suburban school and has made an intuitive comparison can predict the differential effects. It is not difficult to observe the presence of unequal physical and human facilities, nor is it difficult to sense a climate in which learning flourishes and one where learning stagnates from inaction.

Physical Facilities

The schools which have been abandoned to the ghetto residents might legitimately have been abandoned or even condemned in the light of curernt thinking about desirable educational environments. The simple fact that Negroes, Puerto Ricans, and Mexican-Americans move to the oldest residential areas of the city means that the buildings are going to be old. The schools will be unattractive, even ugly, in comparison to the new modern educational homes that we observe in the suburbs, and the psychological effects of living among worn, broken, and dirty objects can be easily imagined. The lighting is usually bad, the heating is often inefficient, and the hallways and even ancient fire escapes portray an image of obsolescence.

Again, the Coleman report adds to our factual knowledge of the differential educational treatment of persons of different ethnic backgrounds. Non-white students appear to have fewer or worse facilities of the following types available to them.

1. Auditoriums, cafeterias, gymnasiums and athletic fields.
2. Shops, power tools, biology and chemistry laboratories.
3. Language laboratories.
4. Physics laboratories.
5. Centralized libraries.
6. Number of books.
7. Full time librarians (primarily a Mexican-American disadvantage).
8. Text books.
9. Up-to-date texts (mainly in the Midwest).[63]

Human Facilities

Given the nature of the difficulties of teaching in ghetto schools (by this most teachers mean discipline problems but may also mean the sheer difficulty of teaching students to perform the basic educational tasks), we constantly observe an exodus of trained teachers

[63] Coleman, *Equality of Educational Opportunities*, pp.66–80.

to the white suburban schools. The ghetto child frequently experiences the substitute teacher more often than a regular teacher. The classes are usually overcrowded, representing the parallel condition in the neighborhood, and pupil-teacher ratios which should be smaller, given the nature of the task, are often larger. The teachers who do find themselves in ghetto schools are often those who are funneled there because of their own inexperience, unpreparedness to teach, or simply because they are black.[64] Often the teachers are awaiting retirement, not wishing to shift their location in the last years of their career. These teachers, given their task and their unreadiness and/or unwillingness to accept it, experience personal frustration and alienation. Unable or unwilling to direct the logical aggression toward administrators or even parents that follows frustration, they often find a likely victim in the student.

Coleman looked at the characteristics of personnel serving schools of different ethnic compositions and concluded that, in comparison to schools dominated by white children, those dominated by non-white pupils

1. were more likely to have Negro teachers;
2. have teachers who score lower on a test of verbal facility than teachers in white schools;
3. have teachers in the Northeast with less teaching experience than in white schools;
4. are "poorly" regarded by most teachers;
5. were more likely to have teachers who teach large classes;
6. had teachers who would prefer to change schools if given a chance.[65]

The *de jure* and *de facto* segregated school in the United States is, as we can infer from the characteristics of facilities and personnel, more than a statistic of racial composition. It is a structure of unequal opportunity. We have talked so far only about how the segregated school is staffed and supplied. The process by which the rates of success and failure are produced are more dynamically illustrated in the way in which students are organized and allocated by the personnel within the school.

Differentiation

Most schools have mapped out routines for differentiating students. The consequence of these routines is that students are

[64] C. E. Vontress, "Displaced Negroes and Urban Schools," *Phi Delta Kappan* (November 1963): 71–81.

[65] Coleman, *Equality of Educational Opportunities*, pp.122–165.

grouped together with those who have similar characteristics or performance records. Most students are required to take some kind of a standardized intelligence test and are grouped by score. Davis and others have long ago exposed the cultural biases of such tests, but nonetheless the tests continue to be used in differentiating students.[66] Once students are grouped, based upon scores on standardized tests, grade point averages, and possibly even interest inventories, they are assigned at the secondary level to a curriculum. These curricula usually define the likelihood of a student's going on to higher education. The patterns are quite obvious. Minority group students are allocated generally to curricula which are educationally terminal, and given the fact that automation is radically reorganizing the world of work particularly at the vocational level, these students are in effect being allocated to highly precarious job opportunities. Given further that they experience discrimination in hiring practices based upon skin color, their opportunities are not appreciably advanced by their school experience.

Differentiation of students into classes or groups which experience different rates of academic success also occurs through a more subtle form of organization than that of testing and grouping. It occurs as a result of the evaluation of students on criteria which are both "moral" and cognitive.[67] Students are placed into a social situation and required to exhibit that they can use their minds in ways that are expected by the teachers. At the same time they are expected to demonstrate where they stand with respect to the internalization of a set of values, sometimes referred to as the Protestant ethic, embodying such qualities as cleanliness, industriousness, punctuality, respect for authority, and so on. Given that these moral qualities are representative of the American middle-class, and since they are necessary to attain and maintain middle-class status, the average minority group child is assigned an inferior status in the classroom which he retains during most of his educational career.

The assignment of students to positions of educational superiority and inferiority uniformly follows class lines. Teachers simply do not approve of the manners, morals, or even language of the disenfranchised minority group child and cannot accept his lack of educational aspiration. She often projects her own failure in the classroom onto the student, emphasizing their unwillingness to meet her expectations.

66 Allison Davis, *Social Class Influences upon Learning* (Cambridge: Harvard University Press, 1952).
67 Talcott Parsons, "The School Class as a Social System," *Harvard Education Review* 29, No. 4 (1959): 297–318.

Racism in the Classroom

Racism is a word that has taken on teeth in the last few years. Because it is often used by those who present themselves in a posture of rage, the word itself has assumed the fury of the user. It is therefore difficult to talk about racism without incurring a number of defensive rationalizations. That is, many persons feel forced to defend themselves against a quality that exists more in systems than in individuals. Therefore it is necessary to make the point early in our discussion of racism that we are talking about a property of institutions rather than individuals. There are of course a number of overtly racist personalities or persons who manifest their prejudices in discriminatory and often hostile acts toward persons of dark skin. Members of the KKK are the most obvious examples. The majority of Americans and probably the majority of school teachers do not display overt discriminatory acts in their relations with non-white people. At least they do not do so knowingly. Most teachers believe in human equality, as do most other persons. But in the way they structure roles and evolve a set of normative patterns of role enactment, institutions have produced a system in which dark-skinned persons are relegated to inferior positions and allocated to inferior statuses. This is the structure of racism. In order to understand this structure we need to look at the specific patterns in which racism occurs and to explore the dynamics of how these patterns are produced and perpetuated.

Social Distinctions

When Kozol confronts his self-styled "non-prejudiced" reading teacher with the very little that a Negro child is getting from his educational experience, she retorts, "He's getting a whole lot more than he deserves."[68]

The implications of this statement are considerable. It gets very much to the heart of the basis on which invidious distinctions are made. In American society the prominent value underlying success is that one gets what he earns. When the reading teacher expresses her belief that the Negro child has not earned the right to receive certain educational advantages, she is pressing this value into action. Persons become defined along a continuum of what they have earned and grouped into categories of "deserving" and "undeserving." Often these categories operate independently of individual merit, and persons are classified as "undeserving" and treated commensurately with that definition simply because they possess the

[68] Kozol, *Death at an Early Age*, p.27.

qualities of others in that category. To be black and to be poor are correlates of that designation.

The criteria by which students place themselves or are placed in one of these categories are established by the institution and translated into larger social values which reflect the components of the Protestant ethic, such as industriousness, respect for authority, goal orientation, delayed gratification, and the like. If students do not display such qualities, they are defined as undeserving of the efforts of the teacher and often have withheld from them the resources of the school. Once students are defined as undeserving, which carries the stigma of inferiority in the eyes of the institutional personnel, certain strategies are employed. These strategies emerge in the same fashion that techniques for dealing with the mentally retarded or even the exceptionally able emerge. One designs categories and then structures an education program commensurate with the problem or educational task that one's definition of such categories evokes. For the "undeserving" poor black the educational task evolves into one of control and allocation. He must be controlled so that he does not disrupt the equilibrium of the school or interfere with the education of the "deserving," and he must be allocated to functional career categories relative to his status and ability. To most educators the solution of the second educational problem lies in the manner in which the student becomes vocationalized. Conant, for example, who conducted an extensive survey into the problems of slum schools, recommended an upgrading of vocational training opportunities in the slum communities.[69]

The whole idea of preparing students for devalued vocational opportunities creates problems in a "damned if you do and damned if you don't" sense. The point is that preparing students for some kind of work appears to be a better plan than allowing them to go into the streets completely untrained for anything. At the same time, when black students are always being trained for low-status occupations, the effect is often similar to the exhibition of outright discrimination. One can advance the core value of the dignity of work, but in the face of the situational reality that the overwhelming majority of black people are forced to enjoy their dignity in low-status careers, such an argument seems hollow. One must recall also that the stigma of the white race in America lies in the fact that they once enslaved the black man. To translate service occupations in which black people service the needs of whites into dig-

69 J. Conant, *Slums and Suburbs* (New York: McGraw-Hill Book Company, 1961).

nified labor intensifies the rage that the black man feels for the indignity of his past. We recall an example in Lorraine Hansberry's early drama about the effects of racial segregation (*Raisin in the Sun* 1958). Miss Hansberry's hero, Walter, exhibits great drive in order to escape the humiliation of being a chauffeur. In social vacuum we can make the argument that a career as a chauffeur does not legitimately invoke invidious distinctions. The problem is of course that no such vacuum does or ever will exist until equality is more than an idea in the minds of outraged blacks or well meaning whites.

The social distinctions that are made in the school appear in acts of omission as well as acts of commission. That is, students are not only differentiated by what one looks for in a social group but also by what one does not look for. The whole idea of the search for and encouragement of talent is the prominent case in point. When a middle-class white student does not exhibit talents or abilities, the average teacher goes looking for them. If a black student does not display the same, the teacher assumes it is because there is nothing there. The fact that she does or does not look for talent is produced by the way that teachers respond to the correlates of social distinctions in the larger society. That is, parents of white students expect achievement, and teachers are then expected to discover the basis for achievement in the child. The black community, however, does not expect great educational achievements from its young, or so the teacher reasons, and consequently she is not pressed to evoke it. The larger society has some standard conceptions about who should be allocated to the professions and who to the streets. Teachers are influenced by these distinctions.

Testing and Grouping

Schools utilize a modern strategy called testing to replace an ancient strategy, that of social typing, or at times, stereotyping. The whole notion of grouping persons together according to some characteristic which they hold in common is based on the human need to reduce complex phenomena to simple units. The problems of teaching large groups of students is logically facilitated by treating persons who appear to be alike in some respect in similar ways. Modern education, however, has advanced beyond the point where we can rely completely on intuition, age, wealth, or ethnic identity as the bases for the simplification of our task. Instead we use the test, the doubtful nature of which was discussed earlier in the chapter. When Negro, Puerto Rican, and Mexican-American students take these tests, they make about the same scores and are therefore grouped (with a "scientific" rationale) together. The problem of such grouping, insofar as this affects the mobility aspirations of those who are so grouped, is that it does not broaden the basis of class or race-linked interaction.

One of the serious retarding effects of this kind of psychometric grouping, which follows ethnic lines, is that educators relate to groups with the same stereotypic view as they would use to describe or analyze individuals. This means, therefore, that the definition of low IQ black students as non-academically oriented focuses the interaction of these students with educators around the theme of producing good citizens and, hopefully, skilled laborers. The mobility possibilities arising out of such a grouping for students who may shift in their motivational base or who might develop new aspirations becomes extremely limited. An educational definition is a ticket to either educational heaven or hell, and not many students can exchange their tickets.

The process of grouping defines students during all of their academic life. Based on IQ tests or standardized achievement tests, students are allocated to reading groups of varying levels or to special classes for remedial or advanced work. Later in junior high school students are classified according to measured ability levels and certain social definitions into varying levels of subject matter classes.[70] Usually by the final semester of the junior high school students are processed into career-oriented categories and funneled into high schools according to this designation. In the high school the organization of psychometric data, including interest inventories and achievement and performance data, leads to grouping into career-linked curricula. By this time flexibility is quite low, and life decisions have been largely determined.

Racist definitions would operate in this process in situations in which persons would make decisions about allocation of black students according to a conception of them as unable—socially, economically, or psychologically—to fulfill the promise of talent. This decision is often avoided by refusal to discover such talent in the first place. When such a process occurs, minority students are often denied the opportunity to be grouped according to the scores they make on the standardized tests.

---

[70] A. Cicourel and J. Kitsuse in *The Educational Decision Makers* (New York: The Bobbs-Merrill Co., Inc., 1963) have demonstrated how grouping of students does not follow completely the manifest criteria established for grouping and how independent assessments and social and psychological definitions of persons operate in such grouping.

The Self-fulfilling Prophecy

It has been suggested in many ways that white middle-class teachers, as a result of social definitions that they make of minority group children regarding their abilities and life chances, communicate to these children a sense of low expectations. When teachers in ghetto schools pass out papers and tell students to fill them up with just about anything they want to, as long as they are quiet, the children learn rather quickly that the teacher does not expect much in the way of achievement or creativity. And the little that is expected is the little that is given. A self-fulfilling prophecy is one that involves the communication of a definition of a person and a reciprocal living up to that definition by the receiver of that communication.

Schools have been shown to be significantly susceptible to the promulgation of this phenomenon. One study investigating this process in the classroom revealed that students of low measured ability would do better in class if the teacher thought the ability was higher than if the teacher knew exact scores.[71] To test this interaction teachers were given forged records of students and the teachers, believing the records, made definitions of these students which must have been communicated as a set of expectations. The expectations appeared to be more important in explaining achievement than the ability scores.

We have already discussed the inferior facilities available to black students, particularly in urban ghetto schools. The process by which these invidious outcomes are produced is often the vicious circle of the self-fulfilling prophecy. If teachers have low expectations for dark-skinned students, then dark-skinned students will internalize these expectations and usually live up to them, thereby reinforcing the original conceptions on which the expectations were based. If not much is expected of the student, either by the teacher, the administrators, or the students themselves, then it is logical that there will be little motivation on the part of schools to provide personnel and materials of superior quality. The long-range effects of this kind of institutionalized racism is a perpetuation of inferior education for the minority student and a deep-seated resentment toward the representatives of the majority culture for having created the conception of inferiority which the minority student accepts in secret.

The self-fulfilling prophecy operates more specifically in terms

[71] R. Rosenthal and L. Jacobson, *Pygmalion in the Classroom* (New York: Holt, Rinehart & Winston, Inc., 1968).

of a set of conceptions regarding the restrictions of life chances. That is, teachers communicate to minority group students that beyond the formal requirements of the classroom is a world of occupations and that educational success, which is not really possible for very many, is required to be successful in that world. This communication usually operates as part of a backfire of some well-intentioned strategies. When one communicates in an abstract sense, as most teachers do, about the importance of education for success in the life after school, the major significance occurs when a student defines himself as an educational failure. Abstract principles, such as future success linked to the requirement of delayed gratification, is an almost useless strategy in the motivation of the poor minority student. All it does is to communicate to the student that as an educational failure he had better find alternative routes to economic success. There is no feeling of being on a success-bound train when one occupies a seat in a vocational classroom in a poorly equipped school in an unattractive community. A student defines himself at this point as an educational loser, and losers do not play the game as well as winners. If you define yourself as a loser you often play to lose. In situations where human beings manipulate every bit of the environment, luck plays almost no part at all. For many minority group students, the only kind of luck could be the presence of a uniquely dedicated and perceptive teacher in their lives. The structure of racism and the forms of confrontation make it necessary that the teacher who does meet that definition be stronger personally and socially than we have been able to expect in the past.

WHITE SUPREMACY—THE PERPETUATION OF SHAME

Almost by definition the structure of racism involves a set of invidious distinctions between persons. One important way in which these distinctions are communicated is through the emphasis on the superiority of cultural forms or traits different from those of the minority student. The Spanish-speaking child, of either Puerto Rican or Mexican-American descent, learns very quickly that his language is not acceptable since it is an important difference between himself and representatives of the Anglo world. Often this is communicated by the fact that educational personnel will not even make an effort to recruit or train bi-lingual teachers. By their omission the child learns that the others do not even think his language important enough to make the effort. By omission again, this time in terms of food, or dress (what dress school personnel will accept and encourage), or the recognition of national holidays, or Mexican poets or writers, or musicians, the Spanish child begins to develop a sense of shame regarding his own cultural habits. The very fact of assimilation into American Anglo-Saxon traditions is itself a racist position. The standards for the evaluation of minority group students is along universal criteria of achievement and moral behavior. Where patterns clash, such as in attitudes toward industriousness or affective-aggressive behavior, there is no attempt to compromise, thereby granting some legitimate value to the other; but rather, students are punished to reinforce loyalty to the one system of values.

The designation of persons as inferior often takes the form of attacking their values. This is class linked as well as racially linked. The two often conspire to produce a set of ethnic-economically based values which are depreciated by schools. The literature of the black man in America, represented by such authors as James Baldwin, Claude Brown, and LeRoi Jones, portrays an affinity for expressive "gut" language, the likes of which teachers have never been able to tolerate in the classroom. When students are not being punished for using vulgar language, they are being told that in order to make it in the outside world they need to discipline themselves and speak correct English, a language which many feel is unnatural and cold. If persons speak an inferior language, be it colloquial English or Spanish, particularly in the classroom, they are defined as inferior persons. This often occurs as a result of apparent teacher disdain which focuses on the language, the social manners, and the disrespect of system values of members of minority groups. Teachers are socialized to believe inherently in the values of the school in the same way that many of us are socialized to patriotic values. When students misuse the language of the school, it is a minor variation on the theme of defiling the flag.

White or national supremacy is characterized by the conspicuous absence of cultural relativism and a unidimensional evaluation standard based on the values of the Protestant ethic. The inferiority of other standards and ethics are apparent from the fact that they are never included in the curricula of the school. They are further derogated by the way in which educators make provisions for the punishment of minority students for violating cultural values, rather than providing an educational experience in which social differences are negotiated by some kind of a democratic process. It is always interesting that democracy is a more viable form of teacher-student relationships in all-white, middle-class schools, than in schools dominated by black and brown minority students.

The imposition of inferiority perspectives on the non-white student population consists largely of an almost total ignoring of that part of his identity that is not part of his rights as an American citizen. Black and brown heroes are not represented in the books used to teach black and brown students. We have only to recall the remark of the reading teacher in Kozol's book to understand the mentality behind this kind of omission. In speaking to the author who wishes to inject a book about Negroes into the curriculum of his class which is 97 per cent black, she says:

"I wouldn't mind using them (the books) if there were all Negro children in your room. But it would not be fair to the white children in the class to force such books on them, too. We do not have all Negroes. If we did, it would be different. I could see using them if this were a segregated school. But it isn't; we have white children. As matters stand it simply would not be right or fair."[72]

What is most pitiful about the inability of many whites to understand the role of the disenfranchised and segregated minority is that without this kind of understanding there is little possibility that racist structures will erode. White educators make concessions out of the militant demands of minority groups, but they do so only out of a desire to maintain stability in the system in the face of potential disruption. The fact that white educators do not initiate programs to reveal the cultural identity of black and brown students without such pressure is but another symptom of the racist structures within which so many are blindly encapsulated.

Racism has provided the American social scene with its soil for conflict. It is often a question of presenting white culture heroes as if they are the heroes of all, and then ensuring that imitation of such heroes is impossible according to social laws. We have provided the black man in America, on the screen and on television, with Caucasian standards of beauty, but we attempt to deny him the right to seek a Caucasian mate. From the earliest grades we provide him with texts and readings that define for him the white middle-class goals; but because he has not been socialized to compete in a contest system of educational mobility, we have denied him the access to these goals. It is one thing to take from a person his identity; it is another to take this and then allow

72 Kozol, *Death at an Early Age*, p.87.

him to fail in his strivings for which he has surrendered this identity.

Most readers, those books used to teach and improve the reading of students, are in any country ethnocentric. It was this assumption, for example, that permitted McLelland to study some aspects of cultural motivation through school readers.[73] Books do reveal what members of the core culture believe to be the best in that culture. And for most countries there is little of what we might call dysfunctional consequences to that kind of ethnocentrism. The United States, however, is a very different story. It is one of the few nations in the world which is almost totally hybrid, one which has seen its original inhabitants become obsolescent in less than four hundred years. Unlike most nations the United States has problems associated with its inability to blend the diverse people together in a way suggested by the myth of the melting pot.

The most painful component of ethnocentrism for Negroes lies in the stereotyped presentation of Negroes to be found in much literature and films. The Bobbsey Twins books, read by many millions of American children, portrays the Negro servants, Sam and Dinah, as jovial, good-natured and illiterate in the early versions, and as subservient and semi-skilled in the later versions. The function of these characters, like Step 'n Fetchit in early films, was purely mock humor, a highly undignified role for a whole race to play.[74]

Ethnocentrism in American readers, unfortunately, has allowed its focus to spill over into areas which are uniquely the province of some citizens but not of others. As the title of one critical paper suggests, "Life is Fun in a Smiling, Fair-Skinned World." This survey of American readers, describing both American and non-American environments, presents some revealing points:

1. South Europeans are organ grinders, peddlers, and fruit and vegetable vendors.
2. Indians are always portrayed as historical figures.
3. Americans are almost always, in origin and appearance, Northern European.
4. Americans are, three-quarters of the time, blondes.
5. Americans are almost always quite well to do, not wealthy, but comfortable.

---

[73] David McClelland, *The Achieving Society* (New York: D. Van Nostrand Co., Inc., 1961).

[74] For a penetrating analysis of the portrayal of racial stereotypes in children's literature, see S. Cohen, "Minority Stereotypes in Children's Literature: the Bobbsey Twins, 1904–1968," *Educational Forum* (Spring, 1969).

6. Life, for the people in these readers, is always easy and filled with fun[75]

It is this ethnocentrism which has come to infuriate the dark-skinned masses in modern times. It is in part a reaction against these insulting ethnocentrisms that has forced minority members to seek their own identity outside the mainstream of American culture. The division between the races has become deeper, and the schools have contributed to this dilemma through lack of foresight and insight into the essential character of American society. We can hope that the influence of the school in its ameliorative efforts will play a major role in reducing the gaps between the races.

THE ROLE OF THE SCHOOL

The task for education may be the most cricital it has been asked to assume since the call came to unify a nation of immigrants at the turn of the century. Education, usually a passive agent of cultural change, structured almost exclusively to reflect and perpetuate the present system of cultural values, cannot do its work by following the mandates of political expediency or even community response. Integration has taken place where there was no integration because the courts commanded, and special programs have been incorporated in schools and universities because the community demanded. But the major changes in educational structures need to flow from an internal rather than external set of demands. The community and for the most part well meaning political figures only vaguely understand the dynamics of process; they do respond with spirit to a conception of profit. In the discussion which appears in the following pages many programs and activities are recommended. There are a compendium of the ideas and work and recommendations of persons working in several ways to the end of making education more relevant and opportunities for mobility more possible for the disadvantaged minorities. But beyond the specifics of innovation and trial lies the necessity to create an ideology supporting changes, supporting commitment to this change, and requiring involvement.

Mr. Nixon and Mr. Humphrey, on the campaign trail in the fall of 1968, spoke to their suburban listeners in an attempt to communicate a respect for the "forgotten American," the man who

[75] Otto Klineberg, "Life Is Fun in a Smiling, Fair-Skinned World," *Saturday Review* 46 (February 1963): 75–77.

pays his taxes, supports the country, and does not engage in the "lawlessness" which concerns him. The concern which we have expressed regarding racism in our major institutions points an accusing finger at this "forgotten" man, accusing him of far more responsibility in the lawlessness which he avoids than perhaps any other social group. His schools are, in the now-classic sense, "lily white," and any attempts to perceive programs intended to make a place for racial minorities as participants in the development of a national identity meet with failure. The structure of racism goes untouched in the schools of the "forgotten American," chiefly because we have not yet conceived in education a way to develop an ethos that sets the development of an integrated society as an educational goal. Instead we have taken the short-range, urgency view and have supported and developed programs for the education of the culturally disadvantaged. But the problems of racial minorities are structurally linked to the institutions of the advantaged majority, and ultimately we need to talk about ways of doing something about those structures.

In its many recommendations to combat racism in American society, the Kerner Commission made several suggestions in the area of education. Some of the major statements were as follows:

1. *The elimination of de facto segregation*—The commission extends this recommendation to include not only ecological segregation but segregation which occurs as a result of ability grouping within an integrated school.

2. *Provision of quality education in ghetto schools*—This recommendation favors compensatory education programs. The commission argues that despite attempts to integrate schools, many racial minorities will attend segregated ghetto schools. Compensatory education is to be viewed as an intermittent step while awaiting programs to increase integration possibilities.

3. *Improving school-community relationships*—This proposition argues the necessity for making schools more responsive to community needs and demands.

4. *Expanded opportunities for higher and vocational education*—Funds should be made available to develop and support talent for professional as well as vocational careers. Also to support intensive preparation for college courses.

5. *Make ghetto residents more employable*—Recommendations are made to develop verbal skills and provide opportunity education for ghetto residents.

6. *Efforts to decentralize control of schools*—The commission views decentralization of control as a way to enhance community-school relationships and communication of the sort that will directly affect programs.

7. *Early childhood education*—A review of their evidence suggested to the commission that racial minorities enter school "retarded." They recommend increasing the support and base of "Headstart Programs."[76]

INTEGRATION OR COMPENSATORY EDUCATION

Most educators agree that integration is a desirable goal. But we are beginning to recognize some of the problems of integration. In the same way that Black Power advocates require equality as a prerequisite of coalition, many blacks feel that integration can be detrimental if some kind of educational equality cannot be achieved first. To this end the early childhood education programs such as Headstart and all possible experimental concept development programs, such as those suggested by Ausubel[77] and Deutsch,[78] are recommended. With entrance to integrated schools as the goal, these programs are intended to make racial minority students ready to compete with their Caucasian classmates for the rewards of education. This requires both skills and motivation, and the two feed each other. For minority group children, however, the task must be more than a duplication of white abilities. Motivation for the Negro and the Spanish-speaking child is linked to his cultural history and requires the development of a sense of person. In white society the Negro is often an object, as are the Mexican-American and Puerto Rican. Members of these groups define themselves as they are defined in their interaction with others. One sense in which compensatory education can be viewed is in terms of the development of the visibility of the child as a subject. This can be regarded as an attempt to compensate for the destruction of any subjective identity which has taken place in the Negro's and Mexican's history among whites. The struggle to develop abilities and motivation needs to be associated with a program to give the child a feeling of the relevance of learning to his own life. This requires that we search for some kind of authenticity in being black and brown and lead children to the realization of that authenticity.

The value of integration has always been considered in the light of what it will mean for the black student—better teachers,

---

[76] *National Advisory Commission Report*, pp. 438–456.

[77] D. P. Ausubel, "A Teaching Strategy for Culturally Deprived Pupils; Cognitive and Motivational Considerations," *School Review* 71, No. 4 (1963): 454–562.

[78] Martin Deutsch, "The Disadvantaged Child and the Learning Process," in *Education in Depressed Areas*, ed. H. Passow (New York: Teachers College Press, Columbia University, 1962), pp.163–179.

cleaner schools, better facilities, association with mobility models. The mixture of racial minorities with the racial majority can only effect the long-range goals of equality and diminished racism if white students can be made to understand the value in their own lives of integration with other races. Until then the function of integration remains uncertain. The first goal of educational integration is to help produce a meaningful society-wide integration. This means not only that the minority group needs to "fit in" but that both groups need to live harmoniously together. This is a feeling of belonging together, and such a notion is required to change the racial mixture into a racial compound. The culture of the white man in America is embodied in his history, and the history of this country is a history of men of all colors. In this sense the history of the black man in Africa is as relevant as that of the white man in Rome or Greece. Integration requires making manifest the reality of differences as well as the reality of similarities. For the white child in an integrated school the educational challenge is to help him work through the monumentally important problem of reconciling differences and integrating these into a meaningful life experience. Schools can make no greater contribution to the conceptual talents of all children.

Segregated education is inferior and non-adaptive for whites as well as Negroes. Put simply, no child can receive a democratic education in a non-democratic school. . . . A racially segregated school imposes upon the white children the inevitable stultifying burdens of petty provincialism, irrational fears and hatreds of people who are different, and a distorted image of themselves.[79]

Regardless of our preferences, it is almost certain that compensatory programs—experiments involving support for such activities as smaller classes, specially trained teachers, supplemental resources, and extensive programs in preschool education—will continue. At the same time efforts to develop some rationale by which integration can be effected without the disturbances brought about by such phenomena as busing will continue. Variations on the current theme of educational parks appear to be the most promising. The educational park concept is one that views the source of educational instruction as several schools rather than a single school, where students attend different schools at different times for different kinds of instruction. It is likely that the government will

[79] Kenneth B. Clark, "Desegregation: The Role of the Social Sciences," *Teachers College Record* 62 (October 1960).

continue to offer incentives to districts to improve the racial balance of schools.

Both compensatory programs and integration activities are viewed at this time as remedial activities, as ways of helping racial minority students improve their life chances. As such, it must be assumed that some segment of the minority student's pride will be actively challenged. One almost certainly knows when he is being treated differently from others, and when the others are the distrusted white child, the pinch is more painful. Compensatory programs may be defined as necessary evils by some blacks or browns insofar as they provide edge, or advantage, which the minority child currently requires, but which in the long run will only serve as a constant reminder that it was and is necessary to compensate the minority child because he experiences unequal opportunities.

Another problem with integration and compensatory programs is that both situations are for the minority child unreal. In some ways it is very artificial to integrate schools if we cannot integrate neighborhoods. If the school is to function as a realistic socialization force, it cannot make a great deal of sense out of the fact that children who cannot live together can learn together. The real structure of integration cannot be legislated. It can, however, be forged by a dedicated effort on the part of educators. In the same way a compensatory program is artificial if it does not reflect what the child will soon learn to be the traditions of education. The kind of focus of concern, individual treatment, and special facilities, similar to that which educationally handicapped children receive, once withdrawn as black and brown students move into the real educational situation, can have disorienting effects. The only solution seems to be the financially burdensome necessity of making all education appear as if adults really cared about their children's education. When the average child can after a day at school come away thinking that society's investment in him was maximum and apparent in the classroom, rather than minimal, conpensatory programs will not seem to be so special.

RECOMMENDATIONS FOR EDUCATION

In light of the many problems inherent in the relationship between races in the United States and in view of the school's critical position in the society, educators must continue to explore new ways to reduce the inherent conflict born of racism. To this end we can reiterate and state anew some suggestions for specific foci in the school. Each proposition must be evaluated in the light of the dysfunctions which present practices have despite the fact that some traditions have been useful to certain ends. For example, grouping has been utilized to facilitate the task of the teacher, who has the responsibility for thirty to forty children daily. If we suggest renovating the grouping policy, this may require that we reduce classroom size. Despite the fact that such a suggestion is unrealistic (given what the society wishes to expend on education compared, for example, to space or war programs), it must be made with the hope that the average citizen will somehow be made to understand that a good education can in the long run solve many of the problems, such as law and order, that he is willing to invest heavily to solve. The following list is incomplete, of course, and students of education and society can add to it in their own way; but we do need to state our recommendations and restate them as often as anyone will read or listen to our pleas.

RESTRUCTURE THE BASIC UNITS OF INSTRUCTION. The school and the classroom have been the basic units of education. It is recommended that new possibilities such as educational parks, or even community-based education of the learning in the homes, stores, parks, and factories in the community sense be considered.

TEACH FOR DIFFERENCES AND SIMILARITIES. This speaks to the necessity of communicating an understanding of the relationship between individual identity and the family of man. Integration is really meaningless if everyone is the same. Integration based on tolerance of difference rather than appreciation for difference is a very different thing. The kind of integration that is necessary in an age when differences can wreak havoc with a society or a world can become a reality only when we discover how to make people want to associate with others who are different because they find they can expand their own human potential within this framework. This means not only that we teach about the racial history of all who compose our society but that we make learning and living together appear to all to be a desirable rather than just a necessary condition of social existence.

RECONSTRUCT STATUS SYSTEMS WITHIN THE SCHOOL. The school provides its members with the criteria by which persons compete for differential positions within the status system of the school. These criteria center upon the traditional evaluative activities that transpire daily, where persons are shifted or stabilized based on a unidimensional and rigid set of standards for cognitive and moral achievement. It is necessary that we consider ways of diminishing the significance of comparative evaluations while at the same time providing different channels by which students can experience a sense of self-worth. We need to discover how self-worth can be developed non-comparatively, that is, by not requiring persons to measure their value in terms of what others have accomplished or in terms of what areas of achievement are highly valued. High achievement in industrial curricula is not valued in the same way that achievement in the academic curriculum is. Either we need to find a way to make different programs more equally respected, or we need to dissolve the boundaries established by students because of their different academic programs.

DISSOLVE GROUPING PRACTICES BASED ON INTELLIGENCE OR ABILITY TESTING. Educators need to conceive of ways of grouping students that will not create social distance between persons in different groups and will not present those inadequately prepared to do well on such tests, such as the minority child, with a one-way ticket to nowhere. Not only does this intensify segregation experiences for both whites and non-whites; it also makes it difficult to utilize differences within the school in a creative way.

TEACH THE VALUE OF INTEGRATION TO WHITES. White students need not only be prepared to accept non-white students; they need to be prepared to demand them in their school. The structure of racism is often perpetuated because no group within the system operates as a force for change. In all-white schools or at least in many the prospects of integration strikes teachers, administrators, and many students as well as parents, as prospective problems. If students understand the value of exposure to different racial groups, they may, as other students in other areas have demanded relevant activities, require the school to seek opportunities for maximum integration. This is of course idealistic. It is hard to conceive of a group of white teachers, administrators, and parents desiring integration at this time. But this may be conceived as the operational goal of programs designed to rid the schools of racist patterns.

REVISE STANDARDS FOR ADMISSION IN HIGHER EDUCATION. The near absence of black and brown students on university and college campuses is a function of admission standards. Like the public schools which prepare students to meet these standards in a unidimensional way, higher education acts to reinforce such a pattern. A reconceptualization of what is required to provide a good learning environment for students may lead to the revision of this standard. This in turn will have a cascading effect on public schools since college requirements provide the external pressures on which public school programs of instruction and evaluation proceed. If for example we should conceive of a desirable learning environment in terms of heterogeneity of social types rather than homogeneity based on achievement motivation, we can begin looking in new directions for admissions criteria.

REVISE THE REQUIREMENTS FOR CONTENT OF BASIC READERS. Many of the hidden and not so hidden traditional culture values are implanted or reinforced by the kinds of books students use to learn how to read. *Dick and Jane* books represent a study in socialization to conformity around limited core values. Even the Detroit readers, which have sought to incorporate Negro life into the classroom, present the same sterile existences that occupy the life of Dick and Jane. If we can separate the infusion of socially acceptable values from the learning-to-read quality of these readers, we will have opened the door for the kind of revision of requirements for such books that is necessary. Before students begin to make social distinctions based on differences in conformity to social standards, they are open to acceptance of the difference of others. Basic readers can be used to promote this acceptability if they are carefully chosen and consequently carefully written.

LINK SCHOOLS TO THE COMMUNITY OR COMMUNITIES THEY SERVE. The first step toward this goal may be the decentralization of control. Leaders in a community are usually more sensitive to the kind of service that schools can perform to the community and to students than are persons working out of a central administration office. Current PTA coalitions are usually a spurious show of solidarity since, particularly in ghetto schools, either the parents do not come or only those representing the most socially mobile members attend. From the perspective of the school many a teacher and administrator can describe the way in which PTA meetings are utilized to cool out the community and give the impression of community interest, which is not really part of the structure of school activities. This linkage can also be effected by intelligent utilization of physical and human resources in the community. For nonwhite students the only significant human influence may be a neighborhood leader, and such leaders can be paid for their help.

Develop an honest sense of concern for human injustice. What would it have meant if most of the schools in the United States had declared a day of mourning when the four little black girls were bombed to death in Birmingham, Alabama? It would have indicated that school children everywhere were able to express their resistance to an inhuman social act. It would have suggested a trend toward involvement in the school rather than the typical pattern of non-involvement in human affairs that the school encourages by its inability to condition students to express feelings toward human injustice. Current events lessons are wholly cognitive responses, an attempt to build an intellectual awareness without suggesting to children that one only knows a tragedy if he is somehow able to empathize with the tragic figure. Problems of race relations are to a considerable extent insoluble, because almost no one in the white society has been trained—or perhaps a better word, freed—to respond with empathy. We recognize immorality, we criticize it, and many teachers throughout the United States probably said, "That's too bad" when speaking to their classes about the Birmingham murders, if they spoke at all. But the only way to stop the injustices that non-whites suffer daily is by building in children the kind of humanistic character that commits them, as children and later as adults, to do something about it rather than sit before their color TV when events are related, and respond that somebody ought to do something.

Carry the fight into hard-core white conservative areas. It is important to note that whites who are willing to become participants in a dialogue on the subject of improving race relations through education are usually those of advanced education and liberal political and social values. There are millions of whites in the North as well as in the South who feel that if one ignores the problem it will go away, particularly if law enforcement potential is increased. The role of education in such communities must be that of attemtping to educate such persons to the way that the lives of all citizens are involved in their own welfare. It is here where the school must refuse to accept the community desire to maintain the *status quo*, and rather than reflect community values educate these whites to the long-range consequences of short-range repressive techniques. Programs designed to teach the value of integration to students should first be brought to the community and have their goals and rationale explained to the parents of school children. It is unfortunate that those who are willing to listen and participate are those who are eager to be convinced and involved. The important job and the difficult one is to make inroads among white groups who are presently defensive and perhaps frightened, and consequently aggressive, about the course that the black revolution seems to be taking. We must work on the assumption that if people will listen to another view, many of them will be convinced. It is a chance we need to take.

IMPROVE THE QUALITY OF TEACHING IN NON-WHITE SCHOOLS. In a class supported by the University of California at Los Angeles which brought together teachers in training and parents of children in the black ghetto, when the question was raised as to whether or not the parents wanted white teachers in the community at all, one parent said, "Really, all we want is for our children to learn how to read and write." Nods around the room supported the statement. Then one of the student teachers responded, "But it's so hard; the children won't pay attention, they show no interest, they yell and carry on."

The parent responded, "You got to do it anyway."

This is the challenge for the white educator and for non-whites who are willing to help him. What must be discovered is how to "do it anyway." The most important step in achieving this goal is the one which puts teachers at the point of saying, "I don't care if they spit in my face every time I try, I'm going to keep trying until I find out how." In order to assist in the struggle of resolving the conflict between the races, white society needs to see itself in the same position as the black society—pressed to the wall, forced to act in a way that is dangerous, uncomfortable, fatiguing and often without observable rewards. Many young people see the necessity of this kind of challenge and are meeting it, but such people are too few. The school has to discover a way to produce a teacher who is not only capable, but committed to teach children who will often hate him and usually distrust him. This requires a program of self-exploration which penetrates deeply into feelings of self and others. Along with the cognitive skills regarding teaching methods, teachers must develop the ability for empathy, the ability to understand cultural relativism, and the ability to act unselfishly.

And the society needs to perceive the necessity of supporting the teachers who put themselves into such a position. They need to be supported by adequate wages, by excellent facilities, by community helpers whom the district will pay. They need to have available experts in every area, autonomy to try new activities, and resource to psychological personnel for continued self-exploration. Only in this way can we provide quality education in the ghettoes.

CONCLUSION

The theme of much of Le Roi Jones' prose and poetry is that the white man can never know the black man. He can never have the same kind of American experience that the black man has had. He can never be a friend to the black man. Many other black authors have drawn the same conclusion. Perhaps the white man cannot know the black man, and perhaps for the present he cannot really have the black man as his friend. Most whites respond that either this is not true, or if it is then there is nothing more that we can do. We need at this time to act as if it were true, and to act anyhow. A great society can be built only with the kind of sacrificial energy that it will take to create a society of equal justice and opportunity even if we receive no thanks from those whom we seek to help, even if we receive constant vindictive retorts for our efforts. In the final analysis most of us know that if we succeed in building this kind of society, then all men will be the friend of all others. This may be Utopian, but the white man's self-actualization is as much on the line as that of the black man or the brown or yellow or red. One's human potential is available to him only as he touches other humans. As long as he defends against the instrusion of others and their needs, he cannot be open to change himself. Working for equal justice is part of the process of being born; retreat from the challenge is being busy dying. We cannot wait around for non-whites to tell us what they want us to do; we can only know that they want us to do something, and now.

The kind of education that is necessary to pull together a divided country is a humanistic education, an honest education, a quality education. The kind of education that we provide for non-white students must be of a sort that will never permit a Mexican-American child to throw away his tacos because he is afraid other students will ridicule him. It will never permit a black child to be bombed without a violent reaction from children everywhere. It will never allow a non-white child to grow up unable to read simply because he did not know how to behave in the classroom.

And what is it that we need to teach the black child? It is appropriate that a black man answer this question, and conclude this chapter:

I would try to teach them—I would try to make them know—that those streets, those houses, those dangers, those agonies by which they are surrounded, are criminal. I would try to make each child know that these things are the results of a criminal conspiracy to destroy him. I would teach him that if he intends to get to be a man, he must at once decide that he is stronger than this conspiracy and that he must never make his peace with it. And that one of his weapons for refusing to make his peace with it and for destroying it depends on what he decides he is worth. I would teach him that there are currently very few standards in this country which are worth a man's respect. That it is up to him to begin to change these standards for the sake of the life and health of the country. I would suggest to him that the proper culture— as represented, for example, on television and in comic books and in movies—is based on fantasies created by very ill people, and he must be aware that these fantasies have nothing to do with reality. I would teach him that the press he reads is not as free as it says it is— and that he can do something about that, too. I would try to make him know that just as American history is longer, larger, more various, more beautiful, and more terrible than anything anyone has ever said about it, so is the world larger, more daring, more beautiful and more terrible, but principally larger—and that it belongs to him. I would teach him that he doesn't have to be bound by the expediencies of any given Administration, any given policy, any given time—that he has the right and the necessity to examine everything.[80]

[80] James Baldwin, "A Talk to Teachers," *Saturday Review* 46 (December 1963): 49.

8

Problems of Alienation

T H E   F I R S T   S T E P toward physical, psychological, or social health is the recognition of the problem, that there is a problem. Sometimes we cannot solve the problem, and the body or the mind or the society dies. And perhaps, at times, it is better that something dies rather than have it live in agony. Sometimes it is necessary for a self or a society that is sick to die figuratively, and out of the grave something alive and healthy may emerge.

In the discussion and analysis which follow a version of society will be presented as sick, in pain, and perhaps struggling in vain for a survival which can be no more than a temporary respite from the ultimate demise of social life as we now know it. In the view of some, who may be overly pessimistic, this may appear to be a tragic condition. The perspective which will guide the evaluation of the condition of "sickness" in this chapter is one that emphasizes the potentially reconstructive value of alienation. This does not mean that alienation of persons from each other and from our social institutions will be defined as good. Alienation, as we will deal with it here, is a condition of pain, of degradation, of despondency, and of pitiful human adaptation. These conditions cannot be lauded in themselves. But we can look beyond the present and suggest that alienation is a symptom which, like physical symptoms, alerts us to the necessity of treatment. In this treatment of the human condition lies the hope of the future, and the urgency with which we regard the necessity of treatment will determine whether we or our children can live in a healthy society or if we will forfeit our opportunities to future generations.

Alienation is a condition which either affects or potentially affects every member of society, since it is present in the structure of the society we inhabit. This position is not the same as one that would argue that we are all potentially poor, or criminal, or sexually or mentally ill. These problems can be explicated by talking about specific groups of people in specific environments, making specific adaptations such as collecting unemployment, seeing psychiatrists, or robbing banks. The point is that alienation is inherent in everyone's environment regardless of his position, income, race, or marital status. Alienation is a function of our time in social history, and we all share this.

For hundreds of years persons have engaged in some kind of struggle to attain security and freedom. They have struggled for national freedom as well as for personal freedom; they have struggled for economic security and psychological security. And in the process they have become meaningfully involved in their struggles. For the past 50 years the American labor movement in the United States has fought for change in the economic order. Members of the movement have fought for freedom from want and exploitation, and ultimately for economic security. Having produced or at least heavily influenced many changes, the American labor union today stands vigorously opposed to change in most areas of social life. Union members, like most Americans, enjoy the security for which they have fought and the freedom from deprivation. Where do they go from there? In what do they become involved? What links them to their fellow Americans? In the process of gaining security most Americans are able to convince themselves that, once attained, this security would free them to develop themselves as human beings, to explore ways of making this a better world for others. Vice presidents, like vice principals in schools, accommodate themselves to patterns which they often dislike, with the intent of making changes once they have attained positions of power. But the process of mobility conditions persons to believe in what they are doing and forces them to extinguish in themselves any inclinations to change the systems which produced them. Many persons dislike themselves for what they have become, but they quickly rationalize and defend this to the point of self-acceptance. As a psychological state alienation often evolves when rationalizations and defenses do not work. It is a condition of awareness at some level that one's social environment needs to be different in order for the person to feel like an integrated human being. It is then in this sense that we speak of alienation as universally potential. The structure of the problem of alienation is couched in the predictability of awareness. That is, when strategies for rationalizing existing social forms, for integrating oneself into some meaningful social stream, and for defining oneself as socially useful are no longer possible, alienation erupts. The point of much of this discussion is that we have reached a time when such strategies are no longer effective, when institutions cannot guarantee commitment to present social forms. The potential of widespread alienation has always been present, but now the means for assuaging its effects are reaching the point of impotence. We must face up to the fact that the age of alienation is here. In the following pages we want to look at its forms, assess the role the school has played and is playing in producing alienation, and speculate about the kind of education that will develop in students the capacity to avoid alienation by evolving a meaningful existence.

THE MEANING OF ALIENATION

The concept of alienation has a long and diffuse history. The basic concept originally developed from work concerned with the cohesion of social systems and the ways individuals are attached to groups. The most prominent association we can make to the attachment principle is the relationship of man to his work. The important idea, important to past as well as present and even projected conceptions of man as worker, is that industrialized society is by definition alienative. Since the Industrial Revolution, or the point at which man turned from an artisan to a figure in a mechanistic economic process, social and political critics have been raising the alienation argument. Marx placed considerable emphasis on the idea of the alientated worker, and this has persisted as a central idea in any subsequent Marxian analysis of modern society.[1]

In Marxian terms the alienated worker was a man whose manual skill and craft intelligence were taken from him, figuratively, and built into machines. Man was left with routine and monotonous jobs. He had lost not only the power to utilize his work skills but also control over the way in which he would use them. Life in the factory was a process of moving to the beat of a drum that one was powerless to control.[2]

Our current concern with the problem of alienation arises not so much from a functional criticism of the workings of capitalism but from the ethical consequences of capitalistic functioning. The early manuscripts of Marx reflected this kind of serious concern with the human dysfunctions of what otherwise appeared to be a highly efficient economic system. We do not wish to extend our own analysis into the area of the efficiency of economic systems. We do, however, want to admit that our concern with alienation does have ethical undertones and sometimes, overtones. That is, we wish to treat alienation as a social problem even though it may be the cost we have to pay for the kind of economic, industrial, and social progress that we make in Western society.

Feuer traces the meaning of the concept of alienation to early Christian thought, in which man was viewed as alienated from God by his original sin. The next important link in the evolution of the concept is traced to Hegel, who shifted the focus from the church to the factory, emphasizing man's passive role in the process of production. Hegel concentrated on the non-creative aspects of man's work, whereas Marx and Engels wrote from a posture of "romantic individualism" protesting the negation of the spirit implicit in capitalistic life.[3]

The broader context of alienation, to Marx as well as the German philosophers writing on the subject in the early nineteenth century, was concerned with man's natural self. Whatever was natural in man that was inhibited, frustrated, aborted, was unfortu-

---

[1] E. Fromm, *Marx's Concept of Man* (New York: Frederic Unger Publishing Co., 1961).

[2] R. Blauner, *Alienation and Freedom* (Chicago: University of Chicago Press, 1964).

[3] Lewis Feuer, "What Is Alienation?" *New Politics* (Spring, 1961): 116–118.

nate; and any man undergoing these processes was thought to be alienated. To Ludwig Feuerback, an influence on the early Marx, this idea was specified as a sexual alienation, where the basic human affection between man and woman was prevented through the external intervention of a system of institutionalized conditions. The castration of man by a formal order of social proscriptions was consummated by the onset of economic capitalism, a circumstance wherein the last of man's human potentiality was taking from him, leaving him estranged from himself, his work, and others. Marx and Engels soon after dismissed the concept from their writings, presumably on the grounds that it was too closely associated with their romantic, humanistic period which was something of a hindrance to the aggressive posture of the socialist movement in Germany.[4]

The revival of the term alienation in recent years should upon inspection reveal something of its meaning. It is important to consider that we are more interested in analyzing a contemporary social and human phenomenon and are therefore more concerned with this than with any precise definition of the term alienation. The fact that it has been used, and perhaps overused lately, may simply reflect the difficulty we experience in isolating what is happening to the members of our society. In fact social scientists have recognized, through their own problems in trying to deal with the concept, that alienation is a very comprehensive term, encompassing a wide range of similar but distinct phenomena. Leaving the history of the meaning of alienation and turning to variations in contemporary meanings, we find that the concept has been used to apply to political, socioeconomic, sexual, aesthetic, and educational spheres. It has been applied to individuals to describe their state of mind and to institutions as a description of the context in which they operate. We need to ferret out the conceptions of alienation that are useful to our discussion here.

Alienation as a concept designating a state of contemporary social relations has been frequently applied as a useful factor in the explanation of various forms of disorganized behavior. The concept is attached to conditions of prejudice, distrust, voting behavior, mental health, worker morale, true believers, and so on.[5] As an explanatory concept, alienation has been conceptualized traditionally as a unidimensional concept, having one broad meaning and not being a multi-purpose concept incorporating similar yet

[4] Ibid., pp.119–125.
[5] M. Seeman, "On the Meaning of Alienation," American Sociological Review (December 1959): 783–791.

very distinct components. Seeman's important analysis of the term has clarified some of the vagueness surrounding our past definitions and usage of the term in social science literature. He distinguishes five separate types of alienation which we can summarize.

Powerlessness

Powerlessness is the expectation that one's own behavior cannot determine the outcomes he seeks. Although one may have clear goals (outcomes), powerlessness is the assertion that, whatever one does, the goal will not be brought nearer to consummation because of those acts. This type of alienation is one in which the actor feels he cannot control events in his environment. If he is successful, for example, he may attribute his success to luck rather than his own determination of the outcome. When people looking for jobs, marrying, driving automobiles, and so on, depict the act as mainly dependent on chance, they are expressing the notion that, these situations being what they are, their own behavior has little influence on the outcome, and so they must depend on coincidence.

Meaninglessness

Meaninglessness is the inability to make any interpretation of events at all. While powerlessness refers to the control of external, though understandable events, meaninglessness precludes even their intelligibility, not to mention their control. Phenomena lack clarity for the person observing the world.

Normlessness

Normlessness is the expectation that socially unapproved behaviors are most efficient in attaining outcomes. Here the actor feels he can control the environment, but control it deviously in terms of social norms.

Isolation

Isolation is the devaluation of societal norms. Where normlessness, for Seeman, refers to the expectation that unapproved behaviors will lead to desired goals, isolation challenges the fact that those goals, or the behaviors leading to them, are desirable to begin with. Norms are generally devalued rather than abused as impractical.

Self-estrangement

By self-estrangement is meant the devaluation of self in terms of ideal standards. This form of alienation is characterized by a negative comparison between that part of the self-image arising out of actual behavior and the ideal standards incorporated through socialization or represented in the behavior of others.

Thus alienation is one's conception of his general attachment to society, and Seeman's distinction between types of conceived attachment has been a conceptual contribution. Many earlier works failed both empirically and theoretically, perhaps because they incorporated many vague and overlapping behaviors, such as weak attachment to group norms, without specifying the variety of meanings that had come to be associated with alienation.

Alienation does not, of course, occur in a vacuum. Once the idea of society had been put forward, it was inevitable that alienation would emerge as a disjuncture in the relations between man and society, and that the cause of this disjuncture would be attributed to certain milieux in the environment. An industrial economy, for example, is said to be so impersonal and routinized that it creates apathetic and indifferent workers, who then become ripe followers of anti-democratic political movements. Those taking this view are tied to Marx for their *logic* of alienation: The structure of society ill begets itself, in such a way as to wreak changes in itself. The form of Marx's argument established the social structure, especially work, as the source of disaffection. Another prominent contemporary view, not so different from the latter, is that a mobile and heterogeneous mass society creates workers who feel powerless; organization men who conform in their behavior, yet feel estranged from themselves; and captains of industry who are anti-democratic in their insensitivity to others and in their political perpetuation of themselves. These statements of cause and effect certainly arouse curiosity, but they imply so many unspecified presuppositions and so few empirical tests that they seem equally applicable to events, even when they contradict one another.

ALIENATION AND ANOMIE

Some social scientists have begun to utilize the term alienation to refer to the subjective aspects of anomie. Anomie emerged as an important sociological concept used to describe certain forms of breakdowns in social relationships. Durkheim, in describing social organization based on the division of labor in a complex industrial society, talked about certain possibilities of disorganization. He used the term *anomie* to refer to a condition in which a low degree of integration between functions obtained as a result of a high degree of specialization, or conflicts between segments of the industrial complex. Anomie occurs then, when the division of labor does not provide an adequate basis for maintaining relationships between persons involved in the industrial task, a situation in which social relations are not maintained by routine patterns of interaction and communication.[6]

Durkheim attempted to employ the concept of anomie in the explanation of changing rates of suicide. Linking suicide to changing patterns of the business cycle, he explained suicide rates as a function of persons being thrown out of adjustment with their typical ways of life. Under such conditions, persons become confused and disoriented and lose all sense of reference for their aspirations and behavior.[7]

The anomie which Durkheim describes is close to Seeman's conception of one component of alienation, that of normlessness. When interpersonal relationships disintegrate and references for behavior become diffuse or disappear, persons cannot appeal to any specific standards to influence their behavior.

The important sense in which alienation and anomie differ, besides the fact that alienation includes more and different conditions, is that alienation is a social-psychological fact and anomie a sociological one. Anomie refers to structural conditions, or the absence of sustaining structures, whereas alienation can only be defined with reference to persons experiencing certain disjunctures in the social system. When alienation is discussed, we are usually referring to the interaction of context or structure with persons, and we usually mean to imply that the perception is not idiosyncratic. That is, we do not want to include in our conception of alienation the way people may feel independent of the context in which they live and work. It is possible that persons do not feel alienated despite an apparent alienative system, and that persons will feel alienated even when there does not appear to be a breakdown in the standards, norms, communication patterns, and access to desired goals. For the most part we will accept as a state of alienation any circumstance in which a significant portion of the members of an institution or a society appear to be unable to feel or to become integrated into that system. Much of our speculation about important cues to the existence of alienation will be based on disruptive and rebellious acts performed by large numbers of persons. When

[6] Émile Durkheim, *The Division of Labor in Society* (New York: The Free Press, 1947).

[7] M. B. Clinard, *Anomie and Deviant Behavior* (New York: The Free Press, 1964), pp.4–5.

such acts are viewed as producing extensive conflict between segments of institutions, the assumption will be made that the problem lies within the institution and not the individual. We could, hypothetically, accept the possibility that large groups of adolescents are acting neurotically because of repressed sexuality stemming from unresolved Oedipal complexes, and that they have randomly chosen anti-social acts to express their neurosis. This direction appears to bear little fruit for the kinds of problems with which educators and social reconstructionists must deal. Our focus will be exclusively upon the degrees of integration of men with their institutions. Most specifically, we will be concerned with the amount of integration that has or has not taken place in the schools of this country. By integration we do not mean racial integration, although this could very well be an example of the alienation of a race. We mean, rather, the extent to which persons, specifically students, feel that their schools have meaning for them, that they can affect their goals through the school, that they do not need to act in a deviant manner to achieve these goals, that they feel a part of the process of education, and that they are able to feel a sense of congruence between themselves and what they are asked to do in their educational life.

ALIENATION AND THE SELF

It has been mentioned that one perspective of non-alienation is integration, specifically the integration of man with his institution. We have not, however, talked about man's integration with himself, except as an extension of the thought that a self-estranged man is one whose institutional life is antithetical to his being himself. But what does it really mean to "be oneself" or to be "fulfilled, self-actualized," or "realized" in the context of a social-problems approach to the study of a man and education? To answer this question, we need to explore the notion of the "self" as it has been described in social and psychological literature. Principally, in this chapter, the idea of alienation is to be understood in the context of the development and presentation of the social self. One problem that we need to analyze is, how can man present his "real self" to others so that inter-personal relations can achieve the status of being non-alienative. Let us then begin to evolve a conception of the self as this has meaning for the kinds of problems produced by contemporary interaction of persons with others and with institutions.

Problems in the Presentation of the "Real" Self

A person relates to others in social situations. In such situations, he calls forth postures which he associates with the same or similar social situations. These postures or presentations of self are revelations to others of the particular definition that he, the person, assigns to his role in that situation. Since all interactions are social, we could assume that role theory could logically account for the self that others perceive at all times.[8] That is, theories that explain the character formation of persons would resort primarily to ideas about the expectations others have for behavior in different social contexts.

On the other hand, trait theory, developed out of standard psychological paradigms, argues that persons have relatively invariant personality characteristics that are only slightly modified by varying social conditions. *Put another way*, each person possesses two selves. One self can be linked to the regularities of social interaction and is founded upon standard *definitions* persons within a particular society make about the normal expectations of others in social situations. The other self (which may or may not be referred to as the "real" self, depending upon our definition of "real"), contains the element of uniqueness. This factor of uniqueness explains variations in the behavior of occupants of social roles.

In relation to the above we are concerned with the question of how persons develop the capacity to transcend the confinements of repressive social expectations and definitions, so that they can avoid self-estrangement and commit themselves to innovations in their social world.

Self-estrangement, as we have described it, arises from a negative comparison of the part of the self-image related to actual behavior to the ideal standards incorporated through socialization, or represented in the behvior of others. Members of professional occupational groups, such as teachers, have undergone a long period of socialization to a professional role. Out of the socialization may develop certain idealized behavioral standards. They evolve a definition of a "real professional self" against which they compare their actual performance. The demands of the professional world, with its bureaucratic bogs, administrative restraints, and requirements for success in a status system, often force persons to abandon their "real" goals, to cease performing in terms of their "real" mo-

---

[8] For a discussion of role theory see T. Sarbin, "Role Theory," in *Handbook of Social Psychology*, ed. G. Linzey (Cambridge, Mass.: Addison-Wesley, 1954).

tivations, and to accede to the limitations of the system in which they occupy a role.

Notions of self-other relationships, integration and alienation, and freedom and self actualization, should be linked to problems of professional socialization. We need to ask: How do persons in standard social situations *develop the capacity* as well as the commitment to deviate from the institutionalized restraints inherent in social systems in order to evolve as "real" people, meaningfully integrated in their institutions?

INTERPERSONAL RELATIONSHIPS

In a discussion of the problem of persons seeking behavioral individuality within and in opposition to systems of prescribed behavior, two perspectives must be defined and taken—that of the structure of institutions and of social groups and that concerning the character of social types. The first perspective relates to external controls over interaction, the second to modal or ideal adaptive standards of persons with a specific configuration of characteristics.

The Structure of Institutions and Groups

Families, churches, schools, peer groups, athletic teams, and the like have systems of beliefs and values about what constitutes desirable goals, and concomitantly about what constitutes desirable behavior. These values, as a collective tradition, mold the direction of the group and set the criteria for the evaluation of the performance of the members. In order to attain the cultural goals of the unit, persons are arranged in coordinated role relationships so that effective communication and control over the behavior of members is possible. These role relationships become patterned through a system of rewards and punishments so that persons perceive themselves in a mirror for performance. When the "mirrored" expectations become internalized, the system is assured its equilibrium.

If role occupants consider legitimate the expectations associated with their roles, the institution may achieve long-standing stability. Legitimacy of expectation is determined by the relative effectiveness in terms of control and communication that networks of role relationships have. The larger society must support this expectation by maintaining agencies and units (such as families and schools) to fulfill important functions along corresponding lines. Inter-personal relations, taking this structural view, are analytically interpreted as functional relationships associated with one of the major functions of social systems.[9]

From the vantage point of social systems, the notion of a "real" self, or even of a person who can become self-estranged or alienated, becomes irrelevant. Innovations or changes within the system can be viewed only as structural accommodations to new system functions. Where new demands are placed on the system or group from the general culture or even from within, a rearrangement of these structural components occurs and new roles become integrated into the network.

The Character of Social Types

The utility of a sociological perspective in developing a model of social or educational change is best expressed by focusing on the individual actor in the social situation, and it can be most effectively demonstrated in a consideration of social types. Given a set of structural conditions (such as those set forth in the previous section), we can then begin to describe the variations in adaptation made by different social types within this structure. Merton's typology of different *modes of adaptation* provides a useful framework within which this concept of variation can be presented.[10]

Merton postulates five social modes which he sees as possible *responses* to standard cultural goals and institutionalized means for attaining these goals. These modes he labels conformist, innovator, ritualist, retreatist, and rebel; and postulates that they emerge out of the position of persons in the social structure and are independent of personality characteristics. Although we might accept this position from the structural perspective, we should also consider the possibility that whereas position in the system explains regularities in social behavior, *individual* qualities can account for deviant cases. Many persons today, for example, despite a position of economic advantage, are turning away from the standard paths to economic success and social prestige. The simple fact that the presentation of the "real" self in social situations is such a common inter-personal problem (and consequently of interest to academics

9 Talcott Parsons, in *The Social System* (New York: The Free Press, 1951), postulates four dominant functions of social systems: *adaptive*—moving the group efficiently toward its goal; *pattern maintenance*—committing the group to the cultural values of the system; *goal attainment*—defining specific goals of the system and committing members to the attainment of these goals, and legitimating the goals; and *integration*—the function of developing solidarity of members so as to ensure the coordination of roles toward the end of accomplishing the purpose of the system.

10 R. K. Merton, *Social Theory and Social Structure* (New York: The Free Press, 1957), p.140.

and to this chapter) indicates we are as concerned about individual irregularities in social life as we are about regularities. To approach the problem of developing an educational experience in which persons develop insights into the structural and personal foundations of their relationships with others, we thus must consider the macrostructures which produce regularities and the microstructures which explain variations. By microstructure, we mean only to suggest that social adaptations can emerge out of idiosyncratic experiences; such experiences force persons to turn away from the paths predicted for them to directions consonant with an awareness of self. Such experiences as therapy, war, divorce, plastic surgery, and LSD have been known to produce important changes in the way persons adapt to standard social roles.

Inter-personal relations often receive their character as a function of the continued interaction of specific social types. Persons who become defined as conformists or rebels, individualists, gamblers or losers, are reinforced by others in their presentation of themselves, so that certain kinds of behavior are maintained. Persons choose roles in social situations and continue to perform consistently as long as their choice continues to be rewarded. Very often roles chosen in childhood (*e.g.,* the scholar, the leader, the athlete, the good friend) persist into maturity. In this sense, the "real" self is submerged in the interest of assuming a comfortable and available role. In the school setting the classroom clown may be the most intelligent student who has chosen an alien role because of circumstance and selection. The simple fact that he is *good* at it forces others to relate to him in such a way as to inspire him to greater acts of clowning. Thus the forces of social approval and disapproval, in informal as well as in formal interaction, conspire to shape a relatively permanent social personality. These forces then in the broadest social psychological sense are the microstructures which influence adaptations to the social world. The professional or the occupational self simply adds functional components to the basic self and the socially determined self. Inter-personal relations thus evolve into a process of presenting all these components to others and responding to the same presentation by the others.

SOCIAL TYPING AND THE DEFINITION OF THE SELF

In the discussion above we have shown that social typing is a functional characteristic of social relations. Sociologically, typing controls the predictability of behavior of persons in social roles. It orders relationships in organizations and provides the basis for maintaining stability of the stratification order. For example, typing persons as destined to achieve occupational goals provides the kind of definition of self that enables those persons to achieve the goals. For example, based on standard stereotypes, the son of a doctor will be socially defined as someone who should be achieving at a given level. The son of a street cleaner will have other expectations leveled at him. Social order is maintained through routinization of expectations for various types in just such a manner, so that inter-personal and inter-organizational communication can be made predictable.

Sociopsychological typing is an obvious aid to the individual in ordering his social relationships. The complex world, particularly the urban world, is most efficiently organized when persons can be categorized. Such typing insures that few interactions require a total inter-relational exploration before communication begins. Typing also appears to be the most efficient way of managing social growth without anxiety. Many children in primitive tribes begin to face their environment by being told that the whole environment is composed of relatives and strangers. When parents want the child to relate comfortably to a stranger, they communicate to the child that he is a relative, an aunt or an uncle. The child can then apply simple, standard definitions of the new person in his world which will reduce his anxiety and allow him to relate comfortably.

Typing, particularly stereotyping, which also increases the efficiency of interpersonal relationships and reduces anxiety, may not be a desirable social mode but it is, nonetheless, the standard mode. Conditioning persons to avoid practices which have been useful for many years is a difficult task, but such conditioning can be useful in encouraging a different kind of inter-personal interaction.

As we have seen, most inter-personal relationships, particularly in bureaucratic structures, occur as a process of relating to types. Klapp's classification of dominant types as heroes, villains, and fools may not be a complete classification system, but it is a useful illustration of the *kinds* of definitions persons use to organize their inter-personal interaction.[11] Heroes, villains and fools are categories of types defined in terms of some attitudinal position or ideology in most bureaucratic interactions. And in most cases the classification occurs as a result of a person's assessment of *that position* in relation to his own. A teacher, for example, may be defined by

[11] Orin Klapp, *Heroes, Villains and Fools* (Englewood Cliffs, N. J.: Prentice-Hall, Inc., 1962).

some females as a hero to whom they relate with affection. She be-comes a hero because she personifies the qualities that many mid-dle-class girls aspire to attain and represent, such as wisdom, moral-ity, and decorum. Many lower-class males, however, may define a teacher as a fool because she has spent so much time getting an education and then makes so little money. Any attempts this teacher may make to present herself in some basic and honest way will be defined by these boys as a simple extensive of the fool model. Con-sequently the influence of the teacher is not only negated but may have a negative effect. (If someone we see as a fool makes a state-ment, the opposite must necessarily be correct.)

We can assume, then, that the dynamics of social typing com-plicate any attempt to help persons relate to others on some basic or even correct grounds. Even if we could socialize persons to for-get about the kind of "front stage" and "back stage" behavior about which Goffman talks (that is, role playing shifts in terms of varying situations), we still would need to solve the problem of how to avoid the dysfunctional consequences occurring as a result of the social typing or stereotyping employed by others.[12]

Personality, the Self and the Other

Personality is a convenient psychological construct which de-fines persons as members of various categories or as holding a posi-tion on a scale of psychological traits. The traits which define per-sonality can be categorized in various ways: as needs, such as sup-port or affiliation; as dispositions, such as aggressiveness or in-trospectiveness; or as orientations, either mechanical or social. As interesting as such trait typing may be, the construct is not espe-cially useful in the consideration of our problem, for our goal is to make possible certain changes in adaptations to others. It does not really matter where a person fits along scales determined by instruments developed by behavioral scientists, for our concern must be with the "self," the phenomenological self, and we must primarily consider the ways in which a person perceives himself in relation to his social world. The phenomenological self is defined not according to a scale of traits, but according to the way in which persons want to be seen by others, and according to the relative importance the person places on the evaluation of specific charac-teristics which he possesses. As Sherif suggests, the human *persona* actively sets levels of attainment and goals of achievement in mat-ters of significance to him.[13] These are components of his self-image

---

[12] Erving Goffman, *The Presentation of Self in Everyday Life* (New York: Doubleday & Company, Inc., 1959).

[13] M. Sherif, *Social Interaction* (Chicago: Aldine, 1968), p. 46.

and as such motivate him to maintain consistency in pursuing objectives. But the self system is not a unitary structure, as Sherif has noted; it contains components (attitudes, identifications, commitments) which contradict one another. These then become the source of internal conflicts. (Contradictory roles, for example, provide one source of such conflict.)[14]

Components of the self system are usually objectified by the person into his social situation for they help maintain the consistency of the self. Social-psychological literature sees these objectified components as reference groups. These are groups with whom persons affiliate, to whom they give loyalty, and in terms of which they define themselves. Often these may be groups with which persons aspire only to affiliate, but the mechanics of identification remain the same. The significant others for the actor who wishes to stabilize his self-system are representative members of these reference groups. From these persons the actor derives cues for his presentation of himself. Often, however, even these constructs are anxiety-producing for actors may find themselves entrenched in roles with contradictory expectations. Even though persons in each group may be defined, at least situationally at one point in time as part of a significant reference group, any contradictions defined as real by the actor become real in their consequence. That is, they cause him to reduce the dissonance he perceives in the impinging expectations, at the same time maintaining loyalty to both groups. A teacher who aspires to be an administrator, or a teacher caught between her loyalties to her professional colleagues and her loyalties to the members of her immediate educational environment might be considered exemplary of such an actor.

The Bureaucratic Self

Weber delineated five characteristics of bureaucratic structures which are relevant to any study of professional alienation.[15] As we consider the cumulative characteristics of bureaucratic systems, we find a portrait of a system that would appear to discourage any attempts to help persons relate to others in ways not completely prescribed by those systems.

The characteristics as outlined by Weber are as follows:

1) Bureaucracy has fixed jurisdictional areas governed by administrative regulations. Each job has a description which contains the duties of that position.

[14] *Ibid.*, p.17.
[15] Max Weber, *Essays in Sociology*, ed. H. H. Gerth and C. W. Mills (New York: Oxford University Press, 1958).

2) A bureaucracy contains a hierarchy of authority. Most authority is invested at the top, and persons in those positions have the responsibility, as one component of their authority, to control the behavior of those below them.

3) Management of the bureaucracy is based on written documents, minutes of meetings where decisions are reached, extensive filing systems, and personnel records.

4) Recruitment to bureaucratic roles occurs in terms of specific criteria and training. These criteria help to control the stability of role enactment, stable in the sense of being congruent with the expectations for behavior held by others in the system.

5) Bureaucratic roles are prescribed by an exhaustive set of regulations, manifest rules which control the behavior of members.

In addition to discovering structural propositions, Weber further reveals the purpose or end of these components of bureaucracy:

The individual bureaucrat cannot squirm out of the apparatus in which he is harnessed . . . the professional bureaucrat is chained to his activity by his entire material and ideal existence. In the great majority of cases he is only a single cog in an ever moving mechanism which prescribes to him an essentially fixed route of march.[16]

In preparing persons to assume bureaucratic roles in ways that may not be prescribed by the inherent conditions of bureaucratic life, educators must discover and present ways in which job descriptions, recruitment criteria, manifest regulations, and the like can be either changed or circumnavigated. In other words students may need to be trained for revolution. If, for example, we communicate to students the notion that bureaucratization requires and depends on highly reliable behavior, we have presented them with a cue as to how to subvert the present bureaucracy. So much, of course, depends on labels. If we were talking about "controlled educational innovation," the above comment would not seem as radical as it probably does.

Commitment to bureaucratic life, to the development of a bureaucratic self, assumes a set of definitions about one's relationship to the organization and to the control mechanisms which assure the presentation of that self. A new conception of man's relationship to work is required if we seek the kind of autonomy for persons that would permit a presentation of self that is not

16 *Ibid.*, pp.228–229.

prescribed totally by forces extrinsic to the individual. Alienation is a common characteristic of contemporary bureaucratic life, and it would seem most obvious then, that the way to reduce alienation would be to change the character of bureaucracy.

INTEGRATION OF THE SELF WITH THE INSTITUTION

As has been suggested, the opposite of alienation is integration, integration in the sense of a *congruency between the self and the role*. Although role expectations may conflict with the self, the person may still be integrated into the system if the structure provides the means for effecting changes, thus bringing the role more in harmony with the self. In other words the person thus integrated has power. An integrated self is, further, a self which perceives a meaningful relationship between the goals of the institution and the self-goals; it is also a self which ascribes legitimacy to the ways and means of accomplishing these goals. It is a self which perceives a congruence with other persons in the institution in terms of agreement about means and ends. And finally, an integrated self is one which can use the institution as a vehicle of self-fulfillment. In simpler terms he finds the institution a place in which he can do what he wants to do and can do best.

WHO IS ALIENATED?

The great bulk of the literature on alienation deals with four groups—workers, non-white minorities, adolescents, and students. We will be concerned with the latter two. Non-white minorities have been dealt with in another chapter, and adolescents and students are germain to the task of the school. It is important to differentiate between the problems of adolescents as a unique sub-culture in interaction with the adult society and students in interaction with the institution of the school. Some alienative conditions arise out of the unique position of one's membership in the adolescent society, and others are distinctly associated with roles within the educational institution. Let us begin by considering the world of the adolescent.

The Adolescent

Adolescence is that particular stage of life that marks the transition from childhood to adulthood. Its significance and interest as an age group is related to its unique status in western industrial civilization. In such societies where the succession of adolescents to the roles of their parents is questionable, the adolescent cannot be described as part of a continuum of social development. Rather than being able to view the adolescent as being embarked on a continuous passage from childhood to adulthood, the unique quality of his transition is that the next stage in his development appears to reside more in his adolescent experience than in the experience of his elders. This is simply to say that the particular interest in adolescence as a subject of inquiry is that he, the contemporary adolescent, is much more than a younger version of his parent. In many ways the adolescent defines himself through his conflict with his parent's generation. Such confrontation helps the adolescent unite his age mates into a distinct society with its own norms, values, and perspective on social life.

The relationship between the adult society and the adolescent is an ambiguous one. American business recognizes the huge market in adolescent products and cultivates his attention. The biggest money-making films are always those that appeal primarily to adolescents. As a customer, the adolescent is well regarded, but as a person he is seen by many adults as potentially capable of injecting a state of chaos into routine and comfortable affairs. They view his music as offensive, his morals as outrageous, and his posture toward themselves as disrespectful. Friedenberg's description of this relationship is, although perhaps overgeneralized, penetrating:

No other social groups except convicted criminals and certified lunatics are subject to as much restriction, and there is strong political support for proposals that would increase these restrictions. If recommendations that the draft age be lowered to sixteen, the legal school-leaving age be raised in most states to eighteen, and paramilitary work camps be established as "schools" for the academically inept all become law, there will be no more male adolescents at large in the country.

And a great many American adults will—or so they now believe—sleep easier in their beds. Willing as they are to trade with him, they have no doubt that the "teen-ager" is an enemy, and they want him confined in schools or suitable recreational or military facilities.[17]

Many American political leaders are quick to affirm that the average teenager is a delightful, healthy, moral citizen and that the bad image that adolescents have in this country is produced by a

---

17 E. Friedenberg, "Adolescence as a Social Problem," in *Social Problems: A Contemporary Approach*, ed. H. Becker (New York: John Wiley & Sons, Inc., 1966), p.37.

few who follow unconventional ways and who attempt to disrupt the normal routines of our society. Such a view is highly suspect, since politicians seldom are aware of the latent structures of social life. Nonetheless it is our intent here to examine the deviant or disorganizing patterns of adolescents in such a way as to expose and explain the conception of the adolescent as a social problem. To this end we will consider two groups separately, the average adolescent and the juvenile delinquent. Many of the problems associated with adolescence are common to both groups, but the utility of such a separation is to help us differentiate between behavior that is normatively disorganizing and that which is legally or "morally" deviant.

Most adolescents do not seem to like the world the way it is, and they resent their elders for having created it in such an unwholesome way. This is not in itself characteristic of the present generation of adolescents. What is characteristic are the things about our society that they do not like. Holden Caulfield, Salinger's popular adolescent, saw the world as being made up of phonies and prostitutes.[18] His definition of prostitute encompassed all of those who sold their talents and individualism in order to be affluent members of a materialistic society. The adolescent who holds such a view finds it easy to turn away from the world of adult institutions and find comfort in a society of his own. In many ways the values that adolescents hold are often congruent with those of their parents. They value popularity, athletic abilities, and to a lesser extent, academic achievement. It is often in the way an adolescent achieves popularity (by subscribing to the expectations of his classmates or peers, rather than those of his parents) that separates him from the adult culture.

The unique characteristics of the adolescent that may conspire in some areas to produce conflict with the adult world are that he has money and considerable leisure to spend it; he treats cars as playthings and status symbols, or as a means to attract dates, rather than as practical necessities; he has his own language and resents it when adults try to copy him; the male is subject to the draft and he is anxious about it; he likes music that infuriates most adults; he is desperate about having fun and will often turn to deviant acts in pursuit of excitement; he follows a set of tribal customs in his pursuit of the opposite sex; he congregates around local stores and eating spots, often intimidating adults by sheer weight of numbers; he is quick to experiment with any form of drugs that may come

---

18 J. D. Salinger, *The Catcher in the Rye* (Boston: Little, Brown and Company, 1951).

his way; he is sexually charged and often indiscriminate in how he releases the tension; he is skeptical of political structures and critical of other institutional structures; his society is socially stratified in the same way the adult society is; and in more recent days, he is in the forefront of "anti-establishment" protests.

This composite picture is not intended to be definitive. Many adolescents are as conforming and conservative on social issues as their parents. But the rate of current shifts in value structures is more likely to push the average adolescent to the extremes of the characteristics suggested above. The problem of adolescents is: How can they be integrated into the society which many of them distrust?

PARENT AND PEER ORIENTATIONS. In a period of rapidly changing values and norms parents appear to be considered by adolescents to be less reliable in defining appropriate behavior than do their peers. It is, after all, the peer group who can talk more relevantly about the expectations for behavior in areas that affect primarily the adolescent. Norms regarding dating, dressing, and sexual behavior are examples.

The average child becomes less involved with family activities as he grows older and turns increasingly to activities which center around his peer group. It is to be expected that the adolescent would orient his actions more around the norms of his principal action group than around those of his family. As a result of his extending his independence through his affiliation with his peer group and because the peer group is able to lend him support in matters and decision making, the authority of the parents decreases. The adolescent is, as most people would be, more comfortable in a relationship in which he holds equal authority with the other members than in one in which his power position is always one of subordinate. The principal socialization then of behaviors which we shall begin to discuss as causing problems takes place within the peer group. What then are the special mechanisms of peer group socialization?

Adolescents who form into social units join for the most part a clique or a crowd. The crowd operates as the central socializing unit in which members are prepared to participate in crowd activities. The clique is the smaller friendship group in which members share information about various activities, evaluate them and decide how and if to participate, and instruct each other as to the best strategy for having a good time. Ordinarily the prime area of socialization exists in the establishment of a heterosexual role. The process by which members become socialized to the expectations of the wider society of adolescents is the same as that followed in other socializing units. In the process of acquiring membership the adolescent must meet the group's criteria for membership and must conform to the group's norms. The result is a basic consensus and a strong group spirit. Roles are ordinarily differentiated into instrumental (task roles) and expressive roles (popularity). The members usually learn the norms associated with the kinds of roles that exist in most organized peer groups: friend, leader, athlete, and cross sex partner.[19]

DELINQUENT AND DEVIANT ADOLESCENTS. When adolescents experience a sense of alienation in their social world, they turn to identifications where they can experience an integrated existence. They look for situations where they can feel that they are participants in decisions which affect them. Often they do not feel that this can be accomplished through their affiliations with adult-dominated institutions, primarily the family. Family relationships are typically the most conflictual during adolescence, and out of these conflicts the search for separate identifications intensifies. Dissension in the family appears to be associated in the minds of adolescents around such issues as "parental imposition of goals, parental interference in personal affairs, parental interference in choice of friends, late hours, excessive restriction of freedom of movement, spending money, parental violation of privacy, differences about boy-girl relations, parental denial of decision, differences about smoking, differences about clothes, arguments over home chores."[20]

Although these concerns were reported in data collected more than a decade ago, it is likely that most of the conflicts today center around similar issues. Some specific differences, such as disillusionment with middle-class values, are currently apparent, and we will deal with this in another context. What is critical to evaluate at this stage of our discussion is the notion of deviance and the way in which this "deviance" is a response to adolescent alienation. The explanations which seem most fruitful in exploring this are those which also help us differentiate between the typical delinquent and the more contemporary "deviant."

In order to be accepted into the mainstream of institutional life, adolescents have always been required to exhibit certain char-

[19]Dexter C. Dunphy, "The Social Structure of Urban Adolescent Peer Groups," *Sociometry* 26 (June 1963).
[20] D. Ausubel, *Theory and Problems of Adolescent Development* (New York: Grune and Stratton, Inc., 1954).

acteristics. They are asked to demonstrate through their behavior that they have internalized the values of the core culture. They must be industrious, ambitious, punctual, neat, honest, respectful, physically passive, not given to displays of emotion, and achievement-oriented. In the school this last characteristic is evaluated as the test of many of the other qualities. It appears, at one level, that adolescents who do not meet these expectations fall into two large categories; those who cannot and those who do not want to. This distinction may form the basis for the major difference between the legal delinquent and the modern moral deviant.

The characteristics of the core culture, which we listed above, are those by which adolescents are evaluated in the status systems created in their institutions, particularly in school. Some form of status is important to all adolescents. Those who do not have the equipment to meet the standards successfully, usually because of a pattern of family socialization different from most middle-class youth, become defined as failures in the status system of the school. These definitions carry over into other segments of their community lives. In such a situation the adolescent failure can do one of two things to change his self-image: He can more successfully meet the standards or deny their legitimacy. The former strategy is unlikely, since if he were able, he would have succeeded this way in the first place. Therefore to retain his self-esteem he defines the standards which he has failed to meet as insignificant. The best way for him to demonstrate his rejection of these standards is to display characteristics diametrically opposed to the original set. Since he is not driven by an original ideology antithetical to standards of achievement, or unrelated to these, he creates a new status system in which his esteem derives from the evaluation of his peers who also reject the traditional standards. As these peers form into delinquent cliques, called gangs, the highest status members evolve as those who are most successful at their particular form of delinquency. Once delinquent sub-cultures emerge, they become differentiated in terms of certain forms of delinquent activity, such as the rackets, fighting, or drugs.[21]

The alienation of the delinquent from the larger society occurs as a result of the failure of his institution to integrate him into its processes, despite his inability to meet certain standards successfully. If he fails in school, for example, he may not even be permitted to play on an athletic team. If students can be said to experience any

---

[21] See R. Cloward and R. Ohlin, *Delinquency and Opportunity* (New York: The Free Press, 1960) for a complete description of the forms of delinquent activity.

real power at all from their position as students, it is certain that those who are unable to meet academic requirements will be restrained from assuming any power or prestige positions. Perhaps the area in which the future delinquent is most highly alienated is that of meaninglessness. Schools have seldom attempted to establish a multidimensional system of achievement with different kinds of activities that can confer a meaningful sense of esteem. It is difficult enough to instill a sense of real meaning into activities which the school values. It is next to impossible to infuse a sense of meaning into activities, such as physical education or dance or carpentry, which the school treats as subsidiary.

THE MORAL DEVIANT. Recent times have witnessed a disaffection of many students from the standards of the prominent institutions, particularly economic and educational, despite the fact that these students are equipped with the proper skills and socialized habits to be successful. It is here where we can perceive the most vivid demonstration of alienation. Whereas many delinquents accept many of the cultural goals, such as economic success, but reject the established methods of gaining such success, the moral delinquent rejects both the goals and the means. He is indeed the rebel, and he is rebelling against the alienating effects of the institutional life which the adult world wishes him to accept. Borrowing this term from Merton, we shall hereafter discontinue using the term "moral delinquent" and apply the designation "rebel" throughout the remainder of the discussion.[22]

The concept of "rebel," as we wish to use it here, is a concept implying commitment to a strategy (not always clearly conceived) alternative to those presented the rebel by tradition and the adult society, rather than solely a defensive reaction against a world in which he is denied participation. It has often been suggested that adolescents "do their own thing" because adults will not permit them access to the behaviors of adults. To follow this line of reasoning, we would have to classify contemporary rebels with the goldfish swallowers of the past. We would see them as passing time until coming of age, when they would gain the rights of passage into the adult society. We would need to view hippies, for example, as a very temporary adaptation, something that they are certain to "grow out of." We would need to view the use of marijuana, LSD, and other psychedelic drugs as being comparable to the fads of every adolescent generation, to be surrendered like toys during the age of responsibility.

[22] Merton, *Social Theory and Social Structure,* pp.155–156.

The rebel believes that he has a better way, better than anything he might achieve under the old order. He is driven by an ideology based on freedom of choice, and his commitment to this ideology often leads him into political action. A normal response to alienation in the past has been a commitment to non-commitment, to being totally uninvolved in the affairs of the world, which most persons believe are out of their control anyhow. This is a glaring adaptation to feelings of alienation. The struggle of young rebels today to rid themselves of this sense of alienation is demonstrated by, for example, the devotion of many adolescents to involvement. Radicalism and alienated apathy are produced by the same social conditions, the disjunctures and apparent irrelevance of institutional life to the development of a sense of self. Much of what we have described as moral deviance in the lives of adolescents is symbolized by the many attempts that they have made to stop the wheels of "progress." Lying down before a steamroller sent to remove a hangout on the Sunset Strip, or before trains taking equipment to Viet Nam, or preventing professors from teaching classes are statements of objection. Adolescents who perform such acts object to being steamrollered into conformity, impressed into the machine of depersonalization. Many of them, like the Young Radicals studied by Kenniston, do not know specifically what their goals are. They know only that they cannot surrender their lives apathetically as have their parents. They feel a sense of personal responsibility to help re-direct the depersonalizing course of history. In many ways they feel they are fighting for their lives, which to them implies a *meaningful* life.[23]

Many adolescents want to wear their hair long, smoke marijuana, dance "immorally," drop out of school, live in communal households, run away from home, resist the draft, and participate in a host of other activities and presentations of themselves which offend the average adult citizen. It is not clear how many do so simply to offend the society which has not made a place for them. But as long as the adult society refuses to grant that the rebellious adolescent has the capacity of becoming more than a simple irritant on the social scene, the communication barrier will continue to become enlarged.

Many adolescent rebels are seen by adults to be motivated by false or unclear goals because of deficient adaptations that they, the adults, have made to their own alienation. If one conceives of rebels as motivated by strong ideological commitments, then he

[23] K. Kenniston, *The Young Radicals* (New York: Harcourt, Brace & World, World Inc., 1968).

begins to ascribe legitimacy to those commitments. If such commitments relate to a struggle against the institutional bindings which
have encapsulated most of us, then such recognition forces the
majority of uninvolved Americans to face up to the way in which
they have ignored responsibility—not only the responsibility to free
themselves, but also of having failed to create a world in which the
children would have a lesser burden of responsibility to carry. It
seems almost normal to deny to all rebels the legitimacy of their
cause, to reiterate the values of the adult society, and to defend
against criticisms of the "establishment." To do otherwise would be
to face the failure of parenthood, and parents do not typically
think in these terms. If adolescents are alienated by a society into
which they are, by definition, not integrated, they have the choice
of buying from the adult culture the strategy which Fromm has
called an "escape from freedom," or to seek that freedom and with
it all the strains of calumny and isolation which committed rebels
experience.[24] Today more than at any other period adolescents are
moving, like the Phoenix, toward the fire, toward the anxiety, rejection, conflict, and family disruption which the struggle for freedom
involves. Most adults do not wish him well, for in his success is
embodied the seeds of their own destruction. For most adults this
destruction consists of eroding the meaningfulness and comfort of
non-involvement.

The Alienated Student

Except on some few university campuses, where student out-
breaks of various intensity and sort have taken place, it appears
that the average student is not highly alienated. Some evidence
derived from high school students suggests that such average students feel involved in the tasks set for them by their institution.
They are, it seems, involved in completing an education. Their
goals are good grades and ultimately graduation, and for many,
access to institutions of higher education.[25] In other words their
goals, in terms of which they evaluate their degree of involvement,
are means rather than ends. The process of educational mobility
and consequently the conception of the means by which this is
attained are such that motivation of students is traditionally and
typically unrelated to any broad view of personal fulfillment.

[24] E. Fromm, *Escape from Freedom* (New York: Holt, Rinehart & Winston,
Inc., 1941).
[25] R. Rhea, *et al., Measures of Child Involvement and Alienation from the
School Program,* Cooperative Research Project No. 5-383, U.S. Office of
Health, Education and Welfare (Washington, D. C.: U. S. Government Print-
ing Office, 1966).

So long as schools are minimally successful in motivating and allocating students through the system efficiently, and fulfilling the function of providing the larger society with committed role players in most areas of the economic system, they are not likely to experience inordinate pressure to make the educational experience more meaningful. Notions of an "integrated self," a "self-actualized" person, or a "healthy personality," while vaguely important to educational leaders, are too unmanageable to incorporate into programs. Nor is there any sign that a shift in cultural values has occurred to such an extent that community or society-wide pressure would require educators to take the task more seriously. The manifest function of the school is to socialize students to the norms and values of their society and to allocate a committed body of students to occupational roles. For the most part this is taking place in the same way that it has always taken place. There is no clear disjuncture between the values of the society and the performance of the schools. Most students are motivated to compliance through their integration into a system whose purposes are seldom questioned.

Students do recognize, however, that their intrinsic interests are subordinated to getting good grades. It is more important to pass a test on a particular book than to participate in an aesthetic experience. Students make a perfectly rational adaptation to the requirements of the system; they know what is expected and they comply. And although he is powerless to change the system and not clear about the relevance of his participation in terms of some intrinsic sense of self, he nonetheless does not exhibit the kinds of behaviors we might expect of alienated youth. Many of the students in the Rhea study, for example, recognized that they were powerless, but they were quite satisfied with their situation because they felt that those who did possess the power were competent and working in the best interests of the students.[26]

On the other hand many students in some high schools and colleges are beginning to resist the institutional temptation to surrender all power and responsibility to a benevolent leadership and to question the legitimacy of a process which has involved students for many years. To this end they have engaged in mass walkouts to protest inferior education in minority ghettos, organized underground newspapers, undergone wholesale suspensions rather than cut their hair, turned to psychedelic drugs while letting their grades drop, dropped out of school in larger numbers (proportional to good-student drop-outs in the past) than before, and in some places, dramatically closed large universities.

26 *Ibid.*

McClelland and others designated a personality component, referred to as "need achievement," which they felt could explain patterns of achievement in industrial societies. This component was linked closely to social and psychological orientations associated with an entrepreneurial society. The entrepreneurial orientation of capitalistic countries appears to explain the process by which need achievement is nourished in persons.[27] That is, young men and women are socialized to the belief that success in the society reveals one's fundamental character and that the rewards of such success (usually economic) are a validation of one's intrinsic worth. This achievement is logically translated into educational behaviors where persons put themselves on the line in terms of standard educational criteria. Such criteria, like the basis of the achievement motivation itself, spring from the same source, a conception of one's worth as a social being.

Such achievement motivation, which has been used to differentiate achieving and non-achieving lower-class youth, is conceived by McClelland as a product of a nation's time in social history and is utilized to explain the rise and fall of economic dominance and the orientation of national states.[28] The fact that we are able to discover these qualities in persons who are not part of the entrepreneurial class, such as in the Kahl study, is important, as it indicates the extent to which the people of a given society are influenced by the standards of the core culture. When the range of persons so influenced extends across class levels, the ability of institutions to control behavior increases. Although the adoption of the need achievement-entrepreneurial orientation has been increasingly extended to the working classes and the non-white minority groups, we have witnessed some erosion in the middle classes. This marks a point of evolution in the total society and can be partly explained in terms of some obvious circumstances.

THE DEFINITION OF AFFLUENCE. An affluent society, as conceived by Galbraith who coined what has since become a common description of our point in social and economic history, is one which defines the worth of humans in terms of the contribution that they can make to the gross national product.

A society which sets as its highest goal the production of private consummer goods will continue to reflect such attitudes in all its public

27 D. McClelland, *The Achieving Society* (New York: The Free Press, 1967).
28 Joseph Kahl, "Education and Aspirations of 'Common Man' Boys," *Harvard Educational Review* 23 (1953): 186–203; and McClelland, *The Achieving Society*.

decisions. It will entrust public decisions to men who regard any other goal as incredible—or radical. We have yet to see that not the total of resources but their studied and rational use is the key to achievement [29]

Galbraith's central concern appears to be in the way in which economic organization evolves independent of any consideration of human goals or of the effects of such organization on the individual. In order to guarantee an orderly and secure progress, industrial organizations have sought to control every aspect of social and industrial life that might affect such progress. To this end the whole idea of the individual has been sacrificed to this "necessary" control. To this end controversy, originality, and even change are viewed with suspicion. When, in the interests of such control, industry turns to advertising to guarantee the market it plans to serve, the people are denied their freedom of choice. They are not even permitted the freedom *not* to choose. They do not know any more what they really want. This is one significant form of alienation that economic development in its contemporary form has produced.[30]

The problem with affluence as a social state and as a condition premised upon modern forms of industrial organization is that it is predicated on the existence of a system which guarantees its viability independent of human intervention. Actually, human intervention is irrelevant; it is not even part of that system, since individual needs or goals are extrinsic to the economic process. But as an extrinsic force not integrated into decisions of economic organization, it can, given a rising tide of disaffection by the "establishment" itself, sow the seeds of conflict.

Many of our current conflicts can be related to the adjustments persons make to living in an affluent society. Affluence should be thought of as a period in which the majority of people are free, not only from life-sustaining needs, but also free from the tensions created when socially-valued objects are unattainable. The American worker, as we have suggested in another section, is secure. He is secure even to the point of disaffiliation from the struggles and negotiations which take place to make him more secure. The whole concept of a common bond in any kind of struggle for upward mobility has been relieved by the attainment of satisfactory wages and benefits, as well as the bureaucratization of bargaining and negotiations.

[29] J. K. Galbraith, *The Affluent Society* (New York: Mentor Books, 1958), p.272.
[30] *Ibid.*

Today's adolescents are maturing in such a context. The kinds of battles, both individual and collective, in which their parents engaged are ancient history to them, even though many parents attempt to keep their own battles alive as a point of reference for youth. This does not work in most cases for at least two major reasons: one, the distance between parents and children, and two, the irrelevance of that kind of conflict in today's world. This generation of adolescents does not view economic security as the same goal that their parents did. They have always had security and most persons do not typically become motivated to attain some condition whose absence they cannot meaningfully evaluate. The fact that most of them still pursue traditional success paths is more a function of perceiving no alternatives than of assessing the value of the goal. Like most persons locked within a bureaucratic mechanism, the role, rather than the self, determines the behavior.

Many young people today define affluence as undesirable. Like Kenniston's young radicals, they are angry and disillusioned about what the benefits of affluence are. They are not necessarily guilty about having been raised in it; they are just unwilling to accept affluence as a worthy life goal.[31] Increasingly it appears that the luxury of a student life, a collegiate existence, is becoming anathema. Fraternities and sororities are beginning to feel the pinch. Many such organizations are beginning to look toward a redefinition of their function, sometimes to the direction of social responsibility, to help the Greek system survive. Fraternities and sororities have traditionally sought acceptable outlets for a kind of tacit motivation to perform some functions in the area of social responsibility. The form of this, derived from the habits of the upper classes, was charity work—for example, holding a fair, the proceeds of which would go to some charitable organization. The fact that the fun at the fair was of infinitely more consequence than the charitable cause is significant because it reveals the structural orientation of the collegiate culture. There were not, through the long history of the Greek system, legitimate channels in the system for persons to pursue commitments in the area of social responsibility. This has changed to some extent in some places. At Berkeley and UCLA, the fraternities and sororities have assumed a large portion of the job that the university has structured for itself in the minority communities. It is, of course, not a radical activity, but a clear-cut establishment function and consequently legitimate in the Greek system. But the fact remains that students in the most affluent collegiate environments have shifted their orientation from conspicuous and irrelevant consumption to reconstructive commitments. They help to staff the facilities of tutorial programs, provide programs for cultural enrichment, and are constantly meeting with concerned groups to discover additional areas of involvement.

Some students do feel guilty about their affluent backgrounds and sometimes go to extremes, either to do penance or to reveal to others that they are no longer entrapped by former values. They may walk around in rags or near rags, live in hovels, drive the oldest cars they can find, and live on a near starvation diet. To these students the success of their parents is close to being despicable. What kind of education then do students who are embarrassed by affluence seek? The answer would be something relevant to aesthetic or humanistic self-development needs. When they cannot find this on the campus, they either drop out or live with their alienation until the time when they can find involvement with others dedicated to the reconstruction of the university. At times, this evolves into radical student action, sometimes leading to violence and disruption of the campus. But the dynamics of this are more complicated than guilt over affluence, and we will deal with this in a later section on student activism.

AUTOMATION AND ALIENATION. Automation affects primarily the person who has been allocated to semi-skilled and unskilled occupations. This person, as a child going through the school and recognizing the patterns of educational mobility, is the one who has been least integrated into the system. He is, as student, given the least attention, criticized most heavily for his failure to meet standards, and denied access to the prestigious functions in which other students participate. His total non-integration into the mainstream of society is consummated by the obsolescence of the jobs he is qualified to hold. Status of occupations is not, in itself, predictive of alienation. Members of labor unions appear to be far more accepting of the *status quo* than do college professors, lawyers, or social workers who man the picket lines of protest movements. Therefore when automation eliminates all possibility of entering the economic establishment, even at the bottom, the consequence is bound to be an awareness of one's powerlessness to control through legitimate channels his own mobility or the processes of the economic order.

Low-skilled occupations are not the only ones to be eliminated or threatened by automation. Automatic processing machines and high-speed computers have implications for a broad range of the total population. A recent estimate indicates that each electronic computer puts an average of 35 people per week out of work. At the same time the advance of efficiency of the machine changes the kind of work and, in all likelihood, the kind of industrial relations for an average of 105 workers per machine. Middle-management skills are also being made obsolete by machines which can improve communication, provide improved information technology, and aid in the decision-making process. Clerical and secretarial staffs associated with these skills will also cease to exist.[32]

The same automated machinery which eliminates many jobs will provide others, but in line with our concern with alienation, the problems for persons involved are similar. The problem for the school is, of course, compounded. It is difficult enough to effect commitments of alienated students to join the labor force. If it becomes necessary to prepare students for careers which we can predict in advance will be made obsolete by the machine, then the school's task may be an impossible one, given its present structural organization.

Augmented technology in industry has had its counterpart in education. As organizations increase in size and knowledge increases and becomes more specialized, the university begins to look ever more like an industrial bureaucracy. When black students at the University of California, Santa Barbara, decide actively to push forward their demands, they chose the computer center to occupy. Regardless of the consequences of this act, the fact that this kind of conceptualization of the heart of the university is implanted in the minds of students suggests broader consequences for the kind of future interaction we observe between students and their institutions.

ALIENATION AND THE ROLE OF THE SCHOOL

Industry has attempted to make some adaptation to the communication problems associated with highly specialized functions. They have attempted to reduce alienation through a process of job or task rotation, personal counseling, and for many middle and top level administrators sensitivity training has been instituted. Whether this becomes a process of "cooling out" these persons, in the sense of reducing frustration while maintaining similar roles, or whether some radicalization in the conception of the relationship of men to their roles is occurring, is unclear. Universities appear to be seek-

---

[32] R. A. Kaiman and J. M. Adams, Jr., "Impact of Automation: High School Teaching and Cooperative Training," *American School Board Journal* 152 (February 1966): 28–30.

ing similar kinds of solutions to the problems of *depersonalization* brought on by the kind of transformation that the American university and college have experienced in the past two to three decades. One conceived solution is to have students involved in their institution. What this involvement means, however, is not clear, and we need to examine the concept in the light of the forces which are currently alienating many college youth.

Alienation of students from their schools does not, of course, begin with their experience in higher education. There are many forces in the public schools which conspire to produce the kinds of psychological states that we have associated with the various components of alienation. Although most students do not appear to be experiencing debilitating effects from their conception of themselves as powerless or from a lack of clarity in their perception of the school's role in helping them achieve some important goal, the fact still remains that many students are affected in important ways. Our position is that the processes of public school education are unconditionally alienative, but that certain mechanisms, such as "cooling out," rigid socialization, reliance upon formal rewards to maintain competitive achievement, and the negative sanctioning of deviance have been successful so far in preventing students from gaining some awareness of the ways in which they are being alienated, or even of their own alienation. When such mechanisms become ineffective, it is likely that felt alienation will spread, and action predicated upon this alienation will begin. It has already begun in many schools. We can illustrate this process vividly with reference to the fact that many college students have gone to jail rather than leave the lines of protest. When a police officer says to a student "get out of here or we'll put you in jail, and you don't want that on your record, do you," he makes the assumption that the old mechanisms of traditional sanctions are internalized in the student. But many of these students are not at all concerned about their "record" in the old way. The threat or even the fact has no potency and consequently cannot be used as an efficient form of control.

We have emphasized the processes by which students have been committed to seek both the short- and long-range goals provided them by the institution of the school. We have suggested that there are significant signs of student unrest at both secondary and higher levels of education. If there are such stirrings, they must be assumed to be related to some definition that students make about the kind of education they are receiving. This would have to do with both the goals they have been asked to seek and to the kind of environment in which they must live. What then are these goals and what are the specific components of the environment that the students find to be alienating?

The overriding goal of education, as it operates to serve society, is to allocate students differentially to occupational roles to produce well socialized citizens. The aesthetic goals of idealistic educators appear to be little more than a by-product of the overall task, one that most teachers and few students take seriously. Appreciation of something is not likely to show up on grade cards, and college admissions officers are not prone to ask if the student is sensitive either to beauty or social experiences. Students are being asked, essentially, to fit into the world outside the school, the world symbolized by the everyday activities of their parents and other peoples' parents. Students learn early that there is some flexibility within the larger social system so that persons can choose a range of occupations, to marry or not, to participate in the political process or not, to vacation where they want, to spend their money as they want, and to associate with whom they choose. As children are growing up, they actually envy adults this latitude, which they view as the prominent result of having aged sufficiently. But young people today appear to be suspicious of that freedom. As they become adolescents and begin to think seriously about the world they have almost entered, they begin to wonder just what kind of star they have been following. They begin to ask themselves and each other about the relationship between the kind of freedom adults have and the kind of world those adults have built. They see a world filled with poverty, riots, ulcers, divorces, hatred, war, inter-personal dishonesty, materialism, repression, political intrigues, assassination of culture heroes, black militancy, drunkenness, drug addiction and crime. They begin to question the soundness of the institutions which have produced such ugliness and uncertainty. The school and its processes begin to come under scrutiny, and those who are still in school begin to think about ways of either extricating themselves from the control the school exercises over them or to become involved in its reconstruction.

The School Environment

In a study of 733 elementary school students it was found that students who felt excluded by the teacher developed a sense of isolation and those who felt excluded by their peers experiencd a sense of powerlessness, centering around classroom tasks and interpersonal relations.[33] The idea of this kind of exclusion appears to be relevant to a consideration of both alienation and the strategies persons use to avoid such alienation. In effect the school provides students with all the appropriate cues for the avoidance of exclusion. Teachers communicate what it takes for students to be accepted by them, and in the process, very early in their educational careers, condition them to conformity. Henry's significant paper on the socialization process occurring in elementary schools describes a situation in which all educational goals are made subservient to acceptance needs. That is, students structure all behavior, including volunteering, criticizing or tattling on other students, helping, contributing to classroom activity, and answering questions, in terms of an interpersonal evaluative process.[34]

Although it may appear from the kind of productivity one observes in the classroom that students are involved in the educational experience, it is not clear what the involvement means. Most of the components of alienation would seem to be affected by some kind of involvement. In their attempt to make involvement a meaningful integrative experience, educators have developed a system of involvement activities. High schools and universities have elaborated on the structural possibilities for involvement found in elementary schools where self-contained classrooms predominate. But most available evidence suggests that participation in these activities has not contributed to the social adjustment of participants.[35] One author went so far as to suggest that students who participated in activities actually felt more alienated than those who did not.[36] This is not surprising in one sense. That is, if we consider those who seek participation to be those who require it, and if we assume that involved persons are more aware of the environment, what it offers and what it does not, then these students will be most aware of the shortcomings of the institution.

Beyond such token activities, how can we make the argument that students are involved in their educational experience? To what extent do they plan it? In what ways do they make their

33 D. C. Epperson, "Some Interpersonal and Performance Correlates of Classroom Alienation," *School Review* 71 (1963): 360–376.

34 J. Henry, *Culture Against Man* (New York: Random House, Inc., 1963), pp.293–296.

35 R. T. Hartnett, "Involvement in Extra Curricular Activities as a Factor in Academic Performance," *Journal of College Student Personnel* 6 (September 1965): 272–274; M. B. Kievit, "Social Participation and Social Adjustment," *Journal of Educational Research* 58 (March 1965): 303–306; M. L. Bach, "Factors Related to Student Participation in Campus Social Organizations," *Journal of Social Psychology* 54 (1961): 337–348.

36 Kievit, "Social Participation and Social Adjustment."

individual interests and needs felt? Do they make or enforce any of the regulations of the school? How do they decide on relevance? Can they censor activities? To what extent can they decide not to participate in activities which they consider irrelevant? Can they choose or dismiss faculty or play any part in the recruitment process? From the beginning of their educational experience students have the choice. They can go along with the formal requirements of the school and gain acceptance, which passes for involvement, or they can decline and fall out of the mainstream of standard rewards for participating.

The latent structure of education has helped to perpetuate many of the worst conditions in American society, those conditions about which idealistic students feel strongly and which are often grounds for student protest and unrest. Schools have maintained the existing stratification order in its unidimensional way of rewarding and punishing. The school has allowed racism in American society to go unchecked. It has produced the kind of conformity which adolescents feel to be strangulating. And it has successfully squelched almost every emotional, affective or aesthetic impulse or creative talent that students have. It is no wonder that the natives are restless. If those who wished to retain the *status quo* in every aspect of social functioning had been more far-sighted, they would have realized that any concession to student expression of dissatisfaction or concern would open the flood gates of awareness. One does not want a little bit if freedom when he recognizes that it makes a difference in his life. He wants it all.

THE STUDENT REVOLUTION

You are quite right in feeling the situation is "potentially dangerous." For if we win, we will take control of your world, your corporation, your university and attempt to mold a world in which we and other people can live as human beings. . . . We begin by fighting you about your support of the war in Vietnam and American Imperialism—IDA (Institute for Defense Analysis) and the School for International Affairs. We will fight you about your control of black people in Morningside Heights, Harlem, and the Campus itself. And we will fight you about the type of miseducation you are trying to channel us through.[37]

So wrote Mark Rudd, one of the prominent leaders of the Columbia rebellion, in the wake of a growing acknowledgement that something significant was happening on the college campuses. Rudd

[37] Mark Rudd, quoted in *National Guardian*, 11 May 1968.

was in effect agreeing with Grayson Kirk, president of Columbia who had stated:

Our young people, in disturbing numbers, appear to reject all forms of authority, from whatever source derived, and they have taken refuge in a turbulent and inchoate nihilism whose sole objectives are destruction. I know of no time in our history when the gap between the generations has been wider or more potentially dangerous.[38]

The Columbia revolt epitomized the conflict between the generations of which President Kirk spoke. It brought to a head the dissensions which had characterized the Berkeley revolt four years before and set the stage for similar conflagrations on campuses across the nation. It is impossible to say, as one can be tempted to, that such disorders culminate in one specific eruption which appears at the moment to be the end of one stage and the beginning of another. Berkeley? Columbia? San Francisco State? San Jose State? By the time this comes to print, other schools will have joined the list. Many eruptions which preceded the Berkeley affair have passed into history as almost another chapter entirely.[39] Student riots in Paris and Japan begin to give the revolution an international flavor, and the full significance of student power is still not clear. The issues are often ambiguous or are spontaneously conceived to bolster action. A visiting military recruiter, minority group tensions, the existence of an "imperialist" navy base, the building of a gym in the ghetto all rush to the fore as provocations. But the seeds of dissent go deeper. They are embedded in the structure of institutional life. And it is this life which students wish to erode. They are criticized by the "establishment" as having no constructive suggestions, no salutary goals. In the minds of those who are comfortable with the *status quo*, the assumption is that one should not change unless there is a clear and significantly better direction in which to move. Every revolution has its causes although there may not be clear alternatives. Participants in revolution are united by the fact they do not want the old; they have suffered under the old regime and want no more of it. The fact that there is little consensus about the new is not a deterrent to action for these young people, as it would be with bureaucrats. It

---

[38] *The New Left*, A Report of the Subcommittee to Investigate the Administration of the Internal Security Act and Other Internal Security Laws (Washington, D. C.: U. S. Government Printing Office, 1968), p.81.

[39] M. Heirich and S. Kaplan, "Yesterday's Discord," in *The Berkeley Student Revolt*, ed. S. M. Lipset and S. Wolin (New York: Doubleday & Company, Inc., 1965), pp.10–35.

is clear that university administrators cannot wait for opponents of their system to come up with a better plan than the one extant. These persons need to focus intently on the causes of student unrest and by attacking these, change the structure of the institutional environment for millions of alienated and potentially alienated students.

"Up Against the Wall"—the Source of Conflict

"Up against the wall," the battle cry for SDS (Students for a Democratic Society, the most militant of white student power groups) posits that students have reached a point in their alienation where they must either take action or figuratively die. Despite the fact that critics of student activism constantly refer to the militants as a small, outspoken minority, student disorders are increasing. Those who are highly alienated and organized to do something about it find a good deal of company when they create a situation in which persons are forced to choose their sides. Students who have not completely dismissed the traditional values of an instrumental education leading to a good job (and this would include many of the young radicals if Kenniston's group is at all representative) find themselves hard pressed to stay out of the fight.[40] The fact that they may endanger their student status is real but not sufficient to deter many of them from acting against their former best interests.

The conditions which provoke active confrontation with the university are not sloganistic revolutionary causes in the mouths of militants, but important alienating influences in the environment of most university students. Clark Kerr, former president of the University of California, replaced ostensibly because he was unable to deal effectively with student dissent, described the modern multiversity as replete with alienating factors. He wrote of a high degree of complexity which was unmanageable for many students, of the hugeness of the institution, of large impersonal classes, and neglect of students by absentee faculty, all conspiring to produce a sense of futility in the average student.[41] Student protests and demonstrations at Harvard prompted President Pusey to analyze the probable sources of conflict. He suggested that a fundamental starting point in such an analysis should be a conception of the contemporary student as one who wishes to be meaningfully involved, that the age of indifference to larger social and political issues has passed. The university in his view has failed students if

---

40 Kenniston, *Young Radicals.*
41 Clark Kerr, *The Uses of the University* (Cambridge: Harvard University Press, 1963).

it cannot provide them with a viable and constructive alternative to indifference. The destructive behavior which such reaction to indifference takes occurs in the absence of such a contribution to student development.[42]

The reasons for student unrest are many and varied. Many authors have attempted this kind of analysis, and we can summarize the independent factors that have influenced their assessment. Some conditions in the university environment are almost taken as built-in factors and turn up in practically every survey of the roots of student protest. Others reflect a special standpoint, and still others will be suggested here. The total may seem terribly weighty, but many of the factors can be eliminated by a single structural change.

The Social Psychological State of Students

Students bring to their environment their unique quality of being a student in this time in social and cultural history. That is, part of what happens to them is a function of how the role of student has evolved, particularly in relation to other roles, such as faculty and administrator.

In a period of rapid cultural change the student exists in a context of controversy, and it is on the college campus where ideas around this controversy become crystalized. His tendency for holding more liberal ideas than those of his family is already present. On the campus away from the mediating influence of his parents, these ideas take on a more solid rationale. He is exposed to the literature which provides a theoretical basis for radical views and action.

The student is also a marginal man in the sense that he exists between childhood and adulthood, between his old family and his new, between the formal institutional controls of family and school and freedom. He is ending his education but is not yet part of the labor force. If he is not ensconced in an academic curriculum such as engineering, law, or teaching, where his path to the occupational world is clear; his perspective is uncertainty. The college student is in a situation of transition where he must adjust his thinking to futuristic plans, but at the same time he must make some kind of successful adaptation to a new situation. Most students have left behind them the old community cues for behavior, their friends and family, and seek new cues to stabilize their existence.[43] When the new context is relatively stable, when few movements or radical

---

[42] Nathan Pusey, "Student Protest and Commitment," *School and Society* 93 (December 1965): 471–474.
[43] Lipset and Wolin, *Berkeley Student Revolt,* pp.5–6.

ideologies are circulating through the ivy-covered halls, the new adaptations will approximate the old. But this is not the case on many campuses, where students in the first stages of their new adaptation are faced with competing pressures. They learn quickly that they can identify with the "establishment" and the traditional goals and processes, or with the alienated and committed students who stand to the left of tradition. This kind of role conflict, like most role conflicts, is resolved situationally. Where the pressures from the left are greatest, as in such schools as Berkeley, Columbia, Brandeis, Wisconsin, and San Francisco State, the tendency to favor affiliation with the radical groups is greatest.

Independent of the students' predilections, the university as a social institution has also evolved, and certain conditions inherent in their stage of evolution are seen by students and social critics as highly productive of problems for persons living in such an environment.[44]

SOURCES OF STUDENT ALIENATION AND CONFLICT

The Impersonal Environment

The small liberal arts college is struggling to survive. The state universities and major private colleges have experienced constant increases in the size of the student body. Several universities have passed the 30,000 mark and many others are hovering near that figure.

When one adds to size the increasing specialization and compartmentalization that have come to characterize these multiversities, the effects on personnel, students, faculty, and administrators multiply geometrically. The assumptions of a personalized environment are that students can establish a meaningful relationship with each other, with the faculty, and with the administrative personnel who make the decisions that affect their lives. However, the envi-

---

[44] For a more detailed exposition of the points covered in this section see Lipset and Wolin, *Berkeley Student Revolt;* K. Kenniston, "The Sources of Student Dissent," *Journal of Social Issues* 33, No. 3 (July 1967): 108–137; R. Flacks, "The Liberated Generation: An Exploration of the Roots of Student Protest," *Journal of Social Issues* 33, No. 3 (July 1967): 52–75; Donald R. Brown, "Student Stress and the Institutional Environment," *Journal of Social Issues* 33, No. 3 (July 1967): 92–107; W. H. Conley, "Pressures from Students for Emancipation from Institutional Controls and Vice Versa," in *Pressures and Priorities in Higher Education,* Proceedings of the Twentieth Annual National Conference on Higher Education (Washington, D. C., National Education Association, 1965), pp.88–91; M. B. Freedman, "Pressures on Students," in *Pressures and Priorities,* pp.148–151.

ronment is one in which students cannot relate well to each other because: (1) they do not meet each other, (2) when they do, it is the classroom where there is very low interaction, (3) they are in competition with each other for the rewards of the system, (4) they seldom have a common ground for communication since they are overspecialized and insensitive to each others' personal needs.

Students do not relate meaningfully with the faculty because: (1) the role relationships are traditionally formal, (2) the faculty are not sensitive to non-academic student problems, (3) pressures for professional mobility require the faculty to focus on research and ignore the education of undergraduates, (4) the faculty are unavailable.

Students do not relate to administrative personnel because: (1) they never come into contact with them, (2) they do not understand the administrative structure, (3) administrative functions are inherent in formal rules and designated role responsibilities rather than in the decisions of individuals.

Students are constantly required to submit to a set of depersonalizing activities, such as filling out many forms, standing in long lines for IBM cards, and receiving IBM printouts for grades. These activities are not potent enough *per se* to infuriate students, except perhaps temporarily, but they do symbolize to the student the fact that he is but a small number in a society of numbers.

Lack of Community

An important conception of the university in the minds of students and faculty alike is one of an intellectual and social community. Having left the protective environment of the home, students seek similar structures in the institution to assure them of both stimulation and security. But the pressures to maintain the present, if not accelerated, rate of institutional output, relegates student needs for affiliation to a low point on the priority scale. At times this affiliation is not critical to student survival, although it would appear to be relevant to the issue of a generalized sense of integration. At other times students, bending before an overwhelming sense of isolation and loneliness, desperately require a place to go, to be in a *Gemeinschaft* environment. But this is by no means assured by the institution. Again this is a matter of low priority. Universities seldom take pains to assure the existence of a meeting place for students where they can discuss significant intellectual and personal concerns. Often business enterprise makes up for the lack of such ecological arrangements to meet these needs. A community is often conceived of as a place where all or nearly all the needs of persons who live in that community can be met. If only occupational mobility needs are structurally accommodated, the university is less than half a community.

Inadequate, Irrelevant Instruction

Large classes appear to be the prominent hallmark of the large university. These classes cannot provide for individual interests, cannot accommodate a range of questions, and without a charismatic teacher cannot hope to excite students about a particular subject. Sometimes classes are broken into discussion sections with teaching assistants assuming the brunt of the teaching responsibility. These assistants are usually in the process of completing their degrees and are more concerned with the state of their personal data than the simple questions of students.

In many ways the teaching assistants are approximating the role of their professors, who are more interested in their research and national prominence than they are with the elementary propositions of their disciplines or in student recognition in their own front yard.

Students frequently feel that their courses are irrelevant, trivial, and meaningless. For many decades students have accepted the definitions of their curricula that were conceived by the faculty and administrators. To the students the course structure was relevant only insofar as they received a degree if the courses were taken and passed. Relevance today, however, is a matter of instrumentality in accomplishing self-fulfilling goals. Students want to do something important; they want to pursue goals that will link them as persons and professionals to the egalitarian revolution. They do not buy the rationale of the disciplinarians that knowledge is its own reward and that contributing to a body of scientific, historical, or literary knowledge is enough. Students are not content to be better thinkers in a vacuum. They want to be better people in a meaningful dialogue with other people. They want, above all, to be productive. They do not feel that one can be genuinely productive in a typical college course. They recognize that learning, as defined by the purposes of most academic instruction, is a suspended, sterile activity, and that such activity is counterproductive. This is to say that one kind of commitment retards the internalization of the other. Scholarship as it is conventionally conceived on the campus is irrelevant to the kinds of important purposes with which students wish to identify.

The involvement of students with the kind of instruction that is available is self-estranging. That is, students are spending time performing tasks which are incongruent with their sense of self, with what they feel they should be doing. This kind of self-estrangement often produces anger, the anger of being co-opted to live in ways that are demoralizing, non-fulfilling, and non-beneficial to others. Many students stand at a point of confronting themselves with what they intend to do about such self-estrangement. The fact that many are deciding against continuing to live in such a state is being reflected in the increasing number of student-institution confrontations.

Bureaucratic Sloth

Many university students experience frustration at the slow rate of institutional change. Their experience with educational systems in the past have familiarized them unpleasantly with the kinds of stagnation with which they must live daily. Students are part of a rapidly changing culture. Inter-personal relations have taken on a more open and permissive posture. Individuals are more aware of their personal needs than before and are skeptical of the school's capacity to innovate in the directions they want to move. Even when they hear professors and administrators support their criticisms and promise changes, they find themselves waiting for change in vain. Bureaucratic institutions have always changed slowly. Bureaucracy has emerged as supra-personal; it does not have the capacity to respond rapidly to the demands of its participants. What is even more frightening is that it may be that bureaucracy has achieved a state of total independence from personal or even cultural shifts in emphasis. If this is the case, then only revolutionary upheavals can achieve the goals of many members or of the culture. If students sense their powerlessness in affecting change when the power structure is unsympathetic, the situation will deteriorate appreciably when they realize that they cannot even have change when the power structure is sympathetic.

Like the majority of American Negroes, students want change and they want it now. For the most part they do not recognize the problems of effecting change within bureaucratic mastodons. They believe that individuals can make decisions, and structures will be promptly overhauled. And even if they are told that this is not the way it is, the student rebel will argue that this is the way it should be. Bureaucrats are interested in doing things in a reasonable manner. By reasonable they mean that it is necessary to consult the limitations of the bureaucratic structure in order to conceive possibilities. On the other hand students often believe that it is necessary to consult the assumptions on which bureaucratic structures are built. If one denies, for example, the assumption that a university must be run on the basis of a hierarchical authority structure and accepts the possibility of a participatory democracy, then we can envision a new set of alternatives for change.

Boredom and Fatigue

The results of delayed gratification are boredom and fatigue. For many students the educational experience, when compared with the excitement of social movements, of rapidly changing norms and values where they can more easily live as adults, is a dreadful bore. This becomes appreciably intensified in the light of how much education one "needs" today. The market cannot accommodate B.A.'s. Persons must have professional degrees, masters, and Ph.D.'s, or specialist credentials. Medical students, for example, do not even think of consummating their studies without a residency. The first step on a ten-mile journey is not as hard to take as the first step on a hundred-mile journey. One can summon up reservoirs of intrinsic motivation to struggle through a third and fourth year, but it requires more from the environment when the prospect is a fifth, sixth, seventh, eighth year, or more.

Many students who pursue professional degrees never think about how they might be allowing whatever spirit they have to atrophy. Delayed gratification is still a highly potent force in the control of middle-class student behaviors. But the foundation rock may be splitting in places. Books like the existential novels of Camus, films, T.V. specials, magazine articles, the folk wisdom of the Beatles, the availability of marijuana, meditation and sensitivity groups, all talking to the student about the meaning of his life and the foolishness of most human behavior, are having a profound impact. One who buries his head in his medical books or law books or physics books for four to eight years beyond the first sixteen years of school is one who is either not receptive to the powerful currents of contemporary life or is too terrified to raise his head and think about what he is or what he wants. When the mechanisms of control, such as delayed gratification, fail to operate within a society, the institution must discover its own methods of motivating students.

Rules and Regulations—College as Parent Surrogate

The college environment as a system of regulation and control will always be defined as authoritarian, regardless of the degree of permissiveness that administrators permit. This is because the permissiveness itself is usually, if not always empirically, determined by the school authorities. The decade of the sixties for most students was a revolutionary period in which groups struck, sat, and even rioted for freedom from authoritarian control of their lives. At the same time college students have reached an age when they begin to question the amount of parental or general control to which they will submit. The university, like the secondary school, has accepted *in loco parentis* responsibility for the behavior of students. And students like the idea less every year.

There appear to be at least three dominant functions of administrative control over student behavior, and each function rests on a fundamental assumption which we might bring into question here.

ORGANIZATIONAL STABILITY. This function is conceived in terms of maintaining the viability of institutional structures. Patterns of educational life are controlled in order to make manageable the passage of large numbers of persons through a complex network of activities and interactions. The assumption here is that social beings require organized and definitive paths to educational goals. If this were not so, we could not guarantee that social roles would be filled and persons would be equipped and motivated to fill them. In order to dispute this assumption one would have to make the argument that college life is different from career allocation, and that free choice of educational patterns would not disrupt the social order. Many students would make the argument that the social order as we know it is not worth preserving to begin with, and even if it were, that freedom in all things educational could be conceived as an educational experience in itself where personal growth would be preliminary to professional development.

MORAL RESPONSIBILITY. Beyond preserving the stability of institutional life as we now know it, control is viewed by many college administrators as a way of socializing students to highly valued ethical standards. In this sense formal controls act as sanctions to prevent students from falling into deviant paths which would be harmful to both the system and to themselves. One moderate rationale for maintaining such constraints is the position that controls are necessary to help students mature, to free them from conflict and disturbance in order to permit reflection and intellectual growth. Beyond this the school must also provide students with stability in their transition from childhood to adulthood.[45] The assumption underlying this functional position is that growth or

45 Conley, "Pressures from Students," pp.88–91.

maturity occurs in the context of stability. Perhaps this is partly true, at least in the area of intellectual development. But many students today do not buy the thought of an educaion devoid of experience and unrelated to feeling. The act of reconstituting in an unstable environment is a force for change, and this is congruent with growth, which is a good part of education. To students who protest the imposition of a set of moral standards which they find stultifying, the notion of stability is meaningless. Students are beginning to discover a rapid maturation process in the kinds of conflict situations which they as radicals impose upon themselves.

INSTITUTIONAL IMAGE. A third function of control in the campus environment is political. That is, college administrators see both themselves and their schools being threatened with lack of support if the image changes. Administrators of state-supported schools know that the state legislature can cut supporting funds at any time. Such support is used as a threat by local politicians whose politics are seldom more than preserving stability and the *status quo*. For private schools regents and alumni donors pose a similar threat. The assumption underlying controls based on these political grounds is that the university, like its counterpart bureaucracy in industry, can survive only if it pleases non-participants who support it. Too many free universities and colleges have emerged in the past half dozen years to permit this assumption to go unchallenged. Perhaps the college as we now know it, as a bureaucratic, instrumental agency of economic institutions, must live with such an assumption. But this is not the kind of school that alienated students want.

Freedom from institutional controls is always conceived in terms of "how much can we permit?" The answer to this question can only be found by examining the conscience of the institution wherever it may exist in order to know which controls are traditional, which instrumental to the purposes of outside agencies, and which specifically valuable to help students mature personally as well as intellectually.

Control over Academic Structure

We examined above the function of university control over the behavior of students. In this section we need to look at the way in which the college determines academic activities for students. The Free Speech Movement at Berkeley emerged out of a developing sense of indignation on the part of some students who resented being excluded from helping to determine the activities in which they were required to participate if they wanted an education. The areas in which students were traditionally denied participation were determination of courses and requirements, faculty recruitment, utilization of student fees, establishment of control regulations, sanctioning of faculty for irresponsibility in teaching, invitations for marketplace recruitment by industry and by selective service agencies, and the creation of new programs. Many of these areas of action now include student participants. Awareness that strategies of protest can affect such participation does not, as we witness, reduce student pressures. It appears that the opposite is more true. Students, like blacks, are beginning to accelerate their demands as they discover areas in which they have power. Students want to be integrated into the decision-making structures that influence their life.

An Environment of Pressure

In the chapter on mental illness we discussed in some detail pressure as it effects students. As a context in which students want to grow, to gain control over their environment so as to reduce the pain emanating from pressures, the university perhaps provides too much challenge. We have suggested that conflict and stress can be beneficial, but in order to be so, the amount must be within manageable limits. But more relevant than the amount of pressure, is the consequence of surviving or prevailing over the pressure. That is, students need to feel that the struggle is worth it in their new terms. The old slogan of building character by persevering is as meaningless to students as studying Greek and Latin to sharpen the brain. Perseverance is not its own reward, and for many students the meaninglessness of both the means and the goals of their current education makes overcoming academic obstacles a futile task.

We have discussed the conventional forms of pressure, where students compete for the rewards of the system. We recognize the consequence of failure for middle-class youth. We are not, however, clear about the extent to which pressure erupts from new and different wells. These are the wells of romantic individualism. Students want to be emancipated, not only from institutional controls but from the goals and values which begin to hamper them in their daily life. They often view the college from the disadvantage point of their encroaching generalized anger. The pressure that they experience comes as much from within as from without. The college environment symbolizes the environment of pressure in which they have lived all their lives. The number of students who are actually at the point of decision because of this intra-personal confrontation is uncertain. But the time when both sets of pressures, from within the person and from the institutional environment, erupt appears to exist for more students now than in the past. It should not be surprising that students are looking about them for something to do about it.

Ivy- towered Isolation

The environment of the campus is unreal for many students. They are not clear, from their courses, living arrangements, and daily routines, what it all has to do with life. Life, for those students who are awakening to the needs of the outside world, exists somewhere else. Like Eliot's character in *The Cocktail Party,* some go off to find life in the bush among the primitives. Many drop out of school and feel impotent and isolated. They are aware of their own failure and the failure of their institutions.[46] Others go about attempting to change themselves and their environment. Students are constantly seeking ways to become involved in the major social issues of the day. They find these issues everywhere around them but not within the ivy-covered walls. They want to do something about problems of poverty, of race relations, about national politics, about the draft, the war, about repressive moral codes. They cannot frequently find outlets within the campus structure. They want to be involved, and they want their school to be involved. They feel shut off from the mainstream of social involvement. Pride in their school, which reflects upon themselves, can no longer be found exclusively in football teams or high academic standards. If involvement of the university in the significant affairs of our time emerges as more than a token thrust, students will have made the difference.

RADICAL STUDENTS AND THE POLICE

The interaction between radical students and the police and the definitions each make of the other, with or without personal interaction, is worthy of exploration. This is so because the inappropriateness of the respective views appears to hide something fundamental about the conditions which have produced the hostility. This analysis is undertaken despite the obvious danger of building

[46] J. W. Wideman, "College Undergraduate Dropouts: Causes, Cures and Implications for Secondary Schools," *National Association of Secondary School Principals Bulletin* 50 (April 1966): 224–234.

an argument on a wrong assumption. Neither the police nor the student nor many critics would assume that their definitions of each other are in any way inappropriate. Or if inappropriate, the argument can also be made that distorted intensity of feeling and response are functional to the struggle each is waging against the other. Although this latter view is useful in describing the implicit rationale for confrontation, it is not useful for making a social-psychological analysis of the way in which position and personality interact to produce attitudes. Man at war, for example, is socialized to define the enemy as everything negative, as worthy of destruction. This makes the task of killing the other psychologically feasible. But it is a different kind of analysis to ask the question: What is there in man that permits this process to work so effectively?

We have talked at some length about the student at a point in the evolution of the student role. We have observed that he is between two cultures, that of childhood and that of adulthood. He is for the first time experiencing a taste of independence. He is entering the college at a point at which college has itself evolved into a depersonalizing environment of efficiency. For those who perceive the alienating effects of such a context, there is a point of decision. Many choose to live with the problems until gaining economic or professional security. Others refuse to live any longer as cogs in the institutional machinery. For them alienation is responded to by some kinds of action which they hope will diminish feelings of isolation, meaninglessness, powerlessness, and the like.

For many students alienation takes the form of reaction to authority. College, like the home, is usually an authoritarian system, bureaucratically organized for control of the lower status participants in the system. Rejection of this authoritarianism is an important stage in the development of a radical posture and radical action. More than any other single group the police symbolize this authoritarian control. Students who are reacting to their feelings of alienation view the police as the blind arm of enforcement of the authority which they reject. Most radical students come from the middle class, whose property the police are dedicated to protect and who seem to represent the core values which law enforcement agencies share.[47] In this sense the police are friends of the middle class and one would expect children to grow with this knowledge. But at this point of the social-psychological development of young radical students, the police are increasingly viewed as enemies. Often the expression Pig, as used by black militants, is adopted by

[47] Kenniston, "Sources of Student Dissent," pp.108–137.

white radicals, and a cop is by definition a categorical enemy with no redeeming features. The prevailing view among police officers appears to be identical. They see radical students as communistic, longhaired and dirty, spoiled, disrespectful, and dedicated to destruction for its own sake. The response to college students at Columbia, Berkeley, and in Chicago during the Democratic National Convention demonstrated how these built-up prejudices can explode in violent action. The police are not unwilling to make their views known to students nor vice versa, as encounter groups have shown and will continue to show despite efforts of moderating influences like Divisions of Urban Affairs in urban colleges to bring the two groups into some kind of meaningful dialogue.

These definitions exist now as stereotypes, and they exist despite the fact that most radical students and most police have not had any direct confrontation with each other. The explanation, it seems, must lie in that segment of the self which each rejects. That is, police and students have something in common, and it is this commonality which each represses in opposite ways. Both police and college students are socialized in similar ways to view authority as useful and necessary. Middle-class students have not traditionally resisted the authority order which has always worked in their favor, at least on conventional grounds. Conflict and confrontation with important social structures has not been part of their history. Violence and aggression are devalued, and smooth passage through normal channels to favored occupational posts is the norm. Any disruption of these patterns is viewed by police and the majority of students as anxiety-producing, and attempts to reduce the tensions are typically supported by both groups.

The radical student sees in the police officer the representation of the authority structure which he is tempted to reject in himself. It is difficult to devalue a structure which has in the past produced and maintained internal security and personal comfort. But once a decision is made, a reaction-formation type of mechanism comes into play in which the person projects the conflict within himself outside of himself. That is, by categorically rejecting any possible definition of the police as well intentioned or a viable force for good, the student washes his own doubts clean. The stronger the tendency to make this definition of the policeman as good, the more intense and appropriate becomes the commitment to define him as bad.

The police officer, on the other hand, undergoes the same process. This can be best shown by reference to the kinds of responses that found their way to the letters-to-the-editor section of daily newspapers when the beatniks settled on the beaches of Los Angeles. The beatnik group, best characterized by Jack Kerouac's descriptions in *On the Road* and *The Subterraneans,* were persons who decided to drop out, to give up working, and settle in poor housing in order to create or to simply exist without working. For months letters poured into the daily papers screaming for action to force these people back into the labor force. The letter writers saw it as despicable that a large group of people would challenge the American way of life by not going to work. What such critics were no doubt saying was: If I have to work, why shouldn't they? But more than this they were responding to a perceived threat to their ritualistic sense of the order of things. Change was too difficult to deal with personally, so a demand was created for the throttling of perceived change agents. These responses were inappropriate because the beatniks were not in reality posing any threat to these persons personally. They were, however, causing whatever doubts these persons had to rise like ugly devils, causing discomfort and anxiety. People have difficulty dealing with their own inclinations to throw off their own difficult-to-bear, but safe burdens. Most workers have at times considered not working, but the anxiety of such a thought provokes them to reject this as an unwise course. In reality they tell themselves that they do not dare try a different pattern of life. It is too threatening to the internalized established way of viewing one's role in life.

The inappropriateness of the policeman's view of the radical student follows the same course. He sees in the student a threat to his own sense of order. This becomes symbolized in hair styles, in beards, in dirty clothes and sandals, and in the many acts of protest against the *status quo.* At some level everyone experiences a desire for more freedom than the social and economic system permits. But in a policeman this is intolerable. To entertain such a possibility places his own life, role, and function in jeopardy. He represses in himself any inclination to value such a struggle by repressing any outward signs of such activity. The young radical falls victim to such a need.

The dynamics of such an analysis should begin to explain some of the motivations of both sides of the confrontation which is sweeping American campuses. The disaffection of persons from the middle strata of society is, for members of the so-called establishment, the most serious threat to their vested economic and psychological interests. The fight between the haves and have-nots usually emerges as a struggle between clearly defined and manageable positions and issues. When the haves revolt against other haves, confusion and even disbelief reign. Adamancy of position will often occur in such an atmosphere, and issues will frequently give way to confrontation between roles over the question of authority alone.

THE FUTURE

From our microscopic vantage point social change appears to progress in a linear fashion. Confrontation gives way to compromise, new confrontations emerge, and other compromises follow. Progress toward the accommodation of the dissatisfied does occur, particularly when the dissatisfied spring from the ranks of the advantaged.

As trends toward depersonalization of society continue, the reaction of those who are negatively affected will intensify, and the ranks of these will grow. Automation will put more people out of work, and higher standards and a greater emphasis on scientific achievement will force more students to turn to delinquent activities or to drop out and pursue aesthetic interests.

Self-exploration movements will require an increasing number of persons to question the gratification they receive from efficiency and affluence alone. The age at which such activities will be conducted, which force students to consider the way in which they will permit themselves to be pressured and directed, will drop to early adolescence.

Alienation will continue to flourish, but the channels by which persons will relieve themselves of the debilitating effects will expand. Persons will join others and pursue what will become highly routinized activities, the goal of which will be integration. But in time even these activities will become bureaucratized, and alienation will again erupt within the context of de-alienating structures. Power and meaning will come and then be lost. Persons will find the handle and ward off self-estrangement for a period of time, and then lose the grip. Normlessness and isolation will be reflected in the way persons choose to temper their bureaucratic lives with humanizing experiences, and in the end they will lose the connection between the two worlds.

Those who wield the least amount of power in the society will gain a foothold and consolidate their gains and after awhile, these too, who want the opportunity to make their own decision about how to deal with affluence, will begin such a process. And the school, like people, will divide the occupationally efficient and the humanistic.

Index

341